For Ellen —

Whose devotion to our great institution has had no bounds. All of us who care about Mt Sinai must always appreciate what you have done and will do.

With deep respect, admiration, affection and gratitude

David
Last door

No More Killing Fields

No More Killing Fields

Preventing Deadly Conflict

David A. Hamburg

ROWMAN & LITTLEFIELD PUBLISHERS, INC.
Lanham • Boulder • New York • Oxford

ROWMAN & LITTLEFIELD PUBLISHERS, INC.

Published in the United States of America
by Rowman & Littlefield Publishers, Inc.
4720 Boston Way, Lanham, Maryland 20706
www.rowmanlittlefield.com

12 Hid's Copse Road
Cumnor Hill, Oxford OX2 9JJ, England

British Library Cataloguing in Publication Information Available

Library of Congress Cataloging-in-Publication Data

Hamburg, David A., 1925–
    No more killing fields : preventing deadly conflict / David A. Hamburg.
        p. cm.
    Includes bibliographical references and index.
    ISBN 0-7425-1674-1 (alk. paper)
    1. World War, 1939–1945—Atrocities. 2. Holocaust, Jewish (1939-1945). 3.
Ethnic relations—Political aspects. 4. Conflict management. 5. Nationalism—
Developing countries. 6. International relations. 7. World politics—21st century. I.
Title.

D803.H36 2002
940.54'05—dc21   2002001811

Printed in the United States of America

⊗™ The paper used in this publication meets the minimum requirements of
American National Standard for Information Sciences—Permanence of Paper
for Printed Library Materials, ANSI/NISO Z39.48-1992.

This book is dedicated to four wonderful people who, over many years, have stimulated, encouraged, and taught me so much about this difficult, crucial problem.

Graham Allison
Alexander George
Jane Holl Lute
Cyrus Vance

Contents

Prologue

Over the past several decades, my basic aspiration for all of us—meaning those who are concerned with international and intergroup relations, those who worry about war and peace, and those who analyze human inhumanity and terrible casualties—has become to think *preventively*. We need to be aware of what is possible now and what may become possible in the decades ahead. We need to push the limits of present knowledge and skill, develop new research, concepts, techniques, and institutional arrangements, and develop and support innovative organizations to strengthen capacities for preventing deadly conflict. In doing so, we can improve the prospects for humanity altogether.

Jennifer Knerr, the superb editor who has overseen all the books of the Carnegie Commission on Preventing Deadly Conflict, published by Rowman & Littlefield, has strongly encouraged me to tell this story in a somewhat personal vein while drawing fully on my scientific and professional background. As she pointed out, it has been my privilege to work with exceedingly interesting, gifted, and dedicated people in many disciplines from many lands. I hope I have learned something from them and in this book I try to tie together several major strands of that experience.

In my medical career, I was first bitten by the prevention bug in the early 1950s when I was doing research with patients severely impaired by polio. At the University of Illinois, we were fortunate to have a superb unit for the care of polio patients. One could not fail to admire their courage and resiliency in dealing with this terribly crippling disease. During this period, Jonas Salk made available the first polio vaccine. The impact on the patients and their families was powerful—so, too, on me. From that moment on, a dollar's worth of vaccine was more valuable than a million dollars worth of iron lungs. By prevention alone could this dreadful disorder be easily defeated!

A few years later, Jonas Salk and I became close friends and remained so until his death several years ago. Indeed, we had a long, very moving, life-review conversation only a few weeks before he died. A major theme of that conversation was his unceasing effort to find ways of preventing adverse outcomes—first through vaccines, but later in other ways, too, and in spheres reaching beyond disease.

In my term as president of the Institute of Medicine, National Academy of Sciences (1975–1980), I initiated a series of studies on vaccines that continues to the present day. We highlighted this strong pillar of prevention, immunization, and ways of widening its use—making better use of existing vaccines and fostering the development of new ones through biomedical and epidemiological research. As this book is being written, the world is nearing the eradication of polio just as the scourge of smallpox was eradicated worldwide by 1980. In retrospect, this may look easy—almost inevitable—but, in fact, many difficult, complex, and controversial obstacles had to be overcome through many generations to reach the efficacy in immunization that is now possible. Maybe this metaphor is encouraging for someday becoming more effective in preventing the scourge of mass violence.

Another powerful reinforcement for the prevention approach occurred for me in the 1960s at Stanford when I became familiar with the work of John Farquhar, Nathan Maccoby, and their collaborators on prevention of cardiovascular disease in adults by changing their behavior for health. Earlier in my career, I had been involved in the care of patients with severe cardiovascular disease and knew of the suffering and premature death caused by these disorders. So, the contrast with prevention was powerful, even though less dramatic than the polio situation.

During my years as president of the Institute of Medicine (IOM), I called this prevention research to the attention of the medical-scientific-public-health community as well as to the policy community in government and health-relevant institutions. We launched a series of analytical studies on the prospects for new vaccines, including for developing countries. This program continues to have a positive effect. From the IOM, and many other foci of effort, there emerged an authentic movement for the prevention of cardiovascular diseases, as well as lung cancer and other lung disorders. The reduction of cigarette smoking is the most vivid example of this movement that has come to involve many institutions in several sectors of society.

The American experience provides reason for some hope in changing behavior for health. One of the clearest examples involves risk factors for cardiovascular disease. Americans finally have begun to address themselves seriously to this problem. In part, this has been done through informal education, the media, and independent institutions, with their relative openness to new evidence. The scientific community has had a vital role in this new awareness. Much of the world's information on risk factors for cardiovascular disease has been generated in this country. Moreover, American researchers have been at the forefront of developing scientific studies of behavior and connecting it with strong biomedical research. Over decades, epidemiological research in Europe and the United States established risk factors for cardiovascular disease. And behavioral scientists have studied ways in which such significant and threatening information could be usefully conveyed to those who need it most in the general population—and to do so in ways that would be personally meaningful and offer concrete steps for overcoming the risk factors.

Over the past several decades there has been a considerable reduction in risk-factors behavior on a per capita basis among adults, especially among relatively well-educated people. Smoking and fat intake have been reduced, while an increase in exercise and preventive care of hypertension have contributed. The decline in mortality from coronary heart disease is especially striking because it occurred after a sustained period of rising death rates from this cause, which extended well into the first half of the twentieth century. Moreover, the changes in behavior required "swimming upstream" against a powerful current of pleasurable habits. A great deal remains to be done, yet this is another promising metaphor for the prevention of deadly conflict.

During my presidency of the Carnegie Corporation of New York (1982–1997), the prevention approach was utilized comprehensively for child and adolescent development to prevent lifelong damage: disease and disability, educational failure, hatred and violence. We achieved this through grants for research and innovation, as well as the sponsorship of special study groups making practical recommendations based on excellent working models and solid data.

Our approach evolved in distinctive ways, which I would like to state concisely to point out what has made this work socially useful and to illustrate how they have implications for my approach to preventing deadly conflict.

1. We tackled very difficult problems because they are vitally important for the future of all our children and hence for the future of the nation and of children everywhere.
2. To do so with any realistic basis for hope, to the extent possible, we built our efforts on a strong science base—and a broad base at that, linking biological and behavioral sciences.
3. We sought to relate this science base to real-world problems, translating research into social action as opportunities could be envisioned. To do so, we fostered communication between scientists and practitioners in education and health, supported creative innovations and working models in communities, and put emphasis on applied research to assess systematically the upshot of these innovative models—asking what sort of action is useful for whom under what conditions.

4. We utilized the wonderful, almost century-long history of the Carnegie Corporation in education (starting with the nearly 3,000 Carnegie libraries) to stimulate and foster a national education reform movement that could be sustained over decades. This came to pass in collaboration with other key organizations and institutions.
5. In doing so, we considered it essential as a practical matter to examine all the main factors that influence learning, both in and out of school. This meant not only working with schools but with drastic and stressful changes in families and communities—in the powerful context of the transforming global economy.
6. We made a decision early on to focus on precollegiate education—and primarily public education, at that. This was the arena most urgently in need of repair—and especially for action to prevent undesirable outcomes. This meant major attention to public education at the elementary and secondary school levels.
7. Even more drastically, we strongly emphasized the preschool years. One of my earliest slogans was, "Education does not begin with kindergarten but with prenatal care." Early childhood education became a pillar of prevention.
8. For each phase of development, we tried to clarify the essential requirements for development and their implications for lifelong learning, health, and decency. We sought to link each phase to the next, constructing a developmental sequence of experiences, opportunities, and interventions that foster constructive, long-term development.
9. We explored in depth a set of pivotal, frontline institutions that have a daily opportunity to meet these essential requirements and sought ways to strengthen their capacity to do so under contemporary conditions of world transformation. These frontline institutions are family, media, schools, health systems, and community organizations (including religious ones). And they in turn need support and help in a serious, thoughtful way from powerful institutions: business, government, the scientific community, and relevant professions.

Here again, we have a promising metaphor for preventing deadly conflict. Indeed, a recurrent theme across all the Carnegie Corporation programs in those years was the prevention of undesirable outcomes: not only in child and adolescent development but in nuclear war and other mass violence. The basic, underlying logic is essentially the same: Prevention is based on anticipation, even long-range foresight. In this effort, the best available knowledge from research is used to clarify the main paths to a particular kind of adverse outcome—that is, major risk factors that enhance the likelihood of a highly undesirable situation.

Having done that, steps are taken to counteract or avoid the risk factors, especially through appropriate changes in behavior. To do so, attention is given to pivotal institutions that can shape and support behavior positively, away from the risk factors and dangerous directions. Thus, in seeking to avoid casualties of childhood and adolescent development—whether in disease and disability, ignorance and incompetence, crime and violence—we focused on such key institutions as family, media, schools, health care, and community organizations to find ways in which they could shape healthy, learning, constructive lifestyles. So, too, in seeking to avoid the deadly conflicts leading to mass violence, we sought ways in which governments, intergovernmental organizations, and the institutions of civil society could help to build favorable conditions in which different human groups can have an authentic basis for hope and learn to live together amicably.

Clearly, prevention of undesirable outcomes involves providing positive conditions under which it is possible to meet the essential requirements for healthy development of one kind or another—be it child development or socioeconomic development of a country—through the cooperative efforts of pivotal institutions that have the salience and the capacity to do the job. The application of such concepts in the public health sphere is familiar—for example, in the provision of immunization through the institutions of scientific research, health care, and education. We have found a wider view of the prevention process useful in our approach to human conflict. In chapter 1, I sketch our efforts to apply the prevention approach to serious conflict in the Cold War and beyond.

Acknowledgments

This book gives me the opportunity to draw together various strands of my experience over several decades. It has been my privilege to work with remarkable people from a variety of disciplines in fostering research, education, and practice on problems of human conflict. I cannot adequately express my gratitude to the many collaborators and friends from whom I have learned so much.

The proximate stimulus for this book was an invitation to give the Godkin lectures at Harvard University in November 1997. For that, and so much else over so many years, I am deeply grateful to my good friend and mentor, Graham Allison. He is one of the most stimulating and innovative people I have ever known.

Our work together goes back to 1978 when we began the Crisis Prevention Program described briefly in the chapter on civil society. In subsequent years, we worked together on the Avoiding Nuclear War Program, both at Harvard and the Carnegie Corporation. In that enterprise, I want particularly to thank Joseph Nye, now dean of the Kennedy School at Harvard, and Albert Carnesale, now chancellor of the University of California at Los Angeles.

These three remarkable collaborators—Allison, Nye, and Carnesale—are excellent scholars, distinguished academic leaders, and public servants. Together, they made a major contribution toward humanity's way out of the immense dangers of the Cold War. Then, in the 1990s, Allison's leadership of the Program on Strengthening Democratic Institutions in the former Soviet Union was ingenious and highly resourceful. In this effort I also learned a lot from Bruce Allyn, Robert Blackwill, Derek Bok, Sissela Bok, Ashton Carter, Abram and Toni Chayes, John Dunlop, Roger Fisher, Arthur Kleinman, Martha Minow, Howard Raiffa, and William Ury.

I am also deeply indebted to Alexander George of Stanford University, a great scholar of international relations and a leader in bridging the gap between theory and practice. He served with distinction on the Carnegie Commission and with characteristic generosity helped many of the Commission's special studies get underway. We first met at the Center for Advanced Studies in 1957, and I have been learning from him ever since.

Both Alex George and Graham Allison once again came to my rescue in reviewing a draft version of this manuscript and making their characteristically constructive suggestions. So, too, did my good friends and collaborators, Warren Christopher, Jane Holl Lute, Connie Peck, Vivien Stewart, and Astrid Tuminez. I am most grateful.

I have already indicated how much this enterprise owes to Cyrus Vance. His great contributions to the United States government, to the United Nations, and many other institutions of public service are well known. The Final Report of the Carnegie Commission was dedicated to him in the following words.

His colleagues on the Carnegie Commission on Preventing Deadly Conflict join in dedication of this report to Cyrus R. Vance. He has devoted his life to preventing, alleviating, and resolving deadly conflict. His integrity, ingenuity, and compassion over many decades have provided inspiration to us and to our fundamental mission.

His wise, encouraging, devoted wife, Gay, was helpful in many ways; so, too, his fine daughter Amy and his long-time assistant, Elva Murphy.

Jane Holl Lute, a remarkable scholar and soldier, served as executive director of the Carnegie Commission with great ability, knowledge, and dedication. My hundreds of discussions with her on problems of preventing deadly conflict have enriched my thinking beyond measure.

In the writing of this book, one associate has been Karen Ballentine, a brilliant young political scientist whose extensive knowledge and incisive intellect have been very valuable. Similarly, David Ekbladh, a superb young historian with a bright future, has been exceedingly helpful. So, too, has Rosalind Rosenberg, a remarkably constructive, intelligent, dedicated, and resourceful person.

Through the decades of working on these problems—including personal involvement in an African political hostage case in 1975—my primary support, encouragement, and stimulation came from my immediate family. My son, Eric, and my daughter, Peggy—two of the most interesting, capable, generous, and loving people I could possibly imagine. My extraordinary wife Betty has helped me in every possible way over half a century. We have had a rare and precious collaboration in family and professional matters. While serving as president of the W. T. Grant Foundation, she initiated a grant-making program on youth violence and published an important book on violence in American schools. Altogether, I have been blessed to have such a family and could not have done this work without them. In the background is the profound influence of my father and his father, deeply humanitarian mentors, and my loving, ceaselessly encouraging mother. Most recently, Peggy and Peter have blessed us with wonderful grandchildren, Rachel and Evan. Similarly, Eric and Jackie are soon expecting their first child. So our lives are enriched. Though I was an only child, I was lucky to have close cousins, like sisters to this day: Neecy, Shirley, and Debbie.

In the decades of my career, I have had opportunities to focus attention on conflict at different levels: family, community, ethnic, religious, military, and political—intranational as well as international—and also to examine human conflict from the view point of behavioral biology, especially in the psychobiology of human stress responses and the evolutionary perspective given by the higher nonhuman primates and by hunter–gatherer societies. I was very lucky to have such wise and generous guides to these various territories. They have helped me get around the contours of complex and fascinating problems.

From an evolutionary viewpoint, I am deeply indebted to Sherwood Washburn, Jane Goodall, and Robert Hinde—all three authentic pioneers in primate research—as well as Richard Wrangham, Barbara Smuts, Anne Pusey, David Bygott, Irven Devore, Walter Goldschmidt, Shirley Strum, Phyllis Jay Dolhinow, Frank Beach, Ernst Caspari, Harold Bauer, William Mason, Peter Marler, Barbara deZalduondo, Dian Fossey, Patrick Lynn McGinnis, William McGrew, Caroline Tutin, Elizabeth McCown, Lita Osmundsen, David Bygott, Palmer Midgett, Deborah Hamburger, Harry Harlow, Theodosius Dobzhansky, Arno Motulsky, and my original inspiration for science, Tracy Sonneborn—a pioneer in modern genetics. Michelle Trudeau collaborated with me in exemplary fashion on an earlier book dealing with biobehavioral aspects of human aggression.

From a biomedical, clinical, and public health standpoint, I am singularly grateful to Jack Barchas, with whom I have shared so much over several decades. Joshua Lederberg has been uniquely helpful for forty years as scientific mentor, inspiring collaborator, and close friend. I have learned much about biomedical and behavioral sciences, especially in relation to stress and conflict, from many friends over the years. I have had a variety of rewarding collaborative efforts with William Dement, Donald Kennedy, Keith Brodie, William Bunney, and Elena Nightingale. I am deeply grateful also to John Adams, Huda Akil, Jeremiah Barondess, David Blumenthal, Monica Blumenthal, Benjamin Bunney, Roland Ciaranello, Charles Czeisler, David Daniels, Kenneth Davis, Joel Dimsdale, Anke Ehrhardt, Leon Eisenberg, Glenn Elliot, Jewelle Gibbs, Chris Gillin, Marshall Gilula, Paul Greengard, Phillip Handler, Eric Kandel, Herant Katchadourian, Helena Kraemer, Alexander Leaf, Alan Leshner, Irving London, Stuart Nightingale, Ernest Noble, Frank Ochberg, Herbert Pardes, Julius Richmond, Morton Reiser,

Fred Robbins, John Romano, Jack Rowe, Kenneth Shine, Solomon Snyder, Marvin Stein, Rosemary Stevens, Albert Stunkard, Sam Thier, Jared Tinklenberg, Daniel Tosteson, Stanley Watson, and Lyman Wynne.

In the world of historical scholarship, I have benefited profoundly from the guidance of great historians: Gordon Craig, William McNeill, and Fritz Stern.

My early mentor in psychiatry, Fritz Redlich, a superb guide, one of the wisest and kindest people I have ever known, has been helpful with extraordinary scholarship on Hitler and with personal encouragement. Three other mentors in psychiatry, characterized by exceptionally broad interests and long-range vision, greatly influenced my work, and I am deeply indebted to them: Roy Grinker, Gerhart Piers, and David Rioch. They all stimulated and encouraged me in my inclination toward interdisciplinary research in the scientific study of human behavior.

Others who were singularly helpful in this early phase of my career include Martha Angle, Therese Benedek, Francis Board, Caroline Boitano, Douglas Bond, Bert Booth, Bert Brown, Sarah Brown, John Clausen, George Coelho, Robert Cohen, John Davis, Joel Elkes, Frank and Sherri Epstein, Robert Felix, Joan Fleming, Stanford Friedman, Thomas French, Erica Fromm, Frieda Fromm-Reichman, Merton Gill, Mildred Grinher, Roy Grinher Jr., Lawrence Hinkle, Myron Hofer, Seymour Kety, Arthur Kling, Robert Knight, Janet Kohrman, Sheldon Korchin, Lawrence Kubie, Seymour Levine, James Maas, John Mason, Robert Michels, Arthur Miller, Elizabeth Murphey, Walle Nauta, Dolores Parron, Harold Persky, Hazel Rea, Margaret Rioch, Robert Rose, Morris Rosenberg, Melvin Sabshin, Edward Sachar, Virginia Saft, Philip Sapir, Lee and Dan Schorr, David Shakow, Roger Shapiro, Earle Silber, Morris Sklansky, Fred Snyder, Fred Solomon, John Spiegel, Albert Solnit, Albert Stunkard, Jana Surdi, Ralph Wadeson, Samuel Weiss, Louis J. West, Harold Visotsky, Robert White, and Stanley Yolles.

In the Carnegie years, I have already mentioned several key people in the work of the Commission. Indeed, I am deeply indebted to every member of this remarkable Commission: Arne Olav Brundtland, Gro Harlem Brundtland, Virendra Dayal, Gareth Evans, Alexander L. George, Flora MacDonald, Donald F. McHenry, Herbert S. Okun, Olara A. Otunnu, David Owen, Shridath Ramphal, Roald Z. Sagdeev, John D. Steinbruner, Brian Urquhart, John C. Whitehead, and Sahabzada Yaqub-Khan. Their vast experience, dedication, insight, and integrity made this effort so valuable.

The members of the advisory council were also exceedingly helpful. I must single out a few who made extraordinary efforts and contributions: Morton Abramowitz, Graham Allison, McGeorge Bundy, Jimmy Carter, Francis Deng, Sidney Drell, Leslie Gelb, Andrew Goodpaster, Mikhail Gorbachev, Lee Hamilton, Theodore Hesburgh, Karl Kaiser, Nancy Kassebaum, Sol Linowitz, Richard Lugar, Michael Mandelbaum, Robert McNamara, Sam Nunn, Olusegun Obasanjo, Sadako Ogata, Condoleezza Rice,

Eliot Richardson, George Shultz, Richard Solomon, Desmond Tutu, James Watkins, Elie Wiesel, and William Zartman. I have had the privilege of serving on the board of President Carter's Center at Emory University and the advisory group of the UN High Commissioner for Refugees Sadako Ogata. These great humanitarian leaders have been inspirations for me.

The superb staff of the Commission, in addition to Jane Holl Lute, were invaluable: Esther Brimmer, Ana Cutter, Robert Lande, Thomas Leney, Anita Sharma, John Stemlau, and Nancy Ward. Without them, the Commission's work could not have been done. They did so much to generate the many high-quality publications that I have relied on in much of this book.

Over fifteen years of Carnegie grant making in this field, I worked closely and profitably with Patricia Aquino-Macri, Deana Arsenian, Deborah Cohen, Fritz Mosher, Patricia Nicolas, Astrid Tuminez, Jane Wales, Suzanne Wood—and especially David Speedie, who superbly chaired the program on Preventing Deadly Conflict in the period of the Commission's work. Judy Smith and Astrid Tuminez did valuable research on these topics as my interests evolved. Elena Nightingale made an extraordinary contribution in shaping Carnegie's grant program on youth violence. Barbara Finberg, David Robinson, and Vivien Stewart were always helpful in more ways than I can specify.

Ekua Annan has faithfully and capably dealt with many aspects of this book, has ably managed my complicated office, has helped me in many ways, and I am most appreciative. Other Carnegie staff members have given me great encouragement, support, and facilitation over many years: Akin Adubifa, Gloria Primm Brown, Bernard Charles, Natasha Davids, Alden Dunham, Jeanne D'Onofrio, Annette Dyer, Karin Egan, Pat England, Irene Germaine, Jeanmarie Grisi, Dee Holder, Tony Jackson, Mary Kiely, Dorothy Wills Knapp, Lorraine LaHuta, Trisha Lester, Michael Levine, A. O. Lucas, Geri Mannion, Alan Pifer, Patricia Rosenfield, Avery Russell, Mary Lou Sandwick, Bob Seman, Judy Smith, and my invaluable long-time assistant and collaborator, Susan Smith.

Vartan Gregorian, my successor as president of the Carnegie Corporation, has taken a thoughtful, constructive interest in the work and given much encouragement. None of this work would have been possible without the strong, consistent, informed backing of the Carnegie Corporation's board of trustees, symbolized by the superb board chairs from 1982 to 2001: John Taylor, Helene Kaplan, Warren Christopher, Newton Minow, and Thomas Kean. Several others trustees took a special interest in this work, and I am very grateful: Teresa Heinz, Robert Rubin, Henry Muller, Shirley Malcom, Vincent Mai, Richard Beattie, James Comer, Peggy Rosenheim, Ruth Hamilton, James Gibbs, Ray Marshall, Eugene Cota-Robles, Billie and Larry Tisch, Fred Hechinger, Richard Fisher, Carl Mueller, and my invaluable, long-time mentor, Sam Nunn.

Carnegie's work in South Africa taught me a lot about this subject. For this experience I am singularly indebted to Francis Wilson, Mamphela Ramphele, Stuart Saunders, Desmond Tutu, Alan Pifer, Avery Russell, Frank Thomas, Wayne Fredericks, Helene Kaplan, Ruth Hamilton, and Frank Ferrari.

In pursuing my interests and deepening my knowledge of developing countries, I was greatly aided in the Institute of Medicine and Carnegie years by Ivan Bennett, Sune Bergstrom, John Boright, Peter Bourne, Sarah Brown, John Bryant, Jimmy Carter, William Danforth, John Evans, Barbara Finberg, William Foege, James Grant, Caryl and Edna Haskins, D. A. Henderson, David Hood, Arthur Kleinman, Thomas Lambo, Martin Lees, A. O. Lucas, Halfden Mahler, Walsh McDermott, Robert McNamara, Elena Nightingale, Frank Press, Julius Richmond, Frederick Robbins, David Rogers, Patricia Rosenfield, Fred Sai, Jill Sheffield, Harold Simon, Maurice Strong, Robert White, James Wolfensohn, and Karl Yordy. In this period, Joseph Califano was a wonderful friend and leader in the "Second Public Health Revolution."

One of the most moving experiences of my life, and at the same time one of the most deeply informative, was the African hostage crisis of 1975. My admiration for those held hostage—Barbara Smuts, Carrie Hunter, Emilie Bergman Riss, and Steve Smith—remains boundless to this day. Their courage, resilience, coping stamina, and generosity of spirit will always be with me. It is a matter of deepest satisfaction that I was able to help in their release and observe their constructive lives ever since. By the same token, I express profound gratitude to Lewis MacFarlane and Beverly Carter, two superb exemplars of the American Foreign Service at its best. In this crisis, Michelle Trudeau was courageous and exceedingly helpful. So, too, were John Bowlby, Norman Hunter, Wayne Fredericks, Phyllis Lee, Abdul Msangi, and Robert and Alice Smuts. As usual, my wife Betty played a crucial role. This experience was my personal and vivid introduction to international terrorism and is particularly relevant to this book.

For insights into international scientific cooperation, I am especially indebted to Bruce Alberts, Jesse Ausubel, Sune Bergstrom, John Boright, Gro Brundtland, John Bryant, Sidney Drell, Leon Eisenberg, John Evans, Marianne Frankenhaeuser, Marvin Goldberger, William Golden, Robert Hinde, Martin Kaplan, Donald Kennedy, Alex Keynan, Arthur Kleinman, Joshua Lederberg, Halfdan Mahler, Abdul Msangi, Rodney Nichols, Wolfgang Panofsky, Frank Press, Ramalingaswami, Julius Richmond, David Robinson, Walter Rosenblith, Joseph Rotblat, Roald Sagdeev, Norman Sartorius, Eugeny Velikov, and Jerome Wiesner.

For the profoundly stimulating, worrisome, and informative efforts to reduce the nuclear danger and end the Cold War, I am deeply indebted to many scholars and participants in that great drama. I have already referred to Alexander George and to the Harvard group spearheaded by Graham Allison. In addition, I owe a great deal to more colleagues than I can remember. Among those who stand out are Ruth Adams, Severyn Bialer, James Billington, Harold Brown, McGeorge Bundy, Ashton Carter, Jimmy Carter, Warren Christopher, Dick Clark, Sidney Drell, Jerome Frank, Richard Garwin, Marvin Goldberger, Joshua Goldstein, Brian Hehir, John Holdren, Arnold Horelick, Joshua Lederberg, Robert Legvold, Robert Lifton, Michael Mandelbaum, Jack Matlock, Doyle McManus, Robert McNamara, Wolfgang Panofsky, William Perry, Gerald Post, Victor Rabinovitch Condoleezza Rice, Eliot Richardson, Jonas Salk, George Schultz, Adele Simmons, John Steinbruner, Philip Taubman, Shibley Telhami, Charles Townes, Cyrus Vance, James Watkins, John Whitehead, and Jerome Wiesner.

From the Congress of the United States I learned a great deal, especially from Sam Nunn and Lee Hamilton. Others who were especially thoughtful and constructive included Doug Beureuter, Jeff Bingaman, Dick Cheney, William Cohen, Peter Domenici, John Heinz, Daniel Inouye, Nancy Johnson, Nancy Kassebaum, Edward Kennedy, John Kerry, Jim Leach, Carl Levin, Richard Lugar, Connie Morella, Nancy Pelosi, Paul Rogers, Paul Sarbanes, Paul Simon, Alan Simpson, John Warner, Henry Waxman, and Tim Wirth.

Several Russian colleagues stand out in my recollections of our shared efforts in these difficult years. Above all, the towering historical figure of Mikhail Gorbachev but also Georgi and Alexei Arbatov, Andrei Kokoshin, Vladimir Lukin, Roald Sagdeev, Valery Tishkov, Eugeny Velikhov, Grigory Yavlinsky, and Vitaly Zhurkin.

In the New York years, I had much encouragement from friends and colleagues at the Mt. Sinai Medical Center and the American Museum of Natural History, especially Karen Davis, Kenneth Davis, Anne Eristoff, Ellen Futter, William Golden, Helene Kaplan, Ellen Katz, Nathan Kase, Frederick Klingenstein, Pat Levinson, Michael Novacek, Stephen Peck, Jack Rowe, Arthur Rubenstein, Lawrence Smith, and Marvin Stein. At Rockefeller University, I had valuable encouragement from William Baker, Alick Bearn, Joshua Lederberg, Neal Miller, David Rockefeller, and Torsten Wiesel. On issues of children and youth, I am especially indebted to Duane Alexander, Paul Baltes, John Bowlby, Sarah Brown, Owen Butler, Lawton Chiles, Donald Cohen, Michael Cole, James Comer, John Conger, Joy Dryfoos, Marian Wright Edelman, Peter Edelman, Leon Eisenberg, Robert Haggerty, Irving Harris, Stuart Hauser, Robert Hinde, Kurt Hirschhorn, Jim Hunt, Klaus Jacobs, Judy Jones, Jerome Kagan, Sharon Lynn Kagan, Michelle Kipke, Eleanor Maccoby, Martha Minow, Anne Petersen, Deborah Phillips, Maria Piers, Rob Reiner, Julius Richmond, Lee Schorr, Isabel Sawhill, Albert Solnit, Vivien Stewart, Ruby Takanishi, Edward Zigler, and always Betty.

While serving on the President's Committee of Advisors on Science and Technology during the two terms of the Clinton administration, it was my privilege to discuss conflict problems with the committee while preparing a paper for the president on the role of the scientific community in preventing deadly conflict. For stimulating input and encouragement, I am indebted to Murray Gell-Mann, John Gibbons, John Holdren, Neal Lane, Shirley Malcom, Peter Raven, Judith Rodin, Charles Sanders, Philip Sharp, Charles Vest, Lillian Wu, and John Young.

Among the nongovernmental organizations that have been particularly helpful in this work, I note with gratitude the Council on Foreign Relations (Les Gelb, Barney Rubin, and Fred Tipson), the Foreign Policy Association (Noel Lateef), the International Peace Academy (Olara Otunnu, David Malone, Rita Hauser), the Woodrow Wilson Center for International Scholars (Lee Hamilton and Anita Sharma), the Aspen Institute (Dick Clark and Michael Mandelbaum), Project on Ethnic Relations (Allen Kassof), the Carter Center (Jimmy Carter, John Hardman, and Harry Barnes), United States Institute of Peace (Richard Solomon), Carnegie Council on Ethics and International Affairs (Ana Cutter), Stockholm International Peace Research Institute (Renata Dwan).

In the years of the Commission's work and its follow-up activities, many leaders of governments and intergovernmental organizations have given great encouragement, stimulation, and guidance. I can mention only a few. United States: Madeline Albright, Warren Christopher, Hillary Rodham Clinton, William Jefferson Clinton, Morton Halperin, Lee Hamilton, Richard Lugar, Sam Nunn, William Perry, Thomas Pickering, Robert Rubin, Donna Shalala, Strobe Talbott, Peter Tarnoff, and Melanne Verveer. United Nations: Kofi Annan, Michael Doyle, Louise Frechette, Boutros Boutros-Ghali, Sadako Ogata, Eleanor O'Gorman, Olara Otunnu, Connie Peck, Kieran Prendergast, John Ruggie, Gillian Sorensen, Gus Speth, and Shashi Tharoor. World Bank: James Wolfensohn. Japan: Hisashi Owada. Canada: Lloyd Axworthy and Michael Small. Sweden: Ragnar Angelby, Anders Bjurner, and Jan Eliasson. Netherlands: Ruud Lubbers. In particular, Kofi Annan has provided worldwide organizational, substantive, and, most importantly, inspirational leadership for the mission of prevention.

In the 1970s, I started a Middle East health initiative to foster cooperation among countries with serious health problems, which do not stop at national borders. It was also intended to extend in due course to related regional problems such as agriculture and water—and that has happened. Concomitantly, we hoped it might improve understanding across adversarial boundaries and perhaps have some potential for track-two diplomacy. I am gratified that this effort continues to the present day. It began with Israel and Egypt and now involves other countries as well. For this remarkable constructive initiative, I am especially indebted to Professor Mahmoud

Mahfouz of Egypt and Professor Alex Keyman of Israel, both of whom had the vision and courage to accept my challenge, and Eli Evans, president of the Charles H. Revson Foundation, for his creative philanthropy. Others who helped greatly at the beginning were Senator Edward Kennedy and Congressman Henry Waxman. Throughout, the National Academy of Sciences has played an important role. I am especially indebted to Bruce Alberts, Phillip Handler, Elena Nightingale, and Kenneth Shine.

During more than four decades of association with Stanford University as faculty member, trustee, and participant in many substantive activities, I have been greatly informed and encouraged by a lot of wonderful people. I have already mentioned many of them and cannot possibly cover them all, but let me now add a few who were particularly helpful: Gabriel Almond, Robert Alway, Richard Atkinson, Albert Bandura, Patricia Barchas, Leonard Beckum, Paul Berg, Bob Beyers, Keith Brodie, Walter Bodmer, Peter Bing, Paul Brest, John Bryson, Paxton Cady, Gerhard Casper, Luea Cavalli-Sforza, Robert Chase, Warren Christopher, Raymond Clayton, Linda Clever, William Dement, Carl Djerassi, Sanford Dornbusch, David Dorosim, Sidney, Harriet, and Daniel Drell, Paul Ehrlich, Thomas Ehrlich, Hazel Eichworth, Glen Elliott, John Freidenich, James Gaither, John Gardner, Julie and Alex George, Ann and Gordon Getty, Robert Glaser, Avram Goldstein, James Gibbs, Thomas Gonda, George Gulevich, Richard and David Guggenheim, Sidney Harriet, Albert Hastorf, Craig Heller, William Hewlett, Ernest Hilgard, Nancy, Robert, Doug, and Laurie Hofstadter, Jetty Hogan, David Holloway, Halstead Holman, Herant and Stina Katchadourian, Donald and Jeanne Kennedy, Mary Kiely, Robert Klein, Bert Kopell, Arthur Kornberg, Anneliese Korner, Helen Kraemer, Norman and Midge Kretchmer, Joshua and Marguerite Lederberg, Seymour Levine, Herbert and Gloria Liederman, Erich Lindemann, Donald Lunde, Richard and Jing Lyman, Eleanor and Nathan Maccoby, James Mark, Frank Matsumoto, Mita Markland, Doyle McManus, Rudy Moos, Barbara Newsom, Frank Ochberg, Charles Ogletree, David Packard, William and Lee Perry, Colin Pittendrigh, Susan Praeger, Karl Pribram, Lowell Rantz, Peter Rosenbaum Alan Rosenthal, Scott Sagan, Alberta Siegel, Eric Shooter, George Soloman, Wallace Sterling, Philip Taubman, Jared Tinklenberg, Joan Travis, Ralph Tyler, James Ukropina, Alfred Weisz, and Alex Zaffaroni.

The Carnegie Commission on Science, Technology, and Government, superbly chaired by Joshua Lederberg and William Golden, with David Robinson as executive director, was a valuable precursor to the Carnegie Commission on Preventing Deadly Conflict. Among other major contributors were Jeannette Aspden, Jesse Ausubel, John Brademas, Lewis Branscomb, Harvey Brooks, William Carey, Ashton Carter, Jimmy Carter, Gerald Ford, Shirley Hufstadtler, Bob Inman, Helene Kaplan, Rodney Nichols, William Perry, Walter Rosenblith, Mark Schaefer, Robert Solow, and Guy Stever.

My education on military matters was enriched by service on the Chief of Naval Operations Executive Panel, chaired by the distinguished head of the U.S. Navy, Admiral James Watkins—who later made major contributions to Carnegie's programs in education; and also by service on the Defense Policy Board, chaired so thoughtfully by Harold Brown with the wise overall guidance of Secretary of Defense William Perry.

The Institute of International Studies at Stanford University provides continuing stimulation and guidance. Key intellectual leaders include its director David Holloway, Herbert Abrams, Coit Blacker, Chris Chyba, Sidney Drell, Melanie Greenberg, Gail Lapidus, Joshua Lederberg, Michael May, William Perry, Scott Sagan, and Stephen Stedman.

In the world of philanthropy, I have already expressed my debt to the Carnegie board and staff. Let me add here a special note of gratitude to my two immediate predecessors as president, John Gardner and Alan Pifer. In addition, I am very grateful to Susan Berresford, William Bowen, Paul Brest, McGeorge Bundy, Lee Clough, Sara Engelhardt, Eli Evans, Murray Gell-Mann, Bob Glaser, Peter Goldmark, Melanie Greenberg, Ruby Hearn, Roger Heyns, Bo Jones, Judy Jones, Richard Lyman, Margaret Mahoney, Russell Mawby, Walsh McDermott, Quigg Newton, Anne Petersen, David Rockefeller, David Rogers, Neil Rudenstine, Jonas Salk, John Sawyer, Adele Simmons, Robert Sparks, Frank Thomas, and Jerome Weisner.

Now, let me turn back a century to the inspirational figure whose pioneering philanthropy made possible much of the work described in this book. Andrew Carnegie came to the United States as a poor boy at age twelve and accumulated one of the largest fortunes in the world. He believed that wealth was a public trust and should be turned to public uses in the lifetime of the wealthy person. So, he invented the concept of a general-purpose foundation, created the Carnegie Corporation of New York, and gave the bulk of his fortune to it.

In 1983, I asked the Carnegie Corporation to return to one of the most fundamental of all Andrew Carnegie's interests, his passion for peace. In his determined, persistent, even zealous quest—a kind of desperate search—he explored many avenues. He created four foundations and three peace palaces and made proposals for the arbitration of international disputes and courts of various kinds, including the World Court, as well as an international police force. His personal philanthropy reflected a unique combination of ideas, institution building, and social action, the spirit of which the Corporation sought to uphold during the years of my presidency.

Throughout this book, I refer to distinguished authors of Carnegie-related papers and books. Indeed, there is a kind of Carnegie extended family of scholars and practitioners who have conducted studies, published reports, participated in meetings, or otherwise aided the quest for understanding. To all of them I express my gratitude.

As it happens, I had an exceptional amount of stimulating and encouraging contact with several of these authors and commentators. I am especially grateful to them. Kofi Annan, Graham Allison, Toni and Abe Chayes, Jimmy Carter, Larry Diamond, Stephen van Evera, Boutros Boutros-Ghali, Alexander George, Andrew Goodpaster, Mikhail Gorbachev, Melanie Greenberg, Bruce Jentleson, George Joulwon, Douglas Lute, Jane Holl Lute, Sam Nunn, Hisashi Owada, Connie Peck, Barney Rubin, Francisco Sagasti, John Steinbruner, John Stremlau, Fred Tipson, Desmond Tutu, and William Zartman. My particular thanks go to these wise and generous people.

The work of this book could not have been done without generous continuing support from the Carnegie Corporation of New York and, in the final phase, from the DeWitt-Wallace Fund, Department of Psychiatry, Weill Cornell Medical College.

The remarks of these past few pages make clear that I have been exceedingly fortunate in personal, professional, and institutional support, encouragement, and facilitation of many kinds. I deeply appreciate these blessings. All this was highlighted most brightly in two rare and special events that were deeply moving for me—and totally unexpected. One was the presentation at the White House of the Medal of Freedom, our nation's highest civilian honor; and the presentation at the National Academy of Sciences of the Public Welfare Medal, the academy's highest honor. For these unforgettable experiences, I express my deepest gratitude to President William Jefferson Clinton, First Lady Hillary Rodham Clinton, and National Academy of Sciences President Bruce Alberts.

Finally, a word about our remarkable editor, Jennifer Knerr: The various scholars associated with the Carnegie Commission are unanimous in praise of her ability, dedication, vision, and judgment. Some of them have worked with her in earlier times. Over the years, she has established a pattern of effective leadership in publication on international and intergroup relations. As I indicated in the prologue, her suggestions changed the nature of this book for the better. It has been rewarding to work with her, and I am deeply grateful. I am also appreciative of the excellent work of the production editor, Terry Fischer. I believe the series of books published by Rowman & Littlefield on preventing deadly conflict constitutes a major contribution to this vital field.

Each month there are new contributors to the great mission of prevention. Though the path is long and tortuous, thoughtful students of human conflict are undertaking the trek. Let us hope that this book adds a few steps and brings a clearer vision to the journey.

1

Growing Up in a Time of Violence: Multiple Perspectives on Prevention

Perennial Predicaments

I grew up in the time of the Great Depression; in the backwash of World War I's desperate anguish; in the era of Adolf Hitler's fanatical incitement to violence climaxing in the grotesque butchery of his World War II onslaughts and his cherished Holocaust.

It was my good fortune that my grandfather had already escaped dictatorship in Eastern Europe to give his offspring the chance of a decent life in a democracy. Most people were not so lucky. In the first half of the twentieth century, the majority of the world's population lived under oppressive governments, whether homegrown or colonialist. At the same time, technological and social change made possible an unprecedented level of large-scale slaughter, from the trenches of World War I to the concentration camps of Joseph Stalin and Hitler, the extremism of Japanese militarists, and other oppressors.

Paradoxically, advances in science and technology also opened an era of vast opportunity. Great achievements were being made in the arts. Modern medicine with real healing power came into existence, and science-based public health measures began to extend the span and the quality of life. Yet these same advances brought painful questions. Was all this great scientific and technical potential to be thwarted by greed, envy, hatred, revenge, and aggression? Would technical progress lead to the degradation of social order and, ultimately, to the brink of human extinction? Does that make any sense? If not, why have we been drawn into one cesspool after another? Is there nothing we can do to stop the carnage? Is it beyond human capacity to create secure and decent living standards for people everywhere and to foster just interactions among diverse peoples?

1

As the world entered the second half of the twentieth century, our hopes rose again. World War II and its attendant horrors were over. The winners were—at least for the moment—cooperating. The losers were given remarkable opportunities to become prosperous democracies. Imperialism was in retreat. Throughout the Southern Hemisphere, nations were liberated from colonial oppression. A comprehensive global institution, the United Nations (UN), was created on the basis of international law and equipped with at least the rudimentary mechanisms for keeping the peace. And human rights were recognized as never before—the fundamental dignity of human beings everywhere became the global measure of civilization.

Then came the Cold War, probably the most dangerous conflict in all of history. There were vivid moments when the human species, after hundreds of thousands of years on earth, teetered on the brink of self-induced extinction. And with the Cold War came vicious proxy wars, civil wars, and then a worldwide epidemic of ethnic, religious, and hypernationalist aggression that left many millions of people maimed, killed, or forcibly driven from their homes. On several occasions in recent years, these fights have not only been ruthless and vicious, they have crossed the line into genocide—the determined slaughter of a whole people for the simple fact of their being distinct.

Yet, even as these atrocities have recurred, most peoples, governments, and organizations in the affluent and powerful parts of the world have been reluctant to face the problems of deadly conflict, typically dismissing any responsibility to act with a variety of self-justifying phrases: "Let it go, they've brought it on themselves"; "They're far away"; "Eventually it will burn out"; "Anyway, they'll always be savages."

As we know after September 11, 2001, hatred and violence are never far away. When will it be enough? Is it possible to understand how we came to be the way we are? Could such understanding help us move beyond our perennial predicaments of hatred and violence?

Research on the Origins of Human Conflict

My interest in the nature of human violence evolved over several decades. This compelling and multifaceted topic engaged and motivated me as I moved from research, education, and university life to work that focused on policy analysis and social action.

In the 1950s and 1960s, the early years of my career, I undertook biomedical research on stress and coping. My research in that period and the powerful experience of seeing the effects of armed conflict on soldiers sent home from the war in Korea caused one strand of my interests to grow in salience. That was the nexus of human anger, hatred, and violence. This was eventually reflected in the title of my research program at Stanford University in the 1970s, the Laboratory of Stress and Conflict.[1] In the 1960s and 1970s, I turned considerable attention to the evolution of human aggressiveness through the study of primates. One of the most fruitful of all the long-term research efforts in primate behavior was at the Gombe Stream Research Center in Tanzania, established in 1960 by Jane Goodall.[2] It was my privilege, during the 1960s and 1970s, to join in a variety of cooperative efforts with Dr. Goodall and Professor Robert Hinde of Cambridge University (one of the great scholars of our time) and Professor Abdul Msangi of the University of Dar-es-Salaam (a wonderful person) to develop research at this site and to stimulate scholars in the study of nonhuman primate behavior and ecology, including its relevance for human evolution. Chimpanzees are the closest biological relatives of the human species. It is rewarding to know that some of our students from that era—including Richard Wrangham, Anne Pusey, and Barbara Smuts—have become leaders in the field.

A characteristic feature of our approach was to apply a multidisciplinary perspective to the study of the social behavior of chimpanzees, both in their natural habitat and in a seminatural laboratory of behavioral biology at Stanford.

At these sites, we were able to observe that behavior patterns of threat, attack, and submission are shared by a variety of higher primates and are similar to some of the aggressive patterns evident in our own species.[3] There are also some similarities between the *contexts* in which threat and attack behavior occurs in higher nonhuman primates and humans. In general, an aggressive response is most frequent when it seems likely to promote individual survival and reproductive success, whether by increasing access to resources or by protecting relatives and friends with whom the individual has affiliative bonds that promote cooperative efforts to achieve mutually beneficial goals.

The most interesting discovery about chimpanzee aggression relates to the fact that chimpanzee males are organized into distinct communities that occupy ranges.[4] They form border patrols to defend these ranges against males from other communities. When males from different communities come into contact, violent fights may occur and individuals are sometimes severely injured. Females and infants are not immune to violent aggression by males from other communities. What is more, during these routine forays, they actively seek out opportunities for aggressive encounters.

These systematic, brutal, and male-dominated attacks among chimpanzees are the closest phenomenon to human warfare observed in any nonhuman primate—though still a very long way from the humanmade institutions of modern warfare. When the chimpanzee evidence is considered along with information on hostile responses to strangers in a variety of nonhuman primate species, it appears likely that the human tendency to react with fear and hostility toward strangers—as well as the related tendency to make in-group, out-group distinctions—has roots in our prehuman past.

Human capacities for aggressive behavior, and our tendencies to respond violently in particular situations, are partly the result of the process of natural selection during our species' long evolution.[5] These legacies need to be taken into account in understanding how our species functions in the vastly different circumstances of today. Behavioral tendencies that may have been highly adaptive in earlier phases of human social development may become maladaptive when environmental conditions change, as they have in our modern, industrial, and increasingly globalized world.

The evolutionary evidence suggests that human capacity for violence is linked fundamentally to our need for human attachment. Much of aggressive behavior is undertaken in the service of attachment. In the name of love, duty, and brotherhood we carry out threats and attacks that now constitute the ultimate peril to our species. Since developing and maintaining a network of close relationships has long been crucial to an individual's survival and reproductive success, it is likely that such aggressive responses would have been favored by natural selection over millions of years. For millennia, human survival depended on belonging to a group, being loyal to a group, and a readiness to defend one's group. We risk our lives and kill our enemies to protect those we care about and to preserve needed social relationships.

In addition to our evolutionary background and its biological legacy, the historical record of the past few thousand years makes it clear that aggressive behavior between individuals and between groups has been a prominent feature of human experience. Everywhere in the world, aggression toward other people has been facilitated by a pervasive human tendency to make harsh dichotomies between a positively valued "we" and a negatively valued "they." In the process, it has been common to dehumanize members of other groups. All this is so because the human and prehuman group has been an essential feature of adaptation among the higher primates. People need people for emotional support, learning vital skills, carrying on in the face of adversity, aiding each other in the work of survival. Belonging to an intimate group has long been exceedingly valuable, and other groups are often viewed with suspicion. Historically, demagogues, tyrants, and fanatics have utilized this tendency for their own purposes, and this trend has shown little sign of abating, as we have seen recently in Yugoslavia, central Africa, and Afghanistan.

Looking Back to See Ahead

Humanity has experienced a very rapid shift from the small primary group that dominated much of human evolutionary history to the mass society of contemporary times. Today, our old biology and customs are set in a new technological and social context. For the first time in history, this context is characterized by multiple global interdependencies. Yet, we enter the high-tech world of the twenty-first century with many of the behavioral tendencies of ancient humans. While we seek ways to adapt harmoniously to the world we have made, we have become capable of destroying it. Within a mere moment of evolutionary time, our scientific and technological ingenuity has produced a huge increase in the destructive power available to our species, available to almost all countries and to many subnational terrorist groups as well. We are rapidly approaching a time when no society on earth will be so remote that it cannot do immense damage to itself and to others, however far away. This is one of the crucial points that must now lead us to a preventive approach.

Human evolution and history provides a meaningful context within which to view contemporary predicaments. By understanding how different our present circumstances are from those in which we slowly evolved, we might be able to modify some of our deeply ingrained behaviors and orientations that have now become so dangerous—for example, prejudice, ethnocentrism, and religious hatred.[6] We may be able to broaden human horizons toward a sympathetic understanding of human diversity, while keeping in mind the basic humanity of our adversaries even when we find ourselves in stressful, threatening circumstances. For evolutionary and historical evidence show that human beings also have a deep capacity for forming mutually beneficial attachments and for promoting cooperative ties that extend beyond one's immediate social group.

In light of the long historical record of large-scale violence, an awareness of today's growing dangers might help us to consider fundamental changes in our attitudes toward and relations with groups beyond our own and to accept the mutual benefit that can be gained through mutual accommodation, respect for diversity, and the active promotion of social justice. A worldwide recognition of unprecedented dangers, and also of the unprecedented opportunities created through science and technology, might even lead to a new vision and novel modes of intergroup harmony. Moving beyond the ancient habits of blaming, dehumanizing, repressing, and attacking is evidently very difficult in practice but far from impossible. For millennia, we were utterly convinced that the earth was flat. So, too, we have believed in invidious in-group, out-group distinctions, and harsh intergroup relations as a way of life.

Tackling the problems of human conflict ultimately requires a sustained, cooperative, and worldwide effort. The quest to find better ways to prevent inevitable human disputes from turning violent needs the knowledge and judgment of people from many different fields, including members of the scientific and scholarly community, the policy community, and citizens of different nations and different political orientations.

Achieving decent, just, and peaceful relations among diverse human groups is an enterprise that must be constantly renewed. People of humane and democratic inclination will need to rededicate themselves to building effective systems throughout the world that can help troubled societies find peaceful, mutually satisfactory ways of resolving conflicts. Since the early 1990s, hard lessons have been learned, new analytical outlooks have emerged, and useful models have been developed. The tragedies of the twentieth century could provide a powerful stimulus for practical arrangements that can help inoculate vulnerable societies against violent conflict and promote conditions for sustainable peace and development.

Applying the Prevention Approach to Deadly Conflict

During my years as president of the Carnegie Corporation of New York (1982–1997), the central organizing principle of our grant-making programs was the prevention of undesirable outcomes. Whether applied to damage in child and adolescent development or to the danger of nuclear war, the underlying logic was, and is, essentially the same.

In my work at Stanford and later at Carnegie we utilized a public health model in seeking ways to prevent violence at several levels of organization: individual, community, and large-scale intergroup relations. The essential features of the public health model have recently been succinctly stated in relation to youth violence.[7] The value of the public health approach was strongly reinforced for me during my years as president of the Institute of Medicine, National Academy of Sciences (1975–1980), when we were able to draw extensively on the world's scientific community to analyze such issues.

The public health model begins with a population-based perspective on problem identification and solution. Research is designed to uncover the large-scale patterns and common risk factors associated with specific health problems. Affected populations are identified, common risks of illness are inventoried, and appropriately designed interventions are then implemented.

Through these basic concepts and methods, great gains have been made in extending the life span and diminishing the burdens of illness. Preventive health strategies have been effective in mitigating epidemics of diseases even when the underlying mechanisms are not well understood. The application of preventive strategies informed by these concepts to large-scale intergroup violence—whether civil or interstate war—is novel and promising.

The preventive approach gives attention not only to the task of altering individual behavior directly but also to harnessing pivotal institutions that can help move behavior away from dangerous outcomes toward more constructive ones. For example, in the Carnegie Corporation's grant-making program on children and youth, the focus on the prevention of undesirable outcomes led us to explore the positive role that cooperative efforts of pivotal institutions can play to increase the likelihood of healthy child development. So, too, in seeking to prevent mass violence, we have sought to discover ways in which the collaborative efforts of governments, intergovernmental organizations, and the institutions of civil society could promote favorable conditions in which different human groups can live together peacefully.

Avoiding Nuclear War

In my annual report essay of 1983, in which I introduced the Corporation's new grant-making program, I asked, "Given the immense risks and costs of the nuclear arms race, is it at least conceivable that the basic relations between the United States and the Soviet Union might change for the better in the decades ahead?" I reported then that the Corporation would direct some support to projects that "explore and delineate long-term possibilities for improving the basic U.S.–Soviet relationship, taking into account their view of us as well as our view of them." I also cautioned that "to do this in a truly thoughtful and realistic way without romantic illusions will be very difficult. Yet the subject is so important for the human future that it can scarcely be ignored."[8]

From 1982 onward, we focused on urgent issues of deep worldwide significance. At that time, the world was in great danger—a severe exacerbation of the Cold War precipitated by the Soviet invasion of Afghanistan.

We proceeded by mobilizing the strongest possible expertise, drawing on the deepest knowledge and the most systematic research, to better understand the sources of nuclear danger, to identify ways to successfully manage our shared predicament, and to do so by forging novel conjunctions of talent across disciplines and national boundaries.

The first set of large-scale grants was aimed at strengthening centers of research to conduct wide-ranging analyses of the possible paths to nuclear war. In what sorts of scenarios was nuclear war possible or probable or imminent? This research was followed by similarly wide-ranging analyses of the potential benefits of various preventive interventions with respect to each of the paths. Special attention was given to the problem of accidental and inadvertent nuclear war, the most slippery of all slopes. We also made grants to assess the potential consequences of nuclear war—the basic, unprecedented facts of destruction that were and remain at the center of the nuclear threat. We sponsored studies on understanding the adversary and on improving our capacity to monitor and analyze the unprecedented changes then unfolding in the Soviet Union and Eastern Europe.

As part of this program, Carnegie invested in a line of inquiry and innovation that had been considerably neglected: crisis *prevention*. Our emphasis on crisis prevention was focused on finding ways to decrease the likelihood that nuclear weapons would actually be used. Our approach did not assume great improvement in the relationship between the United States and the Soviet Union; nor did it assume a great decline in the stockpile of nuclear weapons. It simply assumed that each nation could recognize that a nuclear confrontation like the Cuban Missile Crisis is too difficult to manage safely time after time.

The Cuban Missile Crisis was the most dramatic and dangerous event of the Cold War. How lucky we were to get out of it without an unimaginable catastrophe. In a crisis, there is a virtually irresistible temptation to subject the opponent to strong forms of coercive diplomacy—much like an awesome game of "chicken." Then the likelihood of catastrophic error is great in the setting of terrible stress on decision making and the difficulty of controlling far-flung, high-tension operations. Facing this harsh fact, the superpowers gradually came to recognize that it was profoundly in their national interests to move back a respectful distance from the brink of ultimate shared disaster.

The main concepts of the nuclear crisis prevention approach can be concisely stated. Parties must avoid subjecting each other to nasty, unpleasant surprises. They must reach agreements to deal with predictably sensitive and potentially explosive situations; and if those situations become tense, they must know how to make clear their vital interests to the other side. Such a prevention approach endeavors to strengthen institutional mechanisms that provide for the professional exchange of information and ideas on a regular basis regarding issues that could readily become highly dangerous. The crisis prevention approach has led to broad international interest in confidence-building measures that can be applied to other sorts of conflicts elsewhere in the world. More generally, it attuned us to the mission of preventing mass violence altogether.

In 1985, a remarkable new generation of leadership took control in the Soviet Union. Building on my contacts with the Soviet scientific community, our foundation launched a vigorous attempt to expand cooperative projects between its U.S. grantees and their Soviet counterparts. The Soviet scholars and analysts who were involved in these contacts included several who became key advisors to Mikhail Gorbachev in the early years of his reform efforts. Through the 1980s, we were able to facilitate communication across adversarial boundaries by supporting U.S.–Soviet joint study groups on arms control, crisis prevention, Third World flash points, Eastern Europe, improvement of U.S.–Soviet relations, and building democratic institutions. These joint explorations of vital issues by specialized experts on both sides contributed to the Soviet "new thinking" and to the momentous changes in international relations that ensued. Similarly, we were able to establish regular and systematic linkages between independent experts and American policymakers in both the legislative and executive branches that continue to the present day.

A major grant in the early 1990s brought specialists on cooperative security and conflict resolution together with experts on international regimes for the nonproliferation of nuclear, chemical, and biological weapons systems. Senators Sam Nunn and Richard Lugar participated actively as members of the steering committee for this enterprise, which contributed substantially to the Nunn–Lugar Amendment of 1992 to the Soviet Nuclear Threat Reduction Act. The act provides for the joint dismantling of Soviet nuclear weapons and otherwise for the reduction of proliferation risks in and around the former Soviet Union. The amendment was a remarkable example of creative legislative leadership by Senators Nunn and Lugar in translating research into policy and practice. It led to extraordinary accomplishments in U.S.–Russian cooperation to reduce the nuclear danger, including the end of nuclear weapons in Ukraine, Belarus, and Kazakhstan. I sketch these unusual Cold War experiences because they were the successful precursor to the approach I advocate in this book.

Creating the Carnegie Commission on Preventing Deadly Conflict

The predisposing and precipitating conditions for serious conflict are plentiful and spread widely throughout the world. But must they inevitably pass the threshold from conflict to mass violence? Sometimes it seems so. But appearances can be deceiving. We have all seen, read, and heard so much about the genocidal wars in Yugoslavia: hundreds of thousands killed, hundreds of thousands disabled, even more displaced in their own country or fleeing as refugees to other countries. And all this in the heart of putatively civilized Europe, a continent supposedly able to learn from the horrible lessons of two world wars and the genocides of the past century. Never again? Yes, once again in Yugoslavia.

Are there lessons to be learned from a longer view of the Yugoslav tragedy? Failures and successes in averting mass violence need to be understood so that our capacity for prevention will grow as rapidly as humanly possible.

From personal experience, I know that the debacle in Yugoslavia was not only foreseeable but actually foreseen.[9] In the summer of 1987, a Carnegie-supported conference led by former Senator Dick Clark brought together leading members of the U.S. Congress with independent experts on Eastern Europe to consider the impact of recent events in Eastern Europe. A consensus emerged that a violent disintegration of Yugoslavia was likely to occur in the next five to ten years—that is, as early as 1992—unless the international community made a major effort to improve the situation. This was duly reported to various governments. Nothing significant happened. It was clear that most governments in Europe and North America were not then prepared to get seriously involved in a war-preventing enterprise.

What might have been done in 1987 or 1988? Many possibilities of the sort sketched in these pages were available. My judgment was and remains that it would have been worthwhile to establish a major international forum, sponsored by the community of established democracies, to help the antagonistic parties within Yugoslavia to understand the exceedingly dangerous consequences likely to flow from the fanning of ethnocentric flames, as well as the potential benefits—economic, political, and psychological—of working cooperatively to sort out their problems. This might have led to a reformed federation of states within the old Yugoslavia, or to a fairly amicable divorce of these states. Either of these outcomes would have required, among other things, serious and dependable protection of minority rights and reasonable prospects for a decent standard of living. To be effective, the democratic community would have had to be skillful in mediation and in assembling potential sanctions and incentives for influencing the behavior of the various factions of Yugoslavia. What was ultimately done was much costlier in human life, suffering, and money—and probably much less effective—than what could have been achieved by a concerted, carefully constructed effort in the 1980s.

In the 1990s, Cyrus Vance was asked by the UN Secretary-General to play a peace-making role in Yugoslavia—first in Croatia, later in Bosnia. He and I were close friends and had many discussions about Yugoslavia. As we reflected on these problems, we were increasingly drawn to thinking in preventive terms. What might have been done earlier and more fundamentally to avert this vast human tragedy? What preventive principles, strategies, and tactics might be usefully applied to troubled regions elsewhere in the world? Could the bitter lessons of the Yugoslav tragedy (and similar horrors elsewhere) be turned to the long-run benefit of humanity?

In an effort to provide a systematic examination of these issues and to improve the global capacity for violence prevention, in 1994 we established the Carnegie Commission on Preventing Deadly Conflict. It comprised sixteen international leaders and scholars long experienced in conflict prevention and conflict resolution. Cyrus Vance and myself were its co-chairmen and Jane Holl, its executive director. The Commission's work was greatly assisted by a global advisory council consisting of thirty-six scholars and distinguished practitioners.

The Commission approached its task by asking some fundamental questions:

- What are the problems posed by deadly conflict and why is outside help often necessary to deal with these problems?
- What can be done to resolve disputes at an early stage? What political, economic, military, and social tools are at the disposal of the international community? Which strategies work best?
- What institutions and organizations can effectively use those tools and strategies of prevention?
- What fundamental conditions are conducive to peaceful living? How can the international community help to create these conditions?

Under the auspices of both the Carnegie Commission and our regular grant-making activity, some seventy-five books and reports covering a wide variety of issues related to prevention have been published.[10] In addition, the Commission sponsored a series of international meetings that brought together independent experts and policymakers from around the world to consider these issues carefully. The Commission's main report was published under the title *Preventing Deadly Conflict*.[11] Taken together, this body of work constitutes a unique resource on the theory and practice of war prevention. The present book displays some of the highlights of that large body of work, while seeking to augment its observations with my own on topics such as democracy, preventive diplomacy, socioeconomic development, and ways of achieving international cooperation for prevention. I have been particularly eager to highlight some of the outstanding work published by Carnegie-related experts—for example, new vistas on preventive diplomacy. It also reflects my own perspectives acquired through decades of research, teaching, and participation in problems of this kind.

My recommendations are addressed to many elements of the international community, among them governments, the United Nations, regional organizations, the business community, the global scientific community, educational and religious institutions, the media, and nongovernmental organizations (NGOs). What we seek in this whole enterprise is a way of thinking that becomes pervasive in many institutions and in public understanding.

Like it or not, regional and civil conflicts and religious hatreds have become everyone's business. The idea that states and people are free to conduct their quarrels, no matter how deadly—a notion already very doubtful with the advent of weapons of mass destruction—has become obsolete. In our increasingly globalized and shrinking world, local hostilities can rapidly become international ones with devastating consequences. Similarly, as the cases of Augusto Pinochet and Slobodan Milosevic make clear, the notion that tyrants can commit atrocities, and do so with impunity in the international arena, is beginning to fade away.

A substantial body of careful scholarly research is emerging on violent conflict, on its causes, its nature and scope, as well as its resolution and prevention. The findings are providing new insights and policy guidelines that are useful to practitioners. The field benefits from a dynamic interplay between theory and practice.[12]

In the course of the Commission's work and in the preparation of this book, we approached many difficult issues from a variety of perspectives. Wherever possible, we endeavored to rethink old assumptions in light of the very new and still evolving conditions of a globalizing world. By setting ourselves the task of investigating what might be done to avert mass violence and to promote peaceful and just relations between groups and states, we found ourselves confronting some of the most nettlesome questions of today's world. How, for example, are we to adapt conventional notions of national security to a world of increased interdependence in which national borders can no longer insulate us against the threats posed by weapons of mass destruction, international terrorists, infectious diseases, international crime, and environmental degradation? How do we reconcile our commitment to universal human rights with the challenges that secessionist groups pose to the long-established norm of sovereign statehood and the global order based on it? By what means might we transform entrenched habits of inter-state competition into more cooperative and effective multilateral regimes? How can we promote democratic relations between large and small states as well as ensure economic opportunity with competent, just governance within them? Surely these are exceedingly difficult problems, and no one book can analyze them all, let alone provide all the answers. If it were otherwise, the prevention of mass violence would have become pre-eminent long ago. My goal is to provide a stepping stone from which these complex issues can be engaged.

I have deliberately adopted an actor-centered and institution-based approach to prevention and have sought, as far as possible, to give practical answers not only to the perennial question, what is to be done, but also by whom it may be done and done best. One reason for choosing this method is straightforward pragmatism. When I began looking at the performance of key institutions, I found that with a few notable exceptions, their preventive achievements were modest at best and counterproductive at worst. In fact, until recently, very few of them had developed a strong and sustained organizational or conceptual orientation toward violence prevention. Yet, virtually all of them possess capacities and resources that could be usefully adapted and more effectively deployed for this urgent purpose.

A second, more normative reason for taking an actor-centered approach is to counter the pronounced fatalism and passivity that still pervade our thinking about large-scale, violent conflict. Too often, we let ourselves believe that these conflicts, because endemic, are inevitable and that there is no constructive role for the outside world to play in moderating, resolving, and indeed preventing them. Too often, we ascribe the causes of war solely to ancient ethnic hatreds (important as they are) or to overwhelming systemic constraints—explanations that underrate the significance of leadership choice and collective action. By focusing on actors and institutions, I have sought to stimulate not only policy innovation but also, and more fundamentally, a pervasive way of thinking about violence prevention, one in which the presumption of futility is replaced with recognition of opportunity.

Overview of the Chapters

One recurrent theme of the Commission's work, strongly reflected throughout this book, is that opportunities for preventing violent conflict do exist, that too often they have been missed at enormous human and social cost. In a study prepared for the Commission, two distinguished scholars of international relations, Michael Brown and Richard Rosecrance, challenge those who ignore the opportunities for prevention with the observation that even as complex a conflict as World War II was preventable:

> Most policymakers after World War II contended that the world did not have to countenance the results of the Munich Conference in September 1938 in which British Prime Minister Neville Chamberlain gave way to German Chancellor Adolf Hitler. This and other outcomes could and should have been changed. Some informed observers believe that Hitler was the only figure among the German elite who favored going to war in 1939. If he had been removed, the other leaders, both military and political, would have hesitated to attack Poland, France, the United Kingdom, and their allies. . . . If these contentions are true, World War II might have been averted or altered by hypothesized counterfactual interventions to change the leadership on one or both sides. One does not have to agree, however, with these particular assertions to accept the notion that policymakers can do better. They can learn from mistakes. From a study of many cases, we have come to the conclusion that conflict prevention actions in conflict situations can be both more effective and better timed than they have been.[13]

I take up this question of the preventability of World War II in chapter 2. The immense, almost unimaginable tragedy of World War II and the Holocaust makes perhaps the most vivid case in modern history for humanity to learn how to prevent such catastrophes. If we cannot, there is reason for serious doubt as to whether humanity will survive to the end of the twenty-first century.

Another recurrent theme is the necessity for the international community to strengthen its capability for promoting democratic governance, productive economic development, and nonviolent problem solving in dangerous or fragile areas. These issues are taken up in ensuing chapters. In chapter 3, I discuss the helpful roles that national governments and intergovernmental organizations can play. Chapter 4 deals with the remarkable emergence of nongovernmental organizations with fresh strengths and potentials—and the key capacities of civil societies to stimulate and sometimes transcend governments.

The Carnegie Commission formulated two broad strategies for prevention. The first is operational prevention, or the measures taken in response to an immediate and pressing crisis. The second is structural prevention, or long-term measures to keep crises from arising in the first place or to keep them from recurring. Both have been considered from many angles in the Commission's many publications and in the concomitant analytical work supported by the grant-making program of the Carnegie Corporation. In this book, I highlight important examples of these two modes of prevention. The primary example of operational prevention is preventive diplomacy, an important concept with a set of rapidly evolving practices that I detail in chapter 5. The importance of the evolution and maturation of democratic systems for structural prevention is discussed in chapters 6 and 7. Here, prevention involves the fostering of democratic political and socioeconomic development, that is, a long-term commitment to helping vulnerable and poor nations to develop the resources, skills, and institutions necessary for a vigorous economy and the widest possible distribution of economic opportunity among their citizens.

One lesson that the conflicts of the post–Cold War era have repeatedly taught is that effective prevention requires a high degree of international cooperation, often among governments, international institutions, and NGOs that have had very little experience working with one another. Chapter 8 offers insights into several ways to improve this multilevel cooperation, while also discussing how the financial, legal, normative, and diplomatic resources of the world community could be usefully brought to bear on prevention. It also points the way toward effective leadership for prevention and to wider public understanding. I have deliberately included some overlap among the chapters so that each can be read on a stand-alone basis. Since the topics are interrelated, I have frequently indicated cross-chapter connections. Chapter 9 pulls together various strands from earlier chapters and additional information to point the way toward prevention of catastrophic terrorism, a matter of great urgency now and for years to come. Chapter 10 contrasts the early 1990s with the years 2000 and 2001, giving many illustrations of a growing momentum for prevention. In this sketch, I cite some hopeful developments in a variety of institutions and organizations.

In the epilogue, I highlight a new, landmark report of the UN Secretary-General, Kofi Annan, a truly remarkable leader, on ways in which all parts of the UN can strengthen their own preventive functions and further enhance their efficacy by cooperative efforts across their global facilities. Moreover, they can stimulate new thinking and operations throughout the world, whether within or outside the UN.

One of my strongest desires from the outset of the Commission is to generate new studies as well as draw on existing research to analyze in considerable depth the strongest pillars of prevention. Some of the highlights are summarized in these pages to clarify the best opportunities for prevention. In one of these reports, the Commission's executive director, Jane Holl, and the great scholar of international relations, Alexander George, powerfully make the case that most serious conflicts nowadays are clearly foreseeable.[14] So, I try here to sketch useful ways to respond before it is too late.

For achieving authentic human security and averting mass violence, many peoples and countries need help in addressing the vital tasks described in this book. Such help may come from regional or broadly international institutions, from governments or nongovernmental organizations, from "people power," and from creative individuals. This is difficult and prolonged work, but surely not beyond human capacity. In this book, there are many useful concepts and examples. After all, much of the world has moved a long way in this direction and is far less vulnerable because of it. The contrast between the beginning and the end of the twentieth century in these matters is dramatic and mostly encouraging. The travails of that hateful and bloody century have taught humanity expensive lessons. This book suggests ways in which that hard-won knowledge can be harnessed for humane and constructive purposes to build a better future.

Notes

1. David A. Hamburg and Michelle B. Trudeau, *Biobehavioral Aspects of Aggression* (New York: Alan R. Liss, 1981).

2. Jane Goodall, *The Chimpanzees of Gombe: Patterns of Behavior* (Cambridge Mass.: Belknap Press, 1986).

3. David A. Hamburg and Elizabeth McCown, *The Great Apes* (Menlo Park, Calif.: Benjamin Cummings, 1979).

4. Richard Wrangham and Dale Peterson, *Demonic Males* (New York: Houghton Mifflin, 1996).

5. S. L. Washburn and David A. Hamburg, "Aggressive Behavior in Old World Monkeys and Apes," in P. Jay, ed., *Primates: Studies in Adaptation and Variability* (New York: Holt, Rinehart & Winston, 1968).

6. David A. Hamburg, "New Risks of Prejudice, Ethnocentrism, and Violence," *Science* 231, February 7, 1986, 533.

7. Margaret Hamburg, "Youth Violence Is a Public Health Concern," in Delbert S. Elliot, Beatrix A. Hamburg, and Kirk R. Williams, eds., *Violence in American Schools* (New York: Cambridge University Press, 1998).

8. David A. Hamburg, "Prejudice, Ethnocentrism and Violence in an Age of High Technology" (Carnegie Corporation of New York Annual Report Essay, 1984).

9. Warren Zimmerman, *Origins of a Catastrophe* (New York: Times Books, 1996).

10. These publications are listed in appendix 1.

11. Carnegie Commission on Preventing Deadly Conflict, *Preventing Deadly Conflict, Final Report* (Carnegie Commission Publication, December 1997).

12. Alexander George, *Bridging the Gap: Theory and Practice in Foreign Policy* (Washington, D.C.: United States Institutes of Peace, 1993).

13. Michael Brown and Richard Rosecrance, eds., *The Costs of Conflict: Prevention and Cure in the Global Arena* (Carnegie Commission Series, Rowman & Littlefield, 1999).

14. Alexander George and Jane Holl. *The Warning Response Problem and Missed Opportunities in Preventive Diplomacy* (Report to the Carnegie Commission on Preventing Deadly Conflict, May 1997).

2

The Origins of World War II and the Holocaust: Powerful Stimuli for Prevention

Can We Learn from Bitter Experience?

The twentieth century was the most violent and destructive century in all of human existence. The pivotal event of that bloody century, World War II, was also its most horrific. The war itself cost at least fifty million lives (although a full accounting may never be possible). It also provided the conditions for the Nazi-sponsored Holocaust in which some six million Jews were sent to their deaths, as were hundreds of thousands of non-Jews, including almost all of Europe's Romani (Gypsy) population. Many millions more died or suffered from the dislocation brought about by fighting, disease, deportation, and starvation that were part and parcel of a global war.[1]

The scale of these tragedies cries out for answers. Could this almost unfathomable carnage have been prevented? Have we learned enough since then so that we are in a stronger position to prevent such a catastrophe if similar circumstances arise again? Clearly, this is a large, formidable, and complex question, one to which eminent thinkers have dedicated much thoughtful scholarship. By drawing on their efforts, my purpose here is to reflect on this dreadful era as a way to stimulate thinking about conflict prevention in the twenty-first century.

We must learn from the terrible experiences of the past. One fundamental means of education is studying the diplomatic disasters that led to European war in 1939 and eventually to world war. By understanding how the leaders and citizens of the 1930s comprehended their circumstances and the courses of action open to them, we can clarify the dangers and responses of that period. By learning from World War II, we can improve our capacity to respond effectively to dangerous situations in the future. Perhaps we can surmise how similar catastrophes can be avoided.

In many ways the world community has already learned from the cataclysm of World War II. Numerous international and regional bodies have

been created, which were not available to policymakers in the 1930s, to coordinate international action during an emerging crisis. Leaders now have
recourse in the UN—explicitly established to prevent another tragedy on the
scale of World War II—and a host of other formal and semiformal bodies
to defuse conflict. It would be easy to say that today's world bears little re-
semblance to that of the 1930s in terms of machinery for preventive diplomacy. Yet, that is to miss an important lesson about the origins of the war.

There were many people in and outside of Europe who understood the
nature of the threat posed by Hitler and his fascist regime. However, even
with this understanding there was little action taken to stop this growing
threat. Domestic concerns, wishful thinking, ideological blinders, and simple chauvinism distracted governments and citizens in the established
democracies. They were, therefore, unwilling to take steps that could have
restrained aggression at an early stage. Even with the preventive machinery
that we have developed in the past six decades, this type of disengagement
remains a stumbling block to the effective prevention of conflict. To better
understand the 1930s as a lesson for today, we draw on the many works of
distinguished scholars who have devoted great effort to the study of the
Nazi era, viewing their work through the lens of prevention.

Looking at the historical record, we can improve today's knowledge of
tools and strategies for prevention. By presenting what the main actors did
during that period, we can see what conceivably might have been done to
change the odds toward a less destructive outcome and what sorts of concerns and constraints prevented them from undertaking the necessary actions. We can also begin to understand what we could do in similar situations to avoid such pitfalls. The experience of World War II forces us to think
hard about generic problems of mass violence, the confrontation of ruthless
rulers, mediation of complicated intergroup crises, and the price of inaction.
Perhaps the virulent disease of hatred, intolerance, and violence spread by
Hitler and his allies was beyond any cure available then, but illuminating the
failure to treat it in time can be an instructive start in approaching prevention. The reasons why many in the 1930s failed to act against the threat presented by Hitler are comprehensible, but their failure led to an almost in-
comprehensible bloodletting. Today, with rapid advances in military
technology and the proliferation of weapons of mass destruction, the stakes
are even higher and the margin of error even smaller than in the 1930s.

Faulty Appraisal of Jeopardy and
Constraints on Effective Response

In the 1930s, as in the present, governments typically made an appraisal of
threatening international situations in terms of national interest. Concep-

tions of national interest are often vague and tend to change over time. One overriding priority of any nation is to counter tangible, or at least vividly perceived, threats to the survival of it and its people. The experience of the 1930s and thereafter suggests that such threats are likely to come from certain, often quite predictable, conditions.

An authoritarian junta or dictator oriented toward external expansion and/or a total domestic concentration of power is a powerful warning signal of potential aggression. Coupled with the intense military orientation of these leaders is an attraction to the most powerful weaponry available; today that can mean a desire for weapons of mass destruction. These regimes, unaccountable to most of the people they claim to rule, are often guilty of hyperaggressive and ruthless behavior toward targeted domestic groups and rivals abroad. Especially dangerous is fanatical hatred embodied in charismatic leaders. These are not the only danger signals that members of the international community have to consider, but they should figure strongly in any realistic appraisal of national jeopardy.

Neither national governments nor the world community are powerless in the face of such regimes. But coping with them is still a very difficult process. Critical to this task is an early and accurate appraisal of the threat, a careful analysis of information from a variety of sources, both governmental and nongovernmental, that can provide a clear rationale for action and also minimize wishful thinking. In such circumstances, international diplomacy must be backed with sufficient economic and military strength so that deterrence is credible. Most of all, international cooperation in the face of belligerent states is imperative. It is usually the case that no single nation is adequate to the task of preventive action, at least without incurring prohibitive costs. It is therefore highly desirable to develop and cultivate attitudes, habits, incentives, and institutions that facilitate cooperation in coping with likely aggressors and crisis situations. These desiderata were noticeably absent in the 1930s.

The problems facing Britain, France, and the United States during the 1930s illuminate issues that, in one form or another, are still present in the world today and remain obstacles to effective prevention. In facing the threat that Hitler and his regime presented, all were bound by international and domestic concerns that made resolute action difficult, but far from impossible.

Each of the democracies was haunted by the terror and destruction of World War I. There were deep fears that another war would again savage the populations of Europe. Understandably, powerful pacifist movements took root in many countries, making vigorous preventive diplomatic and military stances difficult. On top of this was the terrible, worldwide depression of the 1930s. This severely exacerbated existing tensions within societies and caused many governments to devote most of their attention to domestic affairs. Altogether, the domestic crises were profound. The bitter recollections of war and the harsh reality of the depression were major reasons for the two most significant powers'—Britain and the United States—isolationism and disengagement from European affairs in the late 1920s and early 1930s.

There was also some sympathy for the aggressor. Among conservative circles in the West, there was relative tolerance—and, in some instances, even admiration—for the brands of fascism exemplified by Hitler and Benito Mussolini. Some believed that the end of the weak and fractious Weimar Republic in Germany was a positive development. Throughout the 1920s, Western statesmen had worried about the situation in Germany. In 1927, Chamberlain wrote the French prime minister, Aristide Briand, stating, "We are battling with Soviet Russia for the soul of Germany." The Nazism of Hitler's Third Reich not only promised a stable Germany but also added a bulwark against the threat of communist expansion in Eastern Europe.[2] Hitler's radicalism was noticed, but it was thought that business, the military, and other powerful interests in German society would eventually moderate any excesses.

Hitler's *Mein Kampf*, though not a detailed blueprint for conquest, vividly laid out his highly aggressive grand design for a Germany-dominated Europe. Even though it provided a powerful early warning, Hitler's doctrine was not taken seriously in London, Paris, or Washington. In many sectors of government, media, and the general public, there was a lack of vigilance about what was happening in Germany. Even when Germany later came to be seen as a serious threat, many in the West hoped that someone else, particularly the Soviet Union, would take the initiative and responsibility for thwarting Nazi ambitions.[3] There was also painfully little sympathy for those singled out as targets of German aggression: European Jewry, socialists, and the vulnerable countries of Eastern Europe. During the Czechoslovak crisis of 1938, Chamberlain remarked to his country that it was both "horrible" and "fantastic" that Britain was considering war because of "a quarrel in a far-away country between people of whom we know nothing."[4]

To be sure, there was varied opinion among the elites of the established democracies. From the outset, many on the political left, as well as conservatives such as Winston Churchill, were critical of fascism and distrustful of Hitler. There were also scholars and statesmen who perceived the danger early and well. Today, historians such as R. A. C. Parker argue convincingly that there was a chance, had the West adopted the firm policies of deterrence advocated by Winston Churchill, that World War II might have been prevented.[5] But in the early 1930s, when preventive action could have been taken with good effect, the influence of individuals like Churchill was still modest at best. As too often happens in history, the danger was adequately grasped only when it was too late to prevent the devastation.

The failure of so many to perceive the gravity of the danger was compounded by narrow and short-term conceptions of national interest on the part of the democracies. It was a fundamentally dangerous time. A world system that was the product of the nineteenth century was being challenged by those powers—Germany, Italy, the Soviet Union, and Japan—opposed to the status quo. In the 1930s, Britain and France worked to preserve world order as they had after World War I. However, they faced in Hitler a man who was more than willing to use massive violence to change that system. What was needed was strong multilateral cooperation in mounting a credible deterrence to Hitler's aggression. However, the isolation, enforced or voluntary, of several of the most powerful actors on the world scene, especially the United States, weakened any international efforts and encouraged Hitler's adventurism. This isolationism also undermined the one international organization that might have enabled those who opposed Hitler to organize effectively against him: the League of Nations.[6] With no one nation willing to stand up to Hitler alone, and international cooperation bereft of the commitment, capacity, and tools for effective preventive action, the seeds were sown for tragedy beyond all imagination.

Recent Research on the Origins of World War II

The opening of new archives has added richness to recent scholarship on the origins of World War II. Many of these contemporary historians emphasize the powerful impact domestic factors had on the decision making of Britain and France in the 1930s. The reality of the fiscal crisis brought on by the depression and concerns about the maintenance of their worldwide empires structured these two powers' responses to fascist aggression. As they made their calculations about Hitler, Mussolini, and Japanese militarists, they gave strong weight to how foreign policy decisions would affect economic conditions at home and preserve their overseas possessions.[7]

The leaders of Britain and France were, to some extent, aware of Hitler's radical ideology of racial hatred and his dreams of world empire, but they were not inclined to take those beliefs seriously even after domestic violence and repression had become hallmarks of the Nazi regime. Through much of the 1930s, the threat posed by militaristic nationalism in Germany, Italy, and Japan was decidedly secondary to efforts by the democracies to consolidate their own domestic social order and defend their colonies abroad. Problems arose for Britain and France not only in Eastern Europe but also in the Near East, Middle East, and Africa. British diplomats and military commanders formulated European priorities in which Germany was included but held in a decidedly subordinate position until 1935, and even then its importance grew only slowly over the following years. The economic aspects of diplomacy included a considerable emphasis on economic appeasement in order to maintain trade to combat the effects of the depression. These factors took on roughly equal weight with traditional areas such as military and territorial ambition and the historic preoccupation with national status and prestige.

What British and French policymakers were responding to in the 1930s was part of a larger shift within international politics that had begun in the late nineteenth century. In Europe, a balance of power system orchestrated by Fürst von Metternich following the Napoleonic Wars and perpetuated by Otto Eduard Leopold von Bismarck in the latter half of the century maintained a general political equilibrium. This system began to fray when Germany and the United States rose as industrial powers, challenging the industrial preeminence of Great Britain. Strains on the system further increased as Russia, Japan, and some areas of Europe also modernized. Coupled with this industrialization was a pervasive belief that it was connected to empire. The British, in particular, were greatly admired for their empire, and many states sought to emulate this example in the hope it would lead to a similar level of development.[8]

Shifts in the international arena were embedded in rapid technological, economic, and social changes brought about by the Industrial Revolution. These changes fed the dislocation of traditional social, political, and diplomatic systems. Democracy and nationalism emerged in this turbulent era as attractive alternatives for those feeling oppressed or left out of the new socioeconomic order. Nationalism spread rapidly among these groups and strained old orders. Altogether, it was a perplexing time; leaders and publics were together threatened by the massive changes taking place around them. These circumstances contributed to the onset of World War I and its unexpected, prolonged carnage.

After World War I, there was a widespread reaction against the suffering that the war had inflicted and a strong inclination on the part of the democracies to seek peace and reconciliation. Throughout the 1920s, there was considerable public support for pacifism that was manifested at the international level in the 1928 Kellogg-Briand Pact, in which twenty-three nations renounced war as a tool of statecraft.[9] Despite these feelings, there was a powerful revanchist spirit in Western countries. Immediately following the war, the victors imposed on Germany heavy reparations payments, stripped it of territory, and saddled it with blame for the conflagration. The punitive nature of this treatment contributed to Germany's sense of grievance, a mood that Hitler both utilized and nurtured in his rise to power.

But this unanimity was not to last. Britain, stung by its own war losses, quickly lost interest in Continental affairs and in maintaining a hard line with the French against Germany. There was increasing sympathy for the plight of Germany, particularly after the 1923 Franco-Belgian occupation of the Ruhr. The differing priorities of the British and French made cooperation against a resurgent Germany in the 1930s increasingly difficult.

The British and French continued to be preoccupied with their empires. In the wake of the war, both countries had added considerable territory to their already vast holdings (much at the expense of Germany) but then found they had declining resources with which to maintain their holdings. The rhetoric and actions of the Communist International (Comintern) also threatened these imperial possessions. Seeing colonial possessions as inherently exploitative, and encouraged by the success of the Russian Revolution of 1917 and the Red victory in the civil war, the Comintern, along with other leftist groups, sought to support indigenous nationalists in struggles against foreign domination.[10] This added to the demands facing the colonial powers. Their own colonial ambitions also served to divide the British and French. Each was mutually suspicious of the imperial plans of the other, particularly in the Middle East.[11] Nevertheless, the physical possession of colonial territory was viewed as a vital interest. Empire was viewed as a fundamental means of maintaining the mother country's economic prosperity, and the costs incurred in the service of empire were still considered acceptable. As Chamberlain noted in 1937, for Britain, the empire was "the seat of our influence in the world."[12]

Outside the European system there were significant forces at work that shaped the outcome of events in the 1930s. Possibly the most important of these was the hesitancy of the United States following World War I to become active in international affairs. By and large, the American public felt it had been tricked into joining that war by an unsavory mix of Europeans, bankers, and arms merchants. The U.S. Congress voted against joining the League of Nations, even though that organization had been conceived of and strongly supported by President Woodrow Wilson.

Yet, the United States did not entirely wall itself off from the world. In fact, in this period it might be better to speak of American policy as being unilateralist rather than strictly isolationist. Immediately after World War I, American distaste for the affairs of Europe led to strong American pressure on Britain and France to repay their war loans quickly. In turn, this drove the Western powers to squeeze Germany for its reparations payments—thereby causing economic hardship and international tension. Eventually, in the 1920s, these problems elicited direct American involvement through the Dawes and Young plans, which sought to reconfigure German reparation payments.[13] Nevertheless, American attention to global affairs, apart from finance, was drastically limited between the wars.

The other great force sitting on the fringe of Europe was the Soviet Union. Its ideology loomed as a threat to many in Western and Central Europe. As noted, Soviet support of the Comintern was also a cause of concern among the colonial powers. To many observers, the Soviet Union was the paramount threat to peace and stability in Europe. There was deep animosity toward it among political and economic elites in Britain, France, and the United States. For years following the Bolshevik Revolution, the Western democracies refused to recognize the Communist Party as the legitimate government of Russia; the United States was the last to do so in 1933. This diplomatic marginalization coupled with the isolating effects of civil war, famines, Joseph Stalin's emphasis on "socialism in one country," and Red terror kept Russia on the fringe of international life well into the 1930s. Nevertheless, its very presence constituted a powerful and feared influence on European affairs. The attempted revolution in Germany following World War I had spawned fears of a communist state straddling Central Europe. When Hitler's regime replaced the unsteady Weimar Republic, there were those in the West who looked on the change with approval precisely because it seemed to promise a redoubt in Central Europe against the influence of the Soviet Union.

Throughout the 1920s, Europe lived in the shadow of World War I. Politically, the war had redrawn the map. It had erased Austria-Hungary and left a host of new, smaller, and mostly unstable states in its place. A new, enlarged Poland was conjured out of the remnants of the former Hapsburg and Romanov empires. Most profound were the social effects of a war in which the human costs had been so terribly high. People spoke of a "lost generation" of young men. Populations had been displaced across Europe and the effects ran deep. When a global depression descended at the beginning of the 1930s, it fanned preexisting discontent across Europe and the world.

The impact of the depression was dramatic when coupled with the vast techno-social-economic changes the world was already experiencing. Widening popular dissatisfaction was harnessed to a genuine mass politics. The new technologies of radio and film added to the ability of people to organize around leaders and ideas. In some places, this mass mobilization had the effect of augmenting democratic processes. Elsewhere it supported the rise of nationalist and fascist regimes.[14] In the 1920s, the dislocation following World War I produced Mussolini and his Italian Fascists. The economic crisis of the early 1930s strengthened the hand of militarists in Japan, who embarked on a program of imperialist expansion. However, it was in Germany that these changes had the most profound consequences: the overthrow of the democratic Weimar Republic and the consolidation of Nazi power.

Hitler's Germany: Early Warning and Inadequate Response

Of the demise of the Weimar Republic, a preeminent historian, Professor Gordon Craig, writes:

> While totalitarian regimes were consolidating their power in Russia and in Italy, an experiment was being conducted in Germany to determine

whether a democratic republic could be made to work in that country. After 15 years of trial and crisis it failed, and the ultimate consequences of that failure were the Second World War and the death of millions of men, women and children. If some benevolent spirit had granted the peoples of Germany and neighboring European states even a fragmentary glimpse of what lay in store for them in the 1940s, it is impossible to believe that they would not have made every possible sacrifice to maintain the Weimar Republic against its enemies. But that kind of foresight is not given in this world, and the German Republic always lacked friends and supporters when it needed them most.[15]

The garbled parliamentary democracy of Weimar, based on a series of post–World War I compromises, had, by the beginning of the 1930s, won few allies. It was greeted with disdain both at home and abroad, from left and right. Much of the German public had grown tired of its ineffective politics. As the heir to all of Germany's political and economic troubles following World War I, the Weimar Constitution was the target of nationalists who were deeply frustrated with Germany's lowered position in the world. Despite its potential, Weimar came to symbolize, to many Germans, all that was bad about modern Western liberal democracy. The republic, dominated by the Social Democrats, seemed unable to reassert German strength on the international scene. The parliament was ineffective due to a proliferation of constantly squabbling parties, leaving the regime unable to deal effectively with the onset of the depression. By the beginning of the 1930s, the government appeared unable to ensure civil peace as paramilitary groups attached to parties from both the left and the right fought in the streets. The possibility of communist revolution loomed large for many across the German political spectrum and abroad.[16]

Of the political alternatives available to the German people, the most compelling was that of National Socialism. As the distinguished historian Professor Fritz Stern has noted, National Socialism offered a powerful temptation for many segments of German society. It promised prosperity in the midst of deprivation, the appearance of strength in an era of weakness and doubt. It drew support from diverse sectors of German society, attracting to its banners workers, students, members of the intelligentsia, the middle class, religious groups, and many capitalists. In the 1932 elections, the Nazis received 37 percent of all votes cast—a significant victory in the highly fractious politics of the time.[17] Hence, Hitler's party came to power legally.

Superficially, once in power Hitler's regime appeared to accomplish much of what it promised. It appealed to German nationalism with much drama and gave Germans a renewed sense of national power.[18] It brought aspects of the economic crisis under control and brought elements of prosperity to many. It brought repressive order to politics and the streets. The image of strength and stability it projected seemed to put an end to fears of social revolution. The removal of the specter of communism was a pleasing development for many within Germany and without.

But this was only one face of the dictatorship. Violence and coercion had simply been moved indoors. The suspicious Reichstag fire in February 1933 (possibly set by the Nazi regime itself) gave Hitler an excuse to issue an emergency decree that gutted the liberties guaranteed by the Weimar Constitution. Protections for free speech, for free assembly, and against unwarranted search and seizure or confiscation of property evaporated.[19] All other political parties and labor unions were banned. Party thugs in the SS and Strumabteiling (SA) were given police powers and their offices became sites of state-sponsored torture and harsh intimidation. Concentration camps for dissidents were quickly established. Jews immediately became targets of official discrimination and found their position in German society under attack. Building on a virulent strain of traditional anti-Semitism, these were the first major steps on the grotesque path to the barbaric Holocaust.[20]

What is more, the existence of these activities was widely known to the German public and any interested observers. Yet, few chose to speak out in opposition. Some wishfully thought the regime would moderate its behavior eventually and be brought under control by other, more sober elements of German society. The international community largely failed to perceive that a government that was lawless and violent at home was also a potentially great danger on the international front.

The excesses of the Nazi regime in its early days in power should have offered a sharp warning to Western leaders, but most did not make the connection between domestic violence and international aggression. There were some leaders, notably Winston Churchill, who came to realize the full extent of the threat. But many in the West continued to assume that Hitler wanted no more than a revision of the Versailles Treaty. Had they taken his *Mein Kampf* and other public statements more seriously, they would have understood that Hitler always had larger, more aggressive ambitions as well as hateful, destructive attitudes. The international community, preferring to either play them down or ignore them entirely, missed these vivid and deadly early warning signals. The danger of hateful, fanatical, charismatic leaders is as pertinent in 2002 as it was in the early 1930s.

Hitler's Foreign Policy

As with so many members of his generation, Hitler was deeply influenced by the experience of World War I. Much of his worldview and foreign policy aims were shaped by the war and, especially, by Germany's defeat in 1918. In Hitler's harshly intolerant view, Kaiser Wilhelm II's foreign policy before and during World War I was disastrous for several reasons: Its objectives and methods were mistaken, inadequate efforts were made to assure public support, and it alienated powerful and reliable allies. Furthermore, Wilhelm II failed to control unreliable elements in Germany. It was this failure of authority that, as Hitler saw it, allowed moderates, internationalists, pacifists, Marxists, and Jews to stab the German Army in the back and foisted a shameful peace on the country. Many of Hitler's calculations were made to correct these perceived failings of Imperial Germany.[21]

One of the issues that had helped Hitler in his quest for power was his attack on the Versailles Treaty. His assaults on the settlement as grossly unfair to Germany found sympathetic ears among nationalistic Germans. Many desired a redress of the slights of the treaty and were willing to support an aggressive foreign policy to do so. There were also those in Europe and America who saw the German desire for redress as legitimate and were willing to indulge this course. However, Hitler's intentions went far beyond simply correcting the wrongs of an unjust treaty and restoring Germany's 1914 boundaries. In *Mein Kampf* he wrote:

> The frontiers of the Reich in the year 1914 were anything but logical, they were in reality neither complete with respect to the inclusion of people of German nationality, nor intelligent with respect to geo-military appropriateness. They were not the result of a considered political action, but momentary frontiers of a political struggle in no way concluded.[22]

He was explicit in stating that Germany must expand eastward, removing the Slav threat by doing so and bringing under German control the most fertile and strategically secure land in Europe. Hitler's rhetoric on expansion did cool briefly after the Nazis took power. Some wishful thinkers viewed this as a sign that the ramblings in *Mein Kampf* were not programmatic. However, this tempered stance was patently about protecting his position in a period when Germany was still weak. His occasional moderate tone later became a means to disarm opponents and lull neighbors, therefore increasing Germany's freedom of action in foreign affairs. Historian Gordon Craig notes that while the Nazi regime occasionally put on a more responsible public face, Hitler's foreign policy ambitions remained consistent.[23]

These dreams of conquest (in some ways not radically different from certain German ambitions in World War I) amounted to a major revision of the existing world order.[24] An empire in Central Europe would give Germany the resources and space it needed to become a power on the order of Britain or the United States. In fact, Hitler saw the United States, with its vast territory and the resources that assured it security and international influence, as an example to be emulated through expansion eastward on the European continent.[25] But such a grandiose plan necessitated the use of force: Unless other powers entirely submitted to this expansion scheme, it could not be secured without massive violence. To assure the eventual success of these expansionist ambitions, the Nazi regime's foreign policy used all means available to seize whatever opportunities appeared or could be created. In a few years, this would come to include war.[26]

This could only come about with quiet on the domestic front. Following his assumption of power, Hitler banned all other political parties and organizations. He struck a deal with the Vatican to dissolve the powerful Catholic Center Party. Marxists and leftists were hounded out of public life. To cement his power, Hitler even turned on the Strumabteiling (SA)—the brown-shirted storm troopers who had fought in the streets for the Nazis during the party's rise to power.

Very quickly after the Nazi party took control of the German government, army officers came to understand that the over-half-million-strong SA could usurp their roles. More importantly, Hitler himself had come to see the strength of the SA's powerful leader, Ernst Rohm, as a threat to his position. During June of 1934, in a spate of bloodletting that left approximately 300 dead, Hitler liquidated the organization's leadership and took the opportunity to kill a number of other opponents of the Nazi regime. He quickly disbanded the SA rank and file in order to ensure the army's loyalty. This "Night of the Long Knives" illustrated that even members of his own party were not safe if they threatened Hitler's plans or authority.[27]

Once Hitler had consolidated power at home, he could turn his attention to other important goals: building up the German military, regaining Germany's freedom of action by withdrawing from international commitments made by his Weimar predecessors, and beginning to test international resistance to his policies. It is here that the boundaries between domestic and international affairs became blurred. Without an effective opposition within German society, Hitler was free to indulge his own desires. Not all authoritarian governments embark on expansionist adventures. Nevertheless, the Nazi regime shows that it is much easier for extreme and dangerous policies to take root in countries where public dissent has been silenced.

Hitler and Europe, 1933–1936:
Fatal Missed Opportunities for Prevention

In his distinguished history, *Germany, 1866–1945*, Gordon Craig offers a number of insights into the opportunities missed in the prevention of World War II. Regarding the failure of the Allies to respond quickly and forcefully to Hitler's emergence in the early 1930s, he writes:

> The first assessments by the Western governments of Hitler's likely course in foreign policy were characterized by an extraordinary amount of wish-

ful thinking. Despite the clear evidence provided by events inside Germany that the country's new rulers were contemptuous of law and morality and the standards of common decency in the treatment of those who disagreed with them, politicians in London and Paris showed no alarm about what this might portend for Germany's future behavior as a member of the international community.[28]

As early as 1933, the British and French ambassadors in Berlin had accurately perceived the threat Hitler posed. To their respective capitals, Sir Horace Rumbold of Britain and Andre Francois-Poncet of France sent reports that left no doubt that Hitler constituted a serious threat to neighboring countries and, indeed, to world peace. Sir Horace reported on concentration camps as early as 1933. He understood that the aims of German policy were to "bring Germany to a point of preparation [for war], a jumping-off point from which she can reach solid ground before her adversaries can interfere." His reports to the cabinet were ominous. Assessing the Nazi regime in 1933, he declared that "there is a mad dog abroad once more and we must resolutely combine either to ensure its destruction or at least its confinement until the disease has run its course."[29] Both ambassadors urged their governments to give serious study to *Mein Kampf* so that they might fully grasp Hitler's real intentions.[30] Clearly, they recognized the connection between the brutality already occurring within Germany and what could happen beyond Germany's borders if Hitler was not stopped and stopped quickly.

In Britain, other well-respected members of the government also understood the gravity of the threat posed by Nazi Germany. In 1933, Sir Duncan Sandys predicted that Hitler would remilitarize the Rhineland. Meanwhile, Sir Robert Vansittart, the permanent undersecretary for foreign affairs throughout much of the 1930s, foresaw a German takeover of Austria at the earliest opportunity and an eventual move against Poland. He felt that only international cooperation could assure peace.[31] Despite these views and differences of opinion within the cabinet, the British government was largely uninterested in these warnings and predictions.[32]

France was more concerned with the challenges raised by Hitler and, in 1934, began a policy of containment against Germany. The foreign minister, Jean-Louis Barthou, attempted to draw up a comprehensive security plan involving all those countries potentially threatened by Hitler. His hope was to contain Germany through a network of mutual defense treaties, supplemented by a regional security pact that would enmesh Germany in diplomatic agreements. However, the plan was stillborn. Barthou could not obtain the cooperation of those countries he hoped to enlist, and Britain continued to maintain its distance from Continental entanglements.[33] These observations make it clear that, despite Hitler's well-known practice of deceptive diplomacy, there was an early recognition by experienced observers of the likelihood of his pursuit of expansion through coercion or war.

The failure to couple this early understanding with effective measures is all the more tragic in light of the fact that Hitler, in his first several years in power, showed signs of vulnerability. As previously noted, in 1934, there was a crisis of authority within the Nazi Party that was followed by brutal repression of opponents. The "Night of the Long Knives" in which the SA leadership was purged was a sign that Hitler's power was not absolute. Earlier that same year, agitation for unification with Austria, which included the murder of that country's chancellor, brought international protest, and the move was eventually challenged and stopped by Fascist Italy. These events point to the possibility that Hitler could have been restrained or even toppled by more concerted, early international action. However, the Western democracies, absorbed in their own political difficulties and economic crises, and seduced by isolationism, failed to act cooperatively against this visible threat.[34]

This weak response only emboldened Hitler. In 1935, he moved to expand Germany's reach. As Ian Kershaw notes in his masterful biography of the man, Hitler sought to surprise his opponents with spectacular propaganda coups.[35] To this end, he launched his "Saturday Surprises." One week, he revealed that Germany had a new air force; the next, that he no longer intended to honor any of the military clauses of the Versailles Treaty and was enlarging his army by fivefold. The German military leadership was stunned by these revelations, not because it disagreed with the plan, but because many generals thought the methods Hitler had chosen were very risky. But, like the German public at large, the concerned surprise of the German military turned into support when it came to be known that no adverse consequences would follow. This was a critical turning point. That the fundamental postwar treaty system could be unilaterally repudiated by a vanquished Germany without any major resistance from the great powers left the door wide open for Hitler to pursue his more grandiose ambitions.

The response of European powers to these unilateral German actions was a conference at Stresa in April 1935. Representatives of Britain, France, and Italy gathered at that Italian town to discuss the effects of these actions on European affairs. France, in particular, was increasingly anxious about the resurgent German military threat. However, that country could only get modest support from Britain. In the end, from the Stresa meeting emerged merely vacuous calls for security based on international agreement for arms limitation.[36]

The noncommittal actions of the British at Stresa were in line with their older policy of disengagement from Continental politics following Versailles. Britain saw a general settlement with Germany as the ultimate way to preserve peace in Europe. For that reason, it pushed for the Allied occupation of the Rhineland to end in 1930, earlier than originally planned. In January 1935, the British government stated that this strip of territory was not central to British interests. Without French participation, the British began discussions with the Germans about air and naval power. The talks ignored military considerations of great concern to the French and eventually produced the Anglo-German Naval Agreement in which Germany agreed to build a navy limited to one-third the size of Britain's. Nevertheless, this was a significant enlargement of German naval power, a matter of great concern to the French.

There was considerable sentiment against war and rearmament in Britain, as shown by the Peace Ballot of 1935. In negotiating with Germany over military buildup, British policymakers were consistent with public opinion that had little tolerance for militant talk.[37] However, leaders had by no means made clear to the public the extent of the emerging threat. The failure of most political leaders to educate the public about growing dangers was a consistent attribute of this period. Even so, there were significant voices against the emerging policy of appeasement. Two leading newspapers, the *Times* and *Manchester Guardian*, spoke out on the dire meaning of German repudiation of the Versailles Treaty.

Nevertheless, many in Britain hoped this would herald the beginning of lasting agreement with Germany. There was a feeling that if Germany was again treated as an equal, it might be included safely in the great power system that Britain was trying to preserve. To this end, when it came to foreign affairs, the British were willing to give Germany wide latitude as long as German policy did not conflict with essential British interests. With its disengagement from the Continent, there was little the British saw as essential at first.[38] But the policy that led to the Anglo-German agreement deeply frustrated the French. It appeared not only to be a final abandonment of Versailles, but even a betrayal of the vague calls for international action at Stresa. Ultimately, it made cooperation between the two most powerful democracies in Western Europe very difficult at a critical time.

The actual declarations and actions by the Germans toward their rearmament in 1935, though threatening in tone, were not as important as the reaction of the Western democracies. The most careful reports noted that the Western democracies had considerable strategic superiority on land, at sea, and in the air over Germany in the near term. It was timid diplomatic activity and the lack of international cooperation that did the lasting damage. Seeing that the British and French could not put aside their differences, and that the United States refused to play any significant role, Hitler was emboldened to take more dramatic steps.

In the disunity of the Western powers, Hitler saw an opportunity to move toward the remilitarization of the Rhineland. He understood that Germany did not yet have the strength for a war over the territory, but he was convinced that the psychological conditions were favorable. In this assessment, he was proven correct. France, while maintaining easily the most powerful

army in Europe, was badly divided. French politics had been terribly unstable in the early thirties, some ministries' lifespan being measured in
weeks. Unrest in the streets and political division assured that, from February 1934 to May 1936, the French government was run by a series of stop-
gap, emergency cabinets, which contributed to French indecisiveness on the
international scene.[39] There was also little faith in British support after
France's concerns over Germany had received such diplomatic short shrift.
In 1936, France, therefore, found itself facing the renewed nightmare of
war with Germany over the Rhineland without a British ally abroad and
with unrest at home.

Had France and Britain chosen to act together, stern military and diplomatic resistance to Hitler's move would most likely have been very effective.
Within the German military there was deep concern over the Rhineland plan.
The Germans had no illusions about their vulnerability. If the French Army
had moved against them, their prompt ouster from the Rhineland would have
humiliated German forces. It was also highly likely that a military-sponsored
coup to topple Hitler would have been the result of a determined resistance
by the Allies. Later, Hitler asserted that the two days after German forces entered the Rhineland were the most anxious period of his life. He is reported
to have remarked that "had the French then marched into the Rhineland, we
would have had to withdraw again with our tails between our legs."[40]

However, within the French government and military, indecisiveness and
timidity prevailed—despite the fact that some French leaders were aware
that German boldness was an attempt to mask its real weakness and apprehension. A mere 3,000 German soldiers were sent into the region, but
French intelligence estimated, by some fantastic arithmetic, that the Germans had 295,000 men available for the operation. Even more important
than overblown estimates of their opponent's strength was a fearful assessment by the French of their own capabilities. Although France's army
was the strongest in Europe, it held that position largely due to the fact
that Germany was only beginning to shake off the effects of its forced de-
militarization and Britain's professional force was traditionally a small
one. Years of neglect and shrinking budgets had reduced the French military to a state that did not inspire confidence in French planners, who
feared a larger war.[41]

There were also members of the government who worried that a forceful
response to the German provocation would actually serve to isolate France
internationally. Mobilization over the Rhineland would be perceived as a
defense of the increasingly discredited Versailles system, they thought. Action in the name of Versailles, in the face of that agreement's dwindling international support, was likely to win France few allies. This only added to
the country's fears that the treasury would be unable to maintain the value
of the ailing franc if a clash occurred. Even if France's military could effec-

tively confront the German challenge, there might be a grievous toll to pay in the form of diplomatic isolation and financial damage.[42]

All these concerns, largely exaggerated, served to justify inaction when the deployment of a single French division might well have put the Germans to flight.[43] Yet, the accumulated fears and wishful thinking made even this small gesture inconceivable. Lack of foresight on the part of the international community in opposing Hitler also played a powerful role. French apathy is considered the major reason the Germans were given a green light to move into the Rhineland. But it also must be remembered that an anxious France was left alone to oppose a resurgent Germany by a world community unwilling to look at the possible long-term effects of German remilitarization on European security. Accordingly, Hitler's bold march into the Rhineland in March 1936 met no opposition.

In many ways, the years 1935 and 1936 were decisive on the road to war and Holocaust. With the move into the Rhineland, Hitler had abolished the constraints on German military and industrial power imposed after World War I. His successful foreign policy increased his popularity at home. From 1936 onward, this led to increasing action in international affairs by Germany. Eastern Europe received more Nazi attention, and Germany became more and more involved in supporting the forces of Francisco Franco in the Spanish Civil War. Hitler's successes lured an originally dubious Italy and Japan into the German camp. In November 1936, these three powers signed the Anti-Comintern Pact aimed at the Soviet Union.

The Coming of War

These successes gave Hitler the confidence to begin planning the realization of the dreams he set down in *Mein Kampf*. In 1937, he met with senior members of the army and government to review his expansionist strategy. Hitler hoped first to take Austria and Czechoslovakia and then move east to acquire the "living space" and natural resources an empire there would provide. These plans were no mere revision of the Treaty of Versailles. Rather, they were part of a more ambitious strategy that would guide Germany on the path to becoming an overwhelming world power. The period between 1943 and 1945 was targeted as the final date for beginning this push for territory.[44]

In 1938, Hitler used a pair of sex scandals to justify the removal of the defense minister and his would-be successor from their respective positions. Following this move, Hitler declared himself commander of the armed forces and replaced the old army high command with the *Oberkommando der Wehrmacht*, with himself in charge.[45] In 1938, he appointed the sycophant Joachim von Ribbentrop to head the foreign ministry, which, in the words of one prominent historian, "reduced the institution to little more than a stenographic bureau that simply did what it was told."[46] These bureaucratic shifts assured that Hitler held almost unlimited power in the making of German foreign and military policy.

At the same time, Hitler's success in upsetting Versailles damaged the credibility of Britain and France with smaller nations. Inaction planted seeds of doubt about the democracies' assurances of support. Indeed, in 1936, Belgium annulled a 1920 agreement for defense cooperation with France.

Churchill would later call World War II the unnecessary war, subtitling his book, *The Gathering Storm*, "How the English-speaking peoples through their unwisdom, carelessness, and good nature allowed the wicked to rearm." In his view, Germany should have been stopped from rearming at an early stage; Britain should never have made the 1935 naval agreement; and Britain and France should have confronted Germany over the Rhineland. In the light of history, Churchill was surely right. After 1936, stopping Hitler was to be a more difficult and expensive proposition. The Western powers' military strength declined relatively as German rearmament increased its feverish pace.

In 1937, Chamberlain came to power in Great Britain. He presided over a Britain troubled by economic depression but one that still held a massive empire. This empire, while viewed as a key to economic recovery, was also a site of vulnerability. Chamberlain adopted an existing policy in which Britain endeavored to prevent simultaneous challenges to its territories by Germany and Japan. In Europe, this led to a policy that was described as "appeasement," largely a continuation of much of what came before.[47] Germany would continue to be given considerable latitude on the Continent as long as its actions did not collide with what were seen as important British interests.

To be successful in the long run, however, appeasement required military strength and political determination. Yet, Britain and France were slow to realize the necessity of rearming to face Germany. Each worried that a confrontation in Europe would weaken its ability to defend its overseas possessions, while increased arms expenditures would weaken domestic recovery. Appeasement, therefore, became a means to buy time rather than a policy for peacefully coaxing Germany into the existing power system—something Germany, with its own ambitions for a "new order" in Europe, did not really want anyway.[48] This whole policy rested on a wishful appraisal of the Nazi threat and a lack of determination to face the danger it posed.

Even without their own military buildup to answer the Nazi threat, Britain and France did have the option of seeking the support of the two powerful states interested in seeing Germany contained: The United States, the Soviet Union, or both could have served as powerful counterweights to

German ambitions. For various reasons, however, neither could be brought into a coalition with Britain or France.

The Soviet Union was an obvious ally against Hitler. Despite their dictatorial similarities, Soviet Communism and German Nazism were anathema to each other. The Soviet Union, still struggling with its own industrialization and the excesses of Stalin's repressive rule, was made increasingly anxious by Nazi rhetoric and rearmament. In 1936, it sponsored the "Popular Front" against fascism, a strategy that accepted temporary collaboration with "bourgeois" regimes as necessary to defend against the greater evil posed by Hitler and his allies. To this same end, the Soviet Union signed a mutual assistance pact with France in 1935. That the Soviets were willing to ally with their "class enemies" against fascism shows just how deeply concerned Stalin was about the threat of Nazism.

However, fear of communism was powerfully rooted in both London and Paris. In France in 1936, the rise to premier of the socialist Leon Blum and the outbreak of the Spanish Civil War waved a red cape in front of Western European elites, who feared that an improvement in the position of the Soviet Union might promote communist revolution in Western Europe. That same year, a new set of Stalinist purges that eventually spilled over into the Red Army's high command did not improve matters. This provided fodder for the conservative French high command: Never positive regarding the Soviet Union, the generals could now further oppose Franco-Soviet military collaboration on the grounds that a hobbled Red Army would not be a useful ally in a war with Germany. In any case, many of France's East European allies were unwilling to contemplate the passage of Russian forces across their territory to do battle with Germany. Even the leftist Blum government remained unwilling to undertake serious negotiations with the Soviets for fear of alienating Britain.[49]

Among the tightly knit British governmental elite, fear of Soviet communism ran deep. Both Chamberlain and his predecessor, Stanley Baldwin, feared that close Franco-Soviet cooperation would draw France needlessly into war, while leaving much of Europe wide open to communism. They also believed that German expansion into Eastern Europe was an expedient way to contain the influence of the Soviets. As Baldwin remarked: "If there is any fighting in Europe to be done, I should like to see the Bolshies and Nazis doing it."[50] Given these biases against an alliance with the Soviets, the British and French never really took this option seriously.

The United States was the other major power that could have played a role in constraining Hitler. Yet, America had never been fully oriented toward involvement in European affairs. In the 1930s, many Americans had come to view their intervention in World War I and the subsequent peace settlements as a tragic mistake. Throughout the interwar period, a recurrent theme in popular literature and movies was that World War I had not been fought for any other purpose than to line the pockets of Wall Street bankers and arms merchants. This idea held powerful sway over public opinion. In 1934, after lobbying by the Women's International League for Peace, Senator Nye of North Dakota began two years of hearings on this subject. Even though no explicit connection between big business and the war was ultimately proven, these proceedings served to solidify the popular belief that this unholy alliance was responsible for U.S. involvement in the war and helped to build support for the first of the Neutrality Acts in 1935. With tensions mounting in Europe, the law banned arms sales to all belligerents in the belief that this type of activity had dragged the United States into World War I. The atmosphere in the country was such that one senator from Minnesota was able to declare, "To hell with Europe and the rest of those nations."[51]

In Franklin Delano Roosevelt, the United States had an internationalist president who did not share the attitudes of such members of the Senate. But Roosevelt had no desire to risk his vital domestic reform agenda for unpopular foreign policy positions. While he recognized Hitler as a threat—having read *Mein Kampf*, he considered its author a madman—he also understood that he faced entrenched isolationist interests, which found their loudest voice in Robert R. McCormick and his *Chicago Tribune*.[52] This powerful lobby served to delineate the limits of the Roosevelt administration's freedom of action. Roosevelt realized that he could not be a full-fledged participant in European affairs, but he was determined to experiment to find America's role in international politics.[53] As early as 1936, he concluded that action needed to be taken to restrain fascism and to assure peace in Europe. What followed was a series of exploratory moves to see what foreign policy actions the American public would allow.

In October 1937 in Chicago, the center of isolationist opposition, Roosevelt gave his famous "Quarantine Speech." He noted that violations of treaties were creating "international anarchy," from which conflict would inevitably result. If war came, the United States would not escape harm; therefore, the United States had a stake in maintaining peace. He warned further:

An epidemic of world lawlessness is spreading. . . .When an epidemic of physical disease starts to spread, the community approves and joins in a quarantine of the patients in order to protect the health of the community against the spread of the disease. . . . War is a contagion, whether it be declared or undeclared. It can engulf states and peoples remote from the original scene of hostilities.[54]

Roosevelt was clearly referring to the aggressive actions of Germany, Italy, and Japan. His answer was a call for collective action to prevent conflict.

Despite his foresight, Roosevelt did not follow up on his dramatic words. When queried by the press the day following the speech, he refused to elaborate on any policy implications. "We are looking for a program," he told the gathered reporters.[55] Roosevelt knew that any major turnaround in American policy would be slow and difficult. But this sluggishness had international repercussions. In early 1938, when Roosevelt proposed an international peace conference, Chamberlain refused to participate, stating, "The isolationists . . . [are] so strong and so vocal" that the United States could not be "depended upon for help if [Britain] should get into trouble." The British prime minister was sure that the Americans were not a useful counterweight to Germany: "It is always best and safest to count on *nothing* from the Americans except words."[56] Convinced that Britain lacked a reliable ally across the Atlantic, Chamberlain further embraced a policy of appeasement.

In March 1938, Hitler, relishing the disarray among the democracies, seized Austria. Again, the reaction of the Allies was one of relative inaction. The world situation had grown more tense in the interim. Japan's expansion had exploded into open war with Nationalist China in 1937, a conflict that threatened British, French, and American interests in Asia. Strong action against Hitler might have left any or all of these countries' possessions in the Pacific vulnerable to Japanese aggression. Nevertheless, there was an increasing belief that a stand should be taken against Hitler. In the spring of 1938, even Chamberlain noted that "force is the only argument Germany understands."[57]

The *Anschluss* was only part of Hitler's larger goals in Eastern Europe. Just after absorbing Austria, the Nazi regime had begun to agitate about the fate of the Sudeten Germans in Czechoslovakia. Britain had little concern for the fates of this minority or for Czechoslovakia itself, but came to understand that the Czechs might drag France into a confrontation due to their long-standing agreements. Throughout the spring and summer, tensions grew as the Czechoslovaks refused to concede to German demands. Both Britain and France had no desire to bow to open threats of force, but neither did they want war. Mobilizations were ordered by both democracies in September, and war fears ran high. Mussolini's call for a conference on the issue allowed open conflict to be avoided. Hitler—despite the fact that he craved a war over Czechoslovakia—consented to meeting concerned parties in Munich. In fact, historians have asserted that violence was averted in 1938 not only because the French and British gave in but also because Hitler did not force a general war at that particular time.[58]

Nevertheless, the Munich Conference that decided the fate of Czechoslovakia was international arbitration at its worst. It was simply a four-power conference, with only Germany, Italy, France, and Britain given seats at the negotiation table. The Czechoslovaks, whose future lay on that table, were forced to sit in the hallway. Neither were the Russians, who also had a clear stake in Eastern European affairs, participants. Various countries in the region from Poland to Hungary who also had interests in the fate of the small nation were left out as well. In effect, four major powers made decisions for many millions of people in several other countries on the basis of their own narrow interests.[59]

While Hitler chose not to fight in 1938, neither did the Western powers have the military wherewithal to force him to back down should he have pursued war. The British and French, struggling to rearm, accepted the severing of the Sudetenland from Czechoslovakia because they feared the strength of German arms.

In the immediate aftermath of Munich, Chamberlain became a hero. His claim for "peace in our time" came as a relief for people across Europe. Following the signing of the agreement, Roosevelt sent him a cable with the simple message, "Good man."[60] In Britain, there was even a song titled "God Bless You, Mr. Chamberlain." Appeasement appeared to have spared Europe another major conflict.

Some historians have viewed the Munich Agreement as one that purchased the Western powers critical time to continue their rearmament, something that may have made the difference for Britain in 1940. While this may be true, Allied appeasement at Munich made war in Europe inevitable. In January 1939, Hitler began to make demands on Poland. In March, German forces, having hardly digested the Sudetenland, swallowed the rest of Czechoslovakia. How late true cooperation came between the democracies is underscored by the fact that it was only at this stage that the British finally accepted full military discussions with the French general staff.[61] Britain also extended a guarantee to Poland, which it had every intention of honoring. However, Hitler no longer feared the gestures of the democracies. Their record of inaction had left him dismissive of their diplomatic overtures. Overall, the foreign policies of the democracies only served to prompt more radical policies of aggression by Germany.

In April 1939, Roosevelt attempted to defuse growing tensions by sending a diplomatic note to Germany and Italy asking them for assurances that they would not attack a list of thirty-one countries for at least ten years.[62] This was part of a series of continuing attempts by the American president to influence world affairs as the international situation deteriorated. The United States had begun to aid Chiang Kai-shek's Nationalists in China against the Japanese and was endeavoring to increase aircraft sales to the French and British in order to stiffen their resolve against Germany.

However, Hitler appreciated the fact that any American international action was severely constrained by the country's domestic isolationists. In 1938, Roosevelt had suffered extreme embarrassment when it was discovered that French military officers were being shown the latest American

combat aircraft. Understanding that Roosevelt's note of April 1939 had little domestic or international support, Hitler called a special session in the
Reichstag to discuss Roosevelt's appeal.

In a long, cynical, and derisive speech heard around the world, he mocked
the president's intentions. He replayed the sentiments of isolationists and
those that sought accommodation with his regime—for his own ends. Germany, he maintained, was only attempting to break out of the "encir-
clement" of other powers. His policy aimed only to bring back "to the Reich provinces stolen from us in 1919." He derided Roosevelt and noted that
the democracies themselves had denied the right of self-determination to
peoples in their colonies. He pointed to the United States' own history of expansion, stating that German peace representatives after World War I "were
subjected to even greater degradations than can ever have been inflicted on
the chieftains of the Sioux tribes." As for the international conference that
the United States sought to arrange in order to defuse international tensions,
he noted that the United States itself had not joined the League of Nations
and had not bothered to negotiate a settlement to its own civil war. Hitler
went on to note that Roosevelt, as the head of the world's wealthiest nation,
had the luxury of being able to intervene in "universal" issues, while Hitler's
own concerns were only those of "my people." Hitler then read off the
names of the states whose security he had been asked to guarantee, but clev-
erly, he omitted Poland.[63]

The Reichstag speech was more than just a signal of Hitler's disdain for
Roosevelt and the international cooperation the president advocated. It was
also a clear indication that the inertia of the international community both
fed Hitler's ambition and provided ready-made rationales for his policies.
Hitler made the same justifications for inaction proffered by Great Britain,
France, and the United States serve for his own actions.

In the summer of 1939, the British and French made belated overtures to
the Soviet Union asking it to join a coalition against Germany. Throughout
the summer, the democracies courted the Soviets and even sent a high-level
delegation to Moscow for discussions. But the ambivalence of the Western
powers, the slight of not inviting the Soviets to the Munich Conference, and
Stalin's own ambitions in Eastern Europe led to an entirely unexpected outcome. Instead of an agreement with the democracies, the Soviet Union
signed a nonaggression pact with Nazi Germany on August 23.[64] The two
irreconcilable ideological enemies of the 1930s reconciled for their own mutual benefit. This agreement cleared the way for German aggression against
Poland.

Britain made its guarantee to Poland into a formal alliance on August 25,
1939. France and Britain were then determined to stand firm against German moves—not from any deep attachment to Poland or an assessment of
its strategic value. Rather, it was an attempt to reassert their great power

status, something that had been seriously eroded by recent events. But it was too late to salvage that prestige in the eyes of the Nazi regime. Many members of Hitler's junta had begun to see Britain and France as weak and indecisive—symptoms of their declining powers—and because of this, by the summer of 1939, Germany had little fear of concerted international action against it. Hitler himself thought that a German attack on Poland would not lead to a military response from the Western nations but only another empty gesture aimed at shoring up their tattered prestige.[65]

War and Its Consequences

In this calculation, Hitler was wrong. Following the German invasion of Poland on September 1, 1939, the British and French issued strong ultimatums. When Hitler ignored them, Europe entered into its second great conflict of the century, one that in two years would envelop the whole globe. The best years to confront Hitler's ambitions for conquest had slipped past, and only total war would suffice to stop the forces he had set loose. Modern, technological war was terrible enough, but the conflagration also allowed the full fury of the Holocaust to be unleashed. In the end, Hitler was thoroughly defeated and discredited, but only at the highest human cost in all of history.

The Allied failure to stop Hitler at the Rhineland in 1936 foreclosed the last good opportunity for the primary prevention of World War II. International action against Hitler was still possible at the time of the Czech crisis of 1938, even extending into the tragic year of 1939. But in the two intervening years, Hitler's military, industrial, and political strength had grown rapidly and so had his confidence and determination to push relentlessly for conquest; the years of his serious vulnerability had irrevocably passed for the Allies.

A speech by Hitler's close confidant and minister of propaganda, Joseph Goebbels, provides a vivid insight into this missed window of opportunity:

> We wanted to come to power legally, but we did not want to use power legally. . . . They could have suppressed us. . . . No, they let us through the danger zone. In 1933, a French premier ought to have said (and if I had been the French premier, I would have said it): "The new Reich Chancellor is the man who wrote *Mein Kampf*, which says this and that. This man cannot be tolerated in our vicinity. Either he disappears or we march!" But they didn't do it. They left us alone, and we were able to sail around all the dangerous reefs. And when we were done, and well armed, better than them, they started the war.[66]

Goebbels understood that international preventive action, had it been taken early enough, could have been successful. Clearly, inaction at that early stage greatly increased the costs that Europe, and the world, later paid.

In 1942, after the United States had been dragged into the world conflict, Winston Churchill gave a speech to a joint session of the American Congress. A body that had been strongly isolationist before the Japanese attack on Pearl Harbor cheered mightily when he stated, "[If] we had kept together . . . if we had taken common measures for our safety, this renewal of the curse of war need never to have fallen upon us."[67]

The enthusiastic reception of the prime minister's words presaged much activity during the war that sought to institutionalize collective action to prevent another violent outbreak. Internationalists, who had been marginalized in the 1930s by intense nationalism and chauvinism in much of the world (including the democracies), gained considerable credibility in the war years when they proposed international cooperation and international bodies to mediate future disputes. Even the father of "realism" in political science, E. H. Carr, changed his tune. In his classic book *The Twenty Years Crisis 1919 to 1939,* which called for a return to power politics as the basis for stability, Carr was critical of what he saw as soft-headed internationalism during the inter-war period. His 1944 *Conditions of Peace* had a different tone, calling on nations to "revolutionize" international affairs by moving beyond a balance of power approach to a view that included space for social, political, and economic change.[68]

Even in the midst of the war, serious thinking occurred among the Allies about the shape of the postwar world. A collection of ideas for a new postwar order emerged from members of the "United Nations"—the name taken by the coalition of aligned countries grappling with the Axis powers. Some ideas ranged from dramatic "one-world" proposals to more traditional ideas of concerted powers acting together to impose stability. These proposals contributed to an atmosphere that eventually pushed the Allied nations bloodied by the war to embark on an effort to plan a new international organization that would move beyond the failings of its predecessor, the League of Nations, and build a stronger set of international institutions. Policymakers of many backgrounds and nationalities, tempered by the crisis of total war, learned from their experiences that international collaboration on many levels was necessary to ensure peace. What emerged from a series of proposals, consultations, and conferences in the war years was the United Nations Organization.

The creation of the UN was not only an attempt to institutionalize collective security but to codify a global regime of conflict prevention. Beyond representation of the countries of the world in a forum that was supposed to provide a means to adjudicate disagreements, the organization was constructed to actively pursue violence prevention around the world. Initially, the "principal organ" of the UN was to be the Economic and Social Council (ECOSOC), which was mandated to address economic questions worldwide. ECOSOC's primacy was an outgrowth of the belief that questions of peace and security were bound to economic and social justice.[69] At the same time, the founders of the UN realized that economics were not the sum of human interaction, as "wars begin in the minds of men, it is in the minds of men that the defenses of peace must be constructed." They understood the following:

> That a peace based exclusively upon the political and economic arrangements of governments would not be a peace which could secure the unanimous, lasting and sincere support of the peoples of the world, and that the peace must therefore be founded, if it is not to fail, upon the intellectual and moral solidarity of mankind.[70]

This more inclusive approach to conflict prevention led to the formation of the United Nations Educational, Scientific, and Cultural Organization (UNESCO). It was the embodiment of internationalist ideas of collaboration and exchange that had been present in the League, except that they were extended to embrace peoples of Asia, Africa, the Middle East, and Latin America who had largely been excluded from activities in the interwar period.[71] All of these ideas were believed to be inextricably connected to basic rights applicable to all peoples, and they were eventually codified in the Universal Declaration of Human Rights in 1948.[72]

Tied to the UN system were several international governmental institutions that were also formed to prevent conflict. Conscious of how the breakdown of the world economic system in the 1930s and the subsequent depression encouraged militant nationalism, the United States took the lead in establishing the International Bank for Reconstruction and Development (which has since become known as the World Bank) and the International Monetary Fund (IMF). Both institutions, accountable to their member states, were meant to oversee a world economy reformed in the light of recent history. Through their work, they were to foster growth and ensure economic stability and security for the world's peoples and prevent the sort of economic slide that had ended in the conflagration of World War II.[73]

The hopes for the new UN organization were as vast as its global responsibilities, but so were the constraints it faced. Even before it was fully formed, the United States and the Soviet Union were using the UN as another arena for their Cold War jousts. As the postwar period wore on, the UN would evolve dramatically and not always in ways that fulfilled its initial conception. Confronting some global concerns, it was hamstrung by political rivalries, shortages of funds, and, at certain points, its own organizational inadequacies. Despite these shortcomings, the origins of the UN as a means to prevent deadly conflict the world over must be remembered. Out of the debasement and chaos of World War II, the United Nations was created with a mission to stop war before it started. Regardless of its limitations during the Cold War, the UN retains this bedrock principle of conflict prevention to this day. In the epilogue, I return to its newest developments that seek to fulfill the original aspirations.

Challenges from the 1930s for the Twenty-First Century: Some Guidelines for Prevention

In this chapter, we examined the catastrophe of World War II and its associated Holocaust. For the generation that emerged from the war, it was a powerful stimulus for prevention, and it remains so to this day. We focused on the dire events of the early 1930s—the crucially formative time for Nazi aggression and destruction and probably the best years for preventive intervention.

We asked some questions based on the historical record of that period and today's knowledge of tools and strategies for prevention. What did the main actors do in that period? What stood in the way of the preservation of peace and justice? What could we do now in similar situations? Perhaps the epidemic of hatred and violence spread by Hitler and his allies was beyond any existing treatment of the time, but maybe advances since then can preserve the health of the international public even in the presence of the same pathogens. Can the experience of World War II and the Holocaust alert us to generic problems of great continuing importance? For example, have we humans learned how to deal with malevolent, ruthless, hyperaggressive dictators and fanatical haters in command of obedient (even enthusiastic) people? Evidence from the second half of the twentieth century shows that this remains an exceedingly hard and dangerous problem.

It is an understatement to say the global context today is different than it was in the 1930s. Colonialism has ended, fascism and communism have been discredited as systems of political organization, and many perceptions have changed in the ensuing decades—all causing momentous shifts in international affairs. Nevertheless there are informative lessons to be learned from the 1930s, when power in the international arena was not focused on two states as it was during the Cold War. These are lessons not limited to that period, and we should take care to remember them even as we digest the lessons of the Cold War and the bloody 1990s.

1. Egregious human rights violations within a country are associated with a high risk of mass violence—both through internal polarization and through external aggression.
2. Prejudice and ethnocentrism are very dangerous, especially in the form of hypernationalistic fervor or other fanatical orientations. These orientations are characterized by sharp dichotomies: us or them, all or none, holy war. They can spread like an infectious disease

throughout populations and national boundaries. Once turned loose in virulent form, they are very hard to contain.

3. Wishful thinking by leaders and by their publics leads to serious blunders. Elaborate rationalizations based on wishful assumptions can foster widespread denial, avoidance of serious problems, and delay in facing them. Later, when it comes time to cope with such problems—if they are addressed at all—the costs and risks are likely to be much greater. A fundamental opportunity to prevent deadly conflict lies in taking early warnings seriously. This requires a differentiated assessment of warnings to discern credible incitements to hatred and violence.

4. A major challenge is learning to make accurate appraisals of hyperaggressive leaders. They are often paranoid, deceitful, grandiose, hateful, and intimidating. When they offer reassurances, it is tempting to believe that the danger has passed. Realistic appraisal must take into account their behavior over a period of years in a variety of conflict situations.

5. Dictators, demagogues, and religious fanatics can readily play on the serious frustrations that people experience during times of severe economic and social hardship. Such frustration is highly conducive to aggressive behavior and makes the public receptive to demagogic appeals. Long-standing tensions between ethnic, religious, or others groups provide a fault line along which harsh leaders may stir up survival emotions, as if to say, "we of the in-group must deal harshly with the out-group in order to survive."

6. The human species is susceptible to genocide; the historical record makes this abundantly clear. The constraints against it are not powerful, especially when there is an autocrat or dictator in control and the culture has established prejudicial stereotypes to provide a convenient target. This combination of factors is particularly dangerous when the international community is weak in its ability to undertake concerted action.

7. Circumstances of extreme turbulence such as war, revolution, a failed state, or economic freefall are conducive to mass expulsion or genocide in the context of highly inflammatory leadership and authoritarian social structures.

8. The absence of clear opposition is conducive to the escalation of hatred and violence. Either internal or external opposition, preferably both, can be helpful in preventing conflict. There can be a constructive interplay between opposition to a violent regime within a country and beyond its borders. For outsiders, it should be taken as a powerful warning when leadership is intransigent and uses terror against such opposition.

9. The best opportunity to prevent genocide is through international cooperative action to overthrow, or at least powerfully constrain, a genocidal regime—if possible, on the basis of strong warning information *before* the genocide is underway.

10. Fear induced by a terroristic aggressor can readily lead to an overestimate of the aggressor's strength or the difficulties to be faced in confronting the problem. This in turn is conducive to appeasement, which only whets the appetite of the aggressor.
11. Alternative approaches and policies beyond appeasement are usually available. It is crucial to consider them seriously, not to avoid them on the basis of ideological preference, personal rigidity, or wishful thinking. There are usually more ways to block an aggressor than initially apparent, especially if the problem is recognized early and dealt with in a resolute manner.
12. Careful preparation for serious danger is helpful, especially since it is so difficult to improvise under severe stress. Having institutionalized structures, criteria for intervention, problem-solving procedures, an array of tools and strategies—all these contribute to rational assessment, sound contingency planning, and effective responses.
13. Leadership is crucial. Leadership must have the ability to recognize real dangers and the courage to address them, not impulsively, but thoughtfully. It requires the ability to transcend wishful thinking. It can be greatly enhanced by building professional competence in the small advisory group and the institutional setting in which leaders make decisions—so that they can get the best available information, analyze it carefully, weigh their options, and reach conclusions for the general well-being. Moreover, authentic leaders must have the capacity to build constituencies for prevention through a base of public information and skill in forming political coalitions.
14. International cooperation is crucial. The multiple failures of cooperation in the face of grave danger during the 1930s, even among major democracies, point vividly to the need for international cooperation—pooling strengths, sharing burdens, dividing labor as necessary to cope with serious dangers.
15. Since dictatorial and/or failed states are so dangerous with their predispositions for mass violence, it is vitally important to build competent, democratic states. To do so, the international community must produce intellectual, technical, financial, and moral resources to aid democratically inclined leaders and peoples all over the world. Such aid, often multilateral in origin, must be sustained over many years, if necessary, as capacity is built within the country or region for coping with its own problems.

The painful lessons of American isolationism and unilateralism in the 1920s and 1930s are even more salient now in the maximally interdependent and superarmed world that is emerging. Many of these considerations apply not only to inter-state warfare but to the intra-state violence now so prevalent.

Applying These Lessons to the Twenty-First Century

Such conditions of violence as existing in the 1930s can occur again. Today, the seductive justifications for hideous atrocities can be provided just as well as they were by Hitler. Indeed, they can be spread more efficiently and vividly now than ever before by advanced communication technologies, and the killing power of worldwide weaponry is moving beyond prior experience.

The events of the 1930s show the probability that World War II was a conflict that was *preventable,* even with the limited tools available at the time. This was strongly emphasized by Winston Churchill. Too often, our view of history assumes that conflagrations are preordained. The purpose of this chapter has been to highlight those moments when preventive action could have been taken and to identify some of the factors that precluded action. One central obstacle to prevention was the narrow, shortsighted definitions of national interest that undermined the high degree of international cooperation necessary to block Hitler's aggressive expansion.

As in the 1930s, we are today living through a period of profound change in our economic, social, cultural, and technological lives. Like the 1930s, the international arena is not bounded by the global confrontation of two superpowers. While the world does not now face a threat like that of Hitler's Germany, we have seen many incidents of mass violence in the past decade—for example, in Cambodia, Africa, Southern Europe, the Caucasus, and by the terrorists based in Afghanistan. The inadequacy of the international community's response in these situations bears a disturbing similarity to the events of the 1930s. But, unlike the 1930s, we now have numerous international institutions, legal norms, economic measures, technological capabilities, and diplomatic practices that, if cultivated and exercised effectively, can serve as vital tools to prevent violent conflict. The remainder of this book is devoted to identifying these tools, the strategies for their use, the institutions and organizations that can do the work, and the leadership necessary to make it all happen.

Notes

1. *Encyclopedia Britannica Online,* "Table 7: World War II Casualties" and "World War II: Costs of the War," www.eb.com, March 29, 2000. Estimates of the deaths caused by the war usually range from 35 to 65 million persons (although some have put the number as high as 100 million). Only the casualty

figures of the United States and British Commonwealth can be referenced with any assurance of accuracy. The dislocation caused by the fighting worked against good record keeping in most places. This is particularly true in Russia and China, which suffered some of the worst losses; neither has been able to make truly accurate counts, especially of their civilian deaths. Potentially, the generally accepted figures could be significantly higher.

2. Michael Jabara Carley, *1939: The Alliance That Never Was and the Coming of World War II* (New York: Ivan Dee, 1999), 5–6; and Gordon Craig, *Germany, 1866–1945* (New York: Oxford University Press, 1978), 521.

3. Carley, *1939,* 30.

4. Sidney Aster, "'Guilty Men': The Case of Neville Chamberlain," in Patrick Finney, ed., *The Origins of the Second World War* (New York: Arnold, 1997), 69.

5. R. A. C. Parker, *Churchill and Appeasement* (London: Macmillan, 2000).

6. Richard Overy, *The Origins of the Second World War,* 2d ed. (New York: Longman, 1998), 96–100.

7. Overy, *Origins,* 16–17.

8. Gordon Craig, *Europe Since 1815* (New York: Holt, Rinehart & Winston, 1961), 442–43.

9. Craig, *Europe,* 552.

10. Sheila Fitzpatrick, "Socialism and Communism," in Richard Bullet, ed., *The Columbia History of the Twentieth Century* (New York: Columbia, 1998), 214.

11. Overy, *Origins,* 16.

12. Overy, *Origins,* 6.

13. Craig, *Europe,* 550–52.

14. Walter Laquer, *Fascism: Past, Present, Future* (New York: Oxford University Press, 1996).

15. Craig, *Europe,* 600.

16. Fritz Stern, *Dreams and Delusions: National Socialism in the Drama of the German Past* (New York: Vintage, 1987), chs. 5–6; and Detlev J. K. Peukert, *The Weimar Republic: The Crisis of Classical Modernity,* Richard Deveson, trans. (New York: Hill and Wang, 1989).

17. Stern, *Dreams and Delusions,* 124.

18. Stern, *Dreams and Delusions,* 172–73.

19. J. Kenneth Brody, *The Avoidable War: Lord Cecil and the Policy of Principle, 1933–1935,* vol. 1 (New Brunswick, N.J.: Transaction, 1999), 102.

20. Lucy S. Dawidowicz, *The War Against the Jews* (New York: Bantam, 1976); Bernard Lewis, *Semites and Anti-Semites: An Inquiry into Conflict and Prejudice* (New York: Norton, 1999); Gotz Aly, *"Final Solution": Nazi Population Policy and the Murder of the European Jews* (New York: Oxford University Press, 1999); and James M. Glass, *"Life Unworthy of Life": Racial Phobia and Mass Murder in Hitler's Germany* (New York: Basic, 1997).

21. Stern, *Dreams and Delusions,* ch. 6.

22. Adolf Hitler, *Mein Kampf,* Ralph Manheim, trans. (New York: Houghton Mifflin, 1943), 649.

23. Craig, *Germany,* 676–78.

24. Craig, *Germany,* 360–66.

25. Hitler, *Mein Kampf,* 139.

26. Craig, *Germany,* 678.

27. Fritz Redlich, *Hitler: Diagnosis of a Destructive Prophet* (New York: Oxford, 1999), 97–99.

28. Craig, *Germany,* 673.

29. Brody, *Avoidable War,* 143–45.

30. Craig, *Germany,* 674–75.

31. Brody, *Avoidable War,* 146.

32. Roy Denman, *Missed Chances: Britain and Europe in the Twentieth Century* (London: Indigo, 1997).

33. Craig, *Germany,* 682.

34. Ruth Henig, *The Origins of the Second World War, 1933–1939* (New York: Routledge, 1991).

35. Ian Kershaw, *Hitler, 1889–1936: Hubris* (New York: Norton, 1998), 550–52.

36. Brody, *Avoidable War,* 279.

37. Brody, *Avoidable War,* ch. 11.

38. Overy, *Origins,* 20–21.

39. Craig, *Europe,* 675–77.

40. Kershaw, *Hitler,* 588.

41. Kershaw, *Hitler,* 588.

42. Stephan A. Schuker, "France and the Remilitarization of the Rhineland, 1936," in Patrick Finney, ed., *The Origins of the Second World War* (New York: Arnold, 1997), 229–36.

43. Kershaw, *Hitler,* 588.

44. Richard Overy, "Misjudging Hitler: A. J. P. Taylor and the Third Reich," in Gordon Martel, ed., *The Origins of the Second World War Reconsidered: A. J. P. Taylor and the Historians,* 2d ed. (New York: Routledge, 1999), 103–4.

45. Overy, "Misjudging," 101–2; Klaus P. Fischer, *Nazi Germany: A New History* (New York: Continuum, 1995), 413–14.

46. Fischer, *Nazi Germany,* 402, quoting Gordon Craig.

47. Overy, *Origins,* 18–19.

48. Overy, *Origins,* 21.

49. Carley, *1939,* ch. 1.

50. Carley, *1939,* 33.

51. David Kennedy, *Freedom from Fear: The American People in Depression and War, 1929–1945* (New York: Oxford University Press, 1999), 387–88, 394.

52. Kennedy, *Freedom,* 404.

53. Barbara Farnham, *Roosevelt and the Munich Crisis: A Study of Political Decision Making* (Princeton, N.J.: Princeton University Press, 1997), 79–80.

54. Franklin Delano Roosevelt, "Quarantine the Aggressors," October 5, 1937. <www.homer.providence.edu/wcb/schools/PC1/his/mmanches/12/files/fdrquarspch.htm> Accessed April 2000.

55. Kennedy, *Freedom*, 406.

56. Aster, "'Guilty Men,'", 64; Kennedy, *Freedom*, 407–8.

57. Overy, *Origins*, 27.

58. Overy, *Origins*, 29.

59. Andrew Crozier, *The Causes of the Second World War* (Malden: Blackwell, 1997), 143–44.

60. Farnham, *Roosevelt and the Munich Crisis*, 119.

61. Overy, *Origins*, 63.

62. William L. Shirer, *The Rise and Fall of the Third Reich* (New York: Simon & Schuster, 1960), 470.

63. Shirer, *Rise and Fall*, 471–75; Kennedy, *Freedom*, 423–24.

64. Carley, *1939*, ch. 6.

65. Overy, *Origins*, 79.

66. Fischer, *Nazi Germany*, 402–3.

67. Quoted in Gary B. Ostrower, *The United Nations and the United States* (New York: Twayne, 1998), 7.

68. Akira Iriye, *Cultural Internationalism and World Order* (Baltimore: Johns Hopkins, 1997), 138–39.

69. Ostrower, *United Nations*, 35.

70. UNESCO, Constitution, Preamble <www.unesco.org>.

71. Iriye, *Cultural Internationalism*, 146–47.

72. Mary Ann Glendon, *A World Made New: Eleanor Roosevelt and the Universal Declaration of Human Rights* (New York: Random House, 2001).

73. John Stremlau and Francisco Sagasti, *Preventing Deadly Conflict: Does the World Bank Have a Role?* (Report to the Carnegie Commission on Preventing Deadly Conflict, 1998), 9–10.

3

Governments and Intergovernmental Organizations: Paralyzed Giants or Serious Players?

Preventing Deadly Conflict: The Legacy of Rwanda

The 1994 mass slaughter in Rwanda ranks as one of history's worst episodes of genocide. In only three short months, an estimated 500,000 to 800,000 people—or about one in ten citizens—were brutally hunted down and killed. For the international community, the cardinal legacy of Rwanda is the knowledge that mass violence of this scale is a deliberate political act, that it can hardly happen without warning, and that the absence of domestic and international constraints permits genocide to recur. This genocide was not prevented. But it was preventable.

This observation is not simply a matter of hindsight being twenty-twenty, nor is it a case of "if only we knew then." The history of politically motivated animosity between Hutu and Tutsi in Rwanda, partly a consequence of the discriminatory and divisive practices of colonial rule, was already widely known for many years before the genocide. Waves of killing and expulsion had occurred in earlier decades in both Rwanda and adjacent Burundi. The potential for renewed violence was clear in the early 1990s. In 1993, the human rights group, Africa Watch, reported that extremist Hutu leaders had prepared hit lists of their political enemies—individuals who some two years later would be among the first victims of the *Interahamwe*. Intensified warnings of a genocidal plot, received months before the suspicious plane crash that killed President Juvénal Habyarimana of Rwanda and President Cyprien Ntaryamira of Burundi, went unheeded by international organizations and by national governments—even those participating in the United Nations Assistance Mission for Rwanda (UNAMIR), a peacekeeping mission that had been authorized a year earlier to support the faltering Arusha peace process. When the deaths of the two presidents triggered the genocide, the response of the United Nations Security Council was to withdraw all but 250 of the 2,500 peacekeepers from

51

Rwanda. Indeed, so intent were the leading nations of the Security Council to evade any involvement that they systematically downplayed the gravity of the crisis, even avoiding use of the term *genocide*—though this was plainly the case. UNAMIR's mandate was so narrowly drawn and its reduced troop-strength so small that it could not intervene to halt the genocide. By this point, there was no peace to keep. And so, this calamity occurred even in the face of clear and authoritative warnings from military commanders on the ground and the UN Secretary-General. The haunting story of these events was recently documented in an exceedingly courageous, thorough, and well-documented report requested by Secretary-General Kofi Annan.[1]

Another four months elapsed before the UN proposed that 5,000 peace-keeping troops be sent to Rwanda with an expanded mandate to protect civilians and to secure humanitarian assistance. Again, however, UN member states declined to support this joint intervention, in part because of the recent and bitter experience of intervention in Somalia. Meanwhile, the slaughter continued unabated. It was only the arrival of the Rwandan Patriotic Front (RPF), a force of Tutsi-led exiles from neighboring Uganda that ended the genocidal campaign.

But the slaughter did not stop there. The ensuing civil chaos sent two million Hutu fleeing into Zaire (now the Congo), Tanzania, and Burundi. Interspersed among the refugees were armed Hutu militiamen who had actively participated in the genocide. They took control of the refugee camps, stole supplies intended for humanitarian relief, and embarked on an insurgency against the new Tutsi-led government in Rwanda. The fervent appeals of UN High Commissioner for Refugees Sadako Ogata for assistance to prevent further conflict also went unheeded, and the violence escalated and spread, particularly into the eastern Congo. When Rwanda and other neighboring countries sent military forces into the eastern Congo to put down the insurgents, they set in motion an insurrection that eventually toppled the government of dictator Mobutu Sese Seko. These events extended the cycle of deadly conflict, as Tutsi fighters and Congolese rebels tracked down and killed thousands of Hutu refugees during the spring of 1997. The violent repercussions of this conflict continue to the present day and now involve a wide circle of African nations. It sparked a regional war that has dragged on over three years and that has consumed as of mid-2001, according to reliable estimates, three million lives.[2]

Soon after the genocide, UNAMIR commander General Romeo Dallaire asserted that, given 5,000 troops and an appropriate mandate, he could have prevented most of the killing. Neither such a force nor the will to deploy one existed at the time. The Organization of African Unity (OAU), the main regional organization, lacked the capacity to undertake preventive action, while North Atlantic Treaty Organization (NATO) members were wholly unwilling to intervene, either as part of a NATO-led mission or individually. When concerned governments belatedly turned to the United Nations Security Council, there was no rapid reaction force ready to deploy.

In early 1997, the Carnegie Commission on Preventing Deadly Conflict, Georgetown University's Institute for the Study of Diplomacy, and the U.S. Army convened an international panel of experienced military professionals to assess Dallaire's claim. After studying the problem carefully, they affirmed that a rapid reaction force of 5,000 troops, if properly equipped and supported, authorized to take all means necessary to restrain or preempt violent acts, and deployed at an early stage, "could have made a significant difference in Rwanda in 1994."[3] While the window of opportunity for effective intervention was small, such an opportunity did exist, and hundreds of thousands of civilian lives most probably could have been saved. A more recent study initiated by the Carnegie Commission dealing with the costs of conflict in many cases of 1990s violence reaches similar conclusions about Rwanda.[4]

What then? These studies of the Rwanda tragedy make it clear that such an intervention could at most provide immediate rescue and humanitarian relief. In the longer term, Rwanda would need a far-reaching political settlement, including international assistance in establishing viable conflict resolution mechanisms and reliable guarantees of human (including minority) rights, as well as economic aid to build the foundations for equitable development. For Rwanda, as for many other places in the world, this is a tall order, one that the international community is currently ill prepared to fulfill. However daunting, these tasks are not beyond human capacities. It is worth recalling that the peaceful and prosperous Europe of today was, not so long ago, the site of some of the worst savagery the world has ever known. In any event, the Rwanda massacres highlight the historical and recent failures of governments and intergovernmental organizations (IGOs) to prevent exceedingly deadly and highly preventable conflicts. Can we do better?

The Necessity of Prevention

While there has long been a vaguely formulated wish for prevention, skepticism has prevailed. Why should we bother? What could we do? Which of us could do it? Because these are the refrains that typically arise to justify third-party inaction in the face of deadly conflicts, they are worth reflecting on at this point.

The first question has a number of variants, most of which boil down to why outsiders should undertake the risks and responsibilities of preventing conflicts elsewhere, in countries whose political, social, and economic misfortunes—however tragic—have little *apparent* connection to the world beyond. The events of September 11 cast a different light on this illusion of remoteness. Saving failed states, protecting human rights, ensuring just political and economic governance are, in the first instance, the responsibility of each society. If any society is to enjoy the benefits of peace, justice, prosperity, and good order, its people must do so on their own terms, summoning their own will and resources, as well as ingenuity and decency, devising their own norms and their own governing institutions. An indigenous commitment is primary; without it, no amount of international assistance can bear fruit. Nevertheless, indigenous efforts are often dangerously insufficient; in cases such as the Rwandan genocide, societies can be so crippled by political repression, economic corruption, intergroup distrust and animosity that a concerted international effort becomes the only avenue of hope. In such circumstances, successful prevention largely depends on how third parties do or do not respond to warnings of social breakdown and incipient mass violence.

To say that the international community is often the only hope for preventing disaster still begs the question of why outsiders should undertake such action or by which agency they should do so. There are several reasons that, when considered together, make a compelling case.

The first might be called *ethical humanitarianism*, based on the well-developed principle that when we are in a position to do something to forestall or alleviate it, we may not stand idly by while innocent people suffer terribly. This norm of mutual aid and cooperation is at the heart of the world's great civilizations and is the necessary bedrock of successful societies. Scholars of human societies view this as a fundamental—necessary—feature of human existence: Without such other-regarding norms of behavior, collective life would scarcely be possible. For this reason, mutual aid has also become one of the central animating principles of modern international society, as reflected in a variety of international agreements, including the Geneva Convention, the UN Charter, and associated UN conventions against genocide and in defense of human rights.

These international norms were widely violated during the twentieth century, most conspicuously during the two world wars and the Cold War. This dubious record has reinforced a certain cynicism, especially among those who believe that the road to perdition is paved with cooperative, internationalist intentions. For those so inclined, the only persuasive rationale for undertaking the arduous and uncertain tasks of prevention is that it should serve *vital* national interests—for example, the enemy is at our shores, or is pointing his missiles at our cities, or is choking off our essential oil supplies. Yet, the practical applicability of this approach is problematic. Prevailing conceptions of the national interest have tended to focus on military strength and physical survival and often on a narrow vision in which robust nuclear deterrence is virtually the only legitimate form of conflict prevention. As the eminent scholar John Ruggie has recently observed, such a high-threshold definition of national interests effectively prohibits us from identifying and addressing the more diffuse but no less dangerous threats that unfettered conflicts pose to international peace and security today.[5]

Since the national interest is so important to the careful formulation of foreign policy, we should be clear that the national interest is neither a self-evident nor an eternal standard of policy choice; national interests are not simply objective imperatives but are also subjectively shaped values. The substantive content of a country's national interest at any given time is the product of public deliberation among competing conceptions of the proper means and ends of foreign policy. These conceptions remain open to the changing nature of the domestic consensus and the international context.[6]

In the decade since the end of the Cold War, much has changed. While the state continues to be the central ordering institution of economic, political, and social life, increasingly it must contend with a variety of transnational, international, and subnational challenges to its sovereign authority and governing capacity. Many of these challenges are of such global scope and complexity that no single state can manage them alone, either to reap potential benefits or to deter potential threats. Driven by rapid technological advances and expanding markets, global interdependence has fast become the defining feature of economic relations, environmental well-being, and cooperative security. These changes have brought new opportunities for economic improvement and for the promotion of human rights and democratic governance. However, some global problems have become even more pressing: the threat of "loose nukes," the massive proliferation of conventional arms and weapons of mass destruction, the global reach of terrorism, global warming, and widespread degradation of the human habitat, as well as profound societal dislocations associated with drastic techno-economic changes, unregulated financial markets, and international criminal activity.

These are new global realities that, perhaps as much as the collapse of communism, have rendered the Cold War paradigm of international security obsolete. As borders become increasingly porous, a rigid adherence to narrow, conventional conceptions of national interests is not an adequate guide to foreign policy choice. Attention must also be paid to the crucial role played by shared norms, principles, and cooperative activities in assuring international peace.[7]

There is thus a need for a new kind of realism, an updated and necessarily broader understanding of how, in this global age, the protection and promotion of national interests will increasingly come to depend on accommodating the interests and welfare of other nations and peoples. Humanitarianism and *Realpolitik* are no longer mutually exclusive policy orientations. As one recent study of international intervention in humanitarian crises puts it:

> The issue is not choosing between vision and reality, between humanitarianism and realism. Policies based on narrow self-interest are costly in

terms of the conflicts that result and the humanitarian expenditures that follow in spite of a commitment to hard-headed Realpolitik. Further a policy that may lead to shame is not realistic. On the other hand, an idealism that fails to take account of the interests of states is a recipe for future failure. Policies must be based on *humanitarian realism*.[8]

From this perspective, third-party preventive involvement in zones of actual or potential conflict should be undertaken not only because it is ethically sound, but because—in an age of increased global interdependence—it is also the prudent response in terms of national security, broadly conceived in terms of the new reality of the twenty-first century so vividly exemplified by the attacks on New York and Washington.

Why prudent? Because, appearances to the contrary, "doing nothing" is assuredly *not* a cost-free strategy.[9] Consider the consequences of the international failure to act to forestall the Rwandan genocide in 1994. Besides the direct and massive toll in human lives, the resulting destruction of the institutional, social, and economic infrastructure will inhibit Rwanda's development and democratization for years to come, while an entire generation—left orphaned, maimed, and traumatized by the violence—is poorly equipped to meet the challenges of postwar reconstruction without extensive and sustained outside assistance.

In failing to prevent the genocide, the world also failed to prevent it from spilling over into neighboring countries. As mentioned earlier, the killing bred more killing. The flight of some 1.7 million refugees effectively exported violent conflict to the Congo, spreading throughout that large country and to ever-wider regional warfare. There was renewed conflict in the summer of 1998 involving Tutsi rebels, the Kabila regime, Uganda, Zimbabwe, and others. These conditions have been highly conducive to continued violations of human rights, serious disease outbreaks, and significant losses in prospective markets and trading partners. To call such conflicts "local" is misleading. Local conflicts can—and typically do—fuel larger security threats: from a greater proliferation of weapons and transnational crime flows to a hospitable environment for political extremism and international terrorism. For people everywhere, security increasingly depends on regional and global considerations.

The failure of outsiders to intervene preventively makes their later and costly reactive involvement all the more likely. In the 1990s, international agencies, NGOs, and outside governments expended huge resources in humanitarian assistance and postwar peace building.[10] Between 1994 and 1996, for example, the United States *alone* spent $750 million on emergency work in Rwanda, a figure that is roughly equivalent to the *entire* annual U.S. aid program to all of Africa.[11] Who pays these bills? It would not be an exaggeration to say that everyone does. The advanced industrial countries, which are the largest contributors to humanitarian aid, pay in the most immediate sense.[12] But it is the poorer countries that typically bear the heavy opportunity costs of war, since every war drains precious resources from the finite amount of international aid available for other vital needs such as education, public health, environmental improvement, and economic development. A telling indicator of this damaging trend is that, in stark contrast to the previous decade, the budget of the UN high commissioner for refugees—which grew from $600 million in 1990 to $1.4 billion in 1996—now regularly exceeds that of the UN Secretariat and UN Development Program.[13]

Finally, "doing nothing" carries the intangible but potentially exorbitant price of lost international legitimacy. At best, the repeated failure of the international community to act consistently and decisively in defense of core principles of rule of law and human rights inspires cynicism; at worst, it encourages the belief that aggression can be undertaken with impunity, if not outright reward. Neither of these prospects should be countenanced lightly. The various legal regimes, treaties, and multilateral associations that together make up the international community are voluntary in nature. Unlike states, the international community does not have the sovereign authority to impose decisions when the consent of its members is absent. Indeed, as recent experience shows only too clearly, without consensus, necessary decisions cannot even be made, let alone implemented. In short, legitimacy is the touchstone of international order. When it is present, individual states reap the benefits of multilateral frameworks for global transportation and communication, disease control, free trade, environmental safety, nonproliferation, and a host of other public goods that contribute to mutual security and prosperity. But when such legitimacy is absent, the international community risks losing not only these shared benefits, but also the collective capacity to effectively deter and punish acts of international aggression. True, states still have recourse to self-help or unilateral defense to ensure their individual security; but, on their own, they cannot hope to generate or enjoy the benefits of vibrant international regimes. Such cooperative regimes augment the capacities of participating states, even the most powerful, and are valuable in protecting human rights and preventing deadly conflict.

The international community ignores violent conflict at its own risk. Unchecked slaughter undermines the utility of the rule of law as an instrument for the protection of basic human rights, as the basis for effective governance, and as a means of regulating cooperative relations between states. Moreover, the failure to respond to mass slaughter—particularly by those states with an obvious capacity to act—can only encourage a climate of lawlessness in which disaffected peoples or contending factions are tempted to take matters into their own hands. Seen from this perspective, the effort to avert mass violence is not just a matter of humanitarian obligation but also one of enlightened self-interest.

By focusing attention on the various costs of inaction, we do not mean to suggest that preventing deadly conflicts is either free or easy. To do so effectively requires an investment of time, material resources, and especially of the political will to stay engaged over the long haul and cope with the inevitable setbacks—all of which entail difficult trade-offs. Were it otherwise, conflict prevention would already be well institutionalized, and these arguments would be unnecessary. Even if the costs of prevention are considerable, they are miniscule when compared to the costs of inaction or doing too little, too late.[14] As many experts on the subject agree, rebuilding societies that have experienced massive bloodshed and destruction is a far more difficult, time-consuming, and resource-intensive proposition than undertaking to help them avoid massive violence in the first place. If we are finally to get beyond the vicious cycle of fighting and human suffering that afflict so many regions of our world, we must begin by recognizing the global nature of the problem and the global nature of any long-term solution. This is not a matter of ideology but of practical necessity in a world pervaded by hatred, easily transmitted justifications for violence, and ubiquitous deadly weapons.

What Can Be Done?

The belief that there is nothing outsiders can do to prevent incipient conflicts from turning violent is another major source of skepticism and policy paralysis. Likewise, those of us who seek to delineate more clearly the tools and strategies of prevention frequently encounter fears that such action will require huge resources, will inevitably deteriorate into an unworkable international bureaucracy, and will make no effective contribution to international peace and security. These pessimistic, vaguely formulated assumptions are prevalent. This is why the Carnegie Commission on Preventing Deadly Conflict devoted considerable time and analytical effort to delineate some of the considerable institutional resources and policy practices that are *already* at our disposal and to offer practical recommendations for improving them.[15] We concluded that much can be done to improve our capabilities for conflict prevention, and that incremental rather than wholesale changes in the work of governments and international bodies can often generate very positive benefits for a modest investment. It is to a consideration of these practical steps that we now turn.

Operational Prevention:
Strategies in the Face of Impending Crisis

Operational prevention emphasizes prompt outside engagement in emergent crisis situations to help foster the political conditions and viable mechanisms through which responsible leaders and social actors can resolve the problems they face without violence. This kind of engagement relies on three key elements: first, an international organization or leader around which an international effort can mobilize; second, a coherent plan of action designed to arrest the violence, address humanitarian needs, and integrate all the relevant political and military elements, taking account of outsider and insider parties at all levels; and, third, adequate resources for the proper implementation of the chosen course of action.

Early Warning and Early Response

The circumstances that give rise to violent conflict can usually be foreseen. This is largely thanks to the greater wealth of information that has been made available in recent years by intelligence agencies, scholars, nongovernmental organizations (NGOs), and the mass media. The first critical task of prevention is to determine where and when the most disastrous conflicts and confrontations are likely to occur. An upsurge of widespread human rights abuses, increasingly brutal political oppression, inflammatory use of the media, an accumulation of arms, and sometimes, a rash of organized killings clearly point to a deteriorating political situation. These are the sorts of indicators that provided a clear warning of imminent conflict in Rwanda and in Bosnia.

In addition to taking seriously early warning signs of trouble, policymakers must identify those local individuals, institutions, and initiatives that, if properly supported, could act quickly to defuse the potential for violence. In particular, moderate and responsible leaders must be strengthened when inflammatory leaders threaten to dominate political and social lives.[16] In almost every conflict situation, there exist pragmatic, problem-solving individuals with the potential to act as effective leaders. Often, however, they lack adequate resources and experience and must function in a climate of intimidation. For their moderating influence to be effective, such individuals need the sustained material and intellectual and moral support of the international community.

Preventive Diplomacy

When crisis threatens, traditional diplomacy continues, but more urgent efforts should also be made—through unilateral and multilateral channels—to pressure, arbitrate, mediate, or lend good offices; to encourage problem-solving dialogues; and to facilitate a nonviolent resolution of the crisis. The Carnegie Commission puts special emphasis in its multiple publications on this important, rapidly evolving approach. This is one of the most important developments in the entire field. See chapter 4, devoted to preventive diplomacy, for a fuller discussion.

Today, far beyond prior experience, diplomacy is tied to a complex web of economic and social relationships that span the globe. States and peoples relate to each other in multiple dimensions at almost all levels of society, and the wealth of contacts may enhance mutual understanding and help establish wider bases for cooperation. There are "bridging people," for example, in the business, scientific, educational, and religious communities, who can be helpful in clarifying opportunities, correcting stereotypes, and building a network of communication among relevant actors. A variety of international NGOs are carrying out such activities on a rapidly increasing scale. This, too, is a dramatic development of recent decades and is discussed in the next chapter.

The Carnegie Commission recommended that governments strengthen preventive diplomacy by using ambassadors, senior foreign office officials, and personal envoys of the UN Secretary-General earlier and more aggressively. States should resist the traditional inclination to suspend diplomatic relations as a substitute for action. Instead, they should maintain open lines of communication with leaders and groups in crisis. Reliable information is essential to manage an impending crisis. It is better to communicate deep concerns and problem-solving opportunities than to make isolating gestures that are all too often ineffective.

Governments and international organizations must express in a clear and compelling way the bad things that can happen and the risks of escalation. This step is essential to clarify crucial issues for the adversaries and build wide support for preventive action in the adversarial areas and beyond—at least regionally and perhaps globally through the UN. This is especially important should it be necessary later to use vigorous measures to draw clear lines against unacceptable behavior. So, preventive diplomacy needs a consistent effort to promote public understanding of the stakes and options, both in the country or region facing conflict and in the countries potentially offering aid. This includes providing clear and accurate information about the developing crisis, how national interests are served through preventive engagement, and what main possibilities are available for dealing with the emerging crisis.

In many cases, governments should move to put the crisis on the agenda of the UN Security Council or on the agenda of the relevant regional organization (RO)—such as the Organization of American States or the Organization of African Unity—early enough to permit preventive action to be undertaken with their formal support, and thus greater international legitimacy. At the same time, national and international agencies should be encouraged to track continuing developments in the crisis and to provide their decision-making bodies with regular updates. Information from nongovernmental entities should be used to augment governmental sources. Illuminating emerging crises helps to clarify the nature and scope of the problem while demonstrating to concerned publics that constructive resolution is possible. Throughout the duration of a crisis, governments and international and NGOs should foster opportunities for dialogue with and between moderate leaders in the affected communities.

The international community should not wait for a crisis. Ideally, there should be *ongoing* programs of international help—offered by governments and intergovernmental organizations (IGOs), usually, but also by NGOs. These help build the capacity of groups to address grievances effectively without violence and establish mechanisms for sorting out conflicts peacefully before they become explosive. Fortunately, there is movement in this direction—techniques of active, nonviolent problem solving; sharing of experience across national boundaries; bringing the world's experience to bear on different local conflicts. As Connie Peck emphasizes, and as is described in later chapters, this is an *assistance* approach, offered without scorn or condescension. In this way, outsiders can help insiders build their own strength to deal with their own problems.[17]

In this vein, there is a growing body of experience to the effect that addressing perceived intergroup grievances and the motivations behind them is useful in violence prevention. Tackling serious grievances as early as possible denies political demagogues the platform of discontent. This approach undertakes a careful analysis of interests (concerns, fears, needs, and aspirations) and develops options that would move toward meeting these interests, thereby reducing tensions.

Basic human needs—for security (physical safety); well-being for one's family or identity group; access to political and economic participation and opportunity; and protection of valued identity, such as cultural and religious expression—can lead to conflict when they go unmet or are deeply frustrated over a long period of time. Intergroup violence is particularly likely when there is a perception of drastic unfairness between groups in close contact. Thus, a basic prescription for preventive diplomacy is to find means of addressing seriously frustrated human needs before inflammatory leaders can exploit grievances. To fulfill the promise of this approach, it is necessary for governments, IGOs, and NGOs to establish reliable mechanisms for doing this work and making sure the public understands what the work is about.

Special envoys and representatives of key states or regional organizations or on behalf of the UN have repeatedly demonstrated their value, particularly in the early phase of a crisis.[18] This topic is considered further in chapter 5 on preventive diplomacy. The Carnegie Commission identified elements of successful mediation. Critical to success is sensing when conflicting parties are open to outside engagement and, once that involvement is assured, maintaining the confidentiality of negotiations. These talks are best executed by judiciously using incentives to carry negotiations through stalemates and by tackling easier issues first. This can provide momentum, since early agreement can facilitate more difficult negotiations later. Throughout, an understanding of the honor and symbolism parties may ascribe to certain issues is vital to maintaining the trust of all parties in an honest dialogue.

Preventive diplomacy itself may cover any number of topics, depending on the specific circumstances of the conflict at hand. These can range from geopolitical questions of peaceful border revisions or the creation of demilitarized zones to questions of disarmament, demobilization, and civil-military reforms. New power-sharing and autonomy arrangements, which assure disaffected minorities that their interests are not at the mercy of a simple majority, and ways of providing equitable distribution of resources and access to opportunity also fall under the rubric of preventive diplomacy.

A useful illustration of preventive diplomacy in practice is provided by the Organization for Security and Cooperation in Europe (OSCE). It has developed "missions of long duration," an innovative form of conflict monitoring that has been deployed in many European countries. These missions protect fundamental human rights through providing an international presence, firsthand information gathering, situation monitoring, and technical assistance to host countries. Senior diplomats with deep regional knowledge and practical experience in intercultural communication, negotiation, mediation, and confidence-building measures typically lead such missions. Of particular significance for conflicts is such diplomats' ability to combine practical conflict resolution skills with strong regional expertise. A leading example of OSCE innovation in this area is the commissioner on national minorities. As led by the remarkable Max van der Stoel, this approach offers worldwide promise and is considered more fully in a later chapter.

Official diplomacy can be augmented by parallel private-sector activity. Leaders have long used track-two diplomacy to take informal soundings of adversaries' intentions to unofficially explore paths toward conflict resolution. It can be the diplomacy of choice, at least for a while, when conflicting parties reject official efforts. Some governments have found NGOs helpful in brokering political agreements and supplementing official activities. For instance, a Norwegian research institute with roots in the trade union movement played a critical part in laying the groundwork for the Israeli-Palestinian Oslo Accords of 1993. Throughout the 1990s, the upsurge in the work of these organizations has been dramatic. Among the NGOs that have made notable contributions to preventive diplomacy are the Carter Center, the Conflict Management Group, the International Crisis Group, the Project on Ethnic Relations, Search for Common Ground, and various groups at Harvard University. They forge relationships between conflicting parties and with interested governments; they provide training in diplomacy and conflict resolution; and they offer good offices to parties interested in peaceful resolution of conflict. These efforts are burgeoning. We have more to say about them in the next chapter on institutions of civil society.

Nongovernmental diplomacy (including track-two, multitrack, and citizen diplomacy) can help to build a foundation of trust through extensive intergroup contacts, social exchanges in many fields, substantial training in the concepts and techniques of conflict resolution, as well as high-technology access to ideas and people via the Internet. Thus, they can help to bridge the gaps between hostile neighbors, and their participants may stay in touch for years across adversarial boundaries. Some emerge as moderate leaders who can serve as bridging people and pragmatic problem solvers.

Operational prevention covers a spectrum of preventive actions—from those that are essentially educational and persuasive to those that have strong restraining or coercive elements. Although preventive diplomacy is weighted toward the former, it merges imperceptibly with the latter. As a practical matter, both scholars and practitioners in this field are inclined to consider the entire spectrum under the rubric of preventive diplomacy—even if they prefer, in value terms, to avoid or minimize coercion. The educational, persuasive, joint problem-solving approach depends on the ability to find (or even convert) reasonable, pragmatic, problem-solving leaders. It works poorly with ruthless, hateful, highly egocentric, ethnocentric, or paranoid leaders. The farther along the spectrum toward this sort of leadership, the more likely restraining and coercive elements will be necessary.[19] We now turn to considerations that involve potentially coercive elements in diplomacy since they may be necessary for effective negotiations in dangerous situations involving malevolent or very rigid, violence-oriented leaders.[20]

Economic Measures: Orientation

In circumstances of incipient conflict, a number of economic tools are at the disposal of states and international organizations that are in a position to influence the potential belligerents to avoid violence. Under certain conditions, sanctions, inducements, economic conditionality, and the dispute resolution mechanisms of international trade organizations may provide effective and timely deterrence. The Carnegie Commission generated special studies to understand and strengthen these modalities.[21]

Sanctions

Sanctions can play an important role in support of preventive diplomacy. A variety of inquiries are underway to sharpen their focus and enhance their efficacy. Governments use sanctions to serve three broad policy functions: to signal international concern to the offending state (and, by example, to others); to punish a state's behavior; and to serve as a necessary precursor to stronger actions, including the use of force. Thus, sanctions are used to signal to the targeted state that more drastic action could be forthcoming if corrective steps are not taken.[22]

Economic sanctions are extremely difficult to employ effectively. In a context of global interdependence, sanctions must be multilateral and sustained if they are to accomplish their goals. Otherwise, they may be readily evaded. This means that successful sanctions depend on the cooperation of key states and relevant international organizations—no easy task. Messages to the offending state should be clear on the behavior necessary for sanctions to be lifted and should sometimes be accompanied by an incentive package for compliance. It is valuable to identify in each case the measures most likely to affect the leaders who are being targeted. Greater international cooperation is required to achieve these aims and minimize loopholes.

Once initiated, sanctions must be sustained until the desired objective has been reached. This requires detailed planning as well as continuous monitoring and enforcement. Sanctions regimes require the joint involvement of agencies throughout governments and international organizations—in particular, those departments responsible for foreign affairs, economic policies, legal issues, and military strategy.

A major problem with sanctions is the collateral economic suffering that they inflict on the innocent populations of aggressor states and on neutral parties. Targeted sanctions are attractive as a way to focus the penalty sharply on those most responsible for violating international norms. Such targeted sanctions include financial sanctions to freeze leaders' personal assets or deny them access to hard currency, bans on travel for officials of the state whose behavior is unacceptable, and arms embargoes. To implement targeted financial sanctions, financial information can be shared among cooperating nations to identify and restrict the cash flows of leaders who threaten to use violence. While these leaders may still be able to hide assets, they would have great difficulty using those assets without being detected. Restricting their access to hard currency can limit their ability to keep arms and ammunition flowing and can also erode their hold on power. In the foreseeable future, technological advances may enhance the efficacy of such sanctions.

From the outset, sanctions must be considered in the context of a broader strategy of influence that takes into account the target government's vulnerabilities as well as the circumstances of neighboring states and regional arrangements. It requires a legal justification, a framework for imposing sanctions, and means of monitoring their implementation. It also requires specifying the steps to be taken by the target state to avoid sanctions or cause them to be lifted. [23] The UN has recently undertaken deeper studies than ever before on ways of making sanctions effective while minimizing collateral damage.

Inducements

Inducement involves the granting of benefits in exchange for a specified policy change to avoid violence and seek fair solutions. Inducements aim to make cooperation and conciliation more rewarding than aggression and hostility. They can take a number of forms. In the economic realm they can include favorable trade terms, including tariff reductions, direct purchases, and subsidies for exports or imports. Political economic or military aid, access to advanced technology, and steps toward membership in regional and international organizations may also be useful. Policymakers may formulate a variety of political, economic, and military elements as part of an overall package of inducements.

One study sponsored by the Carnegie Commission concluded that inducements are most effective when used early and that they are more likely to succeed when used against the backdrop of sanctions—that is, when the tangible benefits of cooperation can be weighed against the stark punishments for pursuing a course of violent action.[24]

The OSCE High Commissioner on National Minorities has sometimes used inducements in a way that directly targets the problem causing friction. The high commissioner was able to offer small sums of money to help Baltic states provide language classes for ethnic Russians so they can pass the language exam required for citizenship, a requirement that is causing intergroup tension and inter-state problems with the Russian Federation. Another example is small amounts of money contributed so that a minority language can be included in a country's school curriculum—thus directly addressing a common minority grievance.

Conditionality

Conditionality links responsible, nonviolent behavior with economic aid and especially with integration into the community of market democracies. This involves not only economic benefits but also the prestige and sense of belonging that accrues from membership in influential international bodies. Through both bilateral programs and international financial institutions, states and international financial institutions are increasingly attaching such peace-oriented conditions to the development assistance they provide to emerging economies.[25] Though there is understandable sensitivity about this approach in developing countries, the positive experience of Eastern Europe in the 1990s shows the practical value of this approach when carefully and judiciously applied.

Economic Dispute Resolution Mechanisms

Every major international trade organization has mechanisms to foster resolution of disputes that arise among members. A requirement for membership is a commitment to pursue grievances through these mechanisms and
to be bound by their findings. These are intrinsically useful economically
and provide models for problem solving in political contexts.

Forceful Measures

Even where supplemented by strong economic measures, diplomatic responses may prove insufficient to prevent the outbreak or recurrence of major violence. Forceful measures may be necessary *to separate or restrain the
adversaries* and thus *provide space for diplomacy*. What principles should
guide recourse to this most delicate of policy options? The Carnegie Commission found several answers to these questions.

First, any threat or use of force must be governed by universally accepted
principles, as agreed to in the UN Charter. Second, the threat or use of force
should *not* be regarded only as a last resort in desperate circumstances. An international rapid deployment force can separate hostile parties before the
conflict spirals out of control. The effectiveness of this option depends on
viewing force as a flexible preventive tool, rather than a residual alternative
when all else has failed. Third, all states and particularly the major powers
must accept that the threat or use of force can only be effective when it is part
of an integrated, preferably multilateral, strategy in which military prevention
is deployed in conjunction with political and economic preventive measures.[26]

The Carnegie Commission sought to contribute to the development of a
system of military intervention that, if clearly needed to stave off war, would
be so predictable, rapid, and effective that its mere existence would act as a
deterrent against mass violence. If necessary, it could quickly separate the
adversaries and open opportunity for diplomacy. Therefore, the Commission
invited General Andrew Goodpaster, a distinguished military leader and
statesman, to consider options for addressing this unfulfilled opportunity.[27]

> One legacy of the Cold War is thinking of the use of military force in terms
> of either doing nothing, or employing overwhelming forces in a decisive
> manner. Such thinking is no longer appropriate. A middle ground involv-
> ing a more modest use of international force—in a limited but persistent
> manner—demands more attention. Such use of force, if required, would
> substantially raise the costs to an aggressor or a group that grossly violates
> human rights.

Goodpaster is clear that this course of action is not easy. One of the major barriers is simple skepticism. If leaders around the world had more con-

fidence in the international community to carry out preventive actions, they would be more willing to commit their states to such a collective effort.

A move that would help instill this necessary confidence is a well-defined management system for the international forces that are typically required for such activity. There are three basic choices for management: the United Nations, a regional organization, or an ad hoc coalition. But any of these variations must be built on solid foundations. There should be a mandate that explicitly lays out the purpose, scope, and (if possible) timeframe of military operations. An effective command structure that permits coordination between military and civilian political leaders must be created. Unified operational control should be the watchword. Most of all the political objectives should be translatable into objectives that the military forces on the ground can achieve.

However, these arrangements are complex. Such an undertaking might be beyond the capabilities of the United Nations, which was never structured to have strong military capability. It is likely that the UN's involvement would be limited to peacekeeping—once there is a peace to keep. Regional organizations have better potential to carry out these operations. Presently, however, these capabilities have not been fulfilled as, with the exception of NATO, in many regions the political will and military capabilities are often missing. Goodpaster is clear that because of these deficits it is ad hoc "coalitions of the willing" that will be most able to handle operations that go beyond peacekeeping, humanitarian aid, or noncoercive military support, at least in the near future.

These ad hoc coalitions are comprised of self-selected states that hold a genuine interest in preventing or stopping a conflict. Usually, an alliance like this will include a major or regional power. Including such a player means that not only are military resources assured but also that financial backing of the operation can be made available. Optimally, these coalitions could be made up of states whose militaries have conducted joint exercises and possess interoperable equipment. They also may be able to graft their undertaking onto an existing command structure (like NATO did in the Balkans) and rely on the assets of better-equipped members.

Nevertheless, these undertakings must be sited within a framework provided by international organizations. The United Nations has a prominent role here. Through the Security Council and the Secretariat, authoritative and public decisions can be made about when, where, and for what purpose multinational forces will be used. The Security Council's decisions can provide an ultimate source of legitimacy for such an operation.

Such a mandate may be necessary. Conflicts that have degenerated to the point at which barbarities of rape as a weapon, ethnic cleansing, and genocide are appearing demand quick and irresistible action. This may necessitate the use of military force to bring the hostilities under control. In this case a writ granted by an international organization is exceedingly helpful.

The major drawback of a "coalition of the willing" is the lack of binding ties between the members. There is always a lurking threat that sustained casualties or differing strategic interests can cause the commitment of its members to wilt. The more difficult a situation, the more likely the national interest may come to take precedence over the common interest. Thus, Goodpaster concisely states the main issues and opportunities regarding the role of force in operational prevention.

In the end, the Commission recommended a rapid deployment capability for the UN under control of the Security Council, thus providing a high degree of legitimacy in a clearly multilateral context. But if this is the best medicine for the long run, what to do till the doctor comes? One or more Security Council members can take the lead in recruiting, training, and regularly exercising a multinational force that would be ready for preventive action whenever political leadership agrees on the necessity of action—doing so through either the UN or an ad hoc coalition. In this way, the international community would not be paralyzed; this military component could be integrated into a coherent strategy with political, economical, and social components oriented toward resolving serious conflicts short of mass violence. The deeply international character of such a force would tend to provide legitimacy, since no single nation would be able to push its selfish interests very far without encountering feedback or restraint. In this context, it is important not only to involve large nations but medium and small states as well.

What Governments Can Do

Because states remain the primary political units of the international system, and the only entities endowed with legitimate military authority, national governments bear the primary responsibility for preventing deadly conflict. When preventive action is needed, it is the governments who initially must decide whether to do nothing, to act alone or to act in concert either with other governments or through international organizations or with elements of the private and nongovernmental sectors. NGOs may opt to become involved regardless of a government's chosen course of action. By practical necessity, however, the major responsibility for preventive action remains with governments. There is considerable scope for government action—though to date much of this potential has yet to be realized. Governments, and especially democratic ones, can use the tools and strategies of prevention far more effectively than they have in the past. Much of this book is devoted to specifying these vital opportunities.

What else can governments and international organizations do to prevent intergroup violence within states? There is a crucial need to devote more attention to the conditions in which different groups—whether ethnically, religiously, or otherwise constituted—will receive fair treatment so that they can come to believe in the mutual benefit of harmonious interactions. In order to develop a positive sense of personal and group identities free of tendencies to denigrate others, one facilitating condition is the development of a robust and pluralistic civil society. We have more to say about this in chapters 4 and 6. It is a fundamental opportunity for peaceful living.

An upsurge of egregious human rights violations is almost always a powerful warning of dire events to come; they are the overtures to civil wars and massive refugee flows. The best protection against such disasters is the consolidation of democratic institutions, capable governments, and free civil societies. The international community must find ways to support the development of these indigenous social and institutional capacities. Specific means of support include technical assistance and financial aid to build the requisite processes and institutions as well as efforts to educate publics about the actual workings of democracy. Support should also involve the promotion of trade and investment, technical competence, the expansion of intraregional and international opportunities, and the extension of meaningful membership in the international community.

Since human rights abuses so often contribute gravely to deadly conflict, a central feature of structural prevention organized by governments and international organizations must be the protection of human rights.[28] The original decision to enshrine a commitment to uphold human rights in the UN Charter reflected more than a humanitarian impulse of member governments. The founders of the United Nations were primarily interested in preventing another world war, and they knew that the Nazis' extreme human rights abuses provided early warning signs of external aggression. They believed that if the international community had acted early and firmly to stop Hitler and his followers from committing *internal* human rights abuses, it might well have been possible to prevent World War II. We have considered this possibility in the previous chapter and have more to say later about ways in which the international community can help troubled states to build attitudes, knowledge, skill, and institutions for democracy and human rights. In this direction lies a strong antidote to injustice and war.

Governments that do not respect the rights of their own citizens are not inclined to respect the rights of weaker neighbors. Even when such behavior is not a precursor of broader aggression against neighboring countries, it may warn of the imminence of massive refugee flows and other serious troubles leading to a tragic humanitarian emergency. The former UN high commissioner for refugees, Sadako Ogata, often reminds governments that today's human rights abuses are likely to become tomorrow's refugee movements.

Thus, the Carnegie Commission urges governments and international organizations to give high priority to building strong institutions and norms for human rights, especially by developing an early warning system of human rights violations and by supporting efforts to advance the rule of law, democratization, and national human rights efforts.

National governments must take the lead in building domestic institutions devoted to the promotion and protection of human rights. This point was emphasized by the World Conference on Human Rights, held in Vienna in 1993. While recognizing the right of each state to pursue this goal in its own way, the World Conference encouraged the strengthening of national institutions based on the Paris Principles developed at the first international meeting of national human rights institutions in 1991. Thus, international norms are increasingly prominent in this vital field.

National human rights institutions should have as broad a mandate as possible, clearly set forth in a constitutional or legislative text that specifies the institution's composition and sphere of action. They should provide recommendations, proposals, and reports to the government, parliament, and any other competent body on any matter relating to human rights (including legislative and administrative provisions and any situation of violation of human rights). These actions should promote conformity of national laws and practices with international human rights standards and encourage ratification and implementation of international standards. In line with international instruments they should carry out the reporting procedures required by these agreements. Publicly they should assist in formulating and executing human rights teaching and research programs in order to increase public awareness of human rights through information and education. They should cooperate in these matters with the United Nations, regional institutions, and national institutions of other countries.

National institutions have an array of other functions that can directly influence the lives of citizens. They may participate in seeking an amicable settlement of a human rights complaint through conciliation, binding decision, or other means. This may mean providing the complainant in a dispute with knowledge of his or her rights and of available means of redress and promoting access to such redress. Rights organizations may be a mechanism for hearing complaints and referring them to a competent authority. They also have a role as a public advocate by making recommendations to the competent authorities, including proposals for amending laws and regulations that obstruct the free exercise of human rights.

The Paris Principles also include detailed guidelines that range from the composition of national institutions and the appointment of members to guarantees of independence and pluralism; and methods of operation, including the need to cooperate with other entities responsible for protecting human rights (such as the institution of an ombudsman and NGOs active in the field). In 1992, the United Nations Commission on Human Rights endorsed the principles as did the General Assembly in 1993. They are an important part of a worldwide ferment on human rights questions, which are now getting more attention from the UN than ever before, as well as vigorous support from most of the established democracies. Still, there is a long way to go.

It is encouraging to note that the UN now has a strong commissioner for human rights, Mary Robinson, and that she is explicitly linking protection of human rights with prevention of deadly conflict.[29] Similarly, Shashi Tharoor, director of Communications and Special Projects in the Office of the UN Secretary-General, recently published an excellent article on the universality of human rights.[30] UN Secretary-General Kofi Annan has spoken clearly on these issues in various parts of the world, including those areas where resistance to human rights has been formidable.[31] This extraordinary and energetic UN leadership, along with the vigorous monitoring, analysis, and advocacy of strong NGOs that focus on human rights, has put pressure on governments beyond prior experience to address these vital needs constructively.

Who Can Do What? Sharing the Burdens, Dividing the Labor

When possible, prevention efforts should emphasize local solutions to local problems, augmenting them as needed with assistance from outside. Clearly, outside governments and international organizations have a role to play in giving needed assistance to societies weakened by poverty, mismanagement, and political oppression, as well as to those destroyed by war. Also important are the resources and expertise of the private and nongovernmental sectors. NGOs, educators, religious leaders and their institutions, businesses, the scientific community, and the media can contribute more to prevention than they have in the past. We have more to consider on these matters in the next several chapters.

As indicated earlier, the circumstances of incipient violence usually do not improve by themselves. Often, the intervention of outside states is necessary and beneficial, provided that the conditions for such interventions are clearly defined, agreed upon, and monitored by the international community.[32] Outsiders who possess special capabilities may have a special role to play. For example, countries that share borders or membership in regional economic or security organizations may possess considerable leverage to broker a settlement as well as a heightened incentive to undertake mediation.

What Established Democracies Can Do

For the most part, *established* democratic states do not fight one another because they see one another as belonging to the same community of shared values, because democratic transparency makes adventurous foreign policies against other transparent democracies extremely difficult to justify, or because democratic states typically have recourse to a highly evolved set of domestic and international institutions by which they may resolve conflicting interests in a peaceable, if not always perfectly satisfactory, manner.

In the 1990s, the peace-promoting effect of democracy has become a major rationale for providing assistance to those less fortunate countries emerging from the collapse of authoritarian regimes and debilitating civil wars to create and sustain their own democratic systems. We consider this more fully in chapter 6 on democracy and prevention.

Given their comparatively longer experience with the norms and practices of representative government, civil society, rule of law, and independent media, the governments and citizens of established democracies are particularly well equipped to engage in long-term structural prevention. By pooling their considerable political and economic strengths, various government and nongovernment agencies from the established democracies could make a major contribution to global peace and well-being, drawing on developed legal standards, accepted procedures, and international norms of fairness.[33] Depending on the degree of interest and competence in dealing with a specific problem, these actors could work in varying combinations, through the UN system, regional organizations, or other mechanisms.

There has recently been broad recognition of the inherent capacity of democratic institutions for structural prevention through domestic conflict resolution. Moreover, there is a special role of the established democracies in assisting the development of rule of law, representative government, and pluralistic competition in postauthoritarian settings all over the world. Yet, the potential role of established democracies in pursuing operational prevention has not had the serious deliberation that it deserves. Given the great potential of democracy for both structural and operational prevention of deadly conflict, we pursue these themes in later chapters on democracy and on international cooperation to prevent war.

The Carnegie Commission invited a study by two distinguished leaders in international relations: Professor Graham Allison of Harvard University and Ambassador Hisashi Owada, then Japan's permanent representative to the UN, to consider the distinctive role of the established democracies in preventing deadly conflict.[34] This highly significant report deserves careful study. Therefore, the following is a summary of the central points of their analysis. During the last half century, those actors that have been most important in preventing deadly conflict have been the democracies. This fact reflects both values and capabilities. Nations with established practices of tolerance and nonviolent conflict resolution within their societies are most likely to reflect similar values in international initiatives. Moreover, the leading democracies of North America, Western Europe, and Asia (Japan and India) have also been most capable.

1. In the coming century, which actors are most likely to be able and inclined to prevent deadly conflict? Again the ever-widening circle of democracies appears most promising. They will not be the only important actors for peace, but together they are more likely to be effective than any other single state, group of states, or international organization. The shared values of democracies facilitate policy coordination, convergence, and joint action. All this is rarely simple or easy, but a fundamental advantage nevertheless.
2. The principal instruments that democracies have used to prevent deadly conflict, and are likely to continue to use in the future, include alliances (e.g., NATO, the U.S.–Japan Security Treaty); global and regional economic institutions that promote prosperity through cooperation (e.g., the General Agreement on Tariffs and Trade [GATT], World Trade Organization [WTO], International Monetary Fund [IMF], European Union [EU]); international institutions (e.g., the UN); clubs (e.g., the G-8, and Council of Europe); and promotion of international norms, both core values such as human rights and institutionalized practices.

Other actors are also important and surely help to prevent wars, but democracies that wield great power are obliged also to assume great responsibility. They are an increasingly important component of the comprehensive approach to preventing deadly conflict with justice developed by the Carnegie Commission.

Allison and Owada point out a number of obstacles. Perhaps the biggest barrier to effective preventive action by democracies is the lack of political will. They are unlikely to support or undertake any foreign policy initiative that is not in their national interest, narrowly defined. There are generic impediments such as constitutional checks that make action difficult and require responsiveness to public opinion, which is often assumed to be reluctant. There are historic impediments to prevention as well. For example, the imperial pasts of some established democracies leave other states suspicious of their motives.

Allison and Owada believe that exhortations to do more prevention are futile unless the problems posed by national interest are addressed. Specifically, they urge that we start with the interest of nations as currently conceived and ask how these may be better formulated to promote effective preventive actions. They suggest we must consider peace-with-justice in terms of a broader view of national interest.

This broader view of self-interest considers several threats likely to emerge in an increasingly interdependent and overarmed world. Nations should understand that the price of letting conflicts burn out of control could lead to direct security spillover in the region. Areas beset by violent conflict may also be breeding grounds for terrorism that is a dangerous development for everyone. (This report, like almost all of this book, was written before September 11, 2001.) Peoples weakened by the deprivations of war may be the origin of health pandemics that do not respect borders. Conflict can also squander business opportunities or resources, causing the loss of economic prospects even for groups not directly involved. Also, there are the enormous costs of recovery in the wake of violence—usually paid for by the democracies. Great power responsibilities come into play. States can lose credibility by failing to help in dangerous situations. Failure to act can have an equally corrosive effect on emerging norms and rule of law. The breakdown of these rules can have repercussions all over the world.

Consequently, reformulating national interests must be considered by world leaders and informed publics as techno-economic globalization draws the people of the earth ever closer together. Allison and Owada suggest specific measures to prevent inter-state conflict:

1. Deter aggressor states by strengthening key alliance relationships among established democracies that provide stabilizing influence (for example, NATO, U.S.–Japanese and U.S.–Korean alliances).
2. Further domestic political reform by strengthening democratic institutions and assisting the consolidation of emerging democracies via economic assistance and security guarantees.
3. Improve arms control, for example, by providing stringent controls on nuclear weapons and materials and by making bilateral aid contingent on responsible defense spending.
4. Foster economic development and integration by promoting the spread of free-market principles and establishing a standing Group of 8 (G8)/Organization for Economic Cooperation and Development (OECD) fund for preventing deadly conflict, and, if necessary, for providing postwar reconstruction.
5. Strengthen international institutions and norms of cooperative security by establishing a global democratic league, including all established and new democracies; going beyond the EU to develop an Atlantic Union based on an Atlantic free trade area and NATO's security institutions; and create a UN/multinational standing/rapid reaction force.
6. Promote preventive diplomacy by focusing efforts on high tension interstate dyads such as Greece and Turkey, India and Pakistan; support preventive deployments (e.g., Macedonia); integrate China into the international community on terms that reduce the chances for violent clashes between China and its neighbors; strengthen regional organizations' capacity to engage in preventive diplomacy; and implement William Perry's concept of preventive defense (professional military-to-military

contacts, civilian control of the military, military budgetary and doctrinal transparency).

Allison and Owada also recommend specific measures to prevent *intra*-state conflicts. These measures draw heavily on those for inter-state conflict and are very similar in nature.

1. Strengthen mechanisms to freeze assets of perpetrators of mass violence, that is, target financial sanctions on leaders.
2. Increase intelligence sharing about impending conflicts.
3. Foster military and defense engagement to promote respect for civilian control, professionalization, transparency, and confidence building.
4. Create a global "Democratic League" that can help with intra-state conflicts.
5. Encourage the spread of democratic government and principles of public accountability and rule of law.
6. Assist emerging democracies to consolidate by providing economic aid and security guarantees.
7. Make bilateral aid contingent on responsible defense spending;
8. Promote the spread of free market principles.
9. Establish a standing G8/OECD fund for prevention and postwar reconstruction.
10. Create a UN/multinational standing/rapid reaction force—not to fight wars but to separate adversarial parties before violent escalation and to make space for diplomatic activity.
11. Strengthen regional organizations' capacity to engage in preventive diplomacy.
12. Support preventive deployment, when appropriate, as a way of separating antagonistic forces and giving space for preventive diplomacy.

The United Nations

The UN is not a world government. It is an intergovernmental organization of sovereign states that works by seeking common ground among them to cooperate in their long-term self-interests. The UN Charter was written by experienced, thoughtful statesmen—largely from established democracies—who had been deeply influenced by two terrible world wars with a grotesquely distorted peace between them. With memories of painful missed opportunities fresh in their minds, they carefully prepared a document that provided a bold vision of a better future and practical means of implementation.

The Charter sets out ambitious objectives. It hopes to achieve international security through the peaceful resolution of disputes. To accomplish this, it emphasizes the rule of law, sanctions, and military action if necessary to suppress aggression. True international stability could not be established without social justice and this means advocating the freeing of colonial peoples, based on equal rights and self-determination; economic and social development; promotion of human rights and fundamental freedoms, regardless of race, gender, language, or religion. All these efforts require fostering cooperation among diverse nations to attain common approaches to solving global problems. Now, with the Cold War over and the world being drawn together by technological and economic forces, we need creative thinking to explore ways in which the UN might renew its founding ideals for prevention and become more effective in these great tasks.

The UN must find ways to strengthen and institutionalize preventive diplomacy rather than reacting to crises that have spun out of control. The UN can best focus on early reconciliation of disputing parties' interests, primarily through diplomatic ingenuity. Can the UN create paths to conflict resolution that are visible, attractive, and useful before conflicts become large and lethal? Can the UN find useful ways to bring the world's experience to bear on a particular conflict at an early stage in its development? Carnegie-supported analyses have examined a number of ways in which these questions can be addressed effectively in the future. For example, the UN has an intermediary role to play in providing assistance—helping in dispute resolution just as it provides assistance in helping states meet their human rights obligations and helping with elections.[35] There is a need for quiet diplomacy and an assistance approach. There are examples of Secretary-Generals using Article 99 of the UN Charter as a kind of informal mandate to act quietly at an early stage without bringing a matter to the Security Council. This practice must be strengthened. These matters are so important they are considered further in the chapter on preventive diplomacy.

The legitimacy of outside assistance is a critical determinant of its success. The UN plays a vital role in establishing the terms of outside intervention and the broad consensus to support it. While UN authorization is typically necessary for multilateral international action, it is not sufficient. The strength of the UN lies both in its role as a legitimating forum that facilitates international collaboration and in its capacity to reflect the interests and intentions of member states, including their commitment to joint and cooperative action. Under the mandate of UN authorization, states, regional institutions, and nongovernmental actors can facilitate local solutions to local problems, using both private and public resources.

When should the UN intervene? The UN Charter gives the Security Council a great deal of latitude in making such decisions. With respect to preventive diplomacy, the Charter authorizes the Secretary-General to bring to the attention of the Security Council any development that may threaten international peace and security. In some cases, an early alert and analysis by the Secretary-General, with consideration of plausible options by the Security Council, can head off incipient conflict before serious damage is done. The following circumstances could provide an appropriate stimulus for Security Council action upon the alert of the Secretary-General: where a regional or internal dispute might entail weapons of mass destruction; where there is evidence of systematic human rights violations or emerging genocide; where large flows of refugees threaten to destabilize neighboring countries; where there has been a forcible overthrow of a democratically elected government; where troops are massed on a border in a threatening military buildup.

In recent years, the traditional doctrine of state sovereignty has undergone significant revision. The international community is now seen as having both a justifiable rationale and a responsibility for constructive intervention in serious internal disputes.[36] As currently practiced, the doctrine of state sovereignty no longer provides a carte blanche for tyrants to oppress their own populations or to commit mass violations of human rights. Increasingly, the United Nations has been applying global norms developed earlier to regulate peaceful relations *between* states to conflicts *within* nation-states. This development should not be construed as a mandate for arbitrary intrusions into the internal affairs of states or for the subjugation of the weaker by the stronger. To guard against the potential for abuse, it is essential that the international community develop a more rigorous set of criteria for legitimate intervention, as well as procedures for practical implementation. On the whole, however, the major problem in the 1990s was not one of excessive or arbitrary violations of state sovereignty but, on the contrary, a marked avoidance of responsibility on the part of the international community when confronted by deadly intra-state conflicts. This problem has so vexed the Security Council, governments, scholars, and concerned publics that we examine it more closely in the chapter on international cooperation for prevention.

The Carnegie Commission published a set of major speeches and reports by UN Secretary-General Annan on ways to strengthen the vital preventive functions of the UN.[37] These statements discuss how a culture of prevention in international affairs can be built and can underscore the vital role the UN has to play in such a formulation. He believes that preventing deadly conflict is the central task of the UN and that these efforts can be strengthened in many ways. For the long term, he emphasizes *human* security as well as the traditional notion of national security. This involves good government that is transparent, impartial, and just; access to economic opportunity; and security in society based on fairness. Human security requires respect for the sovereignty of the individual, not just the nation.

The UN's highest goal is to prevent armed conflict. Its main tools for this purpose are preventive diplomacy, preventive deployment, and preventive disarmament. The UN has an excellent tool in its "good offices" to defuse tensions before they reach the conflict stage, or even make the news. Annan cites the UN envoy who negotiated a settlement between Iran and Afghanistan in 1998. Annan also advocates "citizen diplomacy" by non-governmental actors (such as Jimmy Carter) and preventive action by NGOs as a major component of an international culture of prevention. Preventive deployment may sometimes be useful. Here, the UN or another body can put a "thin blue line" between disputing groups before shooting starts. The example so far was the small UN force in Macedonia that for many years kept the peace. But the crucial long-run question is, what is done with the time bought by such deployment?

Despite scarce resources, the UN also has embraced postconflict peace building to prevent recurrence of violence in areas that have recently emerged from fighting. It is a broad strategy that encompasses various sectors from emergency relief, to demobilization, to mine clearance, to long-term development programs. The premise of this strategy is that human security, good governance, and respect for human rights are interdependent and mutually reinforcing. As a society moves in this direction, it is less likely to slide back into violence. The goal of all these strategies is an inclusive, participatory, and mutually respectful society. Such human communities are less likely to be violent within and to those without. Democracy is an effective, nonviolent form of conflict management. Annan emphasizes that the international community has a powerful role in fostering prevention regimes.

1. It can encourage people-centered security in troubled areas. This means advocating and helping to build democracy, thereby fostering human rights and nonviolent solutions of problems.
2. It should ensure that development policies do not exacerbate risks of conflict.
3. Global corporations, as their power has been increasing relative to states in recent years, should be advocates and exemplars of good governance. They can have a constructive interaction with the UN for this purpose. More recently, Annan's initiative has led to a global compact between businesses and the UN on this vital issue.
4. The international community should be willing and prepared to engage politically and, if necessary, militarily to contain and resolve conflict with a better-functioning collective security regime than exists now.

In welcoming the Carnegie Commission's report, Annan stated that there is no higher goal for the UN than preventing conflict. Indeed, the UN's role in prevention goes back to the promulgation of its charter in 1945. Every development and diplomatic mission the UN undertakes can help to prevent conflict. Nevertheless, the potential for further progress is great.

Repeatedly, the world has allowed differences to develop into violent conflict. There are important reasons for this deterioration. Typically there is a reluctance of the parties in conflict to accept external intervention. In addition, the international community often lacks the political will for concerted action. None of this is helped by the dearth of integrated conflict prevention strategies within the UN system and the larger international community.

The UN cannot provide prevention alone; it must be facilitated by a wide array of institutions in the international community. At some points, the UN must take the lead; at others, regional or nongovernmental groups must be out in front. This work must address the root causes of violence. It may not be glamorous, but only a "long, quiet process of sustainable economic development, based on respect for human rights and legitimate government" can provide the essentials for preventing conflict.

Annan states that human rights are "at the core of our sacred bond with the peoples of the United Nations." These rights give the individual universal and inalienable rights to speak, learn, grow, and act according to his or her own conscience. He believes that the UN should stand up against any actions that abuse these rights.

The UN must have the courage not only to recognize common goals, but it must also recognize that there are common enemies that stand in the way of the achievement of these goals. Those guilty of violations of human rights must be held accountable. This is particularly true in the face of the genocide and ethnic violence that was endemic in the 1990s. Yet, Annan is hopeful that the outrage provoked by these acts is coalescing into norms that find violent repression of minorities unacceptable and that this view will and must take precedence over concerns about state sovereignty. This will be a difficult issue for the UN to tackle, but if it is not dealt with, it is a betrayal of the ideas that inspired the organization's founding in the wake of the catastrophe of World War II.

Regional Organizations

The growing demand for UN intervention, not only in conflict between nations but also in serious internal conflicts, naturally challenges the capacity of the organization to respond. These new challenges also raise questions about the relationship between the UN as a global organization and the various regional organizations that relate to it. A variety of regional arrangements and agencies exist, some more effective than others. There are constructive possibilities for coordinating the efforts of regional bodies and the UN in conflict resolution. Regional organizations in Africa, Latin America,

Asia, and Europe, such as the Organization of African Unity, the Organization of American States, the Council of Europe, and the Organization for Security and Cooperation in Europe (OSCE), all must be explored from this perspective. For the most part, they have not had major responsibilities in conflict resolution or violence prevention, but they could become much more effective in due course. Some have been making serious efforts in preventing mass violence; for example, the Organization of African Unity has created mechanisms for conflict prevention, management, and resolution. This is a thoughtful effort, but, like almost everything else in Africa, very short of resources.

Farsighted analytical work and innovative activities are badly needed to strengthen these organizations for prevention. Therefore, the Carnegie Commission asked Dr. Connie Peck, of the United Nations Institute for Training and Research (UNITAR), to explore these possibilities.[38]

Peck seeks paths that might be desirable and feasible for strengthening regional capability to deal with conflicts. On the one hand, regional entities have the advantage in principle of intimate knowledge of the players and sensitivity to historical and cultural factors that bear on the conflict. On the other hand, they have the disadvantage that they tend to be emotionally engaged, tend to choose sides, and therefore have difficulty in establishing credible conflict-resolving functions. All this needs careful examination in terms of basic principles of conflict resolution and on a case-by-case basis in relation to the idiosyncrasies of particular organizations that have arisen over the years. In any event, strengthening the global-regional cooperative functions would have potential for a variety of purposes, and these are thoughtfully explored in her work, as she considers each major regional organization in its own terms and sees ways to fulfill its inherent potential.

Peck has worked creatively on the conceptual development of Regional Centers for Sustainable Peace—established under the auspices of either regional organizations or the UN. This would be one way to bring together the UN, regional organizations, NGOs, and regional analytical centers. The proposed structure would integrate the most successful conflict prevention instruments, drawing widely on international experience and expertise, but ensuring that they are tailored to local needs and circumstances. The horizontal transfer of knowledge and experience within each region is a distinctive feature of this proposal, in which regional actors who have found solutions to their problems or have developed successful models of good governance could assist their neighbors within the context of a regional effort aided, as necessary, by global support.

Regional centers would have two major foci. The first would be assistance in developing the structural processes for sustainable peace (with good governance at all levels of society). The second would be maintaining peace through assistance in dispute resolution and the development of institutional structures that would allow groups to become more effective at resolving their own problems. Each center could provide an ongoing analysis of existing disputes to both the regional organization and the UN. Peck proposes that these tasks be accomplished as an extension of the UN's Department of Political Affairs.

These functions are sufficiently distinctive that they might call for a new institution. Difficult as it is to create new institutions, the stimulus of looming disaster is powerful; the voice of reason, though small, is surely persistent. Mostly, we have looked to incremental strengthening of existing institutions. Sometimes it is necessary to create a new institution to fulfill vital tasks. Yet with worldwide confidence in Kofi Annan, as reflected in his early, unanimous re-election to a second term as Secretary-General, he might be able to take the lead in creating such regional centers. (Since this was written, Kofi Annan was awarded the 2001 Nobel Peace Prize, further strengthening his leadership stature for prevention.)

Peck's review of the evidence makes clear that ethnopolitical conflicts do not have to be intractable. All but one of the twenty-four communal minorities that were politically active in the Western democracies and Japan in the post–World War II period made gains over the past two decades, due to strategies of accommodation and the kinds of solutions suggested by the Carnegie Commission.[39] These include specific reforms to guarantee full civil and political rights, development focused on reducing poverty, politics that recognize cultural diversity and rights, and political arrangements that provide greater decision making and autonomy over decisions that concern indigenous peoples and other vulnerable groups. Addressing ethnic grievances has contributed to a substantial decline in ethnic conflict in the states involved. Policies that enhance economic development and distributive justice, rule of law, fundamental human rights, and strengthening of democratic institutions all serve to foster security and reduce violence. Regional organizations and the UN have a role to play in such achievements.

Peck describes ways in which regional programs for ongoing assistance in dispute settlement could offer expert help in reducing tension between groups, whether within or between states. These can be broadly summarized as follows.

Providing assistance in intra-state disputes: (1) Listening to and understanding concerns; (2) providing new ideas and recommendations; (3) encouraging the establishment of forums for ongoing dialogue; (4) providing good offices; (5) providing access to expert assistance.

Providing assistance in inter-state disputes: (1) Detecting and analyzing disputes; (2) encouraging parties to de-escalate tensions; (3) facilitating multitrack diplomacy; (4) encouraging and supporting negotiation; (5) offering good offices or mediation directly; (6) acting as a referral source for third-party mediation; (7) helping parties seek conciliation, arbitration, or adjudication; (8) monitoring compliance with agreements; (9) acting as a "trip wire"; (10) providing continuous monitoring of events.

Regional programs for assistance in developing good governance: (1) Providing assistance for the transition to democracy; (2) providing assistance in the development of fair rules, law, and practice; (3) providing assistance in the development of a full range of institutions to administer laws and regulate conflict; (4) separating military institutions from civilian administration; (5) encouraging more honest governance; (6) promoting greater economic opportunity and access; (7) promoting pluralism, cultural understanding, and tolerance.

Augmenting the work of regional centers: (1) Using small assistance missions; (2) using the expertise of regional and international scholars; (3) using the expertise of NGOs and civil society; (4) using the experience of regional leaders.

The Carnegie Commission along with the Canadian Department of Foreign Affairs and Trade, UNITAR, the International Peace Academy, and the International Development Research Centre of Canada held the first ever meeting between staff at the working level from the UN, regional organizations, and NGOs to discuss and compare their methodologies and effectiveness in terms of violence prevention and to stimulate new ideas for regional approaches. The result was encouraging. As the concepts and techniques of prevention are more widely understood, such UN-RO-NGO activities could become a potent force.

Steps Toward Implementing Prevention

Governments, intergovernmental organizations, and regional organizations can be helpful—more so than ever before. The most general and pervasive need is for the international community to be prepared and proactive in helping nations or groups in trouble, rather than waiting for disaster to strike. For the longer term, this essentially means help in acquiring attitudes, concepts, skills, and institutions for resolving internal and external conflicts. It means help in building political and economic institutions of democracy. There can be—and of necessity will be—many different international configurations through which such help may be provided.[40] And it can be done in ways that are sensitive to cultural traditions and regional circumstances.

Governments and intergovernmental organizations should establish focal points for prevention. For example, each foreign ministry should have a high-level office concerned with ongoing analysis of prevention opportunities. Such analysis would be used to stimulate the entire ministry to participate in appropriate ways for implementation and to bring in other relevant ministries as well. This has already happened in some foreign ministries, and the stimulating, alerting functions are valuable. A strong prevention outlook on the part of the foreign minister—for example, Lloyd Axworthy of Canada—is an important asset in making this process work. Here, as elsewhere, and in many ways, leadership is crucial. We have more to consider about leadership in a later chapter.

The Swedish foreign ministry provides an excellent example. It has prepared an action plan for preventing violent conflict. Its core concepts include the following premise:

> Conflict prevention must be based on and further develop the norms of freedom and law which have shaped us for generations and are reflected in international treaties and conventions. These norms apply to the relationships between states and to states' duties toward their citizens. We must work within the international community to develop better methods or early crisis warning and action, both politically and economically, as well as create better legal and institutional instruments for enhancing the observance of our common values.[41]

A steering group for conflict prevention was established within the ministry as a basis for vigorous and unified policy on conflict prevention and for implementation of the policy. Moreover, a small secretariat within the Policy Planning Group of the ministry has been established with a mandate to follow international developments in conflict prevention. The secretariat is involved in implementation of the action plan and the development of new methods and initiatives in this field. It has a stimulating function throughout the ministry and helps personnel to work in a conflict prevention mode through activities such as training programs. The secretariat works in cooperation with concerned authorities, organizations, and research institutes. In a short time, this initiative has elevated the status of prevention in Sweden and also had a stimulating effect on other countries. In practice, the Nordic countries played an important role in preventing deadly conflict in the Baltic countries during the 1990s, as we shall see in the chapter on preventive diplomacy. Moreover, Sweden made use of its presidency of the European Union in the year 2000 to provide an explicit focus on violence prevention by this powerful international organization. In the chapter on international cooperation for prevention, we sketch ways in which such governmental leadership can stimulate intergovernmental organizations and strong nongovernmental organizations to pursue the concepts and operations of prevention with growing efficiency. In these efforts, Jan Eliasson (currently the ambassador of Sweden to the United States) has been not only a national but a world leader.

Under the farsighted leadership of Secretary-General Annan, the UN Department of Political Affairs, headed by Kieran Prendergast, has increased its attention to prevention. Though often preoccupied with crises, it has arranged for prevention-training programs both at headquarters in New York and elsewhere, involving staff from many UN agencies and from member states. Annan and his leadership group have had stimulating effects throughout the UN Secretariat and on the Security Council as well. If this trend continues, it could help to make the prevention outlook pervasive in the international relations of governments and intergovernmental organizations.

Notes

1. *Report of the Independent Inquiry into the Actions of the United Nations during the 1994 Genocide in Rwanda* (UN Doc. S/1999/1257, December 1999).

2. Karl Vick, "Death Toll in Congo War May Approach 3 Million," *Washington Post*, April 30, 2001.

3. Scott R. Feil, *Preventing Genocide: How Early Use of Force Might Have Succeeded in Rwanda* (Report to the Carnegie Commission on Preventing Deadly Conflict, April 1998).

4. Brown and Rosecrance, *Costs of Conflict*, ch. 3.

5. John Ruggie, "The Past as Prologue? Interests, Identity and American Foreign Policy," *International Security* 21 (4): 89–125.

6. David A. Hamburg, Alexander George, and Karen Ballentine, "Preventing Deadly Conflict: The Critical Role of Leadership," *Archives of General Psychiatry* 56 (November 1999).

7. Graham Allison and Hisashi Owada, *The Responsibilities of Democracies in Preventing Deadly Conflict: Reflections and Recommendations* (Carnegie Commission on Preventing Deadly Conflict Discussion Paper, July 1999).

8. Howard Delman and Astri Suhrke, "Early Warning and Conflict Management Study 2: The International Response to Conflict and Genocide: Lessons from the Rwanda Experience" (Steering Committee of the Joint Evaluation of Emergency Assistance to Rwanda, March 1996).

9. Brown and Rosecrance, *Costs of Conflict*.

10. Stremlau and Sagasti, *Preventing Deadly Conflict*, 20–21.

11. John Stremlau, *People in Peril: Human Rights, Humanitarian Action, and Preventing Deadly Conflict* (Report to the Carnegie Commission on Preventing Deadly Conflict, May 1998).

12. Stremlau and Sagasti, *Preventing Deadly Conflict*, 21.

13. Stremlau, *People in Peril*.

14. Brown and Rosecrance, *Costs of Conflict*.

15. Stremlau and Sagasti, *Preventing Deadly Conflict*.

16. Alexander George and Jane Holl, *The Warning Response Problem and Missed Opportunities in Preventive Diplomacy* (Report to the Carnegie Commission on Preventing Deadly Conflict, May 1997).

17. Connie Peck, *Sustainable Peace: The Role of the UN and Regional Organizations in Preventing Conflict* (Carnegie Commission Series, Rowman & Littlefield, 1998).

18. Cyrus R. Vance and David A. Hamburg, *Pathfinders for Peace: A Report to the UN Secretary-General on the Role of Special Representatives and Personal Envoys* (Report of the Carnegie Commission on Preventing Deadly Conflict, 1997).

19. Bruce Jentleson, ed., *Opportunities Missed, Opportunities Seized: Preventive Diplomacy in the Post–Cold War World* (Carnegie Commission Series, Rowman & Littlefield, 1999).

20. Bruce Jentleson, *Coercive Prevention: Normative, Political and Policy Dilemmas* (Peaceworks No. 35, United States Institutes of Peace, 2000).

21. John Stremlau, *Sharpening International Sanctions: Toward a Stronger Role for the United Nations* (Report to the Carnegie Commission on Preventing Deadly Conflict, 1996); David Cortright, ed., *The Price of Peace: Incentives and International Conflict Prevention* (Report to the Carnegie Commission on Preventing Deadly Conflict, Rowman & Littlefield, 1997).

22. Bruce Jentleson, "Economic Sanctions and Post–Cold War Conflicts: Challenges for Theory and Policy," in Paul C. Stern and Daniel Druckman, eds., *International Conflict Resolution After the Cold War* (Washington, D.C.: National Academy Press, 2000), 123–77.

23. Stremlau, *Sharpening International Sanctions*.

24. Cortright, *Price of Peace*.

25. Stremlau and Sagasti, *Preventing Deadly Conflict*.

26. Andrew J. Goodpaster, *When Diplomacy Is Not Enough: Managing Multinational Military Interventions* (Report to the Carnegie Commission on Preventing Deadly Conflict, July 1996).

27. Goodpaster, *When Diplomacy Is Not Enough*, 1–4.

28. David A. Hamburg, "Human Rights and Warfare: An Ounce of Prevention Is Worth a Pound of Cure," in Samantha Powers and Graham Allison, eds., *Realizing Human Rights from Inspiration to Impact* (New York: St. Martin's, 2000).

29. Mary Robinson, "The Next Human Rights Agenda: Preventing Conflict," *New Perspectives Quarterly* 16 (fall 1999): 23–28.

30. Shashi Tharoor, "Are Human Rights Universal?" *World Policy Journal* 26 (winter 1999/2000): 1–6.

31. Kofi Annan, *Towards a Culture of Prevention: Statements by the Secretary-General of the United Nations* (Carnegie Commission Publication, 1999).

32. David A. Hamburg, *Preventing Contemporary Intergroup Violence and Education for Conflict Resolution* (Carnegie Commission Publication, 1999).

33. Michael Walzer, *On Toleration* (New Haven, Conn.: Yale University Press, 1997).

34. Allison and Owada, *Responsibilities of Democracies.*

35. Peck, *Sustainable Peace.*

36. Annan, *Towards a Culture of Prevention.*

37. Annan, *Towards a Culture of Prevention.*

38. Peck, *Sustainable Peace.*

39. Ted R. Gurr, *Minorities at Risk: A Global View of Ethnopolitical Conflicts* (Washington, D.C.: United States Institute of Peace Press, 1993).

40. R. Rubin Barnett, ed., *Cases and Strategies for Preventive Action* (New York: Century Foundation Press, 1998).

41. *Preventing Violent Conflict—A Swedish Action Plan* (Stockholm: Regeringskansliet UD, The Printing Works of the Government Offices, 1999).

4

Institutions of Civil Society: Partners for Peace

Pivotal Institutions

In ordinary parlance, the word *diplomacy* evokes images of government representatives. A phrase like "management of international conflict" evokes images of the United Nations. This is not surprising since the development of strategies to cope with problems of conflict, war, and peace have mainly involved governments, coalitions among governments, and intergovernmental organizations. Governments, coalitions, and intergovernmental organizations remain very important in the contemporary world and they need to be strengthened for prevention. But the dismal record of slaughter on a vast scale in the twentieth century is a testimonial to the failure of the traditional system to prevent deadly conflict. So, we must look to other potentially effective groups to augment the vital efforts of governmental institutions. In this context, the dramatic growth of internationally minded nongovernmental organizations all over the world in the past few decades is a remarkable piece of modern history.[1]

How can nongovernmental organizations, religious leaders and institutions, educational and scientific communities, business firms, and the mass media usefully contribute to the prevention of deadly conflict? How can their capacities be mobilized in societies where violence threatens? It is crucial to identify and support those elements of civil society that can reduce intergroup antagonisms, to enhance attitudes of concern, social responsibility, and mutual aid within and between groups—and to provide the technical and financial resources they need to operate effectively.

Nongovernmental Organizations Oriented
to Conflict Resolution and Violence Prevention

As a dynamic element of democratic societies, NGOs provide a wide range of analysis, services, and advocacy for action on many matters of public concern. Recent technosocial changes have enlarged their opportunities. The rapid spread of information technology, market-driven economic interdependence, and cultural pluralism within and among states have allowed NGOs to become key conveyors of information, ideas, financial resources, and technical assistance. They often function internationally and with cognate interests and are instrumental in relating people across borders by fostering a sense of international solidarity. In difficult economic and political transitions, these organizations of civil society can be helpful in alleviating the threat of mass violence. A matter of particular importance for the international community is the cultivation of peace-and-democracy NGOs in fragile democracies, especially by linking them with counterparts in established democracies.

Groups fostering human rights, democracy, and economic development have become vital in facilitating peaceful transitions from authoritarian rule to open societies. After serious conflicts, they can be helpful in reconstruction and national reconciliation. NGOs can be powerful instruments to prevent backsliding and in due course to make the process of democratic transition irreversible. Human rights groups often provide early warning of rising local tensions. Track-two diplomacy groups offer a political opportunity in which officials on different sides of the conflict can be helped to consider steps toward mutual accommodation. Increasingly, international NGOs work closely with indigenous organizations in different parts of the world to reinforce a sense of common interest and common purpose on the way to a worldwide sense of shared humanity.

Some NGOs have an explicit focus on conflict prevention and resolution. They function in a variety of useful ways. They have the ability to monitor conflicts and provide warning and insights into a particular conflict. In certain situations they can pave the way for mediation and sometimes undertake mediation themselves by convening the adversarial parties in a neutral setting. NGOs may carry out education and training for conflict resolution in an effort to build an indigenous capacity for coping with ongoing conflicts. Coupled with this work may be help to strengthen institutions for conflict resolution or programs that foster development of the rule of law. To further buttress civil society, NGOs may help to establish a free press and train for responsible reporting on conflict. They can provide technical assistance on democratic arrangements that reduce the likelihood of violence in divided societies and may assist in planning and implementing elections. These are all valuable functions that badly need doing in much of the world, especially in emerging, fragile democracies. In addition to the substantive progress that these efforts make in coping with hostilities between adversaries, they generate a cadre of constructive people who carry their attitudes and skills back to their communities and often grow into positions of local or national leadership.

Several examples here may clarify the range and scope of conflict-oriented NGO activities as well as the variety of settings that can foster excellent work in conflict prevention and resolution. Though exceedingly diverse, these examples have in common superb leadership—highly intelligent, dedicated, ingenious problem solvers who know a lot and care a lot about preventing unnecessary human suffering. Although the examples given here are mainly based in the United States, they are deeply engaged internationally. Moreover, excellent examples are also based in other countries—for example, the European Platform for Conflict Prevention in the Netherlands and the Center for Conflict Resolution in South Africa.

The best known of these examples is led and inspired by a highly respected former president, Jimmy Carter. Since leaving the presidency in 1981, he has kept in touch with world leaders, both pleasant and unpleasant. He has taken a keen interest in many dangerous conflicts, kept himself well informed, and kept lines of communication open with relevant political leaders and independent experts. He has repeatedly shown a readiness to enter into difficult conflicts, even to cope with pariahs. He involves colleagues in this work, all the way from outstanding leaders such as Senator Sam Nunn and Secretary of State Colin Powell to students at Emory University. In this way, many people contribute to and learn from President Carter's work. All these activities exemplify humane, compassionate, and democratic values.

The Atlanta-based Carter Center works at the head-of-state level to convene parties in a conflict, either as a precursor to or in parallel with official negotiations. The center is strongly collaborative, reaching out not only to all the parties in a conflict but also to the business and religious communities as well as the international financial institutions as partners in its interventions.

The increased number of intrastate conflicts in the past decade has produced a dramatic upsurge of nongovernmental and intergovernmental groups dedicated to training, research, advocacy, and direct intervention for conflict resolution and violence prevention. Among these, the Carter Center's conflict resolution program and the related International Negotiation Network remain unique in acting at the head-of-state level as a precursor or alternative to official diplomacy. The center classifies its work as low engagement or high engagement. *High engagement* refers to mediation by an eminent person, a request from the conflicting parties for assistance, or a project within the country. Over the past few years, this category has included projects in Haiti, the Korean peninsula, Bosnia, Liberia, and Sudan, some of which were highly publicized. In the first two of these cases, it is probable that war was averted by the intervention—preventive diplomacy of a high order.

For low-engagement projects, the center analyzes conflicts, builds relationships with various parties, and identifies other groups already working in the region. In this way, the center can better determine if and when it should intervene at a higher level and whether its contribution will advance the negotiation process. The center has ongoing activities relating to India, Burma, Bosnia, and the Basque region of Spain, including meetings with various political parties in each country and research to assess the opportunity to be useful. It has often manifested expertise in election monitoring, including village elections in China.

Since the founding of the Carter Center's work in conflict resolution, many different techniques and approaches have been used in answer to the number and complexity of existing conflicts in the world. The center disseminates its findings through a variety of publications. Updates are produced weekly and provide synopses of the military, political, and humanitarian issues of ongoing conflict. The *International Guide to NGO Activities in Conflict Prevention* lists activities carried out by a great variety of NGOs. Disseminated to foundations, practitioners, and governmental organizations, it aims to help focus conflict resolution efforts more effectively. *The State of the World Conflict Report* was published annually for a number of years. It contains summary information and maps on major armed conflicts being waged around the world. It also features papers by conflict resolution experts.

Independent evaluation of the Center's work by Carnegie-related experts confirmed the quality of its work, its ability to conduct useful conflict assessments and help in conflict resolution, and the transfer of its knowledge and experience as a contribution to general knowledge in the field of conflict resolution.

The second example involves a great university, Harvard, and an eminent scholar, Graham Allison. Under his leadership, a variety of highly capable people from senior faculty to young students have been stimulated, even inspired, to work with counterparts in the Soviet Union during the 1980s and in Russia during the 1990s, first to reduce the risk of nuclear war, then to build democratic institutions for their intrinsic value and especially for their contribution to structural prevention of mass violence—the latter being an all too plausible risk in many parts of Russia.

The Strengthening Democratic Institutions Project of Harvard University's Kennedy School of Government has played an important catalyzing role for Western cooperation in Russian democratization since 1990. Building on its accumulated network of contacts with Russian political leaders and parties going back to the emergence of democratic leaders in the

Gorbachev era, this group has conducted research and analysis on these critical problems and shared insights with Russian politicians, helping them to shape and adhere to the rules of multiparty competitive politics and representative democracy.

A decade after sowing the first seeds of democracy and market economy, Russia stands at a crossroad. Its democratic institutions are fragile, the constitution breeds confrontation between the state Duma and the president, the political parties are mostly parliamentary factions centered around a few prominent individuals, and the economy is gripped by serious difficulties.

The Harvard project works with Russian economic and political reformers to produce a framework for the country's development and strives to clarify appropriate Western responses to the challenges facing Russia. The project's research, technical assistance, and outreach activities are concentrated in three areas: Russian democratization, Russian security, and ethnic conflicts in the post-Soviet space.

The project's work on Russian democratization is aimed at promoting a multiparty system and representative democracy in Russia. Building on its past work, including involvement in the first series of competitive elections held in Russia (parliamentary in 1995 and presidential in 1996), the project conducts research and analysis on major elections and works with Russian politicians in shaping the electoral "rules of the game" under which elections are held. The project monitors the activity of political parties and significant individuals as they prepare for the election cycle and analyzes critical issues that have serious consequences for Russian democracy. The products include reports and articles, policy briefings, seminars, and conferences. A specialized conference on Western technical assistance to Russian democratization brought together representatives from foundations that support these activities and groups that carry them out. An important part of the whole enterprise is the building of personal long-term relationships of trust and mutual understanding between Russian and American participants.

As a result of a decade of operations on the ground in Russia and in the post-Soviet states, the project has developed important relationships with key Russian policymakers and major political movements. It has had strong ties to reformist parties, such as Yabloko, Russia's Choice, and Our Home Is Russia, and also relates to some radical nationalist parties. In addition to these connections, the project's research on such topics as the general transition in the post-Soviet states, the development of a multiparty system in Russia, the emergence of new political elites, the evolution of Russian foreign policy, and the dynamics and security implications of ethnopolitical conflict in the region has produced well-respected publications that are useful in Russia and beyond. It had taken the lead in clarifying the "loose nukes" problem and suggesting ways of coping with it—working not only with scholars but with Russian and American policymakers.

This remarkable project has been successful in drawing corporate sponsorships for various activities. Among these are the Russian Middle Class Mortgage Initiative, which works in partnership with the City of Moscow to create, for the first time, a functioning mortgage market that serves as a pilot program for the rest of the Russian Federation; the U.S.–Russia Investment Symposium, which helps attract private-sector international direct investment into Russia through an annual symposium devoted to Western investment; and the Caspian Initiative, which seeks to understand the various political, economic, and security interests in the Caspian Basin, including those of the regional states.

Another important example of conflict-oriented NGOs is provided by the Project on Ethnic Relations (PER). It is dedicated to reducing interethnic tensions in a region that has seen some of the most violent, intractable, and destructive conflict since the end of the Cold War. PER's neighborhood encompasses the culturally and politically diverse space of the former Communist bloc—from Russia and the Baltics through Central and Eastern Europe and the Balkans. But PER deals with a universal problem: how to temper the powerful emotions of ethnic identity with the political self-restraint that is essential to democracy.

It was founded in 1991 by Allen Kassof, who had a distinguished record as the founding director of International Research and Exchange (IREX), which fostered exchanges of scholars between East and West during the Cold War. PER provides an excellent example of how imaginative, persistent intervention by a small NGO can achieve significant and practical results. PER has the unusual attribute of combining direct involvement as mediator at the highest political level with work in community settings. PER's experience shows that, with insight, patience, and durability, it is sometimes possible to modify the behavior of antagonists even in intense, historically rooted ethnic disputes. In a decade of sustained effort, PER has established a well-respected and effective presence in the region.

PER explicitly recognizes that negative political mobilization is the key factor in igniting large-scale, ethnically based strife. Although perceived ethnic differences provide the raw material for such confrontations, violence is by no means inevitable. Those who would encourage interethnic coexistence must find the means to dissuade or prevent political leaders from fomenting or exploiting ethnic tensions. Toward this end, PER has developed relationships with political and other leaders throughout the region. PER has put into practice a complex strategy, working with political leaders and opinion makers at regional, national, and international levels, and backing this approach with activities at the community level.

PER maintains numerous programs. It plays a role in mediating major ethnic conflicts by working with political leaders on a regional level to promote confidence-building alternatives to ethnic and national conflicts. Part of this effort also involves cooperating with Euro-Atlantic institutions such as the Council of Europe and NATO on strategies to manage interethnic conflicts. PER seeks to build confidence between the Romani communities and majority populations, with the aim of reducing anti-Romani violence. Taking a long view, its programs contribute to developing nationwide and local institutions to deal with ethnic conflicts in part by influencing opinion leaders, especially the media. A further element of this endeavor means reshaping ethnic bias in textbooks, supporting applied research on salient conflict issues, and sharing experience widely in the region and with others interested in similar conflicts elsewhere. PER's work helps to shape a new generation of regional experts in conflict resolution and violence prevention.

PER's flagship mediation efforts require intensive and continuous networking with the leaders on both sides of interethnic disputes. This is the single most time-consuming activity of PER's Princeton-based president and its executive director. They spend several months each year in the field and personally lead the mediation projects. Their work is supported by PER's Princeton staff and by small local offices with representation in Romania, Hungary, Slovakia, Bulgaria, Russia, and Poland. These outposts maintain daily contact with strategic institutions and key individuals; they provide a constant flow of current information and analysis.

PER convenes and chairs roundtables for the antagonists, sometimes in their own countries, but sometimes in neutral locations, usually Switzerland and occasionally the United States. Many of the roundtables draw senior participants/observers from the U.S. government, NATO, the European Union, OSCE, and the Council of Europe. Although the roundtables are informal dialogues, in practice they serve as venues for high-level negotiations.

Since its founding in 1991, PER has played a central role in mediating the historic disputes between the Hungarian minorities and the majority populations in Romania and Slovakia. PER also plays a high-profile role in Hungary, which occupies a key bilateral and regional role in the outcomes of these conflicts. In Serbia, PER was the only entity that succeeded in bringing Serbian and Kosovar Albanian political leaders to the table before the tragic outbreak of violence in 1998. Officials and leaders of ethnic groups from all of these countries have requested PER to continue to provide these vital services over the next few years.

The United States Institute of Peace (USIP), led by a highly respected scholar and diplomat, Richard Solomon, provides training for NGOs and others to enhance the skills of professionals who are directly engaged in preventing violent conflicts and of third parties who serve as mediators. The USIP also develops and disseminates research on war and peace issues. It has an extensive publication program. It supports the work of international scholars—connecting them with policymakers and advisors from all parts of the world. It seeks to bridge the gap between research and practice.[2] Although supported in part by the U.S. government, it has a high degree of autonomy and works with the private sector (both nonprofit and for-profit). Thus, it has an intermediate position between NGOs and governments.

USIP's training focuses on improving practical skills in conflict analysis, conflict prevention, negotiation, third-party mediation, and coalition building.[3] Training in negotiation examines successful practices in the prenegotiation, negotiation, and implementation phases. Sometimes the training is used to build or strengthen institutions devoted to conflict management. Projects train trainers who in turn have an impact on a wide range of local institutions in the methods of conflict management. This work is designed to be especially sensitive to local needs and realities.

The institutional setting is an important determinant of success for such training. For training to have a long-term impact, it must be embedded in a setting that can support the work long after the trainers are gone. Therefore, the training should help local organizations build their capacity. Though brief visits from outsiders can be stimulating and helpful, more is needed for long-term capability to deal with ongoing or newly arising conflicts. Toward this end, trainees should not be in a passive position. They should be actively engaged in case studies, exercises, simulation, and discussion of future prospects. Moreover, the training groups should be inclusive, involving women and men from various groups in the area.

An unusual and highly significant NGO is the International Peace Academy (IPA) in New York. It is a close partner of the United Nations, yet fully independent. It has developed an analytical voice on the pressing issues facing the UN. Using its excellent convening power, it is an international forum for discussion; its seminars routinely bring people and organizations together for thoughtful consideration of war and peace issues. It brings together scholars and practitioners. Kofi Annan recently said, "The United Nations community, and in particular the Security Council, have benefited greatly from these contributions."

The IPA has had outstanding leadership from three presidents over thirty years: Indar Jit Rikhye, Olara Otunnu, and now David Malone, as well as its dynamic chairperson, Rita Hauser. An international staff from twenty countries has been engaged in research and policy analysis on crucial issues underlying contemporary conflicts—for example, economic agendas in civil wars, strengthening the UN's conflict prevention capacity, focusing the Security Council's attention on targeted sanctions, understanding the challenges in transitional administrations such as Kosovo and East Timor, and assisting African organizations in developing mechanisms for conflict resolution.[4]

Search for Common Ground is an NGO concerned with helping people on several continents develop skills in resolving their ongoing conflicts below the threshold of violence. John Marks, its dedicated founder and president, describes its "toolbox" as constituting nineteen operational methods, all of which are variations on one method: understanding differences and acting on commonalities.[5]

Marks lists the nineteen tools: (1) radio, (2) television, (3) children's television, (4) forums and roundtables, (5) joint action projects, (6) domestic shuttle diplomacy, (7) conflict resolution institution building, (8) conflict resolution training, (9) training in schools, (10) journalist training, (11) cross-ethnic team reporting, (12) sports, (13) songs, (14) publications, (15) cross-ethnic cooperation within professions, (16) environmental exchange, (17) images of the other: reduction of stereotypes, (18) policy coordination forums, (19) community organizing.

Thus, like some other highly entrepreneurial NGOs, Search for Common Ground undertakes a comprehensive, multifaceted approach, seeking out whatever opportunity presents itself in a particular situation to diminish the risks of violence.

Sarah Mendelson and John Glenn recently evaluated the impact that Western NGOs have had on the process of democratization and the reduction of ethnic conflict in several formerly communist states of East/Central Europe and Eurasia, and similar studies have been made elsewhere.[6] Mendelson, Glenn, and their collaborators produced sixteen case studies, analyzing the effects of Western NGOs' strategies on developments in several sociopolitical sectors including political parties and elections in Russia, Ukraine, the Czech Republic, and Slovakia; independent media in Russia, Ukraine, the Czech Republic, and Slovakia; women's NGOs in Russia, Poland, and Hungary; environmental NGOs in Russia and Kazakhstan; civil education NGOs in Romania, Uzbekistan, and Kyrgyzstan; and conflict reduction in Bosnia, Estonia, Hungary, Romania, Slovakia, and Ukraine. The study combined social science methods with regional expertise in direct observation of Western and indigenous projects.

Several conclusions are emphasized. Western NGOs have played an important role in the design and initial building of institutions associated with democratization—including political parties, regular elections, independent media, and local NGOs. They have so far had little impact on the operational nature of these institutions as they struggle through the long-term process of building democracy. Western NGOs have been limited in their ability to diminish ethnic conflicts within deeply divided states unless they coordinate with governmental and international organizations. In future efforts toward democratization and the reduction of ethnic conflict, Western NGOs should combine local, regional, and global expertise in designing and implementing strategies that specifically address the local situation.

An outstanding worldwide NGO with strong preventive functions is the International Crisis Group. It has burst upon the scene in the past few years and is described in chapter 10.

Religious Leaders and Institutions

The Carnegie Commission convened an international meeting of religious leaders and scholars. They provided depressing evidence that religious beliefs and institutions have played an exacerbating role in many crisis situations throughout history, sometimes inciting communal hatred that led to violence. Fanatical religious hatred is all too familiar in contemporary events. Yet religious leaders have the capacity for curbing passions during times of crisis and for teaching ethical and pragmatic bases for tolerance in a pervasive way.

In communities throughout the world and in their international organizations, religious leaders have powerful advantages for dealing with conflict situations. Because of their prominence within their communities, religious leaders have the ability to deliver a clear message that resonates with their followers. This is due to a longstanding and widespread presence on the ground that includes a well-developed infrastructure providing an effective communications capacity connecting local, national, and international offices. Such a presence confers legitimacy for speaking out on intergroup relations. Most of all, religious groups have a traditional orientation to peace and goodwill. Because of these advantages, established religions could become much more constructive in preventing hatred and violence than they have historically been.

The Carnegie Commission emphasized that religious advocacy for violence prevention is particularly effective when it is broadly inclusive of many faiths. Since interfaith dialogues already exist, such as the World Council of Churches, they provide opportunities for regular discussions on intergroup relations. International religious leaders should encourage frequent interfaith dialogue at the local, national, and regional levels to foster mutual understanding and social tolerance.

Despite history's travails with religious enmity, there are encouraging recent examples of courageous work by religious leaders to solve serious problems in nonviolent ways, especially by fostering democratic trends. For example, some churches in East Germany toward the end of the Cold War were important in averting mass violence while promoting freedom in the transition away from dictatorial rule. Similar functions have been served during the past decade in South Africa, highlighted by the remarkable leadership of Archbishop Desmond Tutu. In the nonviolent, democratic struggle for freedom from apartheid, he provided intellectual and moral leadership, a focal point for open dissent, unity among pro-democratic factions—and he vividly exemplified courageous, nonviolent conflict resolution.

In a book on religion and conflict prepared for the Carnegie Commission, Professor Scott Appleby of the University of Notre Dame cites in considerable detail an encouraging example.[7] This is the Community of

Sant'Egidio that has done outstanding work in brokering settlements in Africa, Latin America, and Europe.

The activities of the Community of Sant'Egidio in the 1990s stand as an excellent example of how religious NGOs can cooperate with secular governments and NGOs. The community fully understands that its track-two diplomacy cannot succeed without the communications capabilities, logistical support, financial assistance, and language skills provided by larger organizations and governments. For this purpose, the Community of Sant'Egidio cultivates partnerships with a large number of groups.

This collaboration was clearly seen in the community's recent work in Mozambique, Angola, Guatemala, and Kosovo. But nowhere was it more apparent than in Algeria. The Community of Sant'Egidio had long seen the country as a place for working on positive Muslim-Christian-Jewish relations. The networking carried out by the organization over time provided new channels of communications for the parties in conflict. Sant'Egidio gave negotiations a serious push. Committed individuals within Algeria itself collected signatures from over 20,000 local political activists on a 1996 "Appeal for Peace." This gave more momentum to talks that were then carried through by other governmental and nongovernmental organizations.

Sant'Egidio relied on governmental sources to supply critical material needs and the track-one diplomatic resources. Not the least of this support was security and protection by the Italian government for members of the community who were under bodily threat from Algerian extremists. Other religious NGOs use external support to allow them to further efforts for justice, conflict prevention, and economic development. More and more, the goals of NGOs like this are peace efforts that can encompass all religious communities.

Religious leaders can profit from these inspiring examples and undertake a worldwide effort to foster respect for diversity and nonviolent problem solving. They should focus intrafaith and interfaith gatherings on ways to play constructive roles in the face of hostility. Co-religionists who promote hatred or give religious justification for violence should be subject to their censure. The paramount goal should be the global promulgation of norms for tolerance, strongly reflected in educational activities for children and adults.

The Media

As with religious institutions, the media have come in for serious criticism for inflaming conflicts. Harshly nationalist and sectarian leaders have used the media in promulgating inflammatory propaganda. Hate radio in Rwanda and former Yugoslavia provide dreadful examples of direct and

powerful incitement to mass violence. Yet even media in democratic societies have been criticized for glorifying violence (although more so in entertainment than in the news).

How can the international community foster a mass media that is devoted to combating intergroup prejudice and ethnocentrism, as well as
communicating the values and skills of conflict resolution? What rewards
are possible for such efforts? We are by now all too familiar with political
entrepreneurs who use the media to exploit intergroup tensions—actions
that often make their own constituencies as vulnerable as the groups that
they target. Can independent media reach publics and "hot spots"? Radio
is a relatively low-cost and widely accessible medium even in the poorest
countries. The international community should support radio and other independent media that combat divisive mythmaking by providing accurate
information about current events, covering constructive aspects of intergroup relations, and clarifying actual instances of violence prevention.

News media can report conflicts in ways that engender constructive public
discussion oriented to conflict resolution. The media can stimulate new ideas
and approaches to serious problems by involving independent experts in their
presentations, seeking to understand the problem and paths toward solution.
The media should develop standards of conduct in crisis coverage that give
adequate attention to serious efforts underway to defuse and resolve conflicts,
even as they give full international exposure to the violence itself.

The Carnegie Commission had constructive interactions with the leadership
of Cable News Network (CNN) International on these matters. Such networks
as CNN International and the British Broadcasting Corporation (BBC) provide leadership on responsible, insightful media coverage of serious conflict.
Through the good offices of President Carter, the president of CNN International, Eason Jordan, met with the full Carnegie Commission and followed up
with the Commission's leadership on several occasions. CNN International
now tries to balance coverage of violence with coverage of paths to conflict resolution. Moreover, it is proactively covering global hot spots in an effort to
clarify ways in which escalation to violence can be avoided. These are valuable
precedents that may, in due course, show the way for other networks.

Research has established causal relationships between children's viewing
of aggressive or prosocial behavior on television and their subsequent behavior. Children as young as two years old are facile at imitating televised
behaviors. Television violence can affect a child's behavior at an early age,
and the effects can extend into adolescence. In general, the relationship between television violence and subsequent viewer behavior holds in a variety
of countries. Cross-national studies show this in countries as diverse as Australia, Finland, Israel, the Netherlands, Poland, and the United States.

There is some research evidence that television need not be a school for
violence—that it can be used in a way that reduces intergroup hostility. The

relevant professions need to encourage the constructive use of this powerful tool to promote compassionate understanding, nonviolent problem solving, and decent intergroup relations. Television can portray human diversity while highlighting shared human experiences. It can teach skills that are important for the social development of children and do so in a way that both entertains and educates. So far, we have had only glimpses of its potential for reducing intergroup hostility.

Professor Gerald Lesser of Harvard University has summarized features of the children's educational television program *Sesame Street* that are of interest in this context.[8] The program originated in the United States in 1969 but appears today in more than a hundred other countries. Each program is fitted to the language, culture, and traditions of a particular nation. The atmosphere of respect for differences permeates all of *Sesame Street*'s many versions. Research from a variety of countries is encouraging. For example, the Canadian version of *Sesame Street* shows many sympathetic instances of English-speaking and French-speaking children playing together. Research demonstrates that the children who see these examples of cross-group friendships are more likely to form such friendships on their own than are children who do not see them. The same is true for Dutch, Moroccan, Turkish, and Surinamese children who see *Sesame Street* in Holland. The findings suggest that appealing and constructive examples of social tolerance help young children to learn such behavior.

Educational television can be developed in ways that reduce intergroup hostility in different cultures as research on *Sesame Street* has demonstrated. The world has only scratched the surface in the constructive use of this powerful tool to promote understanding among different cultures and convey nonviolent ways to cope with life's frustrations.

An interesting example of constructive programming is provided by a 1995 initiative of the Carnegie Corporation and the Voice of America under the leadership of Geoffrey Cowan. This conflict resolution project developed and produced special programs to introduce its worldwide audience to the principles and practices of conflict resolution. Journalists undertook production of stories exploring local efforts to resolve problems, improve intergroup relations, and highlight efforts for peace. A core series of documentary programs in several languages was adapted to the needs of specific audiences. It included a lecture series on media and conflict prevention, a workbook for journalists reporting in emerging democracies, and broadcasting on conflict resolution. Activities included journalist training in Angola and a daily radio broadcast in the Kinyarwanda/Kirundi language aimed at Rwanda and Burundi. This work addressed one of the world's most dangerous areas.

Similar ingenuity was reflected in BBC Radio's educational series on democracy for Russian audiences; and by Ted Koppel's ABC *Nightline* programs on U.S.–Soviet relations during the Cold War and on Israel–Palestinian relations vis-à-vis the Middle East peace process as well as on South Africa during apartheid. The promise of this approach, reaching millions of people in engaging and constructive ways, is genuinely encouraging—including civil discourse between adversaries before a vast audience. Independent, pluralistic media can promote democracy by clarifying issues, attitudes, candidates, and institutions essential for democracy. International election monitors should press for access to the media for all parties as an integral part of free and fair elections.

Karen Ballentine has studied international assistance and the development of independent mass media in the Czech and Slovak Republics.[9] Development of independent mass media has been a major part of efforts to assist the democratization of the postcommunist states. This work has involved international, state, and nongovernmental organizations in journalist training, technological improvement, reforming the legal-regulatory framework, enhancing the financial and managerial performance of media outlets, and developing professional associations for media professionals. These efforts have shared a common outlook that independent and pluralistic media are a bulwark of democracy, serving as a watchdog of abuses of power by elected officials and as an inclusive arena for consideration of public issues. After decades of highly intrusive Communist Party control, the newly liberated media lacked the skills and resources to perform these democracy-supportive functions on their own.

Ballentine found that international support had a positive influence in shaping the norms and practices of the postcommunist media, enhancing their professionalism and their viability, and helping to integrate them into an international media community. She identified four main lessons for effective media assistance, both in these countries and more generally. First, there is a need for strategic planning so that resources can be effectively matched to the most pressing needs of the media sector in each setting. Second, in postauthoritarian settings where the media are likely to be highly partisan, international actors must be careful about mistaking opposition media outlets for independent, professional media. Third, there is a need to integrate media support with other democracy promotion activities, especially those aimed at strengthening civil society organizations and local government reform. Fourth, efforts to foster viable commercial media should be balanced by support for the norms, practices, and effective operation of public service media.

The Business Community

This is a dramatic time of globalization. In recent years, there has been a sharp increase in international trade, cross-border transactions, electronic connections among financial markets, worldwide spread of investment in vast sums, rapid movement of funds every day, and an upsurge of goods and services that are internationally produced and managed. So, economic interdependence is deeper than ever. These economic relations are inherently vulnerable to violent conflict because they can be disrupted with ease. Indeed, the threat of violence is often sufficient to upset investment flows and productive partnerships. In this context of deep interdependence, crises, which occur in one part of the system, may spread rapidly throughout the global economy. Such disruptions can trigger panic, intense resentment, and violent scapegoating of ethnic groups. Years of patient investment can be blown away in days of violence.

Within the business community, there is a slowly emerging recognition of the distinctive interests and responsibilities of business in helping to minimize conditions that lead to deadly conflict—not least because successful business has a vital stake in predictable situations based on general standards of equity in commerce and the rule of law. Emerging markets are highly attractive but they are often in rough neighborhoods. As a practical matter, violence prevention is good for business in the globalized world.

Preventing deadly conflict should be taken seriously by major business organizations in their own self-interest. Yet business has been slow to see its own risks and opportunities in this sphere. For example, firms have tended to look away from serious human rights violations in dictatorships so long as business transactions were profitable. But bitter experience has taught that such gross violations are likely to precipitate mass violence that in turn is damaging to business. Thus, there are moral and economic reasons for attending to human rights, and in the late 1990s several highly respected global corporations adopted codes of human rights and supported equitable socioeconomic development. Responsible investors, especially institutional investors, should vigorously encourage this trend.

Of all the institutions of civil society, the business community is the most perplexing in this context. The gap is very great between its immense capability and economic and political power on the one hand and its minimal role in preventing deadly conflict on the other. Perhaps a new generation of leadership will come to see its own self-interest in a broader framework that includes active pursuit of conditions conducive to peaceful living. One encouraging sign is that a variety of organizations and institutions in the year 2000 reached out to the business community for this purpose. Leading the way is the UN Secretary-General who orchestrated a "Global Compact" with major global corporations. This agreement had numerous large corporations publicly agree to keep their business practices in line with specified basic principles respecting human rights, the rights of labor, and the environment. Moreover, the World Bank, the U.S. Department of State, the Council on Foreign Relations, Amnesty International, the Carter Center, and Oxfam are putting increased emphasis on working with business in relation to conflict. Such cooperative relations may facilitate the work of business in this vital arena. New developments are described in chapter 10.

Educational Institutions

Educational institutions from early childhood to graduate education have a vitally important role to play in the human future, more so than ever before. This not only has to do with the modern, global economy that requires deeper and broader education than ever before; but also with the necessity of learning to live together in this globalized, highly interdependent, culture-mixing world. Historically, education everywhere has to some degree been ethnocentric—and all too often flagrantly prejudicial. If we humans are ever to live together amicably, it will be a wrenching transition from past practices that can only be achieved by using our preeminent learning capacities. Educational institutions must be in the vanguard.

It is time to take seriously the remark of Archibald MacLeish in the aftermath of World War II that was incorporated into the UNESCO constitution: "Since wars begin in the minds of men, it is in the minds of men that the defenses of peace must be constructed." He was writing about the mission of the emerging international institutions that were vividly mindful of the carnage of World War II and the Holocaust, but his words apply to the furious small wars and ubiquitous terroristic hatreds of today. Yet today's education in most of the world has little to say on this subject. Worse still, education almost everywhere has ethnocentric orientations. Indeed, some religious-based schools such as the madrasas of certain Islamic countries may fairly be characterized as education for hate.

Can we do better? Can we educate ourselves to cope with antagonistic intergroup attitudes peacefully? Is it possible for us to modify our attitudes and orientations so that we practice greater tolerance and mutual aid at home and in the world?

The question is how human beings can learn more constructive orientations toward those outside one's group while maintaining the values of primary group allegiance and identity. From an examination of existing research, it seems reasonable to believe that this is possible in spite of very bad habits from our ancient past.[10]

There is an extensive body of research on intergroup contact that bears on this question.[11] Can *contact* between different groups help? Experiments have demonstrated that the extent of contact between groups antagonistic toward one another is not the most important factor in achieving a more constructive orientation. Much depends on whether the contact occurs under favorable conditions. Often, the conditions of contact are not favorable.

If there is an aura of mutual suspicion, if the parties are highly competitive, if they are not supported by relevant authorities, or if contact occurs on the basis of very unequal status, then it is not likely to be helpful, whatever the amount of exposure. Contact under unfavorable conditions can stir up old tensions and reinforce stereotypes.

On the other hand, if there is friendly contact in the context of equal status, especially if such contact is supported by relevant authorities, if the contact is embedded in cooperative activity and fostered by a mutual aid ethic, then there is likely to be a strong positive outcome. Under these conditions, the more contact the better. Such contact is associated with improved attitudes between previously suspicious or hostile groups as well as with constructive changes in patterns of interaction between them.[12]

Related experiments demonstrate the power of shared, highly valued superordinate goals that can only be achieved by cooperative efforts. Such goals can override the differences that people bring to the situation and often have a powerful unifying effect. Classic experiments readily made strangers at a boys' camp enemies by isolating them from one another and heightening competition. But when powerful superordinate goals were introduced that could only be attained by cooperation, enemies were transformed into friends.[13]

Indeed, the findings have pointed to the beneficial effects of working cooperatively under conditions that lead people to formulate a new, inclusive group, going beyond the subgroups with which they entered the situation. Such effects are particularly strong when there are tangibly successful outcomes of cooperation—for example, clear rewards from cooperative learning. This research has important implications for child rearing and education. For example, schools and community organizations can be arranged in a way that meets the favorable conditions for intergroup contact.

Education everywhere should convey an accurate concept of the contemporary human species—a vast extended family sharing fundamental human similarities and a fragile planet. The give-and-take fostered within groups can be extended far beyond childhood toward relations between adults and into larger units of organization, even including international relations. All research-based knowledge of human conflict, the diversity of our species, and the paths to mutual accommodation should be a part of education.

Such education must begin by fostering prosocial behavior in early life. In the context of secure child–adult attachment and valued adult models, provided by either a cohesive family or a more extended social support network, a child can learn certain social norms that are conducive to tolerance and a mutual-aid ethic. Children can learn to take turns, share with others, cooperate (especially in learning and problem solving), and help others in everyday life as well as in times of stress. These norms, though established on a simple basis in the first few years of life, open the way toward constructive human relationships that can have significance throughout the life span. Their practice earns respect from others, provides gratification, and increases confidence and competence.[14]

There is research evidence, both from direct observation and experimental studies, that settings promoting the requirements and expectations of prosocial behavior do in fact strengthen such behavior.[15] For example, children who are responsible for tasks helpful to family maintenance, as in caring for younger siblings, are generally found to be more altruistic than children who do not have these prosocial experiences.

In experimental studies, typically an adult (presumably much like a parent) demonstrates a prosocial act such as sharing toys, coins, or candy that has been won in a game. The sharing is with someone else who is said to be in need though not present in the experimental situation. The adult plays the game and models the sharing before leaving the child to play. The results are clear. Children exposed to such modeling, when compared to similar children in control groups, tend to show the behavior manifested by the models, whether it be honesty, generosity, or altruism. Given the child's pervasive exposure to parents and teachers, the potential for observational learning in this sphere is powerful. Prosocial behavior is particularly significant in adaptation because it is likely to open new opportunities for the growing child, strengthen human relationships, and contribute to the building of self-esteem.

Empathy, defined as a shared emotional response between observer and stimulus person, may be expressed as "putting myself in the shoes of another person." Empathy training has been tested with eight- to ten-year-olds in elementary school classrooms. In one program, children were given thirty hours of exercises in small groups of four to six. A range of activities was designed to increase their skill in identifying emotional responses as well as in taking the perspective of another person. The intervention group was compared with two kinds of control groups. Participants in empathy training showed more prosocial behavior, less aggression, and more positive self-concept than children in either control group. This elementary school training model may provide a guide for the enhancement of empathy in other contexts—for example, learning to take the perspective of different ethnic or religious groups. In any event, responding empathically in potential conflict situations helps to reduce hateful outcomes. This has become an important part of conflict resolution training.

Much of what schools can accomplish is similar to what parents can do—employ positive discipline practices, be democratic in procedure, teach the capacity for responsible decision making, foster cooperative learning procedures, and guide children in prosocial behavior outside the schools as well as in them.[16] They can convey in interesting ways the facts of human diversity and the common humanity we all share. They can convey the fascination of other cultures—making understanding and respect a core attribute of their outlook on the world, including the capacity to interact effectively in the emerging world economy.

Professor Morton Deutsch of Columbia University, a distinguished scholar in conflict resolution, has delineated programs that schools can use to promote attitudes, values, and knowledge that will help children develop constructive relations throughout their lives.[17] Such programs include cooperative learning, conflict resolution training, the constructive use of controversy in teaching, and the creation of dispute resolution centers. Efforts to educate on these matters are most effective where there is a substantial, in-depth curriculum with repeated opportunities to learn and practice cooperative conflict resolution skills. Students gain a realistic understanding of the amount of violence in society and the deadly consequences of such violence. They learn that violence begets violence, that there are healthy and unhealthy ways to express anger, and that nonviolent alternatives to dealing with conflict are available and will always be useful to them.

Research on cooperative learning has developed a substantial body of information during the past two decades.[18] These efforts stem in part from a desire to find alternatives to the usual lecture mode and to involve students actively in the learning process. They are inspired, moreover, by a mutual-aid ethic and appreciation for student diversity. In cooperative learning, the traditional classroom of one teacher and many students is reorganized into heterogeneous groups of four or five students who work together to learn a particular subject matter, for instance, mathematics.

Research has demonstrated that student achievement is at least as high in cooperative learning activities as it is in traditional lecture-style classroom activities. At the same time, cooperative learning methods promote positive interpersonal relations, motivation to learn, and self-esteem. These benefits are obtained in middle grade schools and also high schools, for various subject areas, and for a wide range of tasks. So, wider use of cooperative learning holds much promise.

In 1990, the Carnegie Council on Adolescent Development's Working Group on Life Skills Training, chaired by Dr. Beatrix Hamburg, provided the factual basis and organizing principles on which such interventions can be based.[19] It also described a variety of exemplary programs. One life skill is being assertive. An example of assertiveness is knowing how to take advantage of opportunities—for example, how to use community resources such as health and social services or job training opportunities. Another aspect is knowing how to resist pressure or intimidation by peers and others to take drugs or carry weapons—and how to do this without isolating oneself. Yet another aspect of assertiveness is knowing how to resolve conflict in ways that make use of the full range of nonviolent opportunities in existence. Such skills can be taught not only in schools but also in community organizations and religious institutions.

Supervised community service in schools, starting in early adolescence, can also be helpful in the shaping of responsible, caring, altruistic behavior. It is important to have serious reflection on such community service experience, to analyze its implications, and to learn ways to benefit from setbacks. How we help others is crucial: It must not imply superiority over others; it must convey a sense of being full members of the community, sharing a common fate as human beings together. These principles carry over into higher education, and we have more to say about this in chapter 10, "Prognosis for Prevention."

Scientific and Scholarly Community

We face the problem of intergroup violence in the twenty-first century in a world increasingly saturated with highly destructive weapons. We see in all parts of the world abundant prejudice, hatred, and threats of mass violence. The historical record is full of every sort of slaughter based on perceived differences pertaining to religion, ethnicity, nationality, and other group characteristics. We inherit this penchant for making invidious distinctions from our ancient past and struggle to find ways of overcoming them. In this kind of world, the scientific community has a great responsibility to work in a reasonably unified way so that the physical, biological, behavioral, and social sciences can address these profound and pervasive problems.

The Carnegie Commission stimulated two special studies on these matters: one undertaken by an international research team; another by a panel of the President's Committee of Advisors on Science and Technology reporting to the president of the United States.[20]

The scientific community first and foremost provides understanding, insight, and stimulating ways of viewing important problems—and can do so with regard to deadly conflict. It can generate new knowledge and explore the application of such knowledge to urgent problems in contemporary society. In a world so full of hatred and violence, past and present, human conflict and its resolution is a subject that deserves major research efforts. High standards of inquiry must be applied to this field, involving many sciences functioning in collaborative ways. Crucial world problems do not come in neat packages that match traditional disciplines.

Aggression and conflict resolution have not been major subjects for scientific inquiry; they are largely marginal subjects even in some of the world's great academic institutions. Nevertheless, some interesting and potentially useful approaches have emerged.[21] Among these is the neurobiology of aggressive behavior that gives insight into how cells, circuits, and chemistry mediate such activity. Related to this is research into the biomedical aspects of individual violence, including the role various drugs play in the precipitation, exacerbation, and therapy of this condition. Research into child abuse and its effect on subsequent development also has relevance in understanding aggression as do other factors influencing prosocial and antisocial child and adolescent development.

Behavioral scientists do experimental research on simulated conflicts. This includes the study of negotiations both in real life circumstances and in simulated ones. There has been systematic inquiry into the origin and resolution of past conflicts, ongoing efforts in relation to contemporary ones, and the study of various intergroup and international institutions and processes pertinent to large-scale conflict. All of this is connected to research specifically focusing on war and peace, including ways to diminish the likelihood of nuclear war by arms control, crisis prevention, reducing the risk of accidental or inadvertent nuclear confrontation, and improvement of relations among the nuclear nations. This has been enriched by the study of conflict at various levels of organization, ranging from families and communities to nations—in the search for common factors and even principles so that discoveries at one level may illuminate issues at another level. Nurturing many of these questions is the study of evolution and history of human violence, which illuminates the complex topics of prejudice and ethnocentrism.[22] Taken collectively this work provides powerful and usable insight into ways of modulating human aggression.

The need for knowledge in this field is great and opportunities are substantial, but there are many obstacles to overcome: the inherent complexity of the subject matter; old conceptual rigidities such as the heredity–environment dichotomy; proper ethical limitations of experimental control in human research; ancient prejudices against objective inquiry into human behavior; dogmatic social ideologies; and institutional inertia regarding any kind of major change. In considering human conflict, avoidance and denial tend to substitute for careful scrutiny, authority often substitutes for evidence, and blaming readily substitutes for problem solving. The capacity for wishful thinking in these matters is enormous, as is the capacity for self-justification. But these are not insuperable challenges, and the rationale for overcoming them will become increasingly clear in the decades ahead.

The scientific community has contributed a good deal to coping with the nuclear danger.[23] During the decades of the Cold War, this community sought ways to reduce greatly the number of weapons and especially their capacity for a first strike; to decrease the chance of accidental or inadvertent nuclear war; to find safeguards against unauthorized launch and against serious miscalculation; and to improve the relations between the superpowers, partly through international cooperative efforts in key fields bearing on the health and safety of humanity.

The foreseeable consequences of nuclear war elicited a new level of commitment by the scientific community to reduce the risk. These science-based efforts sought to maximize the analytical capability, objectivity, and respect for evidence that is characteristic of the scientific community worldwide, and indeed the worldwide perspective that is itself integral to the outlook of the scientific community.

In addressing such crucial problems there was a major resource in the scientific and scholarly community of the United States and its links to worldwide counterparts.[24] One way of utilizing these resources was for this community to have ongoing involvement in these issues through broad-based organizations such as the American Association for the Advancement of Science and the National Academy of Sciences. Research-intensive universities played similar roles.

These efforts brought together scientists, scholars, and expert practitioners to clarify the many facets of avoiding nuclear war.[25] To generate options for decreasing the risk, we needed analytical work by people who knew certain fields: for example, advanced weaponry and its military uses; in-depth knowledge of the superpowers and other nuclear powers; geopolitical flash points; the broad context of international relations, policy formation, and implementation (especially regarding the superpowers); human behavior under stress (especially leadership decision making); and negotiation and conflict resolution. Collectively, these efforts provided needed depth and new options for dealing with very dangerous issues. These relevant skills cut right across the sciences: physical, biological, behavioral, and social. Analytical studies were most useful when informed by the perspective of policymakers, and policymakers derived benefit from having access to studies yielding fresh ideas, a wider range of options, and deeper insights. A continuing dynamic interplay between the scientific community and the world of policy evolved.

A prominent example of international scientific cooperation during the Cold War was the Pugwash Conference on Science and World Affairs, recognized in 1995 by the Nobel Peace Prize. Stemming from the initial meeting in 1957 were a continuing series of informal discussions among the world's scientists and the availability of resulting recommendations to world governments. The initial meeting at Pugwash, Canada (which gives the organization its name), set in motion a continuing series of private and informal discussions. It is sometimes hard to trace their influence, but they played a useful role in facilitating the negotiation of the Nuclear Test Ban Treaty, the Nuclear Nonproliferation Treaty, the Convention on the Prohibition of the Development, Production and Stockpiling of Bacteriological and Toxic Weapons and for Their Destruction, and the Anti-Ballistic Missile Agreement. I had the privilege of giving a keynote address at Pugwash's fiftieth anniversary meeting in 2000.

In 1978, Pugwash convened a workshop on crisis management and crisis prevention under my chairmanship, involving scientists and scholars from a variety of countries, but principally the United States and the Soviet Union. By 1978, there was a cumulative record of analytical studies sufficient to derive some tentative but useful principles of crisis management. The central question was whether it is possible to emerge from a crisis in the twentieth century without a disastrous war, let alone a nuclear war.

Scholars sought a consensus on principles of crisis management and then to convey this consensus as clearly and meaningfully as possible to policymakers and policy advisors in a variety of nations, but especially in the superpowers.[26] If crises were to arise again, it would be valuable for leaders to grasp these principles and follow them as well as they could in order to avoid catastrophe. As the evidence of various crises was considered, scholars were deeply impressed with the difficulty of adhering to such guidelines in the event. The immense strains of international crisis and, above all, nuclear crisis test the limits of human capacity to adapt. Therefore, the focus was widened to consider crisis prevention. Whatever the level of armaments, and whatever the animosity of the superpowers, it was simply a matter of prudent self-interest to remain a step or two from the brink of nuclear crisis because the tasks of crisis management are so exceedingly difficult. These concerns in both countries led to a joint U.S.–Soviet study group on crisis prevention. The pattern for several years was to meet about twice a year with substantial preparation between meetings, including visits of younger scholars back and forth to pave the way. These meetings were characterized by civil discourse, mutual respect, and serious analysis of ways to reduce the nuclear danger.

When Gorbachev came to power in 1985, the group began to explore the "new thinking," going beyond crisis prevention to the possibility of basic improvement of U.S.–Soviet relations, and publishing a joint book—a breakthrough at that time.[27] The Soviet and American participants both became more significant advisors to government leadership as the years went by. So, the work exemplified the increasingly useful dynamic interplay between scholars and policymakers in leading countries throughout the world. For example, the American group had links to the Nunn-Warner study group that proposed nuclear risk reduction centers, and these centers were in due course modestly implemented in both countries. The issues of crisis management, crisis prevention, and improvement of relations between adversaries are still fundamental to the problems of major conflict.

In the world of the twenty-first century, it will be crucial to understand incentives for cooperation, obstacles to cooperation, factors that favor cooperation, and strategies that tend to make cooperation useful and effective. Such cooperative agreements in security matters are a means to an end, or rather a variety of ends, but centrally involve reducing the risk of catastrophic war. Lessons of the Cold War—the most dangerous conflict in all of history—can be useful for this purpose. We need to understand how it was possible that five decades passed without a global war; indeed, over the years there emerged some solidarity of interest between the superpowers, which was rooted in the most basic motivations of self-preservation and survival.

The Cold War experience maps a useful role for the scientific and scholarly community in international conflict resolution—as it often acts through NGOs yet maintains open lines of communication with governments. There are a few singular advantages. Policymakers in search of principles and objective analysis can draw on the scientific community for accurate information. Scientists and scholars maintain flexibility for novel or neglected paths toward conflict resolution. They also have common ground suited for building relationships among themselves who, as well-informed and respected people, can make a difference in attitudes and in problem solving at home and abroad.

Two recent penetrating studies of Cold War history show clearly that the momentous reformulation of Soviet policy growing out of Gorbachev's new thinking was strongly influenced by his contacts with the scientific and scholarly community. This occurred primarily through his interactions with leading Soviet scientists and scholars. The contribution of the international scientific community is also clear, primarily through its impact on these Soviet scientists but also through direct encounters with Gorbachev himself.[28]

A remarkable fact of the Cold War is that considerable learning and adaptation took place in order to keep the peace, despite deep hostility and profound strains.[29] Scientists in and out of the governments played significant roles in this achievement. Some useful cooperative agreements were reached, even in the worst of times. Although they fell far short of a comprehensive U.S.–Soviet security regime, they did include partial regimes that embraced norms, agreed-upon rules, evolving patterns of behaviors, shared procedures, and even some specially created institutions. Centrally, these were tacit rules of prudence.

In the late eighties, there were remarkable technical accomplishments in arms control, both structural and operational.[30] The INF treaty was the breakthrough in the structural field. The Stockholm agreements on Confidence-Building Measures in Europe were the principal achievement in the operational field, although the Nuclear Risk Reduction Centers were also significant. Toward the end of the Cold War, the Strategic Arms Reduction Treaties (START I and II) and the treaty on Conventional Armed Forces in Europe (CFE) were noteworthy.

With good reason, much attention was given to the step-by-step development of ways to implement the two nations' shared interests in avoiding accidental war. One landmark in this effort was the upgrading of the hot line in 1984. Another was the establishment of Nuclear Risk Reduction Centers in 1987. Perhaps the most remarkable and enduring land-

mark is the Incidents-at-Sea Agreement of the early 1970s. Dangerous encounters between the two navies, which occurred frequently prior to this
agreement, were moderated and constructively regulated by explicit rules
covering most, though not all, encounters between the two navies. The two
navies pursued this agreement in a highly professional manner even during
periods when the overall political relationship between the countries deteriorated badly.

Overall, it is one of the great challenges for science policy and practice to
organize a much broader and deeper effort to understand the nature and
sources of human conflict and, above all, to develop effective ways of resolving conflict short of disaster. The scientific and scholarly community is
the closest approximation we now have to a truly international community,
sharing certain fundamental interests, values, standards, and curiosities
about the nature of matter, life, behavior, and the universe. The shared
quest for understanding is one that knows no national boundaries, has no
inherent prejudices, no necessary ethnocentrism, and no barriers to the free
play of information and ideas. Recent advances in telecommunications
draw this quest together internationally more than ever.

To some extent, the scientific community can provide a model for human
relations that might transcend some of the biases and dogmas that have torn
the species apart throughout history and that have recently become so much
more dangerous than ever before. Science can contribute to a better future by
its ideals and its processes, as well as by the specific content of its research,
and all these must to be brought to bear on the problem of human conflict.

Notes

1. Jessica Matthews, "Power Shift," *Foreign Affairs* (January/February,
1997).

2. Alexander George, *Bridging the Gap: Theory and Practice in Foreign Policy* (Washington, D.C.: United States Institute of Peace, 1993).

3. David Smoch, *Training to Prevent: Conflict Management* (Washington,
D.C.: United States Institute of Peace, 1999).

4. Kofi Annan and Rita Hauser, *International Peace Academy 2001 Annual
Report* (New York: International Peace Academy, 2001).

5. Personal communication with John Marks, May 2000.

6. Sarah E. Mendelson and John K. Glenn, *Democracy Assistance and NGO
Strategies in Post-Communist Societies* (Working Paper of the Carnegie Endowment for International Peace, 2000); Robert I. Rotberg, *Vigilance and
Vengeance: NGOs Preventing Ethnic Conflict in Divided Societies* (Washington, D.C.: Brookings, 1996).

7. R. Scott Appleby, *The Ambivalence of the Sacred: Religion, Violence, and
Reconciliation* (Carnegie Commission Series, Rowman & Littlefield, 2000).

8. Gerald Lesser, "The Role of Television in Moving Beyond Hate" (paper presented at the Beyond Hate Conference initiated by Elie Wiesel, Boston University, March 19, 1989).

9. Mendelson and Glenn, *Democracy Assistance,* 25–29.

10. Robert A. Hinde and Donald A. Parry, *Education for Peace* (Nottingham, England: Spokesman, Bertrand Russell House, 1989).

11. Marilynn B. Brewer and Norman Miller, *Intergroup Relations* (Pacific Grove, Calif.: Brooks/Cole Publishing, 1996).

12. G. W. Allport, *The Nature of Prejudice* (New York: Doubleday, 1958).

13. M. Sherif and C. Sherif, *Groups in Harmony and Tension: An Integration of Studies on Intergroup Relations* (New York: Octagon, 1966).

14. Hamburg, George, and Ballentine, "Preventing Deadly Conflict: The Critical Role of Leadership." *Archives of General Psychiatry,* 56 (November 1999): 971–76.

15. Margaret S. Clark, ed., *Prosocial Behavior* (New York: Sage, 1991).

16. Ervin Staub, *The Roots of Evil: The Origins of Genocide and Other Group Violence* (New York: Cambridge University Press, 1989).

17. Morton Deutsch, "Educating for a Peaceful World," *American Psychologist* (May 1993).

18. Robert E. Slavin and Robert Cooper, "Improving Intergroup Relations: Lessons Learned from Cooperative Learning Programs," *Journal of Social Issues* 55, no. 4 (winter 1999): 647–66.

19. David A. Hamburg, ed., *Great Transitions: Preparing Adolescents for a New Century* (Concluding Report of the Carnegie Council on Adolescent Development, Carnegie Corporation of New York, 1995).

20. Allison L. C. De Cerrano and Alexander Keynan, *Scientific Cooperation, State Conflict: The Roles of Scientists in Mitigating International Discord* (New York: New York Academy of Sciences, 1998); David A. Hamburg, Sidney Drell, Alexander George, John Holdren, Jane Holl, John Steinbruner, John Stremlau, and Cyrus Vance, *Preventing Deadly Conflict: What Can the Scientific Community Do?* (Report of the President's Committee of Advisors on Science and Technology to the President of the United States, Office of Science and Technology Policy, White House, Washington, D.C., 1996).

21. Hamburg and Trudeau, *Biobehavioral Aspects of Aggression.*

22. J. T. Dunlop, *Dispute Resolution* (Dover, Mass.: Auburn House, 1984); H. Raiffa, *The Art and Science of Negotiation* (Cambridge, Mass.: Belknap, 1982); J. A. Schellenberg, *The Science of Conflict* (New York: Oxford University Press, 1982); and R. Levine and D. Campbell, *Ethnocentrism: Theories of Conflict, Ethnic Attitudes and Group Behavior* (New York: McGraw-Hill, 1972).

23. McGeorge Bundy, William J. Crowe, and Sidney Drell, *Reducing Nuclear Danger: The Road Away from the Brink* (New York: Council on Foreign Relations Press, 1993).

24. Sidney Drell, *Facing the Threat of Nuclear Weapons, With an Open Letter on the Danger of Thermonuclear War from Andrei Sakharov* (Seattle: University of Washington Press, 1983).

25. David A. Hamburg, "Understanding and Preventing Nuclear War: The Expanding Role of the Scientific Community," in *The Medical Implications of Nuclear War* (Washington, D.C.: National Academy Press, 1986).

26. Alexander George, *Forceful Persuasion: Coercive Diplomacy as an Alternative to War* (Washington, D.C.: United States Institute of Peace Press, 1991).

27. Graham Allison, W. L. Ury, and B. J. Allyn, eds., *Windows of Opportunity: From Cold War to Peaceful Competition in US–Soviet Relations* (Cambridge, Mass.: Ballinger, 1989).

28. Matthew Evangelista, *Unarmed Forces: The Transnational Movement to End the Cold War* (Ithaca, N.Y.: Cornell University Press, 1999); Andrew Bennett, *Condemned to Repetition? The Rise, Fall, and Reprise of Soviet-Russian Military Interventionism, 1973–1996* (Cambridge, Mass.: MIT Press, 1999); and Mikhail Gorbachev, *Gorbachev: On My Country and the World* (New York: Columbia University Press, 2000).

29. Alexander George, Philip J. Farley, and Alexander Dallin, *US–Soviet Security Cooperation: Achievements, Failures, Lessons* (New York: Oxford University Press, 1988).

30. Archie Brown, *The Gorbachev Factor* (New York: Oxford University Press, 1996).

5

Preventive Diplomacy:
Early Help with Empathy
and Problem Solving

Preventing Deadly Conflict: One Report or Many?

Cyrus Vance and I went to a lot of trouble to select and recruit a remarkably accomplished set of eminent leaders for the Carnegie
Commission and its distinguished advisory council. Adding up to
fifty-plus richly experienced people from all parts of the world, it would be
plausible to prepare a single consensus report of the Commission, strengthened by the advisory council, and make this the final word of the Carnegie
effort. But I felt impelled to raise the question of collateral publications to
pursue many strands of this very broad subject in greater depth than a single work of synthesis, however excellent, could possibly provide.

In this view, I was especially stimulated by my wonderful colleagues,
Alexander George and Jane Holl. Many of the commissioners did not express
much interest in such additional publications, but neither were they opposed.
So, we pushed on and in the end I believe the in-depth studies were fully as
valuable as the Commission's work of synthesis. (They are listed in appendix
1.) But so far they have received less recognition than the Commission's full
report and it is very important that their data and insights be widely understood. Nowhere is this truer than in the case of *preventive diplomacy*.

The Commission's "final report" (actually one of the first of our series)
dealt with this subject in a reasonable, constructive way—but the emphasis
was more on "diplomacy" than on "preventive." This reflects the vast
diplomatic experience of the commissioners; most of it was late rather than
early, reparative more than preventive. Typically, these gifted people had
been dealt a weak hand by their governments or the UN well after a conflict had become very deadly. In effect, they were asked to improvise—often brilliantly—in the context of extensive bloodshed, deeply ingrained hatred, and intense revenge motives on both sides.

This point was vividly highlighted at the Commission's first meeting. In advance, Cyrus Vance and I alerted the commissioners that we would like each one to reflect on a conflict of personal experience and to emphasize what might have been done at an earlier stage to diminish greatly the risk of mass violence. In the event, the commissioners found it very difficult to think in this way because it was so far outside the sphere of their main experience. It took us about a year to become comfortable in this mode of *preventive* diplomacy.

Therefore, we set in motion several in-depth studies to come at the problem from different angles. Taken together, the four books by Jentleson, Greenberg and Barton, Zartman, and Peck constitute the most informative and analytically perceptive body of work ever undertaken on preventive diplomacy. That is why I emphasize their contributions in this chapter. At the end, I undertake to draw out crosscutting themes, points of convergence among these highly illuminating studies. They fit beautifully at the vital intersection of research, policy, and practice.

Basic Orientation

In recent years, as cruelty and slaughter have become vivid in various parts of the world, there has been growing concern with the need for outside intervention. In practice, this has usually meant *military* intervention to stop an aggression—whether operating across national boundaries or within a nation-state. The risks and costs of such military intervention generate understandable concern, apprehension, and controversy. Moreover, the problem of outsiders violating national sovereignty arouses both legitimate concerns of international law and spurious concerns of dictators preserving their right to abuse people as they wish.

But all of this assumes that the international community will be passive in the face of growing danger and will not respond until a disaster has occurred that can only be stopped with powerful military force. We need not assume such passivity, but instead ask what can be done to recognize growing danger long before a disaster has occurred and respond before military intervention is the only recourse. Much can be achieved by accurate, early information, alertness, and ingenuity in the use of conflict-resolving principles and techniques.

How can the international community enhance its current capacities to prevent the deadliest conflicts? Can we recognize serious dangers early enough? Can we help adversaries to understand the risks of violence before they have crossed the Rubicon? Can we help them strengthen their own capacities for conflict resolution? Can we mobilize international, intellectual, technical, financial, and moral resources to avert disaster and achieve just outcomes? These are profound worldwide challenges.

Dag Hammarskjold first coined the term *preventive diplomacy* in 1960 when, as UN Secretary-General, he sought to find ways to prevent local conflicts from feeding into the larger superpower rivalry. Ironically, it was only with the end of the Cold War and the parallel intensification of ethnic, religious, and regional conflicts that the term gained currency. Indeed, by the mid-1990s, there was a rare degree of consensus among international organizations, states, and nongovernmental actors on the need for more and better efforts at preventive diplomacy. A commitment to policies of preventive diplomacy has since been undertaken by the United Nations, the Organization for Security and Cooperation in Europe (OSCE), the Organization of African Unity (OAU), a number of individual governments, and a variety of NGOs. Yet the implementation of these policies is still in an early phase of development.

An obstacle to preventive diplomacy is the common assumption that, unless a powerful nation's survival is in clear and present danger, the interests of major powers are better served by waiting to see if the conflict will subside or burn itself out. But this is a tenuous assumption. The spread of faraway conflicts often occurs in ways that augment the danger. This happens through combinations of the movement of refugees and weapons to other countries in the region, international terrorism, demonstration effects that foster escalation of other conflicts, and various modes of conflict diffusion. When there is no prevention, the territory in jeopardy may readily enlarge.

The core premise of preventive diplomacy is that international security is today better served by working proactively to avert outbreaks of large-scale violence, state collapse, terrorism, and weapons proliferation than it is by simply reacting to crises once they have occurred. *Preventive diplomacy* is usually defined as the use of proactive, peaceful measures to prevent political conflicts from erupting into violence and to promote peaceful, just dispute resolution.

In operational terms, it resembles conventional diplomatic practice and uses a similar repertoire of policy tools, including information gathering, official and track-two negotiations, mediation, and confidence-building measures. However, preventive diplomacy is distinguished by its forward-looking character, its emphasis on systematic early warning and early response. Traditional diplomacy, by contrast, has typically been ad hoc and reactive, more geared to limited crisis management than to a principled program of fundamental violence prevention.

The onset of mass violence transforms the nature of a conflict. Revenge motives severely complicate the situation. Resolution and even limitation of conflict are then less likely to be effective. So, early preventive action is exceedingly attractive.

We now have a substantial body of studies available on the strengths and limitations of many tools as they have been applied in a considerable number of cases. Practically, we also have a better understanding of how to employ the tools of preventive diplomacy. This chapter deals with such insights. We have laid the foundation for preventive diplomacy in the two preceding chapters. We have seen that governments, intergovernmental organizations, and nongovernmental organizations can contribute.

Studies of Negotiation, Bargaining, Coming to Agreement, and Solving Joint Problems

Negotiation is at the heart of preventive diplomacy whether face-to-face between adversaries or with the addition of a third party in mediation or arbitration. Therefore, we now examine conditions favorable to effective, fruitful negotiation. In the past two decades scholars have undertaken a wide range of inquiry having to do with real-world negotiation in a variety of settings as well as experimental studies on simulated negotiation—and links between the two.[1]

Shared interests often lie behind superficially opposing positions, and any given interest may well be satisfied in a variety of ways. Each side typically has multiple interests. Altogether, a problem-solving orientation is useful rather than putting down the adversary.

To implement this approach, negotiators need extensive knowledge of the situation in conflict, including its social context, and the ability to think creatively about different ways in which the parts might be fit together. Negotiators need to guard against premature closure, against commitment to a single royal road to virtue, against assuming that there is necessarily a fixed pie that must be carved up, and against leaving the solution of the adversaries' problem to the adversaries alone.

The consensus of recent work on factors likely to lead to successful negotiation, and moreover likely to be practically useful in skills that can be learned by negotiators, include the following set.[2]

1. The negotiation actively strives to address legitimate interests of both parties and to resolve them clearly, taking into account shared interests and the conditions required for maintenance of an agreement over extended time.
2. The procedures are efficient and task oriented.
3. The negotiation seeks ways to improve the relationship between the parties over the long term, or at least to do no harm.
4. The negotiators adopt an outlook that both parties can win. Negotiation is not a harsh competition or a theatrical performance, though elements of these often enter in. Fundamentally, everyone concerned should gain something tangible by the time the process is completed.

There must be ways to constitute a "victory" for adversaries if there are to be substantial and durable results.

5. Prepare for negotiation. Negotiations are likely to be more successful if the parties study the facts of the situation, including their social context; set reasonably clear goals; establish priorities among their goals; and draft a tentative course of action, especially with respect to initial steps and, importantly, including contingency plans. This involves serious efforts to understand the adversary, including background, attitudes, and probable expectations. Practice in situations similar to the actual negotiation can be helpful.

6. Keep in mind the needs of the negotiators and the constituencies they represent. These needs are necessarily varied, and therefore a wide range of factors must be taken into account in order to be responsive to them. An orientation of joint problem solving is useful in this context.

7. Consider sources of power and formulate tactics in light of such knowledge. The negotiators represent certain constituencies and indeed usually must keep in close touch with their constituencies. They cannot forget the sources of their power. Therefore, one is dealing not only with the individuals represented in the negotiating situation but a much larger number behind them. The capacity to influence each other's understanding and decisions is crucially dependent on the way these sources of power are perceived.

8. Foster effective communication. Communication between the negotiators must provide reasonably accurate information about needs and priorities, sometimes including the most basic human needs of the adversaries. Though calculated ambiguity is sometimes useful, clarity of communication is usually very important. Searching questions to clarify complex issues and to seek latent sources of potential agreement are essential. As part of probing for underlying intentions and possible changes in outlook, sensitivity to nonverbal as well as verbal cues may help to illuminate where opportunities may exist. Assumptions must be checked and understandings clarified in order to avoid the kind of misinterpretation that can badly undermine trust and even generate a sense of betrayal.

9. Monitor the behavior of other negotiators. The value of knowing your adversary is clear from experience. This means not only the individual directly involved, whose characteristics may indeed be of practical importance, but also the major values, institutions, frustrations, and biases characteristic of that negotiator's principal constituency.

10. Adapt to new conditions. Circumstances arise in which new information must be taken into account, the context of negotiations must be reappraised, or other insights assimilated. Such changes call for midcourse corrections. The abilities to take account of new facts, to

reformulate in light of wider horizons, and to create new proposals are all part of adaptive behavior that favors effective outcomes.

11. Bring agreements to explicit conclusion. When mutually satisfactory solutions have been found to some major issues and further negotiations have become counterproductive for the time being, there is a need to make the agreement explicit. In most circumstances, there is long-term merit in achieving clarity and definiteness in such agreements. Even though a studied ambiguity may help to get an agreement by fuzzing over a difficult issue, it is perilous in the longer term because such ambiguity lends itself to wishful interpretations by both sides and then to charges of violation of agreement and even betrayal. Thus, successful negotiators tend to minimize the potential for future misunderstanding by giving considerable explicit attention to the ways in which such misunderstandings might arise.

One of the most interesting factors that emerges prominently in the research studies, including those that are experimental in nature, is the emphasis on *status, respect, reputation, "face,"* and *appearance of strength.* This set of related needs for esteem may appear intangible and yet can have powerful effects on the progress of negotiations. Experimenters have varied status conditions deliberately in order to examine such effects. This research indicates that concern about appearance of strength or "face" motivates a great deal of negotiating behavior. It tends to be in sharper relief when the negotiators have an adversarial relationship. It is intensified when an adversary acts in a threatening way. These issues centering on appearance of strength and saving of face intensify resistance and competition in experimental games that simulate negotiations. Indeed, sometimes such influences have overriding effects that exceed the tangible issues under negotiation.

Another interesting aspect of the research has to do with the *interdependence* of the party's goals. Experimental research suggests that maximization of joint utilities may be very important. What will the outcome be worth to the contending parties together? For example, powerful effects can be achieved with an instruction like, "You want to win as much as you can for yourself, and you do want the other person to win also." With this kind of orientation, both personal gain and extensive cooperation can be elicited. Overall, the experimental results provide support for the case made by those with extensive experience in negotiation: Concentrating on an adversary's needs as well as on one's own can be useful in arriving at agreed-upon solutions, especially when the needs are to some degree actively interdependent.

There is a great deal of evidence from experimental research to indicate that threats in negotiation tend to elicit counter threats. These intensify a competitive atmosphere, exacerbate concerns about saving face, and engender hostility. Thus, the approach to negotiation that emphasizes threats tends to produce a spiral of conflict. This research fits closely with the view of those who have extensive experience in negotiation. Firmness, principled defense of vital interests, and authentic strength in negotiation need not rest on repeated threats, harsh depreciation of the adversary, or posturing in enhancement of one's own status.

Empirical studies of communication in negotiation have been done. There is evidence on ways to minimize inadvertent misinterpretation, on the effectiveness of gathering information not from a single but from multiple sources, and on bilateral focus. The latter involves restating an adversary's view to the adversary's satisfaction. It signifies a serious intent to understand the viewpoint of the other and may bring to light assumptions that need to be worked on that were embedded in the other's position.

Sending messages effectively has a number of facets. Crucial is stating clearly the specific actions requested of the adversary while at the same time appreciating the opponent's difficulties in complying with such requests. This understanding is complemented by emphasizing the benefits the opponent would realize if the difficulties can be overcome. Still, it may be necessary to make clear the probable negative consequence of noncompliance in these multisided efforts to induce the opponent to reach an agreement.

Situations that put basic human needs in jeopardy often lie at the root of many different human conflicts—interpersonal, organizational, or international. So, conflict resolution centrally involves the search for mutual accommodation in which basic needs of contending parties can be met to a reasonable extent.

Warren Christopher, one of the most respected negotiators of our time, a former secretary of state who has conducted many successful negotiations in both public and private sectors, recently formulated key practical points from his rich experience of complex negotiations.[3]

> War is typically the result of failed negotiations. There are few armed conflicts that are not preceded by some efforts to resolve whatever it is that has led the parties to the brink. Likewise, there are few armed conflicts that, once begun, are not ended by negotiation. . . . The story is much the same in the private realm. A dispute that has to be resolved in a courtroom usually reflects an unsuccessful negotiation. Just as in the international arena, the large majority of private disputes in the United States are settled rather than fought to conclusion. . . . What these observations point to is the extraordinary importance of negotiators—people who can bring disputes to a conclusion short of ultimate conflict.

Christopher delineates key skills and characteristics that help define the effective negotiator. The foundation is mastery of the subject matter that informs any dispute. Even when armed with this knowledge, a negotiator should be ready to seek creative solutions, preferably in the context of joint problem solving. Key to success is understanding the adversary. This is a major factor that can build necessary credibility with other parties. Equally important is credibility that the negotiator instills in his or her own aides. The very human qualities of empathy, stamina, and persistence should never be played down. Nor should sound tactical sense, which is vital in shaping the scope and order of the agenda as well as in the use of technical subgroups and knowing when to use these outside parties to help get to "yes."

Thus, there is a considerable convergence of research and carefully considered experience in suggesting constructive modes of negotiating that offer real promise of meeting basic needs, addressing grievances seriously, and finding paths to mutual accommodation through joint problem solving. This approach to negotiation has much promise for preventive diplomacy, whether utilized by governments, intergovernmental organizations, or nongovernmental organizations.[4]

A Notable Example of Preventive Diplomacy

OSCE High Commissioner on National Minorities Max van der Stoel provided in the decade of the 1990s a remarkably creative precedent for early, ongoing preventive diplomacy in dangerous situations in Eastern Europe.[5] The basic theme running through van der Stoel's work is violence prevention. His constant refrain is that intervention at a very early time of tension can prevent disagreement and conflicts from developing into mass violence. This preventive diplomacy should be done in a cooperative context, understanding that interethnic conflict prevention is not simply a national matter but involves a community of nations and groups that share norms and values that are centered on human rights.

The basis of his conception of minority rights is the OSCE's Copenhagen Document of 1990. This assures national minorities the right to exercise their human rights and fundamental freedoms without any discrimination and in full equality before the law. The document guarantees minorities the use of their mother tongue in private and public life; the establishment of their own educational, cultural, and religious institutions; religious freedom; and the right to unimpeded contact with other minority group members. All fifty-five national members of the OSCE are obliged to observe these protections.

Abuses toward a minority group necessarily turn members of that group against a government and dramatically increase the chance of violence. It is here that van der Stoel sees the intervention of neutral third parties (e.g., OSCE, EU, or the Council of Europe) as vital. They can appeal to moderate elements in society. Van der Stoel also suggests that an approach to the population at large can be helpful since the people are often more moderate than the politicians who claim to lead them. Both his informal, low-key diplomacy and his public education programs are oriented to prevent polarization and radicalization.

The Office of the High Commissioner is constantly receiving and analyzing information as well as visiting trouble spots. This allows accurate assessment of troubling situations and a means to facilitate solutions. The nationalist issues that threaten to boil over may be broken down into core elements that can be dealt with in practical terms. He sees his goal in cases from minority language rights in Slovakia to legislative policy on minorities in Croatia to minority education in Romania as focused on avoiding inflaming the situation and helping the parties to find accommodation in a problem-solving atmosphere.

The support of other international organizations (such as the EU, which may withhold membership to states that are uncooperative) is vital in giving parties a strong incentive to solve their problems. This fits into a framework that encourages states to take care of their own problems by developing their own institutions, legislation, and other mechanisms to assure minority rights.

Van der Stoel has two major points on effective participation of national minorities in public life. First, minorities should have an effective voice in the central government, assured through special arrangements if necessary. Second, minority groups should be allowed some degree of self-governance. This should not be confused with internal self-determination or secession. Secession is rarely a viable option for long-term peace. At the same time, maintaining territorial integrity on the part of a state should not be a justification for the rejection of minority rights.

The key is to strike a balance between the needs of the state and of the minority groups. Van der Stoel feels that insufficient attention has been directed toward nonterritorial autonomy for minorities, that is, a devolution of powers that allows groups authority over some key matters affecting them. He concludes that the best type of early action is the construction of civil societies that protect human rights, including minority rights. These systems give minorities a feeling that they have a stake in the society in which they live.

Van der Stoel notes that disputes concerning minority rights often appear because there are insufficient means for dialogue at a national level in many countries. He brings together experts and representatives from authorities and minorities under OSCE auspices. All sides get to present their cases and intentions to the other disputants. Roundtables and other similar projects are often done in conjunction with other international agencies or NGOs.

For conflict prevention on minority issues to be effective, it cannot restrict itself merely to efforts to stop disputes from degenerating into open conflicts. There must be a cooperative effort to remove the root causes of the dangerous frictions that underlie these disputes. The steady, patient, informative efforts of the high commissioner help adversaries to move gradually in a positive direction.

A Model of Very Early Prevention

The UN's potential for very early prevention is delineated in an important book by Gareth Evans, former foreign minister of Australia, a valuable member of the Carnegie Commission and now president of the International Crisis Group described in chapter 10.[6]

Evans focuses on practical ways to improve the preventive diplomacy capacity of the United Nations, specifically the Secretariat. He elaborates on specific reforms that could be undertaken to enhance the United Nations' ability to act effectively at an early stage. His main emphasis is on the need to expand the human and organizational resources of the Secretariat to allow a more systematic capacity for early warning, early response, and follow-through.

In Evans's view, preventive diplomacy is the least complex, most humane, and most cost-effective path for the international community. He formulates two types of prevention, conceived not as tardy versus timely, but as qualitatively different approaches, each with its own time perspective and objectives and each with its own uses for preventing conflict.

Early prevention aims to preempt the escalation of disputes to the point of armed conflict by providing dispute resolution services when the opportunity is ripe, that is, when the issues in dispute are still limited, localized, and thus tractable. Instruments include the full range of mediation, arbitration, and persuasion mechanisms. Efficacy depends on adequate infrastructure for information and monitoring, high-quality political analysis of long-term trends on the ground, and ability to establish routine multilevel contacts at local and regional levels.

Early engagement is simply better. At an early stage, disputants are more likely to accept third-party mediation while the dispute is still local and limited. Intervention undertaken before issues have snowballed and positions hardened are more likely to achieve positive results. Also, disputes that are resolved early and peaceably are less likely to recur. Overall, this sort of preventive action means the financial and human costs are likely to be much less.

One reason for focusing on the UN is that its charter obliges all members to undertake to resolve their disputes in a peaceful manner. At the same time, the charter does not specify concrete mechanisms that would enable the UN to assist member states in fulfilling this obligation. While the UN may not always be the best agency for preventive diplomacy—nor should it ever be considered the exclusive agency—Evans maintains that enhancing the UN's capacity for prevention is a necessity, since the UN is often summoned to action by member states or finds itself compelled to respond to impending crises in the absence of any other responses.

Evans makes a very interesting proposal for the establishment of regionally focused "preventive diplomacy teams or units" under either Security Council or General Assembly mandate to routinize and expand the Secretariat's capacity for preventive diplomacy.

Senior experts in dispute resolution who have regional familiarity should head these units. They must have sufficient stature to be able to undertake negotiations at the highest level. They could be seconded from regional organizations or member state diplomatic corps or drawn from the senior ranks of academic institutions. They must be given full institutional support (computers, financing, staff access to data banks and outside consultants, communications links, field representatives, and regular travel budgets). The purpose of these units is to provide dispute resolution services, including monitoring, analysis, mediation, good offices, emergent-trend tracking, confidence-building measures and preventive regional regimes design as well as liaison services with other UN organizations for resources and assistance in constitutional, electoral, and development policy reform. In some instances, the units could undertake direct third-party actions or provide a neutral arena for communications or recommend a specific dispute resolution procedure; in others, they might refer disputants to regional organizations better suited to the task.

These units should not have to wait for an invitation to engage disputants, but should have the flexibility for proactive and early engagement. These units should not undertake to act as arbitrators. Instead, they should act as facilitators to the parties in need of third-party assistance. These units cannot be spread too thin. They must focus priorities on the most likely cases of incipient deadly conflict as revealed by indicators such as population displacements, previous or unresolved conflicts, weapons flows, or serious threats of violence.

Preventive diplomacy units should be based in the regions as well as at UN headquarters in New York so that there is a permanent local presence on the ground. Evans suggests stationing these centers near major relevant regional organizations (e.g., Organization of American States [OAS], Association of Southeast Asian Nations [ASEAN]). These regional centers would still remain under direct Secretary-General jurisdiction, closely tied to headquarters.

Evans endorses the UN principle that, wherever possible, local problems should be dealt with locally. He also emphasizes the long-held desire for closer cooperation between regional organizations (ROs) and the UN. This could be followed by more concerted efforts by both the UN and ROs to undertake voluntary, cooperative actions, pooling their strengths and comparative advantages for preventive purposes. Since becoming Secretary-General, Kofi Annan has taken steps in this direction.

Connie Peck, who in the early 1990s worked with Evans on the book *Cooperating for Peace,* developed these ideas further in her important book for the Carnegie Commission, *Sustainable Peace.* The recommendations of Evans and Peck provide several valuable assets. A major contribution is a recommendation for more flexibility and leadership capacity for the UN Secretary-General in preventive diplomacy and increased strength in the UN Secretariat to fulfill this mission. Systematic coverage of each region of the world for early detection of oncoming serious trouble is also a likely result. Together, these provide a fusion of knowledge and skill of three vital kinds: concepts and techniques of conflict resolution; knowledge of particular conflicts, with sufficient grasp of history, culture, and local actors; opportunity for early application of this knowledge in ways that facilitate just, mutually beneficial, nonviolent solutions.

Such a system might well deal with ongoing conflicts below the threshold of mass violence. It could build indigenous capacity for problem solving by training, strengthening relevant infrastructure for coping with conflicts, and making links with international counterparts—all this in the service of democratic socioeconomic development. Moreover, this approach builds strong links between the UN and regional organizations, making it more feasible to utilize the comparative advantages of each in addressing prevention. Peck emphasizes the potential value of dedicated prevention specialists at UN headquarters and in each region of the world, working respectfully in an assistance approach utilizing education and negotiation to address grievances and meet basic needs.[7]

Preventive Diplomacy in a Looming Crisis

Preventive diplomacy is viewed here also in the context of operational prevention geared to the proximate and pressing causes of conflict. This is the period in which violence is imminent or small scale, but still short of massive killings. It is "late prevention" in the Evans-Peck model, yet early in relation to full-scale war. Much is being learned about prevention in this dangerous but not fatal phase. Such diplomacy includes political, economic, and military tools. It calls for integrated strategies in the use of these tools as we have considered in the chapter on governments and intergovernmental organizations.

Given the importance of heading off conflict before it crosses the Rubicon of mass violence, the Carnegie Commission stimulated three major, in-depth studies examining what can be learned from actual experience of the 1990s in preventive diplomacy—early and not so early. These studies looked carefully and systematically at different kinds of conflicts in different parts of the world, facing failures as well as successes to strengthen the capability of policymakers and practitioners in this crucial field.

The three books reporting these studies have a similar structure—an opening chapter by a leading scholar who lays out the problems, useful approaches, and an intellectual framework. This is followed by a series of meticulous case studies, each exemplifying a major facet of the problem, what was done, and what was not done. Finally, there is a substantial concluding chapter that draws together various strands of the evidence from the case studies, relates them to relevant research literature, and describes useful conclusions. Each study has a distinct perspective, and so they illuminate different facets of the problem. Taken together, these three publications plus the Peck study constitute a unique resource on preventive diplomacy. Let us now consider a few highlights from each study, an additional recent study on the UN's role in preventive diplomacy, and then set out some points of convergence.

A Major Study of Preventive Diplomacy:
Opportunities Missed, Opportunities Seized

Professor Bruce Jentleson prepared an important and stimulating book for the Carnegie Commission in collaboration with experts who studied major conflicts of the 1990s. They analyzed ten such cases and assessed patterns across cases in the successes and failures of preventive diplomacy.[8]

The book investigated some of the major hot spots of the 1990s: Chechnya; Nagorno-Karabakh; Baltics; nuclear nonproliferation in the former Soviet Union; Croatia-Bosnia; Macedonia; Somalia; Rwanda; Congo; Korea. These case studies clearly show that preventive diplomacy is not just a noble idea but a practical set of strategies and tactics that are difficult but feasible.

They point out that the international community had specific opportunities at least to limit and probably to prevent serious conflicts. For example, even in the rock-bottom case of Rwanda, there was an opportunity in the early days of the incipient genocide when the Hutu-dominated military still was divided. But the aggressive faction was bolstered by the failure of the international community to respond forcefully to the initial killings. A determined international response against the extremists would have found allies within the military. Similar divisions among political-military elites were noted in studies of other cases. But the moderates were not helped from outside. Indeed, the necessity to help moderate leaders is a recurrent theme of the Commission's work.

There are clear successes, which, quite plausibly, could have been failures if diplomacy had not been skillfully employed. Jentleson shows how there was an interactive effect in these cases by which domestic leaders reached a *cooperation calculus* in part because of incentives, assurances, and other support provided by international intervenors. Throughout these cases, the actions or inaction of international participants have a major impact on whether domestic actors make a conflict or a cooperation calculus.

A case where preventive diplomacy had a clear and noteworthy success was in the Baltic states in the early 1990s. This is elucidated in one of the case studies here. The world learned and remembered the potential for violence in the region from 1990 to 1991 when a Soviet crackdown on independence movements in the Baltic states brought the potential for large-scale violence. The eventual independence of Latvia, Lithuania, and Estonia in 1991 was welcomed, but it also created new ethnic tensions. Significant Russian communities had moved into each state during the course of the Soviet Union's rule of these countries. Nationalistic issues over language, education, voting rights, and citizenship that emerged after independence created serious tensions between the Baltic peoples and these Russian populations. The mix was only made more volatile by the presence of Russian troops, based there during the Soviet period, which had not yet been withdrawn after the collapse of the Soviet Union. This had an impact on larger European security issues since Russia had considerable economic and military interests in the three countries considering their strategic location. However, so did the Nordic states and the other countries on the Baltic littoral that held concerns about the continued presence of Russian forces.

The potential for violence that could not only have serious impacts within the Baltic states but which could also quickly spread brought considerable international attention. Tensions mounted in the early 1990s as Latvia, Lithuania, and Estonia each threatened to establish laws aimed at restricting the rights of the Russian communities. These actions put into doubt whether Russian troops would be withdrawn and raised the specter of ethnic conflict.

The United States took the lead in negotiations that were multisided, with the prominent activity of a number of Nordic countries. The West used incentives based on the promise of membership in international organizations such as the OSCE, the Council of Europe, the European Union, and the United Nations to encourage the Baltic states to abandon these provocative activities. As noted earlier, High Commissioner on National Minorities Max van der Stoel clearly stated that anti-ethnic discriminatory policies of the Baltic states could lead to serious trouble and would preclude membership in the OSCE or other attractive European bodies. It was an interesting use of human rights principles first drafted in Helsinki. They had previously been used to protect Baltic nationalists during the 1980s, but in the early 1990s they were a means to scrutinize Baltic citizenship laws to soothe ethnic relations. Criticism such as this, backed up by diplomacy on the part of the United States and European states—particularly Sweden—had a significant effect on the Baltic governments. Eager to get the credibility and financial benefit that membership in such institutions bestows, they moderated their policies and provided for minority rights in accordance with broader European standards.

This was coupled with international financial support to ease the withdrawal of Russian troops. Their removal had been a major sticking point throughout. Loans were made to help with the costs of dismantling Russian bases and housing Russian troops when they returned home. The United States provided much of this money. International organizations, such as the OSCE, played a significant role by providing oversight and mediation at critical points. The process was not smooth, but it was bloodless, and the last Russian troops left the Baltic states in late 1994.

The events in the Baltic states show how early warning, when heeded, can be an important stimulus for preventive diplomacy. It also highlights the fact that it is most successful when it is multilateral and coordinated. International organizations had an important role in filling gaps in capacities of states that could not or would not undertake certain activities. They often had the credibility to serve as monitors that individual states did not have in the eyes of the disputing parties. However, it was backed by attentive and assertive polices from democratic states. This allowed problems to be tackled from a variety of angles, providing more opportunities for successful outcomes.[9]

The case studies show that there was abundant early warning information in every one of the ethnic conflict cases. In considering such information, it is crucial to analyze the likelihood of escalation to violent conflict, the impact on international interests, the risks and costs of inaction, and the viability of preventive action. The difficulties encountered partly reflect a first-generational problem. No one wanted to believe that genocide would occur. New issues burst quickly onto the scene in a period of rapid historical transition.

Jentleson points out that "the low interests–high costs calculus so often cited as the strategic argument against preventive diplomacy underestimates the interests at stake for the international community and overestimates the cost differential between acting early and acting late." These studies have shown that the interests at stake proved relatively great in three ways—escalation, diffusion, and boomerang—which come through clearly in these cases. Ethnic cleansing and genocide demonstrate *escalation* of the conflicts in Croatia/Bosnia and Rwanda and more recently in Kosovo—far beyond conventional expectations. It is not sufficient to consider only locale and resource endowments in assessing interests. Even remote conflicts can have a powerful impact on national interests when they escalate to such extreme levels.

Diffusion refers to the spread of the conflict to other countries, particularly neighboring ones. The Rwanda genocide triggered warfare through much of central Africa, notably in Zaire/Congo, for years after the initial explosion.

Similarly, Milosevic's plunge into aggression in Kosovo in 1998 was based on his estimate of probable inaction by the democracies—recalling their sluggish responses in Croatia and Bosnia.

The *boomerang* effect is clear in the Chechnya case. The democracies gave first priority to maintaining good relations with Russia, not wanting to add to the burdens on Boris Yeltsin in coping with his country's transformation. But this strategy ended up boomeranging against these very goals. Gail Lapidus, in this study, is clear that the war in Chechnya was severely detrimental to Russia. The war diminished Yeltsin's stature; the military was left embittered, impoverished, and demoralized; resources that could have been better used were burned up in the conflict; and public trust in the government was badly damaged.[10]

These cases highlight miscalculation of costs by political leaders. Jentleson says:

In a sense policy-makers are no different from most people in putting greater weight on immediate costs compared to anticipated ones. It always seems easier to pay tomorrow rather than today—thus the success of credit cards, thus the failures of preventive diplomacy. Sometimes for policy-makers there is the added probability calculus that perhaps the costs won't have to be paid, the bill won't come due, if the issue peters out or at least self-limits. Here too, though, in our cases we see the flaws in this logic, as the bills did come due, and when they did it was the equivalent of exorbitant interest and late fees.

This study also illuminates the *Rubicon* problem. The onset of mass violence transforms the nature of a conflict. Then resolution becomes much more difficult. The addition of revenge motives plunges a conflict situation into a new depth of degradation. Similarly, this research clarifies the *Humpty Dumpty* problem. Putting such severely shattered societies back together again is exceedingly difficult, expensive, risky, and sometimes impossible.

Jentleson and his colleagues clarify through their analysis of the case studies what must be done to make preventive diplomacy work. Successful preventive diplomacy strategy needs to achieve three key objectives. First, it must induce the parties to limit, if not preclude, war and violence. Second, it needs to develop effective means of nonviolent management and/or resolution of issues of contention. Third, common terms of negotiation must be arrived at that allow all sides to gain and to show what they have received from cooperation and conflict management.

Deterring aggression requires that the international community have the credibility to respond coercively if necessary. Members must be ready to include military force in the equation. The members of the international community must also be able to reassure parties in conflict that they can provide protection and inducements, the critical measures that give meaning to agreements and encourage restraint.

Toward this end, it is helpful to clarify international norms in order to provide widely recognized standards against which policies are measured. These norms prominently include the upholding of fundamental human rights and the responsibility of sovereign nations to protect these rights— what is now coming to be called *human* security.

The cases in this study highlight the need for preventive diplomacy to be proactive, prompt, and forward looking. Early indications of progress, though not definitive solutions, give the parties a basis for hope before crossing the Rubicon to mass violence. As a conflict intensifies, the role of special envoys and lead diplomats can be exceedingly valuable. Such diplomatic help may come from many sources: governments, the UN, regional organizations, and NGOs (e.g., President Carter and the staff of the Carter Center).

Typically, cooperative efforts are needed to mobilize the requisite political, economic, and military resources. Whether through international institutions and organizations or an ad hoc coalition of the willing, constructive leadership often must come initially from a major power—though small nations with moral standing and intellectual vitality can also do a great deal. A more concerted commitment to preventive diplomacy is needed from the established democracies.[11]

Jentleson and his collaborators note the importance of the UN in preventive diplomacy; we deal further with the UN in the final section of this chapter. They also conclude that the regional multilateral organizations can be useful here, especially in cooperation with the UN. Three trends have made the role of ROs increasingly important. After the Cold War era, the sources of stability have become more regionally rooted than globally transmitted; also, there is increasing recognition of the link between regional security and the peaceful resolution of internal conflicts because of the problems of escalation and spread; and the basis for cooperation needs to be strongly regional to sustain peaceful settlements.

Jentleson closes this major study with several important concepts.

The key to effective preventive diplomacy is that multiple international actors are involved AND that their efforts are coordinated. Major powers and international organizations need to work together. How they do this, and who the "they" is, will vary from case to case. . . .

As to the actual strategies of diplomacy, our mantra remains *early, early, early*. One of the strongest, least conditional conclusions we can draw is that the longer you wait, the more there will be to do and the more difficult it will be to do well. . . .

First is the importance of mixed strategies, grounded in the need for both deterrence and reassurance, both wielding sticks and offering carrots.

Second, the "lure of membership" in major international and regional organizations is an increasingly influential instrument. . . .

Third, while not always in an explicitly coordinated fashion, NGOs can play key roles, often achieving what governments cannot. . . .

Fourth, diplomacy strategies need to be attuned to the dynamics of the domestic political situation. . . . Those leaders and groups that are more prone to non-violent and cooperative measures (the "cooperation constituencies") need to be strengthened.[12]

Preventive diplomacy must provide strong incentives for peace, often backed by the credible threat of military force and economic coercive measures, for both deterrence and reassurance. The parties to the conflict must sooner or later have confidence in the fairness of international third parties, meaning a commitment to peaceful and just resolution of the conflict rather than partisanship for or sponsorship of a particular party to the conflict. But fairness may not mean impartiality if one side engages in gross violence while the other does not. The parties to the conflict must come to see that cooperation has major benefits for all parties, that noncooperation has adverse consequences, and that the international parties are prepared to enforce those consequences differentially in keeping with actions of the adversarial parties.

Another Important Study: Preventive Negotiation

Professor William Zartman of Johns Hopkins University, one of the leading scholars in this field, together with experts from several countries, prepared an important book for the Carnegie Commission on negotiation to prevent escalation and violence.[13] This research group analyzed different kinds of conflicts: boundary disputes, territorial conflicts, peace processes in ethnic conflicts, divided states, disintegrating states, cooperative disputes, trade wars, transboundary environmental disputes, global natural disasters, global security conflicts, and labor disputes.

The Zartman volume focuses on the core of preventive diplomacy—preventive negotiation. It is a policy for realists—those who find that they can achieve their goals at a lower cost by convincing their opponents of the benefits of accommodation and bringing others on to their side who otherwise might well be swept up into very dangerous situations.

There are six structural criteria that Zartman sees for the efficacy and effectiveness of preventive negotiation:

1. A problem. The most basic point is that all parties involved see and understand that there is an issue that could bring great danger and sub-

stantially increase their costs and that this issue warrants action on their part.

2. Preventability. Once a problem is identified, there needs to be a belief that something can be done to prevent the problem. The sense that a situation is growing worse and there are promising alternatives is important for getting sides to move.

3. Cost-sharing opportunity. If parties are to act, they most often have to be assured that others will join the effort in order to share the burdens of the initiative.

4. New benefits. There is also a need to show actors that there are not merely costs to be avoided but positive benefits that go beyond the expenses and tragedies of violence. The promise of valuable trade or access to desired resources, for example, has been held up as strong incentive to end conflicts.

5. Domestic pressure. If the public does not believe a crisis, potentially dangerous to them, is actually looming, then they are unlikely to support efforts to defuse tension. As we have repeatedly seen, wishful thinking is easy. Public support is crucial to successful prevention. Therefore, the people must be informed of the eventual costs of a problem that bursts into violent conflict. Advocacy groups should be tapped for their support. A broadly based "centrist-moderate coalition" is important and often decisive, in no small part because it can sideline extremist elements.

6. Galvanizing event. A clash, unpleasant incident, or natural disaster can bring all sides dangerously close to hostilities, but they can also clear the decks for preventive action, especially if a known source of help is readily available.

These structural conditions promote processes that stimulate early awareness; this, in turn, fosters opportunities for preventive negotiation. Zartman summarizes six valuable steps:

1. Early awareness. The problem is often not a lack of evidence that a crisis is brewing but the facts that people are not paying attention to these cues and there is a lack of a political culture rewarding proactive involvement.

2. Reduction of uncertainties. This includes gaining information on a situation that allows analysis and understanding, hence a basis for problem-solving action.

3. Reframing the problem. Getting all sides to see that a positive-sum outcome is vital and feasible. This means recasting the issue in a way that distributes costs fairly and integrates all sides into its solution.

4. Building home constituencies. This is not separate from the other steps, and it supports all efforts. Constructing a moderate coalition

and maintaining the support of interest groups are part of this activity.

5. Development of a package of costs and opportunities. Showing sides the costs of inaction as well as the benefits of preventive action are important for bringing parties to the table and building domestic constituencies. There may be a need for third parties or other groups to provide "sweeteners" to entice others into the effort.

6. A regime of continuing prevention. Establishing institutionalized mechanisms for dealing with potential future outbreaks can reassure parties in tackling the specific, immediate threat to peace.

Preventive negotiations must be integrative. Ripeness as a concept has little bearing on these efforts since they must take place before a problem comes to a head and long before struggle has exhausted the adversaries. Thus, preventive negotiation must instill its own sense of urgency about an emerging conflict situation. This requires a culture of awareness that is receptive to early warnings and preventive action.

Since Zartman has made so many significant contributions to this field over so many years, I draw here on another presentation of his about the skills and processes that make preventive diplomacy effective. He gave an incisive account of these in summarizing a Ditchley conference on preventive diplomacy in 1998.[14]

Seek Collaboration

No single agent is likely to be adequate to the complex task of helping others with their conflicts. Interventions, norm setting, and pressures are more effective when employed collectively and most effective when employed by an institutionalized group of which the conflicting parties are members, such as a regional organization or the UN. Multiple agents should be conceived of as elements in a layered process, always keeping in mind the mediator of next resort. Governments, NGOs, state coalitions, regional organizations, and finally the UN Secretariat and Security Council comprise the layers.

Where regional organizations exist, mechanisms for management, shared norms, and principles for conduct are potentially available. OSCE, OAS, and ASEAN are examples—offering potential in Europe, the Americas, Africa, and Asia. When an institutionalized grouping does not exist, constituting a "Friends" group can provide a useful device for mobilizing knowledge and pressure for conflict resolution. Typically, such a group consists of several interested, concerned, well-informed governments.

NGOs and track-two diplomacy are rapidly growing as useful adjuncts to government action and can often prepare the way for official engagement. They include humanitarian agencies, advocacy groups, mediation agencies, reconciliation training projects, and organizations that promote democracy. While NGOs have advantages such as flexibility, pertinent information, ingenuity, and resources, they are not a substitute for official action. There are limits to the privatization of public affairs. In general, in political, economic, or military matters, private involvement is most useful if it is well coordinated with official attention.

Foster Early Awareness

Zartman reinforces Jentleson (as well as Holl and George) on this key point. Early awareness involves a readiness to consider seriously, rather than just file the warnings, an emphasis on looking ahead rather than just putting out fires, an ability to get the warning to the right locus that can formulate appropriate, legitimate, and credible responses. The media have an important role to play in fostering early awareness, by focusing on warning signs such as an upsurge of human rights violations, and by highlighting benefits and examples of violence prevention. Substantial engagement is usually needed early, before parties' positions have hardened and while diversion from a dangerous course is still possible.

Prepare Sticks and Carrots

Prevention and management involve measures to make the present course more unpleasant (sticks) and the future alternative more attractive (carrots). Often functional equivalents—alternative courses to the same goals that do not provoke conflict—can be helpful.

Outsiders Seek Cooperation of the Contending Parties

Preventive measures rarely work by imposition, without cooperation from the parties involved. If parties to the conflict are not convinced of the need for avoidance of violence, regional or internal allies can help. More broadly, prevention is not the job of any limited set of nations, but one that must increasingly involve moderate leaders all over the world, including those in poor and vulnerable nations.

Formulate Principles and Regimes

Every prevention episode contributes to building precedents and principles for dealing with future cases. To the extent possible, preventive interventions should be principled actions based on broader norms and values, taking advantage of previous precedents and principles. Standards created by the UN have a high level of legitimacy and are widely acceptable. Regional organizations can perform the same function for their members, thus giving them a sense of ownership over their norms; regional norms should not, however, conflict with universally accepted standards such as those embodied in the UN Charter.

The Sovereignty Dilemma

This is a recurrent problem in the prevention field and in international relations generally, so we deal with it in several parts of this book. The principle of nonintervention in the internal affairs of states is one that has been accepted by the international community as a common norm and has been useful as a means of inter-state conflict prevention. But the idea of sovereignty has too often been used as an excuse by some leaders to grossly mismanage their affairs (e.g., corruption) and even to slaughter their citizens with impunity. The new concept of sovereignty as responsibility emphasizes the accountability of leaders to live up to international obligations to respect the human rights of their citizens.[15] It suggests that the international community has the obligation to ensure that such obligations are adhered to. Preventive diplomacy needs to integrate these two concepts of sovereignty with special attention to the newer one.

A Third Major Contribution: Words over War

The Carnegie Commission invited Professor John Barton of Stanford University, a distinguished scholar in international law, to undertake a similar study, focusing on ways in which third-party intervention might lead to successful conflict resolution, preventing either the onset or recurrence of mass violence. He enlisted an excellent collaborator, Melanie Greenberg, also a legal scholar. Utilizing scholarship from law and political science, this study analyzes a variety of cases and concludes that the international community can play a helpful role through mediation, arbitration, and the development of international institutions to promote reconciliation.

The case studies in this report focus on cases in which mediation by a nonparty to the conflict constituted the primary form of intervention. These cases are divided into three categories: separation of nations, integration of nations, and mediation in noncivil conflicts. The cases involving separation of nations—Abkhazia, Bosnia, Croatia, and the West Bank—have several elements in common. The definition of sovereignty is a polarizing concept. Minority rights are a basic concern when ethnic groups are separated from their homeland after secession. In all four of these cases, mediation efforts enhanced incentives to compromise.

In the cases involving integration of nations—Cambodia, El Salvador, Northern Ireland, South Africa, and Rwanda—the primary efforts were to end hostilities and to build new, national institutions in the wake of vicious and bloody civil wars. Political power sharing, the vetting and integration of military forces, building new representative bodies and civil institutions, ensuring minority rights, and establishing judicial processes for exposing the truth of prior atrocities and enabling reconciliation became key substantive elements of the mediations.

The cases involving mediation in noncivil conflicts are novel for their subject matter and for the form of intervention. In the Beagle Channel case, a territorial dispute between Chile and Argentina in the late 1970s and early 1980s, the Vatican mediated the conflict and directly averted the outbreak of war. The North Korean nuclear crisis illustrates the value of second-track diplomacy and also the power of a nuclear threat to stimulate international attention and create incentives for cooperation. The Aral Sea Basin water dispute was included not only as a demonstration of how conflicts over natural resources may threaten to become a major source of violence in the future but also because it illustrates a creative approach of the World Bank in mediation.

Greenberg and Barton carefully explored various mechanisms of intervention—clarifying the roles of the intervenors, such as injecting new ideas into the process as well as their ability to achieve settlements through the application of external pressures and incentives. They also clarified obstacles the mediators encountered, such as insufficient funding for the negotiation process, lack of important intelligence information, language problems, or a lack of knowledge about the conflict. They show how the role of international rewards and sanctions is critical in giving leverage to mediators. Economic incentives such as bilateral aid and policies of the international financial institutions can help mediation along with sanctions, embargoes, criminal prosecution of leaders, and military force. A balanced package of positive and negative influences can affect the calculations of adversarial leaders.

Greenberg and Barton look at some unconventional aspects of the mediator's role—for example public information is an important tool of leverage. The cases examine the media in relation to the parties and the mediators and derive clues to effective use of the media during the mediation process—helping to build a constituency for conciliation. They also consider moral suasion by the mediator, most clearly evident in the Beagle Channel case. They sought out instances in which principle, morality, and social pressure for decent behavior played an important role in the mediation process. This is important intrinsically and also because some cynical commentators on diplomacy are depreciatory of these considerations.

This study notes the importance of Zartman's concept of "ripeness," when a conflict is most amenable to mediation. This is a point at which the parties have reached a mutually hurting stalemate. At such a moment, the parties might become favorable to negotiation so as to get a part of their desired gains before further damage is done—or even all is lost. The mediator must then present a mediated agreement as a way out of the stalemate in which both parties have some gain and neither is humiliated.

They point out that ripeness for settlement is not a fixed property of the situation—and here they converge with Zartman. Rather, ripeness can occur at various times along the spectrum of a conflict and sometimes can be fostered by the mediator as circumstances change and perceptions become modifiable. It is useful to think of ripe moments as windows of opportunity that may open from time to time with the help of a mediator, who can then utilize the moment by promoting compromise between the parties.

In an important concluding chapter of this valuable volume, Greenberg and Barton examine the lessons of their case studies for international mediation and arbitration to prevent deadly conflict.

A particularly interesting case is that of the Aral Sea Basin. It is a herald of environmental conflict that is likely to become more prevalent and more serious in the next century. (Professor Donald Kennedy, of Stanford University, led a distinguished group of environmental scientists and political scholars in a study for the Carnegie Commission on environmental quality and regional conflict.)[16] Disputes there also showed that the role of the World Bank has broad implications for the potential contributions of the international financial institutions in preventing deadly conflict. In a report prepared for the Carnegie Commission, John Stremlau and Francisco Sagasti analyze this capacity in depth.[17]

This case illuminates the growing role of international financial institutions in international diplomacy—particularly evident in the World Bank with the farsighted leadership of its president, James Wolfensohn. These institutions are now moving to emphasize human rights and the building of civil society as conditions for economic aid. In the Aral Sea Basin, the World Bank refused to consider economic facilitators until the sovereign nations controlling the Aral Sea Basin worked out a water management agreement among themselves. The Bank assisted this process through quiet diplomacy among the leaders of the newly sovereign states. Accordingly, the Bank encouraged activities by NGOs to build civil society, used its leverage to influence the scope and form of possible solutions, encouraged regional institutions and NGOs to cooperate on water issues, and generally made clear that major economic benefits could flow from regional cooperation. This is a model that deserves emulation.

Greenberg and Barton's comment on these cases is illuminating:

> In the Aral Sea Basin conflict, the World Bank held great leverage in the form of financial assistance, and used it very effectively to encourage the sovereign powers to reach agreement on regional water use. The example

is encouraging, especially because the regional cooperation on water issues could lead to improved cooperation on larger political issues as well. It should be noted that this conflict had not reached the stage of violence, and thus might have been more amenable to outside intervention and leverage. Further, because of the dire financial straits in which the countries found themselves after the breakup of the Soviet Union, they were particularly amenable to and willing to work for the prospect of economic assistance.[18]

The final report of the Carnegie Commission noted the promise of lending and economic assistance in helping adversarial parties to seek superordinate goals of development and prosperity achievable only by cooperating with each other—and perhaps with other regional parties as well.

What about the choice of a mediator? In most of the negotiations, a specific channel and specific individual emerged as crucially significant. Sometimes this reflected that person's expertise in the specific dispute. In most cases, the choice of mediator was based on a combination of attributes: expertise in dispute settlement, possession of a large enough power base to be influential, and especially neutrality and impartiality. For example, former President Carter intervened effectively in North Korea as a well-respected neutral mediator rather than as an expert. Appropriate technical expertise was then added to the situation. In any event, mediators need help from staff and consultants to acquire expertise about the substantive problems of a particular conflict.

This study paid careful attention to the role of international institutions, ranging from the United Nations to cross-national nongovernmental organizations. These various international entities served many functions in the premediation phase, the mediation phase, and the implementation phase of conflicts in the 1990s. In the premediation phase, international institutions help build civil society (a crucial element in violence prevention), provide for constructive discussion of security problems and underlying conflicts, and help with specific problems such as human rights, including those of minorities. In the mediation phase, these institutions offer good offices, peacekeeping services, sanctions and rewards, and intellectual problem solving. In the implementation period of peace agreements, international institutions can aid in truth and reconciliation processes, support security guarantees, provide peacekeeping and economic aid, help in the development of constitutions and legal systems, and assist in the creation or rebuilding of civil society.

International institutions have not only provided mediators for disputes, but they played important facilitating roles as well. Through the General Assembly, the Security Council, Friends groups, observer missions, peacekeeping forces, and UN agencies, the United Nations was present in every one of the case studies except the Beagle Channel. Regional political and economic organizations such as the OAS, the OAU, the OSCE, and the European Union often served in the background, providing support and coordination for political, economic, and military functions. NGOs were valuable in the success of the Oslo Accord, the Aral Sea projects, the South African peace process, and the North Korea crisis. International financial institutions have shown promise in the resolution of resource and environment conflicts, as the Aral Sea process illustrates.

The study documents the rapid rise of nongovernmental organizations in coping with conflict in the 1990s. These organizations acted as facilitators and key institution builders. They helped in developing civil society. They were notable in second-track mediation processes, which preceded and then meshed with official efforts of governments and international organizations.

In the Aral Sea Basin, nongovernmental environmental groups, linked with international counterparts, emerged even before the end of the Soviet Union. After the World Bank process began, they fostered popular support for cooperation and helped to implement programs. In South Africa, NGOs sponsored numerous nonracial dialogues to build support for the abolition of apartheid and to develop interracial activities and democratic institutions.

Greenberg and Barton relate these matters to international law:

> The panel of legal experts who advised our group also pointed out the success of emerging principles of international law, which coincide with political science notions of democratic processes, transparency, and the right of the individual to security. Inherent in the substance of every mediated agreement were: adherence to democratic procedures; fair elections; transparent governmental procedures; the primacy of the rule of law; and the promise of human rights to all individuals. . . .
>
> A key question remains whether future international legal arrangements might serve to help forestall conflict, as by enabling minorities to express grievances legally and politically, rather than militarily or by encouraging development of a civil society and institutions for dealing with disputes. . . .
>
> The rights of minorities or ethnic communities were an issue in over half of the cases studied: Abkhazia, Bosnia, Croatia, Northern Ireland, Rwanda, South Africa, and the West Bank. And the civil rights of communities were also issues in Cambodia and El Salvador. In some of these cases, there has been long-term involvement of international human rights institutions. . . .
>
> More broadly, the use of international human rights law to strengthen civil society appears both useful and desirable. . . . In an era of increased travel, direct broadcast satellites, and the Internet, it should be possible to define and enforce international human rights in a way that makes it more difficult for a nation to opt out of participation in a global civil society.

The international community can usefully intervene in an adversarial situation, well before armed conflict, by helping to build civil society and designing cooperative natural resource projects as well as educating leaders and publics on concepts and techniques of conflict resolution. Among the most important ways that international society can encourage peaceful resolution of disputes is through strengthening national capabilities for understanding and resolving disputes, for example, through strengthening civil society, and developing mechanisms of protection for minorities.

The UN and Preventive Diplomacy

Since these major studies of preventive diplomacy—Jentleson, Zartman, Greenberg and Barton, and Peck—highlight the past contributions and future potential of the UN (among other organizations) in prevention, it is appropriate here to consider ways of strengthening the UN for this purpose.

The UN Charter gives the Security Council a great deal of latitude in making decisions on issues of war and peace. With respect to preventive diplomacy, the charter authorizes the Secretary-General to bring to the attention of the Security Council any development that may threaten international peace. The Secretary-General should have greater functional scope in using this authority than has historically been the case.

As we have noted, certain circumstances can constitute appropriate precipitating events for the Secretary-General to elicit serious consideration by the Security Council. Such a situation might be a regional dispute where weapons of mass destruction are part of the equation. Evidence of mass expulsion or emerging genocide, international terrorism, large flows of refugees threatening to destabilize neighboring countries, or strong evidence of systematic human rights violations might also motivate the Secretary-General. The forcible overthrow of democratically elected governments or severe, widespread, growing damage to the environment, or the provocative action of a buildup of military forces along a border could also attract the attention of the United Nations.

In recent years, a basic extension of prior doctrine has occurred: The international community is now seen as having not only a justifiable rationale but also a constructive responsibility for helping to resolve serious internal disputes of violent potential. Sovereignty no longer entitles tyrants to oppress their own populations with mass violation of human rights. So, the UN has gradually been involved in applying global norms to conflicts within nation-states, taking into account both new and old concepts of sovereignty. Intervention in this context must mean political and probably economic action, whether or not military factors are also involved. Mediation is particularly important.

The United Nations was by far the most important international organization in the cases examined in the Greenberg-Barton study. Many tense

situations during the 1990s were dealt with by the UN Security Council—
some for better and some for worse. The Security Council was central to
negotiations in Rwanda, the West Bank, and Abkhazia. It also provided
the mandate for important peacekeeping operations in Bosnia, Rwanda,
and Cambodia, although there were serious defects in its behavior in the
Bosnia and Rwanda cases. It gave credibility to sanctions levied against
North Korea. The Permanent Five members of the council, acting inde-
pendently as sovereign states while maintaining the council's consultative
processes, were instrumental in devising a framework for agreements on
Cambodia.

Personal envoys of the Secretary-General mediated in El Salvador and
Georgia. They carried out peace missions to South Africa and the former
Yugoslavia and played important observer roles in South Africa, where they
assisted in the institution building envisioned by the peace negotiations.

Friends groups, groups of nations either appointed by or approved by the
Secretary-General, played a constructive part in the Abkhazia and El Salvador conflicts. These groups of diplomats, sometimes acting through the
UN missions and sometimes acting in their direct bilateral capacities, made
significant contributions to the mediation efforts. They coordinated policy,
briefed the Secretary-General on the progress of the talks, helped draft resolutions, and provided resources for the mediation process. In Bosnia, a
"contact group" of nations served a similar purpose.

The United Nations was pivotal in supplying peacekeeping forces to uphold
mediated agreements. They were active in Cambodia, Rwanda, the former Yugoslavia—and in El Salvador, where they were particularly effective. Moreover,
UN agencies played a helpful background role in many of the conflicts studied. For example, the United Nations Development Program fostered NGOs
working in the Aral Sea Basin, and the UN High Commission on Refugees, led
superbly by Sadako Ogata, did heroic work in Cambodia, Rwanda, and the
former Yugoslavia to alleviate terrible suffering. Ogata contributed importantly to the international discourse by emphasizing prevention.

Cyrus Vance and I prepared a report for the Secretary-General, on behalf
of the Carnegie Commission, on the role of personal envoys and special representatives of the Secretary-General.[19] We note that those who drafted the
UN Charter gave the head of an international organization, for the first
time, political-diplomatic prerogatives to conduct impartial third-party mediation on behalf of the international community. Secretary-General Annan
has given strong leadership on strengthening the UN's preventive functions,
including the use of personal envoys and special representatives in conflict
prevention and resolution with the help of a new strategic planning unit and
Senior Management Group, which he established in July 1997. As we see
later, he has done much more since then to move the UN toward preventive
capabilities.

Vance and I advocate a proactive approach for personal envoys and special representatives of the Secretary-General as a low-cost, low-risk instrument for enhancing the UN's role in preventing and resolving deadly conflict. We suggest ways to expand the pool of candidates available to serve in these capacities and to increase the modest funding required to support these appointments. Currently, the contributions of personal envoys and special representatives are undermined by the growing gap between the demand for more effective UN diplomacy, on the one hand, and the limited financial resources as well as qualified candidates on the other.

The most obvious function of representatives and envoys is to provide the Secretary-General with firsthand authoritative information about what is going on in the field. In addition to fact finding, these missions historically have been of value to conflict resolution in at least four ways:

1. Once the parties have accepted their involvement, special representatives and envoys have repeatedly demonstrated the importance of their persistence, patience, and presence in order to keep the peace process alive when it might have collapsed.
2. As representatives or envoys become increasingly familiar with the substantive issues of the dispute, and if they maintain impartiality and credibility with both sides, they can reformulate the vision of a compromise package that otherwise would have eluded the antagonists.
3. International interests and norms are injected into the negotiating process. Typically, neither side in a dispute wishes to be isolated internationally and instead seeks political, economic, and security assistance. Thus, there are significant incentives for settlement.
4. Within the UN, especially the Security Council, the special representative can help to shape international consensus on what would actually be required to achieve a peaceful settlement.

All Secretaries-General have resisted attempts by the Security Council to limit the modest autonomy granted them under the charter. In defending the freedom to select special representatives and to dispatch personal envoys whenever and wherever the Secretary-General chooses, much more is at stake than narrow institutional interests. The sooner the Secretary-General can begin to plan and undertake preventive action, the better will be the chances for peace. A Security Council mandate is not always possible in the timely manner necessary to deploy fact-finding missions. Today's need for third-party mediation to prevent and resolve deadly regional conflicts is greater than ever, and the UN Secretary-General should be granted ample latitude for preventive diplomacy.

Improving the readiness of prospective personal envoys and special representatives poses challenges for the Secretariat. Likely candidates from outside the UN, preferably a geographically diverse group, could be included in periodic workshops and intensive refresher courses on UN operations in preventive diplomacy. Connie Peck points to the potential value of a dedicated, special representative, expert in preventive diplomacy at UN headquarters—and ideally one in each region of the world. This would give a higher level of readiness for early prevention.

The UN should have a well-developed staff college, but so far it has not been able to gain sufficient political and financial support. Efforts are underway to strengthen the staff college. In the meantime, UNITAR plays a valuable role despite modest resources.

The UNITAR Program in Peacemaking and Preventive Diplomacy has, over the past nine years, developed several innovative initiatives to provide advanced training for UN staff and diplomats in the area of conflict prevention and resolution. Connie Peck established the program in 1993 with the creation of the UNITAR–International Peace Academy Fellowship Program in Peacemaking and Preventive Diplomacy, supported by the Carnegie Corporation in conjunction with other foundations and governments. This training program was the first of its kind to expose staff from the substantive departments of the United Nations and diplomats working on UN peace and security issues to the latest knowledge in conflict prevention and resolution. The training, which is held annually in Austria, provides a comprehensive framework on the causes of conflict and the main factors which lead to its escalation or deescalation. It is an interest-based, problem-solving model of negotiation (first developed at the Harvard Program on Negotiation) that provides hands-on practice in the skills involved in conflict analysis, negotiation, and mediation through the use of simulations, small-group work, role-playing, and feedback. Practitioners, such as special representatives or other senior UN staff, present in-depth case studies so that the issues experienced in a real-life dispute resolution can be thoroughly explored.

When the fellowship program was first initiated, there was some skepticism within the UN about the need for this sort of training. However, excellent feedback soon led senior UN staff in the Department of Political Affairs (DPA) to ask for an annual Senior Seminar in Peacemaking and Preventive Diplomacy to help them refine the department's practice at the highest levels. Each year, Peck works closely with senior staff in the DPA to select a topic and various cases that are relevant to the department's work and then brings together a range of senior scholars with senior UN practitioners for in-depth examination of the topic as it applies to the chosen conflict situations.

Also, following the model of the Fellowship Program, UNITAR is now developing a Regional Training Programme to Enhance Conflict Prevention and Peacebuilding in Africa—with the support of the governments of Canada, Denmark, and Germany. The program is based on experience from the Fellowship Program, but training is specifically tailored to the pressing needs of African policymakers.

Picking up on the Vance-Hamburg observation that there was too little knowledge concerning the work of the special representatives of the Secretary-General (SRSG), Peck is carrying out a program for briefing and debriefing SRSGs and envoys. The objective of the project is to preserve their experience and transmit their lessons to new personnel. Funded by the United Kingdom, Sweden, Canada, and Switzerland, it will lead to a well-organized handbook for SRSGs and envoys. This systematic briefing program for new SRSGs will be done in cooperation with the relevant departments in the UN Secretariat. An annual SRSG seminar will be held, so that all special representatives can share their experiences and learn from one another. These innovations suggest ways in which research and training can strengthen the UN operations in preventive diplomacy.

Only with the creation of a special fund for preventive action is the Secretary-General ever likely to have even a modicum of diplomatic freedom to optimize the value of representatives and envoys. Such a fund was established by the government of Norway in the 1990s through the leadership of its then prime minister, Gro Brundtland, who was a valuable member of the Carnegie Commission. This promising initiative deserves broad international support of the kind that Sweden has recently provided.

The UN has not, could not, and should not attempt to monopolize preventive diplomacy. Regional and subregional organizations, national governments, and nongovernmental organizations may have comparative advantages in preventing certain intra-state or inter-state conflicts. But in all cases, it helps for the Secretary-General to have a clear sense of current developments and assurance that an effective division of labor among the governments and organizations is accomplished.

Converging Findings Strengthen Preventive Diplomacy

The cumulative weight of research on *preventive* diplomacy suggests strongly that the international community should not wait for a crisis. It must develop ongoing programs of international help—offered by governments, intergovernmental organizations, and also by nongovernmental organizations. These build capacity of groups to address grievances effectively without violence and establish mechanisms for sorting out conflicts peacefully before they become explosive. They offer hope of better lives to come. Fortunately, there is movement in this direction—techniques of active, nonviolent problem solving, sharing of experience across national boundaries, bringing the world's experience to bear on different local conflicts. Tackling serious grievances as early as possible denies political demagogues and hateful fanatics a platform of discontent. Incitement to violence becomes more difficult.

These major new studies converge on key points of preventive diplomacy. They send a to-whom-it-may-concern message to the international community: to governments, intergovernmental organizations, nongovernmental organizations of many kinds, and leaders in different sectors.[20] Some recurrent elements of the message may be stated simply in a few sentences.

1. Recognize dangers early: Beware of wishful thinking. Highlight the potential value of *early* sympathetic interest by credible outsiders to get the facts straight.
2. Respond to serious danger promptly on the basis of careful decision making, taking into account information from multiple credible sources. Remember that a lack of early warning has rarely been a problem for decisionmakers. The problem has often been failure to make a timely, effective response.
3. In making such responses, do so by pooling strengths, sharing burdens, and dividing labor among entities with the capacity and salience to do what is necessary. This may involve some combination of governments, international organizations, and institutions of civil society, including NGOs.
4. Foster widespread understanding of conflict resolution and of conflict prevention among policymakers and publics. This involves concepts and techniques as well as attitudes and institutions; and leads to building local or national capacity for coping with conflicts in a just, nonviolent way. This also includes the development of negotiation skills in the framework of joint problem solving to meet fundamental needs.
5. Offer third-party mediation early in hot spots. This is flexible and can be provided by governments, intergovernmental organizations, or by nongovernmental organizations. It is less threatening to the adversaries than most other interventions. It can occur early in the course of an evolving dispute. The adversaries can learn a good deal about conflict resolution and violence prevention, sometimes in a brief period. They can become intrigued with new possibilities for mutual accommodation. They can be helped to reformulate the problem in ways that involve mutual benefits.
6. Formulate strategies in terms of superordinate goals for antagonistic parties—that is, goals they both value greatly and can only achieve by cooperation. Such goals may be, for example, the end of killing, reunion of many families, economic benefits, access to scarce water,

coping with deadly infectious diseases, and especially in dealing with mega-terrorism, as we see in Russia's response to September 11.

7. Be fully aware of tools for operational prevention and tools for structural prevention. Consider these systematically in relation to the problem at hand. Strive for integration of political, economic, and military tools in formulating a coherent strategy for operational prevention in the event of impending crisis.[21]

8. Bear in mind the full array of relevant institutions and organizations so that robust problem-solving capacities can be brought to bear on the dangerous situation. Who can best use the tools at hand?[22]

9. To change behavior of adversaries toward moderation, use the incentive of prospect for membership in valued international organizations—a sense of belonging and becoming worthy of respect, thereby enhancing prospects for a prosperous and peaceful future.

10. With respect to economic leverage in preventive diplomacy, consider sanctions and inducements jointly, moving toward a coherent strategy that makes clear to adversaries what they could lose through violence and gain through nonviolent problem solving. Such measures are most likely to be effective if conducted through international cooperation in circumstances that confer legitimacy.

11. In all of this, support moderate, pragmatic, local leaders, including newly emerging leaders, in times of stress. They deserve the support of neighbors and the international community through encouragement, friendship, technical assistance, links with counterparts in other communities, and the ability to elicit economic benefit for their people. These are leaders inclined to consider just settlement for all the parties; they often operate under great pressure and need international help in order to succeed.

12. Keep diplomacy attuned to the situation on the ground, especially the domestic politics of a state in turmoil. Seek to build a cooperation constituency and find ways to buffer "spoilers." Foster domestic pressure for conflict resolution in light of possibilities for a just outcome.[23]

13. In working with adversaries, try to create a credible basis for hope of preventing catastrophe while clarifying the costs of violence. Utilize galvanizing events that make the enormity of danger salient and vivid. Over time, seek a change in attitude in the adversaries—away from revenge toward problem solving for mutual benefit in meeting basic needs.[24]

14. Bear in mind the pervasive need of negotiators and their constituencies for respect and dignity. Even in the stress of sharp differences, hold to the position of shared humanity and the prospect of mutual accommodation.

15. Move beyond rigid formulations of sovereignty and self-determination that pull against each other, clarifying intermediate possibilities that offer a reasonable basis for mutual benefit.

16. Seek ways to strengthen the UN and regional organizations in their preventive functions, including effective mechanisms for linking with NGOs—for example, special representatives and personal envoys of the UN Secretary-General, Friends groups of the UN or regional organizations.

17. As experience accumulates, build increasingly explicit norms of fairness, human rights, and democratic process. Foster worldwide understanding of these norms and seek broad acceptance for formulating international laws on preventing deadly conflict.

18. Upgrade and regularize training in preventive diplomacy of staff and other diplomats associated with relevant institutions and organizations: the UN, governments, regional organizations, and peace-oriented nongovernmental organizations.

19. Strengthen international development banks and international law institutions to take conflict resolution and violence prevention into account in their policies especially involving hot spots. Among other benefits, this strengthens the capacity of mediators in preventive diplomacy.

20. Encourage adversaries to use democratic processes for conflict resolution rather than violence. Over time, mobilize international help in strengthening or building democratic institutions.

As guidelines of this sort come to be incorporated into the thinking of governments, international and nongovernmental organizations—and indeed in public understanding—the risk of drifting into disasters can be greatly diminished.

Notes

1. Stephen Weiss-Wik, "Enhancing Negotiator's Successfulness: Self-Help Books and Related Empirical Research," *Journal of Conflict Resolution* 27 (December 1983): 706–35; William Ury, *Getting to Peace* (New York: Penguin, 1999).

2. Roger Fisher and William Ury, *Getting to Yes: Negotiating Agreement Without Giving In* (New York: Penguin, 1983).

3. Warren Christopher, *The Negotiator* (The Jackson H. Ralston Lecture, Stanford Law School, 1998).

4. Christopher, *Negotiator*.

5. Max van der Stoel, "Democracy and Human Rights: On the Work of the High Commissioner on National Minorities of the OSCE," "Early Warning and Early Action: Preventing Inter-Ethnic Conflict," and "The Involvement of the

High Commissioner Is No Stigma, But an Act of Solidarity," in Wolfgang Zellner and Falk Lange, eds., *Peace and Stability through Human and Minority Rights* (Baden-Baden, Germany: Nomos, 1999).

6. Gareth Evans, *Cooperating for Peace: The Global Agenda for the 1990s and Beyond* (St. Leonards, Australia: Allen and Unwin, 1993), ch. 5.

7. Peck, *Sustainable Peace.*

8. Jentleson, *Opportunities Missed*, ch. 1.

9. Heather F. Hurlburt, "Preventive Diplomacy: Success in the Baltics," in Jentleson, ed., *Opportunities Missed, Opportunities Seized: Preventive Diplomacy in the Post–Cold War World* (Carnegie Commission Series, Rowman & Littlefield, 1999), 91–107.

10. Gail Lapidus, "The War in Chechnya: Opportunities Missed, Lessons to Be Learned," in Jentleson, ed., *Opportunities Missed, Opportunities Seized: Preventive Diplomacy in the Post–Cold War World* (Carnegie Commission Series, Rowman & Littlefield, 1999), 66.

11. Allison and Owada, *Responsibilities of Democracies.*

12. Jentleson, *Opportunities Missed*, ch. 13.

13. I. William Zartman, ed., *Preventive Negotiation: Avoiding Conflict Escalation* (Carnegie Commission Series, Rowman & Littlefield, 2000).

14. *Preventive Diplomacy, Preventive Defense, and Conflict Resolution: A Report of Two Conferences at Stanford University and the Ditchley Foundation* (Report to the Carnegie Commission on Preventing Deadly Conflict, 1999).

15. Lloyd Axworthy, "Human Security and Global Governance: Putting People First," *Global Governance* 7 (January–March 2001): 19–23.

16. Donald Kennedy, *Environmental Quality and Regional Conflict* (Report to the Carnegie Commission on Preventing Deadly Conflict, 1998).

17. Stremlau and Sagasti, *Preventing Deadly Conflict: Does the World Bank Have a Role?.*

18. Melanie C. Greenberg, John H. Barton, and Margaret E. McGuinness, *Words Over War: Mediation and Arbitration to Prevent Deadly Conflict* (Carnegie Commission Series, Rowman & Littlefield, 2000).

19. Vance and Hamburg, *Pathfinders for Peace.*

20. See also Harold H. Saunders, "Interactive Conflict Resolution: A View for Policy Makers on Making and Building Peace," in Paul C. Stern and Daniel Druckman, eds., *International Conflict Resolution After the Cold War* (Washington, D.C.: National Academy Press, 2000), 251–93.

21. Alexander George, *Forceful Persuasion: Coercive Diplomacy as an Alternative to War* (Washington, D.C.: United States Institute of Peace Press, 1991).

22. *Conflict Prevention: Strategies to Sustain Peace in the Post–Cold War World* (Washington, D.C.: Aspen Institute, 1997).

23. Stephan John Stedman, "Spoiler Problems in Peace Processes," in Paul C. Stern and Daniel Druckman, eds., *International Conflict Resolution After the Cold War* (Washington, D.C.: National Academy Press, 2000), 178–224.

24. I. William Zartman, "Ripeness: The Hurting Stalemate and Beyond," in Paul C. Stern and Daniel Druckman, eds., *International Conflict Resolution After the Cold War* (Washington, D.C.: National Academy Press, 2000), 225–50.

6

Democracy and Prevention: The Essence of Nonviolent Conflict Resolution

Democracy: Help or Hindrance?

In the founding letter that I wrote to invite prospective members to join the emerging Carnegie Commission, I put some emphasis on the potential of the established democracies to prevent catastrophes and their responsibility to learn how to do so. Virtually everyone invited did in fact accept, and no letter or call of acceptance expressed any reservations about a large role for the democracies. Yet in the course of events, this became a surprisingly contentious issue.

A few members of the Commission felt that an increased activity of the democracies would end in some hegemonic or neoimperialistic venture, essentially exploiting or dominating poor countries. One went so far as to refer to the democracies as a rich white man's club. Yet most members of the Commission felt that the democracies had not done nearly enough to prevent avoidable catastrophes like those of former Yugoslavia or Rwanda. The result of this strongly felt difference of opinion was to constrain what the full Commission would agree on in its final report. So I urged that we ask leading scholars and other experts to prepare analyses for us on this subject—each author taking full responsibility for the conclusions reached. This led to such important publications as *Promoting Democracy in the 1990s* by Larry Diamond and *The Responsibilities of Democracies in Preventing Deadly Conflict* by Graham Allison and Hisashi Owada. In this book, I highlight their contributions because I regard them as exceptionally promising for future preventive actions, indeed among the most fundamental of all pillars of prevention for the long term.

Among the factors conducive to peaceful living, none is more important in my view than democratic development. Here, I refer to the value of democratic attitudes, practices, and institutions in both political and economic spheres.

These are intrinsically valuable in terms of opportunity, participation, and decent human relations. They also have special and distinctive attributes in the perennial striving of humanity for peace with justice. The chapter deals with political aspects of democracy. The next chapter deals with economic aspects.

Basic Orientation

Democratic traditions evolve in ways that build ongoing mechanisms for dealing with the ubiquitous conflicts that arise in the course of human experience. Democracy seeks ways to deal fairly with conflicts and to resolve them below the threshold of mass violence. This is a difficult process and there are failures, but the general tendency is clear and strong.

Some of the attitudes, beliefs, and procedures of democratic societies are useful in intergroup conflict generally, both within and beyond state borders. Informally as well as officially, processes of negotiation and mediation are common. There is a habit of trying to see the perspective of other people and learning mutual accommodation from early life onward. People become accustomed to a pluralistic society. They learn the art of compromise, seeking something satisfactory for all elements of the society.

Democracies seek to protect human rights, and most do so fairly well, certainly better than nondemocratic societies. They are less likely to cause large-scale egregious human rights violations that lead to intense fear, severe resentment, desire for revenge, and major violence to redress grievances. We pursue this vital point later in this chapter.

Moreover, the established democracies are strong now and getting stronger: economically, politically, technologically, and militarily. They are also in search of better human relations, internally and externally—having learned something from the extremes of hatred and violence throughout the twentieth century. This impulse needs activation to fulfill the promise of democracy in informed, proactive, sustained efforts to prevent deadly conflict through just solutions and improved living conditions.

This chapter takes a few steps down that long and winding road. I am especially indebted to Graham Allison, Robert Blackwill, Larry Diamond, Robert Dahl, Alexander George, Carl Gershman, Lincoln Gordon, Donald Horowitz, Seymour Lipset, Joseph Nye, Hisashi Owada, Robert Putnam, Timothy Sisk, Astrid Tuminez, and Michael Walzer for the shaping of these views.

Essentials of the Democratic Experience

The world rediscovered democracy in the late 1980s. This discovery has stimulated scholars to reconsider what are the essentials of democracy and how they might apply to nations that have had little or no experience with this form of government. Why should there be such a worldwide surge toward democracy?

The basic ideas of democracy are attractive all over the world, even though they are resisted by entrenched autocratic power. Professor Robert Dahl of Yale, one of the leading scholars of democracy, has pointed out a striking fact of modern history: If a democracy can take root in twenty years (one generation), it has a very good chance to be sustained for the long term.

Professor Dahl has devoted his distinguished career to the study of democracy. In a recent and masterful overview, he summarizes key concepts.[1]

1. Democracy helps to prevent rule by cruel and vicious autocrats. 2. Democracy guarantees its citizens a number of fundamental rights that nondemocratic systems do not, and cannot, grant. 3. Democracy insures its citizens a broader range of personal freedom than any feasible alternative to it. 4. Democracy helps people to protect their own fundamental interests. 5. Only a democratic government can provide a maximum opportunity for persons to exercise the freedom of self-determination—that is, to live under laws of their own choosing. 6. Only a democratic government can provide a maximum opportunity for exercising moral responsibility. 7. Democracy fosters human development more fully than any feasible alternative. 8. Only a democratic government can foster a relatively high degree of political equality. 9. Modern representative democracies do not fight one another. 10. Countries with democratic governments tend to be more prosperous than countries with nondemocratic governments.

Dahl considers a great deal of scholarship on the serious difficulties of making democracy work in practice over long periods of times. He understands that representative government, upon which democratic rule is based, also has a "dark side." Under a representative system, citizens necessarily delegate discretionary authority over important issues. This power is given not only to elected representatives but also indirectly to administrators, bureaucrats, civil servants, judges, and international organizations. Thus, democracy is connected to a nondemocratic process, bargaining between political and bureaucratic elites.

This elite bargaining, officially, takes place within democratic institutions and processes. But in practice limits are broad; popular oversight, participation, and control are not strong. In reality, bureaucratic elites have considerable leeway to act.

Nevertheless, the bureaucrats are not appointed despots who are outside of public control. Regular elections keep the bureaucracy deferential to public opinion. Also, a multiplicity of bureaucratic interests serves to mutually check and balance one another. Elected officials are also part of this broader bargaining process, and they remain a channel through which people can push their own desires, goals, and values. While political and bureaucratic elites are more powerful than ordinary citizens, they are far from despots.

Dahl is aware of the vicissitudes of democracy in the twentieth century. More than seventy times democracy collapsed or was undermined, paving the way for an authoritarian regime. But all told, the period was a profound success for the idea of democracy. Rather than an age of failure, by the end of the century it was one of triumph. Democracy's ideas, institutions, and practices have flourished and achieved a global reach.

What conditions favor the rise of democratic institutions? Democracy works best when elected officials control the military and police. Domestic society contributes when it solidly supports democratic beliefs and political culture in the absence of a deeply hostile subculture. A modern market economy and society tend to contribute to pluralistic governance. Beyond these domestic concerns, the lack of foreign control or a foreign threat is a powerful boost to democracy.

Any democracy needs a systematic, fair process for governance with the consent of the governed. There must be a system of representation but no single kind will suffice for everyone. Around the world, in governments generally recognized to be democratic, there are many different representative arrangements: parliamentary or presidential; centralized or federal; single member districts or proportional representation; exceptional majorities required for certain purposes viewed as particularly vital; plebiscites for constitutional change; special arrangements to protect the rights of vulnerable minorities. Across these variations is a common theme of fairness, of broad participation, of access on a large scale to the decisions that affect the lives of the population in important ways.[2]

The equality of human beings is a principle of democracy that cannot deny the immense biological and cultural variability of human experience and human attributes. But it does speak to questions of political equality with equal access to elections in some kind of one person, one vote formula, as well as equality before the law with authentic access in practice to judicial and other remedies, especially those that can redress grievances and resolve conflicts without violence. This is a fundamental and exceedingly practical aspect of democratic functions.

Closely related is the concept of equality of opportunity. The principal pathway to implementing equality of opportunity has been free public education over a considerable span of years, often supplemented by legislative and judicial remedies against patterns of discrimination. Like everything else in democracy, this quest for equal rights and equal opportunity has to be updated from time to time in light of changing conditions.

The inalienable rights referred to in the American Declaration of Independence are fundamentally protections against abuse by government. Protection is typically offered in one way or another to all individuals and to minority groups. Since executive power, going back to ancient times, has been exceptionally susceptible to abuse, there is usually legislative oversight and press freedom and basic rights of people to assemble and petition—all designed to protect against the many variations on the theme of executive abuse. Rule of law excludes arbitrary arrest and imprisonment, unreasonable searches, or other major deprivations without due process.

Facing Obstacles and Difficult Transitions

There are many obstacles in the way of well-functioning democracy that provide an antidote to complacency or smugness. However fundamental the advantages of democracy truly are, they remain imperfect, requiring constant vigilance and ongoing adjustments to avoid erosion of democratic values and practices. The necessity to raise large sums of money in order to conduct modern, media-based campaigns besets a growing number of democratic states. The persistence of prejudice dogs democracy in virtually every society in one form or another. Powerful special interest groups can damage the process. The inability to form governing coalitions in some parliamentary systems can make pluralism unworkable. All these concerns show that even in the oldest and most powerful democracies the system must be constantly adjusted. This emphasizes the recurrent need to rebalance powers among the constituent elements of the society, including the balance between majority rule and protection of minorities.

Present circumstances in the world require consideration of emerging, transitional, and limited democracies.[3] The history of Western Europe reveals a variety of transitions to democracy—variations on the theme of building democratic institutions. Additional examples have emerged in recent decades. For example, in Brazil from the mid-1970s to the mid-1980s, there was a vigorous transition from authoritarian military rule to a civilian constitutional democracy.

One of the factors that come into play in such transitions is the positive correlation between market-oriented economies and effective political institutions of a democratic nature. There remains a good deal of uncertainty about the patterns of interaction between political and economic institutions, but it is certainly desirable to place both in a democratic framework—that is, multiple choices, opportunities, and decentralized power. There are cases in which a reasonably effective, market-oriented economy has functioned in an authoritarian setting, at least for a decade or two. Some observers even elevate this to the status of a principle—that is, that the difficulty of moving from a command economy to a market economy requires a period of nondemocratic political rule. Let us hope that this is not the case, because a great deal of suffering can be inflicted on many people in a repressive political system, as we see today in China, even though economic gains are being made. In any event, it is difficult to conceive of a long-term, flourishing market economy in the twenty-first century in the absence of a democratic political system, because participation in the world economy requires so much openness in the flow of information, ideas, capital, technology, and people.

Democracy is structured to avoid massive concentration of political and economic power. A highly centralized, command economy is not compatible with authentic democracy. There is simply too much power concentrated in the government that employs everyone, controls all resources, and readily abuses human rights. Pluralism is at the heart of democracy; it permits and fosters the dynamic interplay of ideas, enterprises, parties, and a great variety of nongovernmental organizations on the basis of reasonably clear, agreed-upon rules—reflecting a fundamental attitude of tolerance, mutual respect, and sensitivity to human rights.

Democracies with strong market economies see to it that there are safety nets for those in seriously disadvantaged circumstances; moreover, they make public arrangements for vital human requirements such as education, health care, and the protection of public health, as well as unemployment insurance. They employ progressive taxation in the interest of public fairness and seek ways to foster equality of opportunity. Indeed, all modern democracies make deliberate efforts, however imperfect, to balance efficiency with social justice.

Democracy needs a supportive culture in which elites accept the principles underlying free speech, religious freedom, the rule of law, human rights, and other fundamentals. In fact, cross-national studies of the correlates of democracy reveal that cultural factors may be even more important than economic ones. The problem, however, is that cultural norms in favor of democracy do not evolve quickly. Indeed, many countries have undergone a relapse to authoritarianism after making the initial transition to democratic governance. One-third of working democracies in 1958 had become authoritarian by the mid-1970s. But since then there have been major gains, often fostered by international cooperation.

The importance of political culture poses a profound challenge to the recent democratic transitions in former communist countries. However, belief systems do change; the development of capitalism, a large middle class, an organized working class, as well as increased education and wealth can promote secularism, civil society, and other prerequisites for democracy. This seems to be the case in recent transitions in the Confucian societies of Taiwan and South Korea, both markedly aided by established democracies such as the United States.

One major problem associated with legitimacy is the protection of minority rights from infringements by the majority. Minorities who feel excluded from access to political power will withhold support from a democratizing state; this is true of recent transitions in Eastern Europe and the former Soviet Union. Various efforts have been made to solve this problem—for example, the creation of constitutional structures that give minorities veto power in the policy process when their vital interests are at stake.

Civil society builds democracy by allowing the evolution of democratic values through nonviolent conflict among nongovernmental entities. Groups compete with each other and with the state for the power to carry out specific agendas. Within the context of institutionalized competition, tolerance and acceptance of opposition develop. Civil society provides the opportunity for coalitions of individuals to undertake innovative activities, for instance, in the service of equal opportunity or protection of human rights.

Political parties are crucial components of civil society; they are vital mediating institutions between the citizenry and the state. In the former Soviet bloc countries, the absence of strong political parties impedes democratic institutionalization. The existence of at least two parties with a devotedly loyal mass of support is a crucial condition for stable democracy. Excessive political fragmentation with the emergence of many parties is likely to impede the efficacy of democratic governance, especially if the parties are intolerant of each other.

Institutions of civil society have an increasingly important role to play beyond their national boundaries. They can work with counterparts on an international basis, not only to build democratic institutions but also to help prevent deadly conflict in other ways. We considered these opportunities in the chapter on institutions of civil society.

Facilitating the Emergence of Democracy through International Cooperation

Can we formulate a decent minimum of democratic facilitation for all (or almost all) countries? Should the international community adopt a worldwide democratic orientation? If so, that would entail a vigorous, sustained effort for education of publics through the media and the formal educational systems about the essential democratic experiences. What are the vital structures and functions for the emergence of a viable democracy? How can the international community make these widely known and understood? Certainly, there is a vaguely formulated aspiration that has been sweeping the world in recent years. The international community must address the translation of this aspiration into the reality of emerging democracy. Scholars such as Larry Diamond of the Hoover Institution, Stanford

University, have addressed this problem in a penetrating way. He did so in a report prepared for the Carnegie Commission.[4]

It is reasonable now to think about a democratic community—those nations that have reasonably well-established, clear-cut democracies—even though they differ considerably in their variations on the basic democratic themes. It is no coincidence that such a democratic community includes the nations of the world that are strongest economically, militarily, scientifically, and technologically—not to mention their relatively high quality in terms of decent human relations. For such a fortunate community with so much relevant experience about coping with the problems of modern societies, there is a moral imperative to address in a systematic, deliberate, long-term, high-priority way the path to democratization around the world. What can be done to foster a democratic atmosphere, democratic values, and a climate of democracy worldwide? This does not mean a rigid, narrow approach; not a one-size-fits-all. Rather, it means variety among democracies depending on historical circumstances, cultural traditions, and human ingenuity.

Since resources are limited, the democratic community will have to make priorities in such efforts. One consideration is the importance of a particular country in the world at large—for example, the manifest significance of Russia on many dimensions. There are also important considerations involving the practical prospects for successful democratic development. Some priority will be given to investment where it is most likely to make a beneficial difference in the foreseeable future. There is also a need to consider some sampling of countries in each region of the world that can serve as a beachhead for democratic impulses, a model for the region of constructive ways to tackle the problems involved in building democracy. Special efforts will be needed when a promising, though fragile, democracy is experiencing a reversal that jeopardizes its future. All such efforts are more likely to be effective if there is extensive international cooperation within the democratic community.

Should every democratic government have an agency whose primary purpose is to facilitate the development of democracies throughout the world? Such agencies would be likely to develop the necessary sensitivity to cultural differences, the history of particular countries, and the skills necessary to be generally helpful. The trend of recent years has been toward the creation of such units—in or close to government. The National Endowment for Democracy of the United States is a case in point. It reaches out to emerging, fragile democracies to help them strengthen their capabilities in diverse ways. It also works collaboratively with other established democracies, such as India. Western European democracies have strong units of this kind, as do Canada, Japan, and Australia.

The National Endowment for Democracy (NED) is a good illustration of democracy-promoting organizations set up by many democratic countries.

The U.S. Congress created it in 1988 to "strengthen democratic institutions around the world through nongovernmental efforts." As a private, nonprofit organization, which also has an annual appropriation from the government, it makes yearly grants to hundreds of groups that support democracy in Africa, Asia, Central and Eastern Europe, Latin America, the Middle East, and former Soviet Union.

The guiding principle of the Endowment is the belief that freedom is a universal, fundamental human goal. A way to achieve it is by developing democratic institutions, procedures, and values. Democracy is a more complex process than a single political election. It should evolve from unique needs and traditions of diverse political cultures and not be based on a model of the United States or any single country. New democracies should be able to draw up the whole world's experience in building democratic institutions. NED creates a bond between indigenous democratic movements abroad and U.S. citizens based on the common commitment to government created and maintained by the people and the ideal of freedom as a way of life. In the Endowment's early years of grant making, the ideal of promoting democracy worldwide was considered by many to be controversial. Today, it has become an established field of activity throughout the world. As NED has continued to evolve into a more complex and mature institution, in addition to grant making, it aids the work of activists for democracy by helping to deepen their understanding of democratic development and bring about a sense of common purpose within the worldwide movement for democracy. The support for NED's efforts is dramatically stronger than it was a decade ago.

NED has developed seven strategies for achieving its goal of furthering the cause of democracy:

- *Helps democrats in closed societies.* Significant democratic breakthroughs have occurred in various countries—in central Europe, Soviet Union, Latin America, Asia, and Africa—with the help of NED's early investment in struggles for democracy. Currently, the Endowment has its focus on the remaining communist and authoritarian countries such as China, North Korea, Cuba, Sudan, and Burma. The work encourages the development of civil society and defends human rights in a practical approach to democracy building.
- *Consolidates democracy.* In its work with developing democracies NED focuses on two primary objectives: (1) to strengthen institutions and procedures that will help to ensure fair and free elections, and (2) to gradually bring about liberal democracy through fostering social pluralism, strengthening rule of law, and protecting civil liberties. In the next phase of development, the Endowment supports groups that try to build a healthy market economy, independent trade unions, and a free

press along with institutions that encourage accountable politics, clear economics, corporate governance that is responsible, and a military controlled by its civilians.

- *Applies a multisectoral approach.* NED's four core institutes (National Democratic Institute for International Affairs, International Republican Institute, American Center for International Labor Solidarity, Center for International Private Enterprise) offer expertise in the fields of business, labor, political party development, and electoral reform. Relationships with these institutes lets Congress and others know that the Endowment is fair in its judgments in addition to being open to diverse approaches to democratic development. Groups abroad also are given support for their work in human rights, independent media, the rule of law, and a broad range of civil society initiatives.
- *Cooperates with other democracy foundations.* NED seeks to foster cooperation among existing democracy foundations worldwide and to encourage democracies, already established, to create similar institutions. In the early 1990s, NED held a kind of "democracy summit," the first of several among democracy foundations in the United States, Germany, Great Britain, and Canada. Not only was information shared, but opportunities were provided to coordinate strategy and assistance to Burma, Belarus, and Serbia—some of the most difficult places to promote democracy. Efforts have expanded recently to include new foundations in France, Sweden, the Netherlands, Austria, and Australia.
- *Cultivates partner organizations in new democracies.* Organizations in new democracies are seeking to share their expertise with others in countries where democracy is just developing—a kind of peer learning. Polish NGOs are leaders in this mentoring trend as they work to bring about democratic civic education in central Europe and in other parts of the former Soviet Union. NED encourages such "east-to-east" partnerships through grants to Polish groups and various NGOs in other Eastern European countries.
- *Advances research on democracy.* NED founded the *Journal of Democracy* in 1990. It publishes new research on democracy, debates important issues, reviews current literature, and reports on major events and recent developments that influence the worldwide development of democracy. The success of this highly respected publication set the stage for the development, in 1994, of the International Forum for Democratic Studies. This center is a leader in analysis of the theory and practice of democracy throughout the world. The Forum's other activities include conferences, books on democratization, a Visiting Fellows program, a library and online database, and a network of collaborative research centers based in new democracies. The Forum illustrates

NED's belief in the interplay of research and practice for the benefit of democratic development.

- *Builds a worldwide movement for democracy.* The World Movement for Democracy, created in 1998, is a proactive network of individuals and organizations whose goal is to collaboratively tackle the most difficult challenges to the advancement of democracy and human rights. This global movement creates a group of democrats—from the most developed to the least developed democracies—who are drawn together by their belief that the common interest is served by the gradual expansion of systems based on freedom, self-government, and the rule of law.

The potential of new communications technologies to help build democracy is extraordinary. It stems from the connection between democracy and the flow of information. We deal with this in a later chapter.

Although governments certainly have a major role to play, these efforts should not be thought of as purely governmental or even resting on intergovernmental international institutions, important as they are. There is a significant role for a great variety of nongovernmental organizations. And they, too, need international cooperation to be effective.

What are the most useful means for promoting democracy? In the case of new, emerging, and fragile democracies, it is valuable to strengthen the political and civic infrastructure of democracy. This involves technical assistance and financial aid to build the requisite processes and institutions, including widespread education of publics about the actual workings of democracy. It involves many kinds of help. Building the means to conduct elections at both the national and local level along with the establishment of legislative bodies at the national and local level is only a start. The development of support services that nourish the political system such as the Congressional Research Service in the United States are part of this project as well.

Aid must be directed at the prolonged task of establishing the idea of rule of law embodied in an explicit and legal framework. This includes a constitution, the creation of an independent judiciary with real capacity for implementing laws fairly, along with oversight institutions to provide for public accountability. Reforms must follow in the bureaucracy to ensure public administration of a professional nature. Civilian institutional capacities must be created to deal with security questions, both within and beyond the borders of the country, to temper the military. Special measures to protect individual human rights, minority groups, and vulnerable sectors, including mechanisms to deal with conflict that can be perceived as fair to all and effective in preventing violence, must be evolved.

Political culture must reflect these changes. Political parties should be assisted in the service of democratic participation, but with no attempt to favor one party over another so long as they are all within the democratic family. This can help to bring into existence institutions of civil society (nongovernmental organizations) that address issues of concern to the population such as working conditions, the environment, human rights, science and technology, and independent media.

Toward these ends, it is desirable that the democratic community establishes, singly and together, special funds for economic assistance that will be used to strengthen democracies that are making a serious effort to make their democratic institutions enduring parts of the society and culture. Such funds may be administered through nongovernmental organizations as well as government agencies and international multilateral organizations. Both funding and technical assistance must be sustained over a period of years to support the complicated processes of democracy building. There is much more to it than one successful election.[5]

The international democratic community must make a serious effort to intervene as best it can to protect fragile democracies when they are seriously jeopardized by tensions from natural disasters or violent ethnic conflicts or strong authoritarian currents within the society. It is important to have a system of early warning so that the democratic community can recognize when a democracy is slipping into crisis. International mediation at an early stage could usefully be developed as an art form beyond present efforts.[6] Building new democracies must include the fostering of innovative institutional arrangements that can take account of dangerous sensitivities likely to engender serious conflict and build mechanisms to accommodate ethnic, religious, linguistic, and political diversity.[7] The embassies of well-established democratic countries could serve as a focal point in each emerging, fragile democracy. They have the potential to serve as sites of intellectual, technical, and moral support, not only in building democratic institutions in relatively good times, but also for preventing deadly conflict when warning signals become clear. This was the case in the 1996 Paraguayan crisis in which the embassies of Brazil and the United States played an important role in defusing a potentially violent situation concerning presidential succession.[8]

In recent decades, there has been a remarkable upsurge of international attention on protection of basic human rights. The Helsinki process has been a remarkable success story, and not the only one. Yet, the question arises as to how human rights can be protected on a secure and enduring basis—not just as a function of emergency interventions by the international community, and not just as a side effect of anti-Communist efforts during the Cold War. While it is useful for bilateral and multilateral diplomacy to pursue individual cases of human rights abuse, the emphasis should be on systemic reforms. In the first instance, these involve ways of treating human beings fairly, with a minimum of force in the handling of prisoners, the elimination of torture, the avoidance of imprisonment on political grounds, highly professional police operations, and a well-functioning independent judiciary. There is no clear way to provide an enduring basis for protection of human rights other than the establishment of effective democratic institutions. Therefore, the democratic community should put strong emphasis on upholding basic human rights and the fundamental dignity of human beings everywhere.

The European experience in the second half of the twentieth century provides specific models for judicial means of protecting human rights. One is the United Kingdom's Privy Council that was retained by Commonwealth countries after they achieved independence; it provided an appeal that was meaningful in human rights problems. Another is the European Convention on Human Rights, an extraordinary advance in international law that gives enforcement machinery to individuals in their right of appeal against their own government. The European Commission on Human Rights and the European Court provide enforcement machinery for human rights.[9] These mechanisms are now being adapted to take account of the wider scope of emerging democracies in Europe. Its experience can usefully be considered in other parts of the world.

Another remarkable step, largely a product of the 1990s, is the international monitoring of election campaigns, including preparation for the election as well as its conduct, and indeed follow-up measures so that the election is not wasted. Democratic governments, the UN, regional organizations, and NGOs (notably the Carter Center) have made dramatic contributions here. Similarly, democracy declarations are beginning to have effect. One was the British Commonwealth's Harare Declaration of 1991. It asserted the respect of all member states for democratic processes and institutions, the rule of law with independent judiciary, fair and honest government, protection of basic human rights including equal opportunities for all citizens regardless of race, color, creed, or political belief. This declaration appears to be having some impact on the democratic transition in Africa. A similar case is the Santiago Declaration of the Organization of American States, also instituted in 1991, which commits all members of the organization to upholding democracy in the region. Any nation that puts democracy in jeopardy has to contend with not only the threat of expulsion from the OAS but also the mobilization of international financial institutions against it.

Democracy as Conflict Resolution

Widespread understanding must be achieved that democracy is able to cope well with conflict at a nonviolent level through institutional mechanisms. It is a game that all can play with reasonably good results so long as they accept the rules of the game—and the rules of the game are mutually agreed upon, updated periodically by common consent. These ideas are attractive in virtually all cultures once they are adequately understood. They include explicit respect for the dignity of individuals and the protection of basic human rights.

The experience of Zambia in the early 1990s illustrates the way in which the advent of democracy can prevent a civil war. In this case, a peaceful transition occurred from an authoritarian state run for a long time by a single leader to a multiparty democracy. Of course, the long-run consolidation of democracy in such a poor country with minimal democratic traditions will be difficult but crucial. Outside help proved to be useful in the initial transition, mainly coming from highly respected nongovernmental organizations such as the Carter Center. NGOs have become increasingly concerned with helping nations on the precipice deal with conflicts within themselves, particularly those conflicts arising out the reawakening of old, lingering prejudices and the political exploitation of harsh, ethnic nationalism. In the absence of democratic mechanisms to sort out these conflicts within a country, they can readily spill over into violence.

Virtually all of the comprehensive peace settlements in which the UN has participated in recent years involved democratization as a crucial part of the settlement—for example, El Salvador, Cambodia, Namibia, Mozambique, and Guatemala. Indeed, the final major publication of Secretary-General Boutros Boutros-Ghali was "An Agenda for Democratization."[10]

There is a strong case for the role of core democratic values in resolving intergroup conflicts and preventing their escalation to violence. Although the history of each region has left a distinctive legacy of cultures, languages, and religions, the fundamental democratic principles can be useful to all—applied in ways that fit indigenous circumstances. The development of electoral systems and the monitoring of elections constitute only one crucial piece of this puzzle.

Another crucial element is the development of strong civic organizations in societies that have been harshly limited by authoritarian regimes. This takes time, to be measured in decades and perhaps even generations, like so much of the development of democracy. To do so requires much work at the grassroots level, preferably in collaboration with similar entities in other countries that have more democratic experience. This means that the public of previously nondemocratic countries comes to understand what is involved in democracy: What the rights, responsibilities, and opportunities of citizens are; how they can express their views; how they can learn about vital subjects and formulate constructive approaches. Such cooperative work on the part of the democratic community also involves high-level collaboration to stimulate the development of parties, parliaments, and responsible leadership. So, it is both a matter of grassroots and high-level connections to produce a stable democracy in which a broad range of citizens participate actively in important decisions.[11]

Such efforts call for communication from established democracies about what is involved in crucial aspects of the democratic experience: how to take different political arguments into account, to accommodate the views of different sectors of the society, to work out choices that are fair to all, to be aware of mechanisms for nonviolent conflict resolution. This also involves a commitment to the inherent legitimacy of the society, with leadership that reflects its people and their continuing input; attitudes and mechanisms to protect basic human rights; enough of a personal stake for individuals in the future of the nation that sacrifices can be made in the nation-building process; and perhaps most important of all, tolerance for diversity, especially religious, ethnic, and political differences. The international democratic community can help to create an atmosphere in which these ideals are meaningful and worth striving for even though they are hard to attain and in which there is faith in successive approximations over extended time toward a better way of life.

In the short run of democratic transitions, there is great need for mediators who enter into disputes, however informally, as impartial outside parties trying to help the contending parties see that they have similarities as well as differences, that they have the capacity, intelligence, and decency to find common ground. It is particularly important to develop a shared consensus around processes that can sort out difficult problems, to move toward institutions that can put such processes on a reliable and readily available basis for the citizens of the country. In short, from an early stage in democracy building, it is important that people widely understand the possibilities for nonviolent conflict resolution and the practical value of mutual accommodation among different sectors and peoples within a state. Moreover, they can be helped to see that very often cooperation can lead to greater benefits in the long run; even that there are superordinate goals of compelling value to all concerned that can be achieved only by cooperation. Examples from other countries and other regions give a reality to this possibility, including visits by emerging leaders to such sites in order to get a vivid sense of what is possible and how democratic processes can work.

The first step in building the conflict-resolving process of democracy is to establish election systems. Outside advice, influence, and concrete help may well be necessary so that the parties can feel comfortable that their interests will be preserved. An election system in effect is a negotiation for democracy, and it is useful for the participants to get explicit guidance on negotiation and mutual accommodation as they go through the experience of their first elections. Underlying factors involved in most conflicts can be shifted to the election arena and then to the nonviolent mechanisms of ongoing electoral politics. Great care is needed to be sure that the people involved perceive the new elected government as truly representative of the entire population, that there is at least the beginning of a culture of fairness, and that local or regional governments have the capacity to deal with any grievances that may exist with respect to central authority.

One of the merits of a strong international participation in the first democratic election is reassurance to the voters that they can vote in secrecy without fear of retribution. Indeed the voters need to be protected not only during the election but afterward, and here the international community has a heavy responsibility. The election process must be open, readily understandable, and patently fair. This includes the registration of voters, the right of the parties to campaign freely throughout the country without intimidation, the access of all to the print and nonprint media, the presence of independent monitors at voting places and experienced, fair-minded international observers at every focal point in the process. An outstanding example was the role of the United Nations in carrying out these tasks in Namibia. This is a model for the resolution of conflicts throughout Africa and elsewhere.

There is a great need, all the way from fundamental principles to operational details, to educate for democracy. Indeed, in the era of modern telecommunications, it might be feasible to have a worldwide democratic network under highly respected auspices—perhaps a mix of governmental and nongovernmental supporters. Such a network could present many interesting examples of ongoing efforts to build and strengthen democratic institutions in rich and poor communities alike. It could present basic concepts, processes, and institutions. This could be done in a variety of languages and adapted to many cultures. Thus, it might be feasible rapidly to enhance the level of understanding throughout the world of what is involved in democracy and its potential benefits for all, including and especially its capacity for nonviolent conflict resolution.

Military and Democracy

If the international democratic community is serious about helping to sustain the peace in conflict-ridden nations by building democratic institutions that work, it must be attentive to the situation of the military in such countries. This involves the interlinked questions of democracy, development, and demobilization. The military forces in these countries have often been engaged in bloody battles under authoritarian regimes. They may have been in positions of very high status, perceived as protecting their people from disaster. Now with a democratic transition, they must learn respect for civil authority, for rule of law, for new kinds of command responsibilities, for responsible management in a democratic setting.

To do so, they need to work collaboratively on the basis of mutual respect with comparable military leaders and organizations from democratic societies. This gives them a sense of belonging to a valued profession and having clear paths toward functioning in a different way with decent prospects, albeit with some personal losses. It is also important to provide training for civilians who will be managing military resources, often in situations where civilians have had no access before. So, the application of democratic principles to military education becomes a vital matter.

Cooperative learning modes across international boundaries can be used to establish professional standards for the military of formerly authoritarian regimes, including the discipline of working well with civilian authority and taking into account the well-being of the entire society, not just the military or military-industrial sector. These questions have been at the center of "preventive defense" as formulated by William Perry as U.S. secretary of defense and elaborated in an important book with his collaborator, Professor Ashton Carter of Harvard University.[12]

Preventive defense involves establishing ongoing relationships between the military establishments of the democracies and those of other states to encourage military acceptance of civilian authority and removal of the military from domestic politics; promoting openness about defense budgets, capabilities, and military doctrine; negotiating confidence-building measures such as advance notice of military exercises and limits on their size, scope, and duration; and generally strengthening civil-military relations within countries on a democratic basis.

Often it is valuable to get the most reasonable, constructive military leaders involved in negotiations to sort out an ethnic or other "internal" conflict. They can be practical in pointing out the illusion of some short-term victory or the fallacy of the last move. They can help political leaders accept the reality of the situation on the ground. They can cope with the military aspects of conflict resolution; for example, working out specific methods of making a cease-fire effective, dealing with demobilization, and later creating a new national armed force under democratic authority.

There are important military factors in sustaining the peace and gradually building democratic institutions. For example, the retraining of military personnel so that they can participate effectively in a civilian economy and provide skilled labor for economic development is a crucial consideration. So, demobilization must address retraining as well as reasonable benefits that can provide some sense of security in a strange new world for the military. For example, there are questions of mustering-out pay, modest pensions, a modicum of medical care, and housing. If military people in large numbers are simply dumped on a society in the midst of a drastic transition, they can once again resort to violence and become a highly destabilizing factor. These considerations are important not only for individual governments that wish to help but also for the UN, the World Bank, the IMF and a variety of NGOs that function internationally.

Democratic Engineering and Power Sharing

Many paths to mutual accommodation in heterogeneous countries are available. These include a broad range of options from federation or confederation, regional or functional autonomy, and institutionalized cultural pluralism within each nation and across national boundaries. Yet all of these variations must be grounded in democratic institutions.

The option of confederation is important in today's world. In general, this is a form of democratic government that can accommodate a variety of orientations and cultural preferences, including highly parochial ones. It can foster tolerant and widely participatory orientations. In effect, it is a kind of decentralized, loosely organized, inclusive democracy. Such democracy can be accountable to the people, can have effective protection of minorities, can live by the rule of law, can represent its people fairly and relate to other peoples in the same vein. Within it, local areas may have a high degree of autonomy, distinctive cultural groups may have extensive jurisdiction over their own affairs—yet they can draw on the strength that comes from pooling resources in a larger economic and social entity. One factor that can be helpful is the fostering of a lively civil society in which a great many NGOs and voluntary associations pursue diverse interests and values in a legal context that protects them and a psychological context that blesses them with respectability.

Switzerland provides a particularly interesting example of how this has been done, facing up to very complex and difficult situations. By some measures, Switzerland is the oldest democracy of the modern age. Not only does it have four distinctive cultures within it, but three of its four linguistic groups live in immediate proximity to a much larger nation that constitutes their cultural center.

There is also a long history of bad relations between Switzerland's bigger neighbors—France, Germany, and Italy—which could easily have caught up a segment of the Swiss population in one of their various conflicts. Indeed, on several occasions Switzerland was in danger of being split up. Yet, it was possible to maintain the integrity of the state through respect for the principle of territoriality. This involved a great deal of local autonomy so that there was no rational basis for any minority group to feel threatened. Switzerland's neutral status was also helpful in this regard.

Authority has been widely distributed and fairly shared on the basis of systematic planning and explicit principles. These are well known and widely understood among the different populations. There has been a concerted effort to work out a basis for living together amicably and deriving major economic benefit from cooperative efforts. At the center of this complex adaptation is an agreed-upon, pervasive, durable pattern of arrangements in government and other sectors that leads to shared power on an equitable basis among the various groups.

In view of the epidemic of ethnocentric violence in the 1990s, it is vital to learn lessons form the world's experience with mitigating such violence where—as is commonly the case—different ethnic groups have lived together for a long time. In the most deadly conflict cases, ethnically based political parties pervade civilian politics and there are no interethnic parties. If an intense fear of competition exists between different ethnic groups, the danger is great. When there is also a legacy of domination, the risks of severe conflict are formidable. The real or imagined loyalty of one ethnic group to an outside entity can fuel antagonism. So, too, can demographic changes that stimulate fear in one group that it will be swallowed up by another.

Civilian, nongovernmental actors must be fostered to play a role in every major facet of these societies. They can be particularly significant in the protection of human rights, including minority rights. In tense, multiethnic societies, political institutions may well find it useful to shift to a percentage-based proportional representation in parliaments and to take other measures that avoid harsh majority domination. Another possibility is to decide on a fixed number of seats for each minority living within a republic. This kind of effort often requires continuing participation by the international community to help in formulating standards and monitoring implementation. Multiparty systems and free elections are necessary but not sufficient conditions for building a stable peace. An array of projects is needed to serve as bridge builders between the peoples of the different ethnic groups that have been suspicious of each other. Local branches of international organizations may be particularly helpful.

The development of market economies with special attention to fairness in the distribution of opportunities is valuable. The international community over the longer term can help emerging nations or autonomous regions to generate a regional political economy, communication systems, education systems, information systems—in many ways to foster technical cooperation throughout the region. Whatever can foster a more cosmopolitan identity rather than a narrowly defined ethnic identity is helpful. Since the media have such a powerful reach almost everywhere, the international community must search for ways to make this a constructive role with bridge-building functions across ethnic barriers.

The approach that is so badly needed is one focused on democratic pluralism. This means developing a culture of fairness, mutual accommodation, and even mutual aid among diverse groups sharing a common space. There are many ways in which this can be done. It is possible to build democratic institutions with strong protection of human rights for all, clearly including minorities. This can include a measure of autonomy for distinctive groups, including access to the media and the schools that gives promise of enduring appreciation of valued cultural attributes.

In many multiethnic societies, the procedures of majority-rule democracy have been effective for managing intergroup relations and maintaining social cohesion. Yet, there are societies with deep ethnic divisions and little experience with democratic government in which simple majority rule is inadequate to maintain peace with justice. Where ethnic identities are strong, national identity is weak, and political leaders divisive, populations may vote largely along ethnic lines. Domination by one ethnic group can lead to a tyranny of the majority, and this is conducive to deep resentment. A preferable solution may be the adoption of mutually agreed upon power-sharing arrangements that encourage broad-based governing coalitions.

A Carnegie Commission–sponsored study by Timothy Sisk identified several conditions under which power-sharing arrangements are most likely to be successful. Crucial is a core group of moderate political leaders who are genuinely representative of the groups that they purport to lead and who embrace pluralism. Supporting this are practices that are flexible and allow for equitable distribution of resources. These arrangements work best when they are developed locally and are region-specific. In due course the parties can gradually eliminate the extraordinary measures that some power-sharing arrangements entail and move toward a more integrative and liberal form of democracy.[13]

Historically, there is little precedent for deliberate, systematic, well-organized international efforts to help substantially with the process of democratization. It is important to draw on the remarkable efforts that have been springing up all over the world in recent years. What are the most valuable lessons to be learned? What is the role of the UN? What is the role of the established democracies? How can each facilitate the work of useful NGOs? How can the latter be coordinated if necessary with each other and with governmental bodies?

If democracy is viewed as an optional preoccupation of self-righteous democratizers—or even as an intrusive activity of sugar-coated, neoimperialists—then all this is much ado about nothing (or worse). But if we view democracy as a powerful constructive mechanism for sorting out the ubiquitous, ongoing conflicts of our highly contentious human species, then the challenge becomes a vital one with positive implications for the human future.

People Power for Prevention

One of the most powerful forces to prevent conflict is mass action by the people on behalf of democracy and against tyranny. The recent past has given numerous examples of how peaceful protest by a nation's populace can have profound political consequences and defuse or prevent conflict in potentially violent situations.

In East Germany in 1989 there were growing tensions as the country's citizens sought to leave the country and other East bloc nations opened their borders. Sharp clashes occurred that autumn as the communist regime in East Germany sought to prevent its people from leaving the country to travel to the West via Hungary. The situation was dangerous since the East German government had a history of violent repression against internal dissent. Its leader, Erich Honecker, kept to this tradition and generally resisted Mikhail Gorbachev's examples of liberalization. Street protests became commonplace as Germans sought not only the right to move freely but also began to agitate for democratic reform. Leading the way in organizing these protests were a number of protestant pastors who used their churches as sanctuaries for this purpose and also used their stature to maintain the peaceful nature of the protests even when faced with repressive government measures. Prominent in this movement was the Nikolai Church in Leipzig, which served as a rallying point for protests. On October 9, nearly 70,000 people gathered peacefully in a protest that started at the church. Organizers made sure that the crowd maintained composure while exerting strong social pressure. The security forces backed down from confrontation. Within days, crowds calling for reform on the streets of Leipzig had swelled to over 150,000. It was not merely activists or students in the streets but people from all walks of life who joined in the demonstrations.[14]

The peaceful example of Leipzig encouraged further action around East Germany. The streets of various cities were soon swollen with their citizens. They remained peaceful, which not only gave the regime no legitimate cause for a crackdown but also gave the protesters and their message considerable moral authority. In the face of this swelling evidence of people power, the outwardly steely East German regime tottered and then fell in November 1989.

Elsewhere in the Soviet empire, attempts by communist governments to stifle reform and protest were met by peaceful civic action. State coercion in Czechoslovakia was overcome in the peaceful "Velvet Revolution." In Mongolia reformers used hunger strikes and civil disobedience to force democratic concessions on the communist regime (although the communists later won the free elections).[15]

A new report from the United States Institute of Peace (USIP) clarifies the nonviolent revolution and the transition to democracy in Serbia. Its essential points follow.

1. "Yugoslav president Slobodan Milosevic fell from power in October 2000 after a concerted campaign of strategic nonviolent action that

was similar to democratic revolutions in other countries, thus offering a paradigm for foreign-supported strategic nonviolent action against autocratic regimes.

2. The opposition's effectiveness depended on a broad coalition of political parties, nongovernmental organizations, media, and labor unions.

3. While foreign assistance helped to build and sustain the broad anti-Milosevic coalition, indigenous organizations and action were mainly responsible for driving events.

4. The transition to democracy in Serbia is far from complete, and continuing pressure from civil society is crucial to sustaining the process.

5. The organizations that generated the movement against Milosevic need to reengineer themselves to be effective in a more democratic environment.

6. These same organizations have a crucial role to play in pressing the new government to undertake effective anticorruption, accountability, and truth and reconciliation efforts, as well as military and police reform.

7. Foreign assistance should focus not only on political parties but should continue to support a broad range of NGOs, labor unions, think tanks, and media.

8. Long-term peace and stability in the Balkans continue to require the establishment of genuine and stable democracies in Serbia and the entire Balkan region."[16]

These activities and other incidents of "people power" in the Philippines and elsewhere show the formidable strength of an aroused but nonviolent population. While there have been times in which mass demonstrations have been squashed, notably Tiananmen Square in China, it is usually difficult even for repressive and authoritarian governments to stand against such protests.

Protests of this sort build on the nonviolent movements of Mahatma Gandhi against colonial rule and Martin Luther King Jr. against racial discrimination. They show that these movements can be forces for democratic change but also for the prevention of deadly conflict.[17] Challenging imperial power, racism, or authoritarianism is a dangerous proposition. These are often difficult social issues for the society at large to confront. The violence used to sustain repressive systems can be the spark for a cycle of violence that ends in open conflict or even civil war. In East Germany, Czechoslovakia, Mongolia, and most recently in Serbia, leaders and activists—and the people themselves—understood the true power of mass, nonviolent protest. They made sure that their demonstrations remained peaceful in the face of provocation. In this way they prevented the possibility of violent conflict and moved toward a just regime.

Fostering Democratic Consolidation

In an informative new study, Larry Diamond formulates indicators of democratic consolidation in emerging democracies.[18] He identifies the conditions under which democracies move beyond fragility. Diamond asserts that this is likely to occur when most leaders of opinion culture, business, and social organizations accept the legitimacy of democracy, when all major leaders of government and politically significant parties believe that democracy is valuable and that the constitutional rule and institutions deserve support. This is not a simple task as these beliefs must be publicly expressed and supported under stress. Governmental and other leaders must respect each other's right to compete peacefully for power within the framework of established law and generally accepted norms of political conduct. Leaders cannot accept incitement to hatred and violence as political methods; nor should they attempt to use the military for political advantage.

These conditions are most likely to be met when 70 percent or more of the public believes that democracy is preferable to any other form of government and no more than 15 percent of the public prefers an authoritarian form of government as well as when no antidemocratic movement, party, or organization has a significant mass following, and citizens generally do not use violence, fraud, or illegal methods to pursue their political interests. Needless to say, these conditions are not easy to achieve. They require sustained long-term efforts and outside support. While there are democratically inclined people in virtually every culture, they face formidable obstacles, and their success rests heavily on help (not imposition) from the international community.

The next phase of democratization in the early twenty-first century may be singularly difficult because almost all of the countries that had favorable economic, social, and cultural conditions for democracy have already moved a considerable distance in the democratic transition. Yet Diamond's comment is trenchant and hopeful:

> However, no calculus of regime futures should dismiss the possibility for surprise. Few foresaw the collapse of Soviet and East European communist regimes, and the rise of democracy in Russia in particular. Not many Asia specialists were predicting in the mid-1990s that General Suharto would be ignominiously toppled from power. Few were the Africanists in 1990 anticipating an imminent "'second liberation.'" Many democratic transitions during the third wave figured to happen sooner or later, when dictators died, military rulers exhausted the patience of previously democratic societies, or international backing for authoritarian rule peeled away. But others were simply unexpected. . . .
>
> The element of surprise thus justifies some broad distribution of democracy promotion efforts, so that repression is condemned, democratic

opposition is encouraged, and foundations for pluralism are fostered in as many non-democracies as possible. This increases the odds that authoritarian regime crises will lead to democracy when they do emerge unexpectedly. In addition, international pressure for democracy and human rights will be more credible and effective to the extent that it has some consistency across different regional and political circumstances. . . .

Diamond's study of recent democratic consolidation ends on a note of optimism. People throughout the world committed to democracy have a view of the international system that is democratic in some important ways. It is a system composed of free societies within democratic states that carry out their relations with one another in an atmosphere bounded by law and common principles of decency and justice. States that aspire to membership in this community of nations must show that they govern with the consent of the governed. There is an evolving international architecture that has established the right of the international community to promote and defend democracy and human rights.

This tide is rising around the world. The agenda for democratic reforms is broad and must continue to expand to meet the needs of women and minority groups. Diamond is clear that gains, even in established democracies, must be guarded. Campaign finance must be controlled to prevent corruption and safeguard the electoral process in some countries. Economic reforms and social justice must be part of the agenda. The vast gaps between rich and poor must be tackled in a sustained way.

Regardless, norms concerning human rights and democracy will become increasingly prevalent in the international arena. Here, the established democracies will be important centers to promote this change. The tortuous path to democratic development has been illuminated and many countries are moving well on it—with others to come. To the extent that the established democracies can help the emerging democracies to navigate this path, a precious route to world peace will be enhanced.

The Development of Human Rights in a Half-Century Perspective

In her important new book, Mary Ann Glendon enriches our understanding of human rights.[19] It is the story of a document that provides the foundation for the modern human rights movement and people who were gathered in 1947 at the behest of the newly formed United Nations, chaired by Eleanor Roosevelt, to draft the first "international bill of rights." These remarkable individuals were able to overcome their personal, political, and cultural differences to usher in a new era of rights from the ruins of two world wars. This Universal Declaration of Human Rights was adopted by the General Assembly of the UN on December 10, 1948, and continues to grow in worldwide influence fifty-plus years later.

Originally, this human rights project was only a concession to small countries and a response to the demands of many religious and humanitarian associations that the Allies make good on their promise to assure that the community of nations would never again fall prey to such massive violations of human dignity as those of World War II and the Holocaust. The five most powerful nations—Britain, China, France, the United States, and the Soviet Union—believed that their national sovereignty would remain intact.

Exceeding the expectations of almost everyone concerned, human rights became a huge political factor with unexpected prominence in ensuing decades. The Universal Declaration became the most vivid symbol of changes that would allow people with little power to be recognized and heard.

The Allies' 1946 Nuremberg Principles of international criminal law for the trials of German and Japanese war criminals and the 1948 Genocide Convention joined the Universal Declaration in efforts to ensure that nations' treatment of their own citizens be open to scrutiny by the world community. However, the Universal Declaration was a more ambitious effort, with its goal aimed toward *prevention* not punishment. It proclaimed, "Disregard and contempt for human rights have resulted in barbarous acts which have outraged the conscience of mankind."

The Declaration, comprised of thirty concise articles, inspired postwar and postcolonial constitutions and treaties, including, importantly, the new constitutions of Germany, Japan, and Italy. Freedom movements organized themselves around its principles and spurred the fall of totalitarian regimes in Eastern Europe and the end of apartheid. This declaration is the primary inspiration for most rights movements today, and it is the premier point of reference for international discussions on how to live together in an increasingly interdependent world.

As early as the seventeenth and eighteenth centuries, great charters were created marking humanity's initial attempts at codifying beliefs in human rights. These charters proclaimed that all men were born equal and free and that the role of government was to protect these liberties. In 1689, the British Bill of Rights was created; the year 1776 bore the U.S. Declaration of Independence; and the French Declaration of the Rights of Man and Citizen was written in 1789. Taken together, they provided the foundation for a modern language of rights on which the Universal Declaration of Human Rights was built.

From the beginning, this language broke off into two dialects. Continental European thinkers influenced the first with its focus on equality, "fraternity," and certain rights tempered by duties and responsibilities. The state was cast in a positive light as protector and guarantor of the rights of the needy. At the end of the nineteenth century and the beginning of the twentieth century, as a reaction to the severe effects of industrialization, continental European Socialist and Christian Democratic parties worked toward the creation of social and economic rights.

By contrast, the Anglo-American dialect of rights language highlighted individual freedoms as opposed to equality or social solidarity. In addition, government was not considered to be as benevolent a force. The core differences of these two dialects had largely to do with degree and emphasis. However, the spirit of the traditions spread into their respective societies.

A convergence of these two strains began when Latin American countries achieved independence in the nineteenth century. Most of the countries kept the European-style legal systems while adopting the United States' constitutional model and adding provisions to protect workers and the poor.

The individuals who created the framework of the 1948 Universal Declaration achieved a unique combination of previous considerations about rights and duties. After carefully considering sources from cultures in virtually each corner of the world, the result was a set of core principles that they believed to be so basic that all nations would accept them. A unified document was quickly created and replaced all previous ones as today's human rights instrument. A clear measurement of the success of the human rights idea is the fact that nations and interest groups more and more frame their agendas and seek to justify their actions in terms of human rights.

The Declaration was meant to provide a common standard that "can be brought to life in different cultures in a legitimate variety of ways." A common and unfortunate misunderstanding is the belief that it was designed to impose a single model of conduct. Eleanor Roosevelt clearly understood this dilemma and concomitantly maintained that people need to understand and know the ideals contained within the document and push for them to be actualized. It is all the more important today with the world's contrasting influences of homogenized global forces on the one hand and an increase of ethnic assertiveness on the other. So, it is vital to have clear standards that can lay the foundation for mutual understanding between different cultures. Mrs. Roosevelt once remarked that the UN itself is " a bridge upon which we can meet and talk."

At its core, the Declaration is a document that tries to improve the "odds of reason and conscience against power and interest." Between World War II and the definitive onset of the Cold War, there was barely enough time for major international institutions such as the UN and the World Bank to become established and for the creators of the Universal Declaration to complete their extraordinary task. Almost immediately following its adoption, the brief window of opportunity was shut and remained closed for forty years.

The mounting hostility between the United States and the Soviet Union created a huge obstacle to the drafters of the Declaration as they strove to create a clear set of principles with universal applicability. In addition, they were challenged to overcome linguistic, cultural, and political differences in addition to personal animosities. Yet they succeeded well enough to show that peoples with drastically opposed worldviews can agree upon a few basic standards of decency that are a part of being human—or should be.

Over the ensuing half century, these proved to be contagious. Today many people throughout the world in many ways pursue them earnestly and courageously: within government and nongovernmental agencies, nationally and internationally. Respect for human rights is in itself a major pillar of prevention against violence. It is also a model of the way in which other supports for preventing mass violence may arise in the coming half century. The concomitant movement for human rights and democracy are clearly interrelated. Democratic institutions are the principal means for durable, reliable protection of human rights. In so doing, they contribute mightily to the prospects for just peace.

Human Rights: Prelude to an International Regime for Preventing Deadly Conflict

We have repeatedly noted the link between virulent human rights abuses and the instigation of deadly conflict. Conversely, we have emphasized the importance of reliable safeguards for human rights and the prevention of mass violence.[20]

Few would have assumed that the valiant efforts of Eleanor Roosevelt and her international collaborators in the years immediately following World War II would have set in motion such a pervasive worldwide movement for human rights that is gaining strength every year. Let us briefly look at the evolution of this movement because it is intrinsically important and it may pave the way for a broader international regime to prevent the deadliest conflicts.

The Universal Declaration of Human Rights, which covers the spectrum of rights, bans all forms of discrimination, slavery, torture, and other cruel, inhuman, or degrading treatment or punishment and guarantees every human's right to life, liberty, nationality, freedom of movement, religion, marriage, assembly, and many other fundamental rights and freedoms. One-hundred-thirty states have signed the Universal Declaration since its adoption by the UN General Assembly on December 10, 1948. The International Covenant on Economic, Social and Cultural Rights and the International Covenant on Civil and Political Rights with its two Optional Protocols together form the International Bill of Rights, the cornerstone of the worldwide human rights movement foreshadowed in the UN Charter. Many regional organizations incorporate the International Bill of Rights in their charters and proceedings, and some include additional human rights provisions. For example, the Helsinki Accords—the founding documents of the Conference on Security and Cooperation in Europe (CSCE, now OSCE)—provide, as does the Universal Declaration, for freedom of thought, conscience, religion, and belief.

In the post–World War II setting, human rights have increasingly transcended the boundaries of the nation-state and become a legitimate domain of politics not only for nation-states, but also for international, regional, private transnational, and individual actors. While nation-states continue to be key decisionmakers in contemporary world politics, nonstate actors nonetheless exert significant influence on states' human rights policies.[21] In Forsythe's perspective, a human right is a way to deal with a person's or persons' relations to public authority—and indeed to the rest of society. It involves a fundamental claim that an authority, or some other part of society, do or refrain from doing something that affects significantly the dignity of a human being. He focuses on the political struggle for defining and implementing human rights on a global scale.

Some claim that the notion of human rights is a Western concept that cannot be applied to all nations and cultures and, if it is, a form of cultural imperialism transpires. A growing sector of world opinion believes, however, that human rights are a basic entitlement of all humanity. Indeed, the universality of human rights was unanimously reaffirmed at the Vienna Conference on Human Rights in 1993. The issue is validity, not area of origin. Nearly all non-Western states have signed the UN Charter, with its human rights provisions, and voted for or verbally endorsed the UN's Universal Declaration of Human Rights. Even China signed the basic agreement in 1997 and 1998. Many non-Western states have also included human rights provisions in their constitutions. Some do not adhere strictly to them, but there is internal as well as external pressure to do so. Further, the case for universal human rights underlines the need to restrain state power as well as the power of majorities in society by having recourse to a set of personal legal rights.

Human rights instruments provide a blueprint for good governance. If states use this guidance, they would reduce grievances and thereby the risk of violence. The Human Rights Covenants are basically a prescription for a well-functioning democracy.

Modern technology of international communication and transportation have illuminated standards of decency and augmented human rights demands all over the world. Although the Universal Declaration of Human Rights was adopted in 1948, it was not until 1967 through 1970 that human rights took a prominent place in international relations. Two sweeping covenants on civil-political and economic-social-cultural rights came into legal force for adhering UN states; and the Economic and Social Council

(ECOSOC) authorized the UN Human Rights Commission to examine specific states" human rights records. Then, ECOSOC implemented a systematic procedure for processing private complaints of states' gross violations of human rights. So, it is no longer fashionable for tyrants, petty or grand, to perpetrate atrocities on their own people under the guise of national sovereignty and domestic jurisdiction. They still do so but the risks are greater for them, both from their own people who know what is possible in the world and from the pressure of the international community.

UN human rights activities from 1945 through 1967 consisted mainly of standard setting—that is, the development of declarations and treaties which attempted to specify the human rights content of the UN Charter. Beginning in 1967, the UN expanded its role to include investigation of states' human rights records, the examination of specific problems such as torture or disappeared persons, and provision of technical assistance to states who want to improve their human rights situation. The UN's role in human rights has consistently moved from promotion to protection. Protection includes implementation and enforcement.

This now includes active assistance in helping states to meet their obligations—by helping them incorporate the standards into national constitutions, laws, bills of rights; helping them set up National Human Rights Commissions; and in the training of judges, lawyers, police officers, prison personnel, and armed forces; and in helping them establish parliamentary committees. In line with the assistance approach, this kind of help at the national level really starts to bite in terms of creating national rules and mechanisms to protect and enforce human rights (and national constituencies to demand it). It is hard to discount the importance of these developments.

In the 1990s, a breakthrough came in the creation of a UN high commissioner for human rights. This was a contentious struggle. Not surprisingly, one of the leaders in this creative effort was Jimmy Carter. Kofi Annan appointed a strong and vocal high commissioner, Mary Robinson.

The UN has been most successful on two fronts. It has been instrumental in educating the international community on human rights as well as using human rights as an indicator for granting or withholding legitimacy to specific parties. Taken altogether, these accomplishments have a more long-term than immediate impact. The UN is limited in its power to protect human rights directly because it is not an independent actor with its own resources so much as a collection of member states; further, it is a large, heterogeneous body whose human rights activities often lack effective coordination. Yet, it has raised aspirations, stimulated worldwide interest, and functioned more effectively after the Cold War—reaching its peak with the courageous leadership of Kofi Annan.[22] Its capacities have grown markedly and are now being tested as never before.

Forsythe's study concludes that the internationalization of human rights has caused an "incremental revolution" in international relations. International law has shown an increased human rights content, and states' legal obligations include observance of fundamental rights that preserve human dignity. Moreover, international, regional, and private international bodies have emerged as effective actors in promoting and protecting human rights. Human rights issues have also influenced states' foreign policies (e.g., the disbursement of foreign aid). In analyzing internationally recognized human rights, he puts forward several conclusions. Despite shifts internationally, national public authority is still responsible for key decision making. However, this authority is usually fragmented and parts of it are open to influence from the outside. Private persons and groups are influential at the margins more than the center of human rights policies, yet they are significant. Intergovernmental organizations as part of this private effort have increased their human rights activities and can influence international relations in the long term. While most human rights situations are still viewed as primarily domestic, there are clearly international dimensions, and these are growing. Human rights are more important than ever in international relations. A large part of this significance is the fact that they intersect with such established concerns as state security, economic health, and a viable environment.

Francis Deng, a distinguished African diplomat who served on the Advisory Council of the Carnegie Commission, prepared in 1993 a study in his capacity as representative of the UN Secretary-General on human rights issues related to internally displaced persons.[23] This document focuses on those who have been forced to flee their homes suddenly or unexpectedly in large numbers as a result of armed conflict, internal strife, systematic violations of human rights, or natural or human-caused disasters and who are within the territory of their own country.

Using a broad definition of human rights (including economic, social, and cultural rights), Deng believes that states forfeit their sovereignty when they fail to provide or protect these basic rights. Thus, in the case of internally displaced persons, the international community has a moral and legal right to intervene on behalf of citizens whose rights are ignored, neglected, or violated by the state.

Tens of millions of people, largely women and children, were displaced within their own countries in the 1990s. This is a massive problem. According to a report by the UN Secretary-General, there are six primary causes of displacement (armed conflict and internal strife, forced relocation, communal violence, natural disasters, ecological disasters, and the systematic violation of human rights). Of these, armed conflict, with the attendant violation of human rights, is the most pervasive.

Internal displacement leads to severe violations of human rights. Most of these are obvious, including the right to food, shelter and adequate living conditions, and health care. But it also challenges more mundane but equally important rights that include the right to life and personal integrity; the right to work and to an adequate wage; freedom of residence and movement; family unity; the right to education; and freedom of thought, expression, association, and assembly. Where the causes of internal displacement are natural, governments are often willing to provide assistance and to solicit the aid of the international community. However, when internal dislocation results from armed conflict in a divided country, governments can readily become indifferent or even hostile to the plight of internal refugees. Those displaced find themselves falling into the cleavages of armed conflict or suffering at the hands of the combatants. In these cases, international help is most needed, but often most difficult to provide.

Deng recommends several measures. First, there should be a full examination of current international norms that apply to internally displaced people. Second, governments and international bodies should decide on additional standards that might be needed to address the specific problems of internally displaced persons. Third, a clear set of guidelines should be devised to apply to all internally displaced persons, regardless of the cause of displacement, the country in question, or the prevailing social, political, legal, or military situation. States would be held accountable for these guidelines, as would insurgent groups that have control of areas where displaced persons are located.

The issues surrounding displaced persons are a frontier of human rights activity in which serious efforts are being made. There are a number of necessary activities here. Information on internal displacement and allegations of abuse must be cataloged and disseminated. In the search for remedies, governments and displaced populations must be brought into discussions, and links with UN bodies as well as regional and international organizations should be forged. There is a need for specific field missions to intercede with governments on behalf of the internally displaced, which may include stationing in troubled areas human rights monitors from a variety of organizations. Groups involved should also be prepared to submit a well-documented annual report to the Commission on Human Rights. Such a report can apply pressure on offending governments and insurgent groups. Sometimes public pressure of this kind has been remarkably effective. In the late 1990s, UN High Commissioner for Refugees Sadako Ogata took a prominent and constructive role in this field.

Human Rights: The Cold War Experience

A particular interesting and surprising achievement of the human rights movement occurred in a Cold War context that has come to be called the

Helsinki process. William Korey traces the uneasy start of the Helsinki process in 1973 and its apogee in 1990 and 1991.[24]

The Conference on Security and Cooperation in Europe (CSCE) was the start of the Helsinki process that began in 1973, at the initiation of the former Soviet Union. Soviet leadership wanted to secure an agreement that would legitimate Europe's post–World War II borders and, therefore, Soviet hegemony. Ironically, two decades later, this very process would catalyze the dissolution of the Soviet empire and its satellite system, as well as the ideological structure on which they rested.

U.S. policy toward the CSCE was lukewarm at the outset. President Richard Nixon and Secretary of State Henry Kissinger viewed arms control and economic agreements as the cornerstone of U.S. policy toward Moscow, and they did not want to complicate this policy by supporting the Helsinki process and its emphasis on human rights. In contrast, Western European leadership wanted to push human rights to the center of the Helsinki process, and European leadership remained important throughout.

The first major agreement hammered out through the Helsinki process was the Helsinki Final Act, a 40,000-word document signed by CSCE heads of state on August 1, 1975. This historic document marked the first time that respect for human rights and fundamental freedoms was recognized as a key principle for regulating relations between states. Many resisted this act, both before and after it was adopted. The Soviet Union, for instance, objected to the language on human rights, but eventually accepted it as part of a quid pro quo for Western acceptance of the inviolability of borders in Europe. The United States itself downplayed the significance of the Helsinki Final Act. Kissinger feared that it would lead to an excessive focus on human rights, spurring confrontation and jeopardizing the bilateral relationship with Moscow.

Between 1975 and 1990, the CSCE traversed an occasionally rocky but ultimately successful path. Success came about in no small measure because of a transformed American policy—one that moved from apathy to active and explicit support and participation. Several factors explain this evolution. First, a mostly congressional body called the Commission on Security and Cooperation in Europe (commonly referred to as the U.S. Helsinki Commission) worked actively to reshape U.S. policy. The commission worked not only to reorient U.S. foreign policy, but also to effect domestic change in the human rights sphere. This commission had counterparts of sorts in the Soviet bloc in the form of Helsinki monitoring groups. These included the Moscow Helsinki Watch group, Charter 77 in Czechoslovakia, and, later, Solidarity in Poland. These groups worked with the U.S. commission and U.S. NGOs (e.g., U.S. Helsinki Watch) to stir Western conscience on the human rights issue.

A second factor that changed U.S. policy is the power, diplomacy, and skills of individuals. High on the list is President Carter. His election in

1976 and subsequent leadership moved human rights and the Helsinki process to the forefront of Washington's agenda. His secretary of state, Cyrus Vance, became a vigorous advocate of this position. Two other leaders were former Supreme Court Justice Arthur Goldberg, who represented the United States at Helsinki's first review conference in 1977–1978, and Max Kampelman, who led the U.S. delegation to the Madrid review meeting in 1980–1983. Justice Goldberg made a historic contribution by insisting that, when reviewing the implementation practices of governments, specific names be named and specific cases of violation cited. He offended many diplomats, including some within U.S. ranks, but he nonetheless set a standard of toughness that made the CSCE a forum with genuine teeth. Kampelman continued the practice of mentioning names and cases. With diplomatic skill and intellectual acuity, he built a cohesive group of NATO allies for vigorous pursuit of human rights.

After Gorbachev came to power, there were notable improvements in Soviet human rights policies. Moscow allowed more emigration for Soviet citizens who desired to be reunited with families in the United States, and, in addition, Gorbachev's new thinking led to progressive developments in 1986 at a CSCE conference on confidence-building measures in Stockholm. At this conference, agreements were reached to reduce the risk of surprise attack. The Soviet Union also acceded to unprecedented verification procedures and called for a renewal of conventional arms reductions talks under the Helsinki umbrella.

During the Vienna review meeting in 1986–1989, the United States pursued a policy of linkage between human rights and arms control. Secretary of State George Shultz saw this as an effective track toward satisfactory quid pro quos between Moscow and Washington; the former wanted more progress in arms control, while the latter sought greater Soviet observance of human rights. Shultz's policy of linkage proved successful, particularly after the summer of 1988, when Gorbachev succeeded in overcoming his conservative opposition at home. The Vienna stage of Helsinki yielded very impressive gains for human rights. First, the Soviet Union complied with standards on emigration, freed political prisoners, and stopped foreign radio jamming. Second, the Vienna concluding document far surpassed the Helsinki Final Act in its provisions on the freer movement of people and ideas. Finally, Vienna created unprecedented implementation provisions, which effectively undermined the traditional argument of communist states that internal affairs, including human rights, were not the business of the international community.

Three CSCE conferences on the human dimension followed the Vienna review meeting: Paris (1989), Copenhagen (1990), and Moscow (1991). These conferences further consolidated CSCE accomplishments in the human rights sphere. The CSCE and its contributions to human rights protection facilitated the revolutions in Central and Eastern Europe in 1989. For example, Hungary cited CSCE standards on the rights of anyone to leave any country to refuse East German demands that its "vacationing" citizens, who really intended to go to West Germany, be returned. Overall, the Helsinki process basically kept its promises in the first stage of its work, 1973 to 1991. Its behavior moved beyond anti-Soviet rhetoric to establishing principles and practices for the actual protection of human rights throughout Europe. Elsewhere in this book, we point out some recent accomplishments of what is now the Organization for Security and Cooperation in Europe. It is a constructive part of the new European system for human rights and democracy that has transformed that historically bloody continent and proved a stimulating model for other continents as well. The story of the Helsinki process is a significant part of the worldwide movement toward an international regime for human rights and democracy that points in the direction of a regime for preventing deadly conflict.

Notes

1. Robert A. Dahl, *On Democracy* (New Haven, Conn.: Yale University Press, 1998).

2. Dahl, *On Democracy,* 38, 44–61, 113–14, 145–47.

3. Lisa Anderson, *Transitions to Democracy* (New York: Columbia University Press, 1999); Jack Snyder, *From Voting to Violence: Democratization and Nationalist Conflict* (New York: Norton, 2000); Ben Reilly and Andrew Reynolds, "Electoral Systems and Conflict in Divided Societies," in Paul C. Stern and Daniel Druckman, eds., *International Conflict Resolution After the Cold War* (Washington, D.C.: National Academy Press, 2000), 420–82.

4. Larry Diamond, *Promoting Democracy in the 1990s: Actors and Instruments, Issues and Imperatives* (Report to the Carnegie Commission on Preventing Deadly Conflict, July 1996).

5. Thomas Carothers, *Aiding Democracy Abroad: The Learning Curve* (Washington, D.C.: Carnegie Endowment for International Peace, 1999).

6. Greenberg et. al., *Words over War.*

7. Timothy D. Sisk, *Power Sharing and International Mediation in Ethnic Conflicts* (Washington, D.C.: U.S. Institute of Peace, 1996).

8. Arturo Valenzuela, *The Collective Defense of Democracy: Lessons from the Paraguayan Crisis of 1996* (Report to the Carnegie Commission on Preventing Deadly Conflict, 1999).

9. Peck, *Sustainable Peace,* 106–13.

10. Boutros Boutros-Ghali, "An Agenda for Democratization" (Report of the Secretary-General, support by the United Nations System of the Efforts of Governments to Promote and Consolidate New or Restored Democracies, December 17, 1996).

11. Mendelson and Glenn, *Democracy Assistance.*

12. Ashton Carter and William Perry, *Preventive Defense: A New Security Strategy for America* (Washington, D.C.: Brookings, 1999).

13. Sisk, *Power Sharing.*

14. Mary King, *Mahatma Gandhi and Martin Luther King, Jr.: The Power of Nonviolent Action* (Paris: UNESCO, 1999), 419–20.

15. Peter Ackerman and Jack Duvall, *A Force More Powerful: A Century of Nonviolent Action* (New York: St. Martin's, 2000), 421–54.

16. Albert Cevallos, *Whither the Bulldozer? Nonviolent Revolution and the Transition to Democracy in Serbia* (United States Institute of Peace Special Report, August 6, 2001).

17. Carnegie Commission on Preventing Deadly Conflict, *Preventing Deadly Conflict*, 125–27.

18. Larry Diamond, *Developing Democracy Toward Consolidation* (Baltimore: Johns Hopkins University Press, 1999).

19. Mary Ann Glendon, preface to *A World Made New: Eleanor Roosevelt and the Universal Declaration of Human Rights* (New York: Random House, 2001), xv–xxi.

20. Hamburg, "Human Rights."

21. David P. Forsythe, *The Internationalization of Human Rights* (Lexington, Mass.: Lexington Books, 1991).

22. Annan, *Towards a Culture of Prevention.*

23. Francis M. Deng, "Further Promotion and Encouragement of Human Rights and Fundamental Freedoms, Including the Question of the Programme and Methods of Work of the Commission" (Study to the Economic and Social Council, Commission on Human Rights, 1993); Francis M. Deng, *Protecting the Dispossessed: A Challenge for the International Community* (Washington, D.C.: Brookings, 1993).

24. William Korey, *The Promises We Keep: Human Rights, The Helsinki Process, and American Foreign Policy.* (New York: Institute for East–West Studies, 1993).

7

Toward Competent, Decent, and Prosperous States: Updating Socioeconomic Development

On the Ground in Tanzania: The Anguish of Development

On May 19, 1975, a heavily armed group of insurgents crossed Lake Tanganyika in the middle of the night and kidnapped four of my students conducting primate research at the Gombe Stream Research Center in Tanzania. I went immediately from California to Tanzania to see what I could do to help. Who had taken these students and why? Were they still alive? What, if any, actions could we take to find and free them?

It turned out that the lead hostage taker was Laurent Kabila, who a quarter century later became president of the Republic of Congo. His brief moment of glory ended with his own assassination in early 2001 after he had enmeshed the Congo in a war that has drawn in several neighboring states and caused immense suffering. The main object of his wrath in 1975 was then President Julius Nyerere of Tanzania as well as President Mobutu Sese Seko of Zaire. We were caught in the middle, pawns in a deadly postcolonial power struggle for the control of Zaire/Congo. It was only after months of intensive negotiations and some cloak-and-dagger activity that we were able to obtain the release of all four students.

These several months exposed me vividly to some of the sources of violent conflict: social breakdown, abject poverty, rampant disease, oppressive dictatorships, fear and hatred, and egregious violations of basic human rights. I was never the same again. Coupled with my research, this profound experience turned me toward a deeper quest for understanding the causes of human conflict and an active search for more effective practices of conflict resolution and violence prevention.

When I got back to Dar es Salaam at the end, when the fourth and final hostage was released, I found a letter from the then president of the National Academy of Sciences, Dr. Philip Handler, offering me the presidency of the Institute of Medicine. Shortly before the hostage episode, I had been approached about this possibility and had declined to be considered, even though I was certainly honored. I loved what I was doing and had no desire to move. But when I got this letter from him at the end of the hostage episode, just a few months later, it was a different matter. The core of his message was that an extraordinary experience of this sort might make me want to reconsider how to make the best use of my career. I did not know whether that was the right move, to the Institute of Medicine, but Handler was right, I needed to rethink.

Should I devote the remainder of my career to positions where I could, however slightly, have an impact on those terrible problems? Could I deal with policy questions and practices in professions and institutions that would have some impact on hatred and violence and abject poverty and terrible diseases?

One indelible imprint of the primate research in Africa and the hostage episode was my concern about developing countries. When I moved to the Institute of Medicine in 1975, I initiated a program in international health that continues to the present time. When Jimmy Carter came to the presidency in 1977, he and his colleagues—especially Dr. Peter Bourne, Secretary of Health and Human Services Joseph Califano, and Surgeon General Julius Richmond—took a keen interest in what we were doing. A cooperative relationship ensued in which the United States rapidly expanded its health activities in developing countries. President Carter has remained deeply engaged in this field to the present day, especially in Africa. Over the years I have tried to help him with this work and now serve on the board of the Carter Center.

I also became deeply engaged in the work of the World Health Organization (WHO), again focusing on developing countries. I served for the better part of a decade on the Advisory Committee on Medical Research of the WHO, working with wonderful colleagues from all parts of the world such as Dr. Ramalingaswami of India, Dr. Sune Bergstrom of Sweden, Dr. John Evans of Canada, Dr. Thomas Lambo of Nigeria, Dr. Norman Sartorius of Yugoslavia, Dr. Halfdan Mahler of Denmark, and Dr. Gus Nossal of Australia. Among other activities, we assisted a major program of research on tropical diseases headed by Dr. A. O. Lucas of Nigeria. Later, I recruited Dr. Lucas and his collaborator Dr. Patricia Rosenfield to head Carnegie's program in developing countries. During the fourteen and a half years of my Carnegie presidency, we maintained a program on African development, with special attention to South Africa. The foci of our efforts were these:

- Building democratic institutions.
- Strengthening the role of women in development, with special attention to health and education.
- Investing in science and technology for development

These continuing interests are reflected in this chapter. Their urgency is greater than ever in light of the recent devastating wars in Africa, which reflect failures in development, and the clear evidence that development failures readily breed rampant disease and international terrorism. Yet, we have learned a lot from some very promising democratic developments in South Africa and a variety of other countries in Asia and Latin America. It is surely time to put this knowledge to work in preventing deadly conflict.

Cumulative Evidence and Emerging Concepts of Development

The establishment of new democracies requires decades or even generations, so we must be persistent and resourceful in working with democratic reformers all over the world. The gradual emergence of democratic and prosperous countries will reduce the likelihood of catastrophic terrorism and devastating wars. This requires special attention to the Southern Hemisphere and the post-Communist countries.

We have learned important lessons from successes and failures of socioeconomic development in Asia, Africa, and Latin America during the past half century. Yet much of the world's population still cannot rely on ready access to food, water, shelter, and other necessities of life. Why are there still widely prevalent threats to survival when modern science and technology have made such powerful contributions to human well-being? What can we do to diminish the kind of vulnerability that leads to desperation and hatred? The slippery slope of degradation so vividly exemplified in several areas of abject poverty in Africa and Asia leads to great danger of infectious disease pandemics, civil war, terrorism, mass migration, and humanitarian catastrophe.

Development efforts to meet decent living standards require significant help from affluent states, international organizations, and multinational firms. Development assistance, especially capacity building, is crucial for very poor countries. Yet fundamental, long-term solutions hinge on states' own development policies, attentive to the particular needs of a society's economic and social sectors with careful management of natural and human resources. These policies can be influenced constructively by the international community.

Many nations in the global south and in devastated countries such as Afghanistan have been late in getting access to the unprecedented opportunities now available for economic and social development. They are seeking ways to develop in keeping with their own cultural traditions and distinctive settings. They need help in finding ways to adapt useful tools from the world's experience for their own development. It is surely in the interest of countries near and far away to facilitate the development of knowledge, skill, and freedom in these countries so they can become contributing, responsible members of the international community rather than breeding grounds for social pathology, epidemic disease, and widespread violence.

In this context, the Carnegie Commission emphasized that economic growth without widespread sharing in the benefits of that growth will not reduce prospects for violent conflict. Indeed, intense resentment and unrest can be induced by drastically inequitable economic opportunity. This reinforces the desirability of helping poor countries to foster political as well as economic development. It is important to keep in mind that an avoidable excess of human suffering generates resentment that can easily become the seedbed for hatred, violence, and terrorism.

During the 1990s, a substantial effort has been made by individuals and institutions to understand the development experience of the second half of the twentieth century and to learn from it—both its successes and failures. One major feature of this effort has been to take a broader view of the development process, recognizing the crucial importance of *human development*, linking social and economic considerations. One influential source of analysis has come from the human development reports of the United Nations Development Program (UNDP). Under the remarkable leadership of Mahbub ul Haq of Pakistan, with the eminent economist Amartya Sen as a major advisor, a series of reports in the early 1990s made the case for the human factor in development with hard data and close observation of the development process over decades.

The approach is carried further in a new book by Sen, who received the 1998 Nobel Prize in economic science.[1] He views development fundamentally as a process of expanding the real freedoms that people enjoy. Therefore, development requires removal of major obstacles to freedom: poverty, poor economic opportunities linked with systematic social deprivation, neglect of public facilities, social intolerance, tyranny, and repressive states. He illuminates the paradox that, despite great economic growth and indeed opulence on a worldwide basis, vast numbers of human beings lack elementary freedoms. Thus, their potential to fulfill their personal capacities and to contribute to economic growth and social development is stunted. To liberate this unfilled human potential, it is essential to enhance political participation, to receive basic education and health care, and to live in a context of respect for human rights. These circumstances are not only of value to the individual, but they contribute powerfully to the economic progress of the society. Like the UNDP reports, he advocates public policy to foster human capabilities and substantive freedoms. In doing so, he highlights five distinct types of freedoms viewed instrumentally: political freedoms, economic facilities, social opportunities, transparency guarantees, and protective security. He identifies empirical evidence showing how these instrumental freedoms interact to advance individual capability and social well-being.

This outlook converges to a considerable extent with recent developments at the World Bank. These have been pursued in a series of important analytic papers by the distinguished economist Joseph Stiglitz, who until recently was senior vice president of development economics and chief economist at the World Bank.[2] In 2001, he was the recipient of the Nobel Prize in economics. This work makes clear that the evidence of the last quarter century is unequivocal with respect to dramatic advances made in many parts of the developing world. There is no longer any basis for pessimism referring to never-to-be-developed countries. There have been remarkable gains in life expectancy and per capita annual incomes. But there are regional differences, with sub-Saharan Africa lagging far behind most others. Overall, evidence indicates that rapid development is possible, and understanding has deepened about the factors that make such development actually occur. The record of the past quarter century shows that aggregate economic growth benefits most of the people most of the time and usually is linked to tangible progress in social dimensions of development. Indeed, per capita growth above 2 percent usually benefits poor people. Further, egalitarian societies can generate high levels of savings and investment.

Stiglitz points to examples such as South Korea to show how progress has been made in some countries on both income and nonincome measures of development. (We consider South Korea later in this chapter.) These two kinds of measures tend to reinforce each other. Investments in people, particularly in terms of education and health, stimulate economic growth. This, in turn, provides resources that can be further invested in people toward a higher level of development.

The experience of the past few decades has also shown that highly centralized state planning is not an effective development strategy. Its failures have occurred not only in the communist countries but elsewhere. There is increasing recognition that private investment is an important part of economic development, alongside public sector investment.

The conditions that lead to high rates of private investment are particularly important. They involve a policy environment that is credible to investors, an open competitive economy, and an honest effective public sector—the latter involving sound macroeconomic policy, with fiscal and monetary discipline, but also transparency and an effective legal-judicial system. This provides the opportunity to enforce contracts. Without that, nepotism and cronyism become very prominent and sooner or later weaken the economy. Studies have shown that high levels of corruption and the absence of the rule of law are highly detrimental to investment as well as to human rights.

Openness to competition in the world economy is by and large another positive force. Stiglitz points out that the successful East Asian countries have been much more open than the less economically successful countries in

South Asia, Latin America, and sub-Saharan African. Openness also facilitates acquiring knowledge anywhere in the world and adapting it for local use—a prominent feature of East Asian economic success. This attribute becomes all the more important in a world of rapidly evolving economic opportunities related to new technology, and it cuts both ways in the opening of markets by rich countries as well as poor.

An effective public sector provides adequate defense without huge investment in military hardware, is attentive to equity and has mechanisms for redistribution of income, has a viable legal-judicial system, has reasonable regulation of financial markets and protection of the environment—all are beneficial for the population in social and economic terms. The point is even more vivid in relation to the provision of universal opportunities for education and health.

Stiglitz and Squire make an important observation about financial markets. While financial markets are central to a flourishing market economy, nearly all successful economies are well regulated. Rather than strangling investment, these regulations make sure that fair competition is maintained and consumers are protected, assure the sound condition of financial institutions, and allow that a cross-section of groups has access to capital. Their summarizing comment is of special interest:

> We have broadened the development agenda to include democratic, equitable, sustainable development that raises living standards on a broad basis, and we have brought to bear a wider set of instruments—not just sound macroeconomic policies and trade liberalization, but also strong financial markets, enhanced competition, and improved public services. There have been major advances in our understanding of development.

The World Bank's *World Development Report 1996* as well as the 1999/2000 report provide useful insights. They derive lessons of experience from economies in transition from central planning to market-based operation—building essential institutions to support efficient markets with adequate social safety nets. What does the experience of transition to date suggest for the many other countries grappling with similar issues of economic reform? The newest report assesses current reformulations of development thinking, including the world trading and financial systems, with special attention placed on cities.[3]

1. Consistent policies, combining liberalization of markets, trade and new business entry with reasonable price stability, can achieve a great deal—even in countries lacking clear property rights and strong market institutions.
2. Differences between countries are very important, both in setting the feasible range of policy choice and in determining the response to reforms.

3. An efficient response to market processes requires clearly defined property rights—and this will eventually require *widespread* private ownership. [italics mine]
4. Major changes in social policies must complement the move to the market—to focus on relieving poverty, to cope with increased mobility, and to counter the adverse intergenerational effects of reform.
5. Sustaining the human capital base for economic growth requires considerable reengineering of education and health delivery systems. International integration can help lock in successful reforms.

I have been deeply impressed with the great preventive value in initiatives that focus on children and women, not least because these groups make up the greatest proportion of victims of conflict and because women represent a large and neglected potential for economic, intellectual, and political as well as social contributions. A growing body of evidence shows that the education of females is a highly valuable investment for developing countries. It enhances women's skills and choices, improves their health and nutrition. Health studies show that the more educated the mothers, the less likely that their children will die, regardless of differences in family income. Education helps delay marriage for women, partly by increasing their chances for employment, and educated women are more likely to know about and use contraceptives. With education and modest borrowing opportunities, women contribute significantly to economic growth.

Enhancement of respect and opportunities for women can have a powerful effect on family planning in the broadest and most fundamental sense. Science and technology can contribute greatly to the reduction of environmental threats by developing technologies that pollute less and by designing measures to mitigate environmental degradation. Indeed, the judicious use of science and technology is a key element in development, yet curiously neglected in many countries as if it were a luxury for rich countries. On the contrary, participation in the world economy now requires a modicum of technical competence everywhere.

In my view, the essential ingredients for development center around knowledge, skill, and freedom. Knowledge is mainly generated by research and development; skills are mainly generated by education and training; freedom is mainly generated by democratic institutions.

Significant improvement has occurred in many measures of health, education, and well-being around the world, due largely to the spread of modern science and technology. Infant mortality rates have declined, while life expectancy has increased. Many diseases have been brought under control, with the total eradication of smallpox being the most dramatic case. (Ironically, bioterrorism may now bring it back.) Nutritional indicators have improved in most places (though serious problems remain in sub-Saharan Africa). Educational levels are rising and education has become more widely available. These trends deserve reinforcement by policies fostering science and technology for development as well as education at all levels. International cooperation is essential for the effective implementation of such policies. Nowhere are these concepts more vivid and challenging than in relation to HIV and AIDS. It is crucial to build local capacity by promoting individual and group competence; generating relevant, new knowledge; diffusing knowledge to potential users and refining this knowledge through application; creating institutions to support education, research, and knowledge diffusion; and enhancing the capacity of public and private organizations to reach sound decisions based on objective analysis.

Promoting competent governance has become crucial in development, along with the building of fundamental skills for participation in the modern global economy. This means that a state must build a professional, accountable civil service that can provide an enabling economic environment and handle macroeconomic management, sustained poverty reduction, education and training, technical competence, and protection for the environment. To bring these complex, crucial tasks to fruition requires sustained international (even global) development cooperation, involving government aid agencies, UN agencies, nongovernmental organizations, educational and research institutions, and private firms. Knowledge and skill come from many sources. International support networks can foster much of what needs to be done in every field of development.

Professor Jeffrey Sachs, director of the Center for International Development at Harvard University, has recently delineated what he calls a "New Global Consensus on Helping the Poorest of the Poor."[4] He describes four pillars of this consensus. One is economic reform along the lines suggested in this chapter. Another is maintaining a population that is sufficiently healthy and educated so that it can participate in the world economy. This pillar may be undermined by the now rampant AIDS epidemic or widespread malaria, degraded tropical soils, or extreme scarcity of clean water. The third pillar of development is technology. A multifaceted system of private, public, and academic institutions provides the foundation for technological advance. Financing typically comes from the government and foundations, as well as capital markets. Technological development in and for the poorest countries must specifically address such problems as the impact of infectious diseases, enhanced crops that can withstand the stresses of climate, and energy alternatives that can reduce the rate of deforestation. Sachs's fourth pillar of poverty reduction is structural adjustment, especially export diversification. This requires an industrial strategy to foster new kinds of industry, and it requires open markets in the developed countries for manufactured exports from the poorest countries, especially textiles and garments in the near term.

The broader view of development that emerged in the 1990s is well exemplified in the World Bank's leadership by James Wolfensohn. He has formulated a long-term, holistic, and strategic approach in which all the component parts are brought together.[5]

> Building new schools is of no use without roads to get the children to schools and without trained teachers, books and equipment. Establishing banks and financial institutions without a banking system that is supervised will lead to chaos. Initiatives to make progress creating equal opportunities for women make no sense if women have to spend many hours a day carrying clean water, or finding and gathering fuel for cooking. Seeking universal primary education without prenatal health care means that children get to school mentally and physically damaged. Establishing a health system but doing nothing about clean water and sewerage diminishes enormously the impact of any effort. Seeking equity when government is riddled with corruption and has inefficient and untrained officials is an objective that will never be realized.

The World Bank must focus on structural factors. Larger efforts for change are dependent on good and clean government; an effective legal and justice system; a well-organized and supervised financial system; a social safety net and social programs. The World Bank must also give determined attention to human factors from education and knowledge institutions to health and population issues. The well-being of people must also take into account their physical surroundings that can require efforts to improve water and sewerage; power; roads, transportation, and telecommunications; and other environmental concerns. The program Wolfensohn advocates and puts the formidable resources of the Bank behind is an open, participatory process of formulating and implementing development strategies. This is a process that will systematically involve governments, multilateral and bilateral participants, civil society, and the private sector.

President Carter is leading an effort of this sort in Guyana with promising results. This work flows from a task force of the Carnegie Commission on Science, Technology and Government.[6] Such farsighted, integrative efforts as those of Carter and Wolfensohn update decades of development experience in a modern synthesis that could finally lead the way out of the morass of abject poverty, dictatorship, and civil war.

UN Secretary-General Annan linked equitable economic development with conflict prevention in an address at the World Bank in 1999.[7] He endorsed President Wolfensohn's call for the Bank and its partners to start asking hard questions about ways to integrate a concern for conflict prevention into development operations.

> If conflict is often caused by different groups having unequal access to political power, then it follows that a good way to avoid conflict is to encourage

democracy—not the winner-take-all variety, but inclusive democracy, which gives everyone a say in decisions that affect their lives. . . .

Democracy is, in essence, a form of non-violent conflict management. But a note of caution is in order. While the end result is highly desirable, the process of democratization can be highly destabilizing—especially when states introduce "winner-take-all" electoral systems without adequate provision for human rights. At such times different groups can become more conscious of their unequal status, and nervous about each other's power. Too often, they resort to pre-emptive violence. But that should not discourage us from urging the right sort of democratization, as part of our development policies. . . . If war is the worst enemy of development, healthy and balanced development is the best form of conflict prevention.

Building democratic societies with market economies in a technically competent and ethically sound way is a clear path to structural prevention. In this direction, albeit with large bumps in the road over long and hard distances, can be found the conditions conducive to peaceful and productive living.

Learning from Successful Cases: The Stimulus to Adapt and Update Elsewhere

One of the stark, vivid lessons the 1990s taught us—and one that we should have known before—is that disintegrating, incompetent governments constitute a great danger, especially when they are poor and getting poorer, discriminatory, and getting repressive.

They involve many kinds of suffering for their own people—and they tend to fall into the hands of hard, indecent "leaders" whose proclivity to mass violence is insidious at home and abroad. These countries, if they slide into degradation, are candidates for mass expulsion and refugee flows that are tragic and destabilizing for the region; genocide; fostering of international terrorism; and breeding grounds for exceedingly dangerous infectious diseases of worldwide jeopardy.

So, tackling this problem is not alone a matter of altruism and generosity on the part of the more competent and affluent international community, but also a matter of utmost significance to the maintenance of a decent and secure world.

This is not primarily a problem for traditional overseas development aid—though that is still important and cannot safely become a moribund victim of "compassion fatigue." Publics in highly capable and rich areas such as the United States, Europe, and Japan must realize what a tiny fraction of their human and financial resources go into tackling this fundamental problem that, in the long run, affects everyone for better or worse—

much worse if we follow the path we are now on. The distinguished economist Paul Krugman of Princeton University estimates that an additional dime a day per American citizen would make a profound difference in world development capacity. As it is now, the United States is far behind other established democracies in per capita support of development.[8]

Have such problems been overcome at some times and places? For heuristic purposes, let us examine an example that may at least open the door to this vital problem, even though it differs in some respects from current situations.

South Korea, in particular, is emblematic. It went from being a society shattered by partition and war with a per capita income equal to that of Ghana in 1950 (one of the lowest in the world at the time) to a modern, industrial, export-driven economy in the space of a generation. To observers around the globe this was stunning. Its major development over the past five decades does not provide a literally transferable model for other international efforts, but does offer some suggestions that can inform future aid activities. There are factors in its development that can be adapted to other situations of development.

By 1953, South Koreans had endured, in the space of a decade, the impact of World War II, the troubling division of the peninsula into rival northern and southern armed camps, and then a massive international war that killed millions. It was a country severely impoverished and deeply troubled. Its problems were serious and exacerbated by the recently concluded war. It is similar in some respects to countries today, such as Cambodia, that are only beginning to recover from prolonged conflicts. However, South Korea, because of historical circumstances, had access to considerable outside support that kept it from lingering in this troubled state. We view the aid to South Korea in historical context because it shows some of the structural reasons why aid worked and the atmosphere in which it was seen to be necessary and justified.

Explanations of the success of South Korea have dealt with cultural factors that predisposed the country to modern development. Positive influences are seen in Confucian tradition and long-standing commercial attitudes; also of cultural emphasis on education. However, there is one clear historical dividing line—the Japanese empire. Korea had long suffered at the hands of powerful neighbors. Imperial Russia and Japan split Korea into respective spheres of influence at the 38th Parallel at the end of the nineteenth century. It was only after Russia's defeat at the hands of Japan in 1905 that Japan had uncontested authority in the region. In 1910, de facto control of the peninsula became colonial control when Japan annexed Korea. Russia and China, the latter traditionally Korea's patron and protector, due to military weakness did not protest; Britain, dependent on Japan's presence in a military alliance to maintain the balance of power in

East Asia, let the issue pass, and the United States, despite an 1882 treaty to support Korea, had previously come to an agreement with Japan that promised the island nation a free hand in Korea if Japan gave up any complaints over the United States' newly acquired colony in the Philippines.

Japan's rule is an extremely sensitive issue. There is a great deal of awareness in South Korea of the brutality of Japan's imperial government. One Japanese minister recently had to resign after a furor erupted in South Korea when he said that Japan's empire had "done some good things for Korea." There is ample reason for sensitivity. Japan colonized a complex society with a well-defined culture. Japanese methods of control were often repressive and, at points, brutal. There were attempts to replace the local culture by banning the Korean language and educating only in the Japanese tongue and customs. Yet, Japan also put into place or further developed many aspects of modern society. Beyond a comprehensive mass education system that reached a majority of the Korean population (although few were let into technical or postsecondary education), Japan also established an effective national police force that reached down to almost every village. Japan also built up the transportation and communication infrastructure.

Korea was seized for strategic reasons and put to work as a cog in Japan's imperial system. The colonial authorities either created or reorganized farming that provided for intensive cultivation and export of crops. In fact, rice production in Korea by the 1930s was more productive per acre than in the United States (which had a fairly large and advanced rice export sector). In the 1930s, Korea was singled out for large-scale industrialization. The Japanese built large chemical, steel, and electricity production facilities, mainly in the north. By the end of World War II, Japan had done some of the important groundwork for a modern, industrial, and export-based economy—albeit at a heavy social cost.

The end of the World War II saw the end of the Japanese empire. Korea was slated for independence in the 1943 Cairo Declaration but was split between the United States and the Soviet Union at the 38th Parallel (a hasty decision made without full knowledge of the situation on the ground or the previous division at the same point). The division of the Korean peninsula by the United States and Soviet Union eventually solidified into two separate and opposed regimes in the north and south. In the north there emerged a pro-Soviet regime under Kim Il Sung, who inherited much of the industry built up by the Japanese. On the southern half of the peninsula a pro-American government under Syngman Rhee took power. Rhee, a nationalist and long-time opponent of Japan's rule, inherited a country that was mainly rural and agricultural in orientation. However, both new countries suffered from the fact that they had once been a unified economic entity (some of North Korea's recent problems with agriculture are echoes of this split). Neither could meet their needs without outside support. Also, from the beginning, the two regimes sought to undermine each other. There were rebellions, border fighting, and rabid propaganda meant to overthrow the other and establish one government as ruler of a united Korea.

These desires spilled over into international war in June 1950. Kim, after securing the support of Mao Tse-tung and Stalin, launched an assault on the south after a long period of border skirmishing.[9] The United States quickly intervened, an action that eventually brought Communist China into the war. The Soviet Union participated by loaning pilots and aircraft to the Chinese, but did not directly or officially intervene in the war. However, to Americans the war in Korea seemed to be absolute proof of coordinated communist expansionist plans in Asia. The North Korean invasion of the south sharply exacerbated the Cold War.

Beyond the U.S. military commitment to Korea, there began a massive aid program to reconstruct the south. There had been American economic aid before the war, but these new programs dwarfed those preceding them. South Korea became the largest development project in the world in the 1950s.

Americans had a fairly long history of aid to Asian nations, a good portion of which was connected to the region under discussion. NGOs had been active in famine relief and development in 1930s China, and much of this expertise carried over into U.S. and UN aid agencies that operated there in the late 1940s. Many ideas and staff found their way to Korea. This is a reminder that the prominence of NGOs in this arena of international relations is not altogether a recent occurrence. Moreover, some development successes are based on long-term engagement on particular issues. Much development was collaborative between local authorities, the U.S. state, and NGOs. Many ideas implemented in the postwar period came from previous experimentation, which probably contributed to their success. In short, the development efforts undertaken after the Korean War had to cope with historical and recent devastation and oppression. Yet, it had latent assets in historical and cultural factors that provided useful precursors for development. Identifying latent positive factors can be useful in most development efforts anywhere in the world.

The Republic of Korea (ROK) was one of the largest recipients of U.S. foreign aid in the twentieth century. Although they were couched as "reconstruction" programs, they sought to make a new and stable state, a "South Korea," where none had existed before.[10] From 1945, there were ongoing U.S. rehabilitation efforts in the southern half of Korea. The United States had supported agricultural and educational reform up to the start of the Korean War. With the start of the international war in Korea in 1950, the scale of the reconstruction programs vastly increased. The United States brought the UN into the development program by helping to fund the United Nations Korean Reconstruction Agency (UNKRA), which was to carry the banner of a unified effort to rebuild Korea. However, within a few years American policy shifted to emphasize a bilateral effort to help Korea (the UN remained, but in a shrinking role). Hundreds of NGOs operated in Korea, from missionary groups, to Cooperative for American Relief to Everywhere (CARE), university groups, even the Boy Scouts—all bringing their accrued knowledge and enthusiasm. These efforts were not unlike concurrent NGO activity in such places as Taiwan and India. Korea's reconstruction was a massive, high-profile, sustained, and collaborative effort between intergovernmental groups, governments, and NGOs.

The war-damaged and underdeveloped country was transformed into a modern society by this effort. Koreans viewed the Japanese influence in a very negative light, especially in the realms of language and education. Major reforms in education were undertaken to combat this legacy. Education was widely emphasized and technical schools were established to provide the engineers and technicians that simply did not exist, since the Japanese had refused to educate Koreans in these areas. Also, thousands of Koreans were sent overseas to study, mostly in the United States. In these exchanges, they not only acquired knowledge and technical skills but also absorbed the values of democracy.

The Americans emphasized agricultural development, as the majority of the population was rural. They encouraged rice exports to Japan (even to the point of encouraging people to eat barley so that their rice could be sold abroad). Conservation projects for forestry were instituted, fisheries were supported, irrigation plans instituted, and fertilizer provided across this sector of the economy.

Industrial development was also sought, but it was beset by a lack of trained engineers and a lack of electricity. The division of the peninsula at the 38th Parallel had deep and prolonged effects. Most of the electric current had been generated in the north, and, with the emergence of separate regimes in 1948, this had been switched off. Into the 1950s the United States struggled with a shortage of current, which hampered efforts in many spheres of activity.[11]

By the end of the 1950s, the Americans were complaining about the lack of progress in the Republic of Korea. Despite high hopes and massive aid at all levels of society, South Korea was seen as a lingering problem. Clearly short-term expectations had been unrealistic in the immediate post–Korean War period. Yet, wonder of wonders, by 1965 South Korea had come to be seen in Washington as a developmental success. Possibly the biggest reason for optimism was the new military regime of Park Chung Hee. Park had come to power in 1961 after overthrowing a short-lived democratic government that, in turn, had replaced the authoritarian clique around Rhee in

1960. The Americans were at first cool to Park and the colonels who led the coup. As Park's emphasis on modernization came into focus, he gained increasing favor with the Kennedy and Johnson administrations.

Park and the men around him followed a program the Americans desired. The basic goal of this new Korean government was economic growth. Park spoke of a program by which the "modernization of man" would provide for economic expansion. Park was willing to have South Korea play the critical role forced on it by the needs of an American-dominated East Asian regional system. Trade with Japan was emphasized.

Park understood that the Cold War needs of the United States in East Asia gave him considerable power in dealing with his American patron. There was a great deal of rhetoric of cooperation that surrounded this relationship and also considerable cooperative action. Park dispatched a 50,000-man expeditionary force to support the U.S. effort in Vietnam. South Korea also benefited hugely from American offshore procurement for the war in Southeast Asia (it was in a position similar to that of Japan during the Korean War). Some of this procurement in the Republic of Korea was a reward for its unequivocal support in Vietnam. Many large Korean conglomerates were either founded or hit their stride during this period.[12]

The middle years of the 1960s also brought increasing Japanese involvement in Korea. With normalized relations, Japanese capital flowed into Korea, supporting the impressive economic expansion. By 1963, imports from Japan had tripled. Japan was playing the role of regional center envisioned by the United States. Part of this position included its central role in founding the Asian Development Bank (ADB). By the end of the 1960s, some 40 percent of all of the ADB's loans would find their way to Korea. Regionalism appeared to be paying off. Indeed, by the mid-1960s, the United States was no longer providing economic assistance aid grants to Korea. Military aid continued, but further U.S. economic support came only in the form of loans, a sign the United States saw the Korean economy as basically sound.[13]

Park led what has come to be seen as a primary example of the "developmental state." South Korea's state had considerable power (and faced little domestic opposition) to mobilize resources toward the goal of economic growth. One of the major reasons for the success of this program is the fact that the United States and Japan were willing to secure financial resources for the country. Nevertheless, the domestic organization of the Republic of Korea's developmental state is crucial. These observations provide a useful example of a dynamic interplay between insiders and outsiders in development.

Park made his regime dependent on the business community without forcing state planning on the marketplace. Some have characterized it as "government as the chairman of the board." The state, through direct contacts, personal relationships, and even ownership of stock in the business sector, created a relationship in which the government and business depended on one another without one sector dominating the other. It did not foster an open, democratic, or honest system, but it did lead to economic growth. In the meantime, democratic undercurrents were gathering momentum that would come to eventual fruition.

Park and his junta were far from democratic. The United States, as the leading patron of his government, understood this and essentially made a deal with the military regime. The United States, while never comfortable with the lack of democracy in South Korea, placed a greater value on building a stable non-Communist state in East Asia. After the Korean War, the United States simply would not allow South Korea to degrade or collapse. There was a deep American military and financial commitment to the struggling state. However, it also meant that the democratic shortcomings of Park were overlooked.[14]

In the 1970s, the American strategic retrenchment known as the "Nixon Doctrine," the oil shocks, and inflation had detrimental effects on Korean growth. In response, there was the nationalist "Big Push" by Park to create independent heavy industries (chemical, shipbuilding, steel, and defense). This had some success but also came at a high price socially. To force through these programs in an increasingly difficult domestic and international economic environment, the Park regime increasingly turned to the suppression of dissent and strong-arm tactics. The ballot box was ignored and the regime waged a "dirty war" against opponents; some simply disappeared. Indeed, the current president of South Korea, Kim Dae-jung, as an opposition leader in the 1970s, was nearly a victim of this repression. He was kidnapped by South Korean intelligence operatives in 1973, and his political murder was only avoided when the U.S. and Japanese governments vigorously intervened. In the 1980s, he was sentenced to death by the military regime, but, again, domestic and international pressure caused the sentence to be commuted to life imprisonment, and he was later released.[15]

This violence of the government against its own people reached a crescendo in 1979 during the Kwangju uprising in which perhaps several thousand people were killed by the regime's troops. The tensions whipped up by the regime could not be avoided, not even at the center of power itself. Park himself was a victim of violence that same year, shot dead by his own intelligence chief.

The inequities in South Korea, perpetuated by the military regime, became increasingly intolerable to growing sections of the population—particularly its professional and middle classes. Protests became commonplace and eventually forced changes on the military regime in the 1980s. Democracy came slowly. It was only with the election of Kim Dae Jung in 1997 that an opposition party took the reins of the government. Politics remain tense, but on the whole the country's democratic success now finally matches its economic success.

Some asserted that the authoritarianism of the military regime in South Korea (and elsewhere) was a prerequisite for its impressive economic growth. Only that sort of authority, it was assumed, could discipline a country to develop. However, looking back we can see that it also heavily increased costs. South Korea under military rule gained an improved standard of living. Yet, that same rule heightened tensions, leading to violence within the society that claimed a significant number of lives and had profound costs that are still being paid today. Economic development, as the case of South Korea shows, could not—and cannot—alone produce social harmony. It is a reminder that democratic, pluralistic policies are not a luxury in international development. Without them the potential for serious conflict is likely to be heightened.

American aid to South Korea in the second half of the twentieth century shows the importance of long-term relationships in helping troubled states. The prognosis in the 1950s that Korea could recover from partition and war in only a few years was shown to be badly misguided. Aid had to be stretched over decades. It was also effective because it was multisided. While aid from the U.S. government predominated, it must not be forgotten that other states in the region (notably Japan), the UN, NGOs, and international financial institutions played important roles at certain times.

The depth and prolonged character of American aid also means the United States must take some responsibility for South Korea's domestic strains. Even with reservations, the United States accepted an authoritarian and often corrupt military regime in South Korea in keeping with its view of Cold War requirements. However, it is also true that the U.S. government as well as sectors of its civil society (notably the media, NGOs, and academics) were also active over a long period in bringing pressure on the regime to moderate its course politically. This was part of a larger burst of international criticism in the 1980s and 1990s that made the junta's position increasingly untenable. Democratic change in South Korea was largely the product of arduous work of the Koreans themselves but international concern had a vital role to play. Today, we can draw from both the positives and the negatives of the Korean experience to illuminate the potential of development to prevent violent conflict.

Many of the imperatives that drove the commitment to develop South Korea are missing in today's world. The deep commitment by the United States to South Korea and the East Asian region was largely a function of the Cold War. This made the huge outlays in money, resources, personnel, and time appealing to different groups in government and civil society within the United States. Today, a similar set of motives is lacking. Yet, it is possible to imagine other motives that might impel the international community to make such a deep engagement in countries similar to the South Korea of a half century ago. In chapter 9, we consider this problem in the context of preventing international terrorism.

Implications of the Korean Experience

The example of South Korea shows that the presence of a "development mentor" can be an element of success. The economic aid, technical assistance, military support, and general guarantees provided by the United States and allies in the decades following World War II were important. Now, though, the United States and other industrialized states do not seem to have the same sense of urgency in dealing with developmentally troubled countries. Should they? Could they be effective? I think the answer to both questions is yes. Let us see now some of the implications of the U.S.–Korea experience that might be adapted for wider use in our current context. In doing so, this heuristic exercise should be related to experience elsewhere and to the burgeoning research literature on socioeconomic development.

While there is no overarching development model to be carried away, there are indeed lessons to be taken from the history of South Korea that deserve consideration in other settings. Within the historical specifics of the Japanese empire, the demands of the Cold War, Korean culture, and American policy there are important points for future development activities elsewhere.

Prompt Success (and Sometimes Long-Term Success as Well) Is Often Built on Cultural Attributes

It is useful to take such cultural attributes into account when formulating development strategies. The achievements of South Korea (as well as Taiwan and Japan) are due in part to a reverence for education that is deeply held in these cultures. Therefore, American and local efforts had a solid foundation on which to set themselves. This is also true of a decade and a half of work by NGOs on Mainland China before they began similar programs elsewhere in Asia. Success was sometimes built on established attitudes and methods.

Long-Term Commitment Is Necessary

In the case of South Korea, American commitment to building a stable, modern economy was deep and prolonged—nearly two decades of American aid grants and assistance before 1965. This was followed up in the 1960s and 1970s with U.S. financial and military aid that took certain pressures off the economy. Long-term commitment of the international community is likely to be necessary in much of Africa, Asia, and Latin America.

Development Is Not Just a State Activity

It is apparent that the U.S. government was the dominant player in these efforts in terms of resources. However, every step of the way there were a variety of NGOs and other institutions that played key roles in providing expertise, funds, and attention to issues that supported the larger project of development. NGOs were not simply tools of the U.S. government. Many agreed with the overall goals but did not agree with particular policies or priorities of the U.S. government and made their views known. The role of the Asian Development Bank in the 1960s and 1970s reflects the importance of intergovernmental organizations and international financial institutions in supporting development.

Regional Economic Cooperation

U.S. policies in East Asia, like its efforts in Europe, were based on regionalism. This was partly meant to lower the costs of foreign policy, by sharing burdens with other states and actors in particular areas. But it was also meant to make development in the region mutually supportive. Americans tried very hard to stretch their aid dollars by getting, for example, Koreans to buy Japanese goods for reconstruction that might have been made with materials from other states in the region. The emphasis on Japan as a regional economic center had profound impacts that are still felt to this day in Asia Pacific. The advantages of regional economic cooperation were, as we have seen elsewhere in these pages, exceedingly important in Europe after World War II.

Democracy Is Not a Luxury

South Korea shows that even considerable economic growth and development will not, in and of itself, prevent violent conflict. If not coupled with democratic principles and practices, development can contribute to tensions within society. There is no reason from this case to assume that development requires autocratic control or political repression.

The purpose of discussing South Korea is to stimulate thinking about underlying factors in successful development. While there is immense variability from case to case around the globe, there are recurrent themes, perhaps even general principles that deserve serious consideration by those struggling with these difficult problems and dangerous situations. The stakes are too high to ignore any clues that might be helpful.

Sustained International, Multisectoral Cooperation Can Foster Equitable Development

Although the case of South Korea mainly involves one large country as the source for outside help, there is no reason why this has to be the case. Indeed, in the twenty-first century the outside help is likely to be international and multilateral: a cooperative coalition of willing states, international financial institutions, effective NGOs; regional organizations; and private firms. The mix will be different from one case to another. But the international community can surely build on such experiences as South Korea to work closely with developing countries in a sustained way toward democratic socioeconomic development.

To be effective, a great deal of institution building is necessary. This is primarily local but will often require considerable leadership from outside, helping the host country draw from the world's experience in ways that mesh with local cultures to the extent possible.

Such institution building must foster human development through education and health, in addition to legal and administrative structures compatible with international investment for economic development.

Since the developing country government in many cases will be shaky and possibly corrupt at the outset, it is important that much of the foreign aid flows through nongovernmental organizations—both local and international. Financial and technical aid should be addressed toward strengthening both public and private sectors with visible evidence of fairness, for example, in land distribution and educational opportunities. The creation of a special agency or coordinating body at a high level of quality on an international basis can be an effective vehicle for honest, open, and democratic development.

The international partners will be wise both to stimulate the production of goods and services in the host countries and to open markets of advanced countries so they can make large purchases over time as the developing country gains skill in bringing useful products to the market. Formation or strengthening of regional development banks is a valuable policy—more on this later.

The outside, helping partners will do well, on the one hand, to foster a constructive interplay of developing country governments with the business community, internal and external; yet, on the other hand, vigilance is needed to minimize corruption, inequity, and hyperelite concentration of wealth and power.

One of the fundamental underpinnings of successful socioeconomic development is education, from preschool through graduate school. This must include women on an equal basis, not only as a matter of equity but also as a matter of economic stimulus.

Given the crucial role of science and technology in the economy of the twenty-first century, an important component of this effort must be education in mathematics, science, and technology. This should cover the entire gamut of the sciences from physical to social and inclusion of science-based professions, especially engineering, medicine, and public health.

To develop research capability, it is essential for each developing country to connect its emerging scientific community with the international scientific community. This happened productively not only in South Korea, but even more so in the early postindependence experience of India and Israel.

The role of an effective technical community in moving toward prosperity is clear. Moreover, the international ties that develop in this way can be helpful in other ways, not the least of which is fostering democratic norms and helping to sort out inter-state conflicts without violence.

A Frontier of Development:
The Role of Foreign Assistance in Conflict Prevention

In 2001, there is ferment among the established democracies in finding better ways to stimulate interest in development and to delineate the most promising pathways. This is manifested especially in leading nongovernmental organizations, universities, foundations, and intergovernmental organizations. Let me now give a sampling of these ideas and observations.

In January 2001, the United States Agency for International Development (USAID) and the Woodrow Wilson International Center for Scholars jointly sponsored a conference in Washington, D.C., entitled, "The Role of Foreign Assistance in Conflict Prevention." Participating were eighty experts from USAID, the State Department, the National Intelligence Council, congressional staff, academic institutions, the business community, and nonprofit organizations.[16]

The purpose of this conference was to shape a new vision for foreign assistance by developing a long-term strategy keyed to conflict prevention and building capable societies. The new vision involves reformulation of traditional development assistance programs, especially by enhancing collaboration and coordination of action within and among governmental and nongovernmental foreign aid providers. Several recurrent themes emerged from this meeting.

Recognize the Importance of Preventing Deadly Conflict

In order to quench fires before they become unmanageable, an early warning system needs to be developed to alert policymakers to key areas of potential conflict. Development strategies for a particular country or region need to focus on ways that aid can exacerbate or ameliorate ongoing tensions. Aid can be used in ways that foster mutual understanding and mutual benefit among adversaries—and provide nonviolent means of addressing grievances.

Expand the Definition of National Security

The traditional approach tends to ignore long-term problems such as demographic pressures, environmental threats, and terrorism. It also fails to account for the increasingly transnational nature of these problems—and the profound effects of globalization and deep interdependence. So, a broader view is needed.

Construct Capable States

Institution building occurs through fostering democratic governance. This empowers citizens, provides checks and balances, and minimizes abuses of power. Concomitantly, the development and maintenance of market economies with legal structure and fair ground rules is a high-priority prerequisite for institution building.

Capable states are characterized by representative governance based on rule of law; market economic activity; thriving civil society; security, well-being, and justice available to all citizens; the ability to manage internal and external affairs peacefully.

Build Local Capacity

Cooperative efforts between aid provider and host country can lead to building of essential institutions with major roles for local actors. Citizens can learn self-governance, with outside assistance playing a facilitating but not a dominating role.

Engage Multiple Actors

To implement the new vision of institution building to combat transnational problems, the knowledge and skill of multiple actors is needed. This means that aid agencies and high-level leaders should stimulate the involvement of a variety of government agencies, operationally pooling their resources. It is also essential to stimulate the private sector (business, private voluntary organizations, nongovernmental organizations). Many different contributions are needed for the design and implementation of the new foreign assistance vision.

Develop Better Mechanisms for Collaboration

Given this essential complexity for effective development, a new system for interagency collaboration is needed. The distinctive cultures of the agencies currently involved in foreign assistance should promote information sharing, plan explicit and systematic coordination, allocate tasks efficiently to avoid duplication and conserve precious foreign aid resources. The most useful means of promoting lasting democratic socioeconomic development set out in the previous chapter are highly pertinent here.

Successful development entails building local capacity and promoting competent governance, which over time provides the essential enabling environment. This requires sustained international development cooperation, including NGOs, government aid agencies, private firms, and educational and research institutions. The international community is best suited to provide the essential ingredients for indigenous development: knowledge through research and development; skills through education and training; and freedom through democratic institutions.

Development Assistance as
Structural Prevention of Deadly Conflict

This meeting, like the Carnegie Commission, emphasized development that aims to prevent the emergence of mass violence through deliberate strategies of structural conflict prevention.

Aid providers must help to build capable states that can construct (with outside collaboration as needed) conditions of security, well-being, and justice for all citizens. Moving toward these vital desiderata greatly diminishes the risk of mass violence, both within the countries and beyond. It is the intersection of these three conditions that is crucial for prevention. All require serious, sustained attention from those, internally and externally, who are striving to foster democratic socioeconomic development.

- Security is about safety from fear or threat of attack. But it is also about mutual accommodation so that different people can live together with a sense of fairness and mutual respect.
- Well-being is about health and also about equal opportunity. This means opportunity for education, training, and constructive employment. Young men without skill or decent prospects are susceptible to incitement to violence.
- Justice is about the right of each person to have a say in how one is governed and the right of each person to exercise that voice without fear of reprisals. Justice is also about accountability of those in power. This is crucial because of the long and recent history of grave abuses of power manifested in widespread human rights violations, often leading to war.

Building "stable" societies is not to suppress change or preserve the status quo, but rather to encourage the indigenous development of institutions and processes to help societies manage change in peaceful ways. Outsiders must offer the kind of help that promotes these conditions while recognizing that the major responsibility, effort, and credit for success ultimately resides with the insiders—those who are helped by outsiders for as long as necessary but who learn to help themselves as rapidly as possible. By constructing competent, decent states, the entire international community benefits. Thus, substantial economic aid and technical cooperation can be seen as an excellent investment in the prospect of peace and prosperity.

Growing Recognition of Links between
Development and Violence Prevention

Growing recognition of the need for explicit links of development with violence prevention is reflected in an excellent new report commissioned by UNDP and carried out by the highly respected Canadian analyst, Bernard Wood. Submitted in 2001, *Development Dimensions of Conflict Resolution and Peace-Building* is incisive in its formulation of concepts. Wood's report is part of serious attempts by the UN's specialized agencies to contribute to a "culture of prevention" in their own outlooks and activities.

> The developmental perspective on conflict prevention starts from the premise that conflict prevention itself is not just an aberration, but a normal and inescapable fact of life and development. Thus the goal of peace building and conflict prevention in a developmental perspective is to help prevent the slide into *violent* conflict (or oppressive forms of "order") and not any illusory ambition of trying to prevent conflict altogether.

Wood gives a set of guiding principles for development cooperation. They reflect the emerging consensus in this field.

1. Maximise indigenous "ownership" and participation—the people and countries concerned need even more right and ability to decide, when they will bear such huge costs if things go wrong. Remember that communications can now reach almost everybody;
2. Minimise dependency, striving to find and support local capacities, and focus aid on sustainable activities;
3. Maintain long-term engagement and trust and strive to make "partnership" real;
4. Seek to reduce the dangers of violent conflict and mitigate its results, recognizing that many of the best preventive results will be gradual, and hard to prove;
5. Work for the respect of human rights;
6. Preserve an even-handed commitment to development values and goals;
7. Strengthen coordination and coherence with other external actors (including non-governmental ones) working against violent conflict, on the basis of comparative and collaborative advantage;
8. Improve responsiveness and flexibility, while maintaining a long view;
9. Listen and learn about specific country situations, while adapting relevant lessons and good practices from elsewhere;
10. Promote more development-friendly policies and coherent practices in fields beyond traditional development assistance (e.g., trade, finance, environmental regimes, international crime fighting) that have major impacts on the prospects for development and peace building;
11. Avoid making promises of aid that cannot be delivered or sustained.

Wood addresses the turbulence that is virtually inevitable in the course of development—and ways to cope with it short of violence.

> Development itself is change, and de-stabilizes. Even when broadly thriving, development raises expectations and highlights disparities, sometimes adding to the factors that may trigger violent conflicts. When development stagnates or regresses, the pressures are usually even more intense. Thus building up its capacity to manage continuing (and today's accelerating) change, while protecting human rights and avoiding violent conflict, is now seen for any society as both a vital means and a continuing goal of development.
> It is because these policy challenges for developing countries are so central, and so difficult, that the issues of governance have become increasingly prominent in development thinking in recent years. In fact, the primary rationale and purpose for foreign assistance can be seen as helping developing countries to strengthen the governance capacities they require to master these strategic preconditions for sustainable development. . . .[17]

Voices from Latin America: Equity in Development

In these pages a good deal has been said about Africa and Asia. Now let us hear from Latin America. The distinguished economist, Francisco Sagasti, has led an interdisciplinary team over several years in formulating Agenda Peru. Its conclusions have wide implications for developing countries. The experience of recent decades shows the possibility of designing economic and social strategies capable of leading to integrated and sustainable development. In the view of Sagasti's team, such strategies should be organized around four central themes: economic modernization and a competitive productive structure; social justice and the provision of basic social services to the entire population, particularly those living in poverty and unemployment; sustainable management of natural resources and the environment in order to assure development for future generations; and territorial ordering, decentralization, and the provision of physical infrastructure, designed to make better use of heterogeneous geographical space.

> This is a participative task that calls for the collaboration of institutions of the state, the private sector and civil society: all of these actors on the national stage will need to implement a series of institutional reforms. Institutions linked to national, citizen and personal security will also require reforming. Lastly, the design and implementation of a development strategy should incorporate a change of mentality and a recovery of moral and ethical values, as well as a series of reflections on our national identity.

While focusing on Peru, Sagasti draws on his extensive experience with the World Bank, Canada's excellent International Development Research Center, and the Carnegie Commission on Science, Technology and Government to formulate conclusions supported by worldwide evidence bearing on the best opportunities for constructive socioeconomic development. He has put special focus also on the accomplishments and potential of multilateral development banks.[18]

Multilateral Development Banks

In a new study, he provides a broad strategic framework for examination of issues affecting the future of the multilateral development bank system. It is based on a review of the growing research literature on the subject, as well as new research conducted by Sagasti's group.

Multilateral development banks (MDBs) are international financial intermediaries whose shareholders include both borrowing developing countries and donor-developed countries. They mobilize resources from private capital markets and from official sources to make loans to developing countries on better-than-market terms; they provide technical assistance and analysis for economic and social development; and they provide a range of special services to developing countries and to the international development community.

> This is a time of unprecedented stress on the entire MDB system. At no time since the founding of the World Bank over fifty years ago have multilateral institutions been forced to contend with so many pressures and paradoxes. They are challenged as never before by their poorer member countries to help catalyze successful integration into the global economy and, at the same time, to help alleviate the deep socio-economic fissures that such integration can also cause. New levels of openness and transparency are demanded over the full range of MDB operations, while the institutions remain bound in many instances to protect the confidentiality of privileged relationships with clients. They are asked to exercise regional and global leadership by uniting international development efforts and also to reflect the myriad interests, differing viewpoints, and often-conflicting priorities of a vast array of other actors. They are required to seek out and function effectively in partnerships with governments, decentralized authorities, the private sector, bilateral and other multilateral agencies and NGOs, and to do so at national, trans-national and grass roots levels. . . .
>
> The MDB model is a most useful institutional innovation to assist developing countries. In spite of many problems and shortcomings, independent analyses have consistently confirmed a reasonably positive track record and the fact that there are no other institutions that provide a comparable range of products and services to member countries. With the possible exception of similar organizations that would benefit from automatic

resource mobilization mechanism (e.g., international taxes), there are no alternative institutional innovations in sight that could provide the combination of financial resource mobilization, capacity building and institutional development, knowledge brokering and the provision of international public good. . . .

Therefore, MDBs will continue to be needed to provide finance and a range of complementary services and products to developing countries for many years to come.

Equity Tools for Development

In another analysis based on Latin America experience, Nancy Birdsall and Augusto De La Torre clarify the limitations of existing development policies.[19] They offer ten "equity tools" to clarify what governments could do to reduce poverty and inequality without sacrificing economic efficiency and growth. Their tools aim not only to reduce poverty, but in a larger sense to build more just societies. They search for ways in which the poor and the middle class, not only the elite, have full access to economic, social, and political opportunities. Their focus is the domestic policy agenda in Latin America but also on the actions of industrial countries. These are the equity tools for a better development policy.

1. Rule-based fiscal discipline. Fiscal indiscipline—when governments consistently spend more than they collect and more than they can easily finance through sustainable borrowing—has high costs for the poor and the emerging middle class. . . .
2. Smoothing booms and busts. Booms are better for the rich, busts worse for the poor. Fiscal and monetary policies and tough banking and other financial standards to manage volatility and minimize crisis cannot be improvised. They should be locked in when times are good.
3. Social safety nets that trigger automatically. A modern system provides an income floor for working and middle class households as well as the poor. During slumps, spending should kick in automatically for emergency public works employment and subsidies to families to keep their children in school.
4. Schools for the poor, too. Today's centralized systems reinforce inequality. Critical reforms include more schools autonomy, lower subsidies to the better-off for higher education, and more public spending on preschool programs. Education policy must also embrace the Internet, with public subsidies to ensure that every school and every community benefit from this revolution in access to knowledge.
5. Taxing the rich and spending more on the rest. The region relies heavily on consumption taxes that are regressive. Closing income tax loopholes

and reducing evasion would increase revenues without adding to the tax burden of working and middle-income households.

6. Giving small business a chance. Weak financial and judicial systems and onerous red tape block talented small entrepreneurs from expanding their businesses. Improved enforcement of credit contracts and shareholder rights, the end of insider credit from state-owned banks, and access to information and professional services would help create more small firms and more jobs.

7. Protecting workers' rights. The poor bear the cost of a job-contracting environment that has too little worker protection and too many legal rules. Latin America needs more aggressive protection of workers' rights of association and collective bargaining, more independent and democratic unions, and more social protection to replace inflexible rules that discourage job mobility and growth.

8. Dealing openly with discrimination. A serious attack on poverty and inequality has to include a visible attack on discrimination. Political leadership can help break down the social and political barriers that hurt blacks and members of indigenous groups—and, in some arenas, women.

9. Repairing land markets. A new generation of land reform programs can make rural land markets truly competitive—finally giving the rural poor a fair chance. The new approach emphasizes credit and community involvement and relies less on centralized bureaucracy.

10. Consumer-driven public services. Shortcomings in infrastructure, public health, and such regulatory services as consumer protection have cost the poor and the near-poor dearly. Poor and other low-income consumers must now be at the heart of a new culture of service delivery.

This study also emphasizes reducing rich-country protectionism, for example, in agriculture and textile imports. These barriers reinforce inequality in Latin America and worsen poverty. Also development goes beyond economic policy—it includes the necessity for promoting democracy, extending civil liberties, reducing violence, ensuring the rule of law, fighting corruption that poisons an equity-enhancing strategy, and enhancing civil society.

Finally, the study highlights the need for political leadership to build the necessary constituency for equity, making the vision of equal opportunity attractive not only to the poor and the middle class but to the politically powerful elite. The researchers believe that good, humane economics is likely to be good politics in the long run. In my judgment, these policies would in time reduce dangerous tensions and bitter resentment that can so readily lead to violence.

Science and Technology for Development

I have earlier emphasized the fact that to participate in the global economy with reasonable prospects for prosperity, virtually every country in the world—and certainly every region—will need a modicum of technical competence. The opportunities provided by science and technology in the coming century will be vast, reaching far beyond all prior experience.[20] It will at last be feasible largely to eliminate poverty. But how does this enormous potential become fulfilled?

In a recent editorial in *Science*, Mohamed Hassan, president of the African Academy of Sciences, makes this powerful statement:

> Many of the continent's most serious problems, including malnutrition, disease, and environmental degradation, cannot be met without the presence of a critical mass of African scientists working on issues of direct concern to the continent itself. Science alone cannot save Africa, but Africa without science cannot be saved. . . . And that is why it is important for the governments of Africa to nurture environments that not only provide sufficient financial resources but also allow scientists from Africa and elsewhere to interact freely and without constraints.[21]

But how is a poor developing country to proceed in moving to diminish the gap? The scientific community is overwhelmingly located in and focused on affluent countries. Indeed, to say *affluent* is almost tantamount to saying *technically advanced*. Now there is a serious movement in the scientific community to focus much more intellectual and technical firepower (rather than explosive firepower) on the problem of developing countries. It has been my privilege to stimulate such interests and commitments in the scientific community over three decades, and I have never seen so much promising activity.

One of the most encouraging enterprises is the new Inter Academy Council (IAC), a cooperative effort of eighteen major scientific academies, north and south, intended to provide the most penetrating, objective analysis of developing country problems—and global problems as well. Here, as elsewhere, leadership is vital—and Bruce Alberts, president of the U.S. National Academy of Sciences has provided it on the basis of intellectual acuity, social responsibility, and respect for the people of developing countries. He co-chairs the IAC with the president of the Indian Academy of Sciences.

In one of its earliest statements, the IAC points out that all nations and societies will face local, regional, and global problems in the coming century: providing adequate nutrition and producing sufficient housing, material, and energy resources for a larger world population; mitigating environmental damage; protecting the health of an increasingly urban and mobile population—and much more. Addressing these problems requires generating new knowledge and applying current knowledge for problem solving on a global scale. All nations must develop sufficient capacity in science and technology to increase, utilize, and adapt the world's scientific and technical knowledge to their own problems and to help with global dilemmas.

While much knowledge, skill, and capacity for improved problem solving are now available in the world's scientific and engineering communities, there is a great need for new resources and greatly strengthened institutions. Many nations lack the scientific institutions and infrastructure to benefit from what is already known—much less to adapt new discoveries to their local needs. Insufficient cooperation exists among the world's scientific research institutions, including those in the developing nations. Moreover, linkages between social needs and long-term research agendas requires much more scientific attention than they have so far received. Inadequate use is made of new communications networks that provide an opportunity for the world's scientific community to share its socially valuable knowledge and skill on an unprecedented scale.

The IAC is organizing and will implement an advisory project designed to produce a global strategy for improved access by all nations and peoples to the benefits of science and technology. Four major topics will be addressed.

Human Resources

What are the specific needs for scientific and engineering talent in nations with different trajectories of development? How do we attract young talent, which exists everywhere, to science and maintain continuing interest of such people in the understanding of science and the uses of science for humanity? How do we best develop continuing education and collaboration opportunities for scientists in developing nations? How do we reduce their professional isolation? What national programs and policies have been successful in slowing the scientific brain drain occurring today from many developing countries to the industrialized nations?

Research Institutions

What models of successful institution building can be replicated all over the world? How can the international community of scientists contribute most effectively to such institution building? What can we learn from searching examination of past successes and failures? How can investments be increased for scientific institutions in developing nations—and what are the roles of national governments, international organizations, and the private sector in this regard?

Scientific Cooperation

What are successful models for increasing scientific cooperation among developing nations as well as between developing and industrialized nations? What kind of international cooperation can link social needs with scientific, engineering, and biomedical research agendas?

Global Communications

How can we greatly increase the availability of information technology services and information resources for developing nations? How can we increase synergies for scientific information sharing on a global level? What approaches would make it possible for developing nations to leapfrog the development gap with judicious use of information technology?

Mode of Operation

For each of the specific topics addressed, the IAC will strive to create an improved understanding, shared by national governments, the private sector, and civil society—especially of the scientific and engineering human talent required for addressing these challenges. Emphases will be placed on institution strengthening of the scientific and engineering communities in developing countries, thereby facilitating their ability to formulate and implement wise and effective policies. This work will also strive to be helpful to international organizations. From the outset, there has been a good working relationship with the UN Secretary-General.

Located at the Royal Netherlands Academy of Arts and Sciences in Amsterdam, the IAC will bring groups of scientists, engineers, and health experts together to provide analysis to international bodies, such as the United Nations and the World Bank, on matters of science, technology, and public health. This new NGO will work on a project-by-project basis funded by international agencies and interested foundations. When it receives a project request, the IAC assembles an expert panel to study the problem. Panel members serve on a voluntary basis. Each study panel prepares a report of its findings, conclusions, and recommendations. Following a peer review of the draft report, it is released to the sponsoring organizations and the public. Although primarily designed to respond to external requests, the IAC will also undertake self-initiated studies. Altogether, this remarkable social invention provides the opportunity to illuminate vital paths to development.

While analysis of this sort can be helpful to socioeconomic development in many ways, it is particularly vivid and poignant in the case of the global AIDS pandemic. Tragedies of this sort can provide a powerful stimulus to the scientific community and to policymakers all over the world. If the singular power of science and technology can be devoted not to destructive capacity but to a worldwide commitment to peace and prosperity, the human prospect could well become better than it has ever been in recorded history.

Notes

1. Amartya Sen, *Development as Freedom* (New York: Knopf, 1999).
2. Joseph E. Stiglitz and L. Squire, "International Development: Is It Possible?" *Foreign Policy* (spring 1998).

3. World Bank, *World Development Report 1996* (New York: Oxford University Press, 1996); World Bank, *World Development Report 1999/2000* (New York: Oxford University Press, 2000).

4. Jeffrey Sachs, "A New Global Consensus on Helping the Poorest of the Poor" (address to the Annual Bank Conference on Development Economics, World Bank, Washington, D.C., 2000).

5. James D. Wolfensohn, *A Proposal for a Comprehensive Development Framework* (Washington, D.C.: World Bank, January 21, 1999).

6. *Partnerships for Global Development: The Clearing Horizon* (a report of the Carnegie Commission on Science Technology and Government, 1992).

7. Annan, *Towards a Culture of Prevention.*

8. Paul Krugman, "The Scrooge Syndrome," *New York Times*, December 2001.

9. S. N. Goncharov, John Lewis, and Litai Xue, *Uncertain Partners: Stalin, Mao, and the Korean War* (Stanford, Calif.: Stanford University Press, 1993).

10. Edward S. Mason, Mahn J. Kim, Dwight Perkins, Kwang Suk Kim, and David C. Cole, *The Economic and Social Modernization of Korea* (Cambridge, Mass.: Harvard University Press, 1980), vi.

11. Anne O. Krueger, *The Developmental Role of the Foreign Sector and Aid* (Cambridge, Mass.: Harvard University Press, 1982), 5–81.

12. Jung-En Woo, *Race to the Swift: State and Finance in Korean Industrialization* (New York: Columbia University Press, 1991), 43–117.

13. Woo, *Race to the Swift*, 73–115.

14. Woo, *Race to the Swift*, 116–17.

15. Woo, *Race to the Swift*, 118–47.

16. *The Role of Foreign Assistance in Conflict Prevention* (Woodrow Wilson Center for International Scholars Conference Report, Washington, D.C., January 8, 2001).

17. List is derived mainly from the DAC Guidelines, 1998, 22.

18. Francisco Sagasti and Gonzalo Alcalde, *Development Cooperation in a Fractured Global Order* (Ottawa, Canada: International Development Research Center, 1999); Francisco Sagasti, Pepi Patron, Max Hernandez, and Nicolas Lynch, *Democracy and Good Government: Towards Democratic Governance in Peru* (Lima, Peru: Agenda Peru, 1995), 119.

19. Nancy Birdsall and Augusto de la Torre with Rachel Menezes, *Washington Contentious: Economic Policies for Social Equity in Latin America* (Carnegie Endowment for International Peace and Inter-American Dialogue, 2001), 3–17.

20. Rodney W. Nichols, *Linking Science and Technology with Global Economic Development: A US Perspective* COSTED Occasional Paper No. 5 (Committee on Science and Technology in Developing Countries, September 1999).

21. Mohamed H. A. Hassan "Can Science Save Africa?" *Science* 292 (June 2001): 1609.

8

International Cooperation for Prevention: Emerging from the Shadows

Personal Window on Leadership for Cooperation

Through his scientific advisors, I met Mikhail Gorbachev during his first year in office. There followed a relationship in which I was able to bring him into contact with leading Western scientists, scholars, and other leaders. Two distinguished physicists, Yevgeny Velikhov and Roald Sagdeev, were instrumental in making this possible. Later Sagdeev was a valuable member of the Carnegie Commission. Gorbachev was intellectually curious and open-minded—a very different kind of Soviet leader. After he left office, the Carnegie Corporation helped him establish a center in Moscow, which is a focal point for democratic reforms and analysis of international security under the drastically changed conditions of the new century.

In 1994, I asked him to reflect on a decade of intensive involvement with political leaders all over the world. One of his outstanding conclusions was the large extent to which they see "brute force" as their ultimate validation. His observation, based on abundant experience, highlights a long-standing, historically deadly inclination of leaders of many kinds from many places to interpret their mandate as being strong, tough, aggressive, even violent. Gorbachev, in control of a vast nuclear arsenal, as well as immense power in conventional, chemical, and biological weapons, was wise enough not to interpret his own leadership in terms of brute force. But there is no shortage of leaders who do. They will have massive killing powers at their disposal in the twenty-first century. Yet, there is a positive side of leadership, and this chapter explores constructive possibilities.

On behalf of the Carnegie Commission on Preventing Deadly Conflict, Jane Holl and I personally invited five world leaders—Boutros Boutros-Ghali, George Herbert Walker Bush Sr., Jimmy Carter, Mikhail Gorbachev, and Desmond Tutu—to consider leadership in preventing deadly conflict.

Their essays in this publication are diverse.[1] Yet all conclude that an individual leader's choices are crucial to creating the conditions that enhance or undermine peace.

International leaders can call attention to the problem of international group violence and tap into latent public inclination toward prevention. They can cogently explain the need for prevention. They can build the constituency necessary to prevent violence before it erupts. Addressing this point in his essay, former United Nations Secretary-General Boutros Boutros-Ghali highlights the need for vision, communication about problems and solutions, and eliciting international cooperation. Former U.S. President Bush stresses the importance of building relationships and maintaining credibility so that in times of crisis allies can be persuaded, not bullied, into cooperation to achieve a common goal. In his essay, Gorbachev addresses nonviolent responses to the breakup of the Soviet Union, in contrast to the massive violence that might readily have occurred. He emphasizes that modern leaders need the intellectual and moral authority to persuade rather than to compel.

Former U.S. President Carter explains why he believes it is necessary to engage all sides in a conflict, even international political outcasts if necessary. He points to the value of understanding the different perspectives of adversaries in fostering productive negotiations. Archbishop emeritus of Cape Town, Desmond Tutu, emphasizes that great leaders often speak the language of moral suasion and have personal credibility, solidarity with the people they are leading and an ability to nurture the best in others.

My own contact with these five leaders and others like them has impressed me deeply with the constructive potential of democratic, humane, well-informed, and courageous leaders as problem solvers and peacemakers. Leadership must come to mean drawing on the best resources: intellectual, technical, and moral as well as material resources; being thoughtful, fact-based, active, creative, and respectful to others in helping to clarify great dangers and ways of coping, and thus providing a moral and operational basis for dealing constructively with international and intergroup tensions. They must learn how to elicit cooperation across diverse boundaries in order to prevent deadly conflict and build constructive societies. That is the focus of this chapter.

Basic Orientations for a Transformation of Intergroup Relations

The twentieth century has witnessed the bloodiest, most destructive wars in recorded history.[2] As the world begins the third millennium, many unresolved intergroup and interstate conflicts continue to fester, taking a toll in human lives, in suffering, and in resources. For too long, the international community has deluded itself with the complacent belief that dreadful events in faraway lands are not the whole world's concern, that the problems of other peoples do not have consequences for all. This shortsighted view has left the international community ill prepared to deal with conflicts when they occur; leaving it to muddle through from crisis to crisis, applying emergency first aid. Instead, what is urgently needed are more fundamental solutions; norms and institutional arrangements that protect human rights, firmly embedded in democratic institutions with the protection of national and international law; and easy access to mechanisms of conflict resolution to cope with ongoing disputes.[3] If the 2001 terrorism originating in Afghanistan has not taught us a lesson here, it is hard to imagine what would do so.

The prevention of mass violence has a deeply rooted moral basis. It is also immensely practical. Where peace and cooperation prevail, so do security and prosperity.[4] We can learn from the steps taken after World War II that laid the groundwork for today's flourishing European cooperation. Leaders such as Franklin and Eleanor Roosevelt, George Marshall, Harry Truman, Robert Schuman, and Jean Monnet looked beyond the wartime devastation and the hateful fanaticism that had caused it and envisioned a Europe in which regional cooperation would transcend adversarial boundaries and traditional rivalries. They foresaw that large-scale, sustained economic cooperation would facilitate not only postwar recovery but also the long-term democratic prosperity that has helped Europe to achieve peace and security dramatic in contrast with its bloody and degraded experience in the first half of the twentieth century. Recognizing that there had to be global cooperation as well, they created a new international organization—the United Nations. The institution was given broader powers than its predecessor, the League of Nations. The focus was not just on diplomacy, however, as the framers of the UN took a wide view. They included work on international health, international development, and human rights as fundamental parts of the UN's mission. Behind all of the organization's efforts there lay the explicit goal of preventing violent conflict between the world's peoples and the recognition that it can only be achieved through substantial international cooperation.

Building support for this vision was very difficult. It required determined efforts to educate publics, mobilize key constituencies, and persuade reluctant partners. The United Nations, the Marshall Plan, NATO, and the European Union show vividly what sustained international cooperation can accomplish, mediated crucially by visionary and courageous leadership.

The record of the second half of the twentieth century provides a substantial basis for hope. The decline of tyranny and the extension of democratic government, the protection of human rights, the promotion of social justice and economic well-being—limited though they are—suggest what human ingenuity, decency, and dedication can accomplish.[5] Yet the prevention of mass violence on a worldwide basis represents a drastic break from our long history as a species.[6]

The worldwide historical record is full of hateful and destructive activities based on religious, ethnic, national, and other distinctions that are often associated with deeply felt beliefs about superiority (the inclination to superiority is one of the deepest vulnerabilities of the human species), a sense of jeopardy to group survival, and justification by supernatural powers (especially the holy wars that have once again erupted). All that is an ancient part of the human legacy—and very dangerous. What is new is the rapidly accelerating destructive power of weaponry: conventional, nuclear, chemical, biological—and the means of accurately transporting them over short or long distances. Moreover, the worldwide spread of technical capability, the miniaturization of weapons, the widely broadcast justifications for violence, and the upsurge of fanatical behavior are occurring in ways that can readily produce large-scale conflicts of high lethality everywhere on earth. As a species, we have a rapidly growing capacity to make life miserable and disastrous—even to cause human extinction.

In the century to come, human survival may well depend on our ability to learn a new form of adaptation, one in which intergroup hostility is largely replaced by mutual understanding and cooperation. Curiously, a vital part of human experience, learning to live together, has been badly neglected. There are initiatives in this field that offer fundamental, long-term promise. Some of them have been described in this book. Others are covered in the seventy-plus books and reports of the Carnegie-supported efforts of the 1990s. The course that desperately needs to be steered is one toward democratic pluralism. This means developing a culture of fairness, mutual accommodation, and even mutual aid among diverse groups sharing a common space—ultimately all human groups sharing planet earth. It is possible, though difficult, to build democratic institutions in every part of the world with strong protection of human rights for all, minorities as well as majorities.

An ongoing, vital aspect of all efforts to prevent deadly conflict must be education of publics throughout the world. From scientists and professional educators to the UN to grassroots NGOs to international university networks and religious institutions, there is a profound need to address the ascending dangers of violence, constructive ways of dealing with ubiquitous human conflicts, respect for universal human dignity, and paths to peace with justice. The profound threat of prejudicial ethnocentrism and religious fanaticism as a precursor to hatred, violence, and mass killing has to emerge as one of the major educational thrusts of the next century: through the media and community organizations as well as educational, scientific, and religious institutions.

The international community can formulate general standards with sensitivity in their application to a great variety of cultures; it can develop a strong preventive orientation, monitoring hot spots and becoming involved early as conflicts emerge. Increasingly, participation in the international economy can be used to ensure adherence to standards of decent behavior in intergroup relations as well as individual human rights. Ways can be found to facilitate mutually beneficial associations of diverse neighbors.

It is of utmost importance for contending parties throughout the world to understand the nature, scope, and consequences of ethnocentric violence. Especially significant are the action-reaction cycles of violence with buildup of revenge motives and the tendency to assume hatred as an organizing principle for life and death. In these circumstances, violent extremists and fanatics are likely to take control of the situation. There are the slippery slopes of proliferation (the spread of deadly weapons), escalation (the upward spiral in killing power of the weapons employed and numbers harmed), and addiction to violence when the powerful dependence on hatred and killing can become a source of fundamental satisfaction. When stewed together, the result can be the degradation of life for all concerned— even annihilation in areas of intense fighting.

Most people in the world live in multiethnic societies. To make constructive use of this interesting fact requires a multidimensional approach, starting with physical security including economic, political, and military aspects and drawing on ongoing mechanisms for sorting out conflicts without violence in the framework of democratic institutions widely perceived to be fair. Thus, democratic institutions must find ways in which all groups are represented and in which there are protections against the abuse of power. They must provide a code of human rights for individuals and groups and create mechanisms of implementation, especially respected courts in an independent judiciary. To look after the vital interests of different groups, they must provide an atmosphere of negotiated solutions with training, skills, and accessible mechanisms. Constitutional arrangements and a democratic legal system can strongly facilitate a climate of negotiated problem solving.

Several desiderata for implementing such a system of democratic, nonviolent problem solving have been set out in recent scholarship.[7]

- Orienting to prevention through early warning of emerging conflict.
- Creating visible, respected fora for discussion of problematic disputed issues involving all the relevant parties.
- Encouraging the expression of grievances in organized settings that foster empathy and restraint, utilizing to the extent possible culturally accepted mechanisms for reconciliation.

- Facilitating processes of joint problem solving in which representatives of different groups explore together their interests, basic needs, and fervent aspirations—seeking to understand underlying motivations and their shared humanity.
- Identifying common goals such as economic development of the region and strengthening democratic institutions.
- Utilizing external resources to create incentives and skills for cooperation.

A fundamental requisite of mutual accommodation is development of a genuinely free civil society within a democratic framework in which there is truly equal citizenship, respect for human rights, protection against the abuse of power, freedom to express differences openly and constructively, and a fair distribution of opportunities. Each case presents a distinctive set of opportunities and constraints, and each solution is inevitably reached only after difficult deliberation. Whatever the outcome, it must eventually satisfy the reasonable claims of most citizens, though not necessarily the intolerant militants or harsh extremists.

Superordinate Goals, Enlarging Identity, and Mutual Accommodation

There is an urgent need to create the conditions under which various identity groups can sort out their differences and learn to live in a state of harmonious interaction with their neighbors. Ways must be found to foster self-esteem, meaningful group membership, and internal cohesion without the necessity for harsh depreciation of out-groups and without resort to violence in the event of a clash of interests.

To an increasing extent, we must learn to broaden our social identifications in light of shared interests and superordinate goals across all of humanity. We must come to think of ourselves in a fundamental sense as a single interdependent, meaningfully attached, extended family. This is, in fact, what we are; but to state this fact is not to assimilate it as a psychological reality. Through most of human evolution and historical times, our primary (and usually strong) identification has been with a relatively small (even intimate) group. So, it is difficult to expand our horizons on a regional, let alone a worldwide, basis.

Superordinate goals have the potentially powerful effect of unifying disparate groups in the search for a vital benefit that can be obtained only by their cooperation. Such goals can override the differences that people bring to a contentious situation.[8] What could constitute shared goals of this extraordinary significance? The avoidance of nuclear destruction is one. So, too, is the avoidance of infectious pandemics. Protection of the environment is emerging as another, since it could involve jeopardy to the human habitat. The creation of new forms of community, social cohesion, and solidarity in the face of vast impersonal modern society is another. The threat of worldwide economic deterioration or recurrent financial crisis might also become salient. At a regional level, the desire to improve economic prospects can impel two or more nations to cooperate in the development of agriculture, transportation, electricity, and water resources, increasing confidence and mutually beneficial interdependence.

These are mainly survival goals, updated to the modern era, where the reference for adaptation goes beyond the sense of belonging in the immediate valued group to identification with a much larger unit or ideal. The ancient propensity toward narrow identity, harsh intolerance, and deadly intergroup conflict confronts us with new dangers and challenges us as never before. By the same token, this new and dynamic century will create a great opportunity to identify superordinate goals and their unifying possibilities in the world of small- and large-scale wars that have proven so contagious in recent years. How can all of humanity benefit—indeed survive—by adopting fresh attitudes, practices, and institutions?

This analysis suggests the importance of having crosscutting or overlapping group memberships in the modern world. Such relations connect subgroups of society or connect nations in ways that overcome in-group/out-group distinctions and prejudicial stereotypes. They involve the opportunity for members of alien, suspicious, or hostile groups to spend time together, to work together, to play together, and even to live together for extended periods of time, gaining a sense of shared humanity.

On the international level, there must be concerted efforts to expand favorable contact between people from different groups and nations. Some measure of comprehension of a strange culture is vital. Educational, cultural, and scientific exchanges can be helpful. At a deeper level, joint projects involving sustained cooperation can provide, if only on a small scale, an experience of working together toward a superordinate goal. There are many ways to break down antagonisms between groups or, preferably, prevent them from arising in the first place. International organizations—nongovernmental as well as governmental—can do much to promote empathic personal contact and overlapping loyalties that cut across in-group/out-group antagonisms.[9]

There are other ways to create positive connections between groups. Families, schools, community organizations, religious institutions, and the media throughout the years of human growth and development are pivotal institutions that can shape attitudes and interpersonal skills toward either decent relations or hatred and violence.[10] In the twenty-first century it will be necessary in child raising to put deliberate, explicit emphasis on developing prosocial orientations and a sense of worth based not on depreciation of others but on the constructive attributes of oneself and others. Taking turns, sharing, and cooperating, especially in learning and problem solving—these norms, established on a simple basis in the first few years of life, can open the way to beneficial human relationships that can have significance throughout a person's life.[11]

A greater comprehension of other, often-unfamiliar cultures is essential for reducing negative preconceptions. Those who have a deep sense of belonging to groups that cut across ethnic, national, or religious lines may serve as bridges between different groups and help to move them toward a wider, more inclusive social identity. Building such bridges requires many people interacting with mutual respect across traditional barriers. Developing a personal identification with people beyond one's primary group has never been easy. Yet, broader identities are possible, and it is necessary to encourage them on a larger scale than ever before.

At a time when many countries are struggling with new and uncertain challenges of democratization, the international community must champion the norm of responsible leadership and support opportunities for moderate leaders to engage in negotiated, equitable solutions to intergroup disputes. Leaders who demonstrate good will and decency should be recognized and rewarded. By the same token, conditions should be fostered that allow electorates to hold their leaders accountable when and where they depart from norms of peaceful conflict resolution. The international community must expand efforts to educate the public everywhere that preventing deadly conflict is both necessary and possible.

One role of the teacher is to facilitate the learning of new mechanisms for resolving conflict. This means showing respect for the essential humanity in every person. An example of this can be found in a City Montessori School in Lucknow, India, that has imbued its principles in practice for half a century.[12] From kindergarten onward, the school instills in Hindu, Sikh, and Muslim students the religious and cultural tolerance found in the teachings of Mahatma Gandhi. Classroom activities include collaborative problem solving; teachers commend and reward students for consideration of others. Parents and grandparents are involved in curriculum design, and the school encourages them to reinforce the principles of toleration and cooperation at home. All over the world, tolerance is beginning to be taught, and prejudices and stereotypes are being challenged.

It is important for people not only to learn about tolerance, but also to have practical ways to deal with the tensions of everyday life so they do not escalate into violence. The ubiquitous tensions between groups can become serious if a threat to security or existence is perceived. The perspective of a third party can ease tension through better communication, understanding of the other party's perspective, and the establishment of a process for joint problem solving.

The current revolution in information and communication technology facilitates bridge building on a global scale. Young people are participating in exchange programs with students from other countries, more business people make deals across borders, and more tourists visit foreign lands. In this way, stereotypes can be replaced by genuine understanding. Such connections reduce the risk of demonizing other cultures.

To a considerable extent, this has happened in the dramatic transformation of Western Europe in the second half of the twentieth century as previously mentioned. Europe still has disputes, but for the most part, violence is no longer considered an option for resolution. This model of international cooperation offers a powerful stimulus to other areas of the world. In a variety of ways, international cooperation can foster opportunities for peace with justice and fulfillment of human potentiality.

Implementing Operational and Structural Prevention

How can the international community enhance its current capacities to prevent the deadliest conflicts? Preventive diplomacy is the prime example of operational prevention—oriented to coping with serious conflicts and imminent crises before they cross the threshold to mass violence. It has shown great promise despite the fact that the world is poorly organized to take advantage of its potential.

I have summarized several major new studies that converge on key points of preventive diplomacy. They combine established knowledge with new insights. They send a strong message to the international community: to governments, intergovernmental organizations, nongovernmental organizations of many kinds, and leaders in different sectors. This information should become part of the basic knowledge and skills of organizations and institutions that have opportunities and aspirations to diminish risks of war. These guidelines should be useful on a worldwide basis for many years to come. Learning how to implement them will be a task of utmost importance. Readers should take away from this book a sense of the tangible promise of preventive diplomacy for coping with emerging crises before they become catastrophes.[13]

In earlier chapters, I have considered many factors conducive to long-term peaceful living, structural prevention. Among these, none is more important than democratic socioeconomic development. The evolution of democratic attitudes, practices, and institutions is crucial in both political and economic spheres.

Although there are many other elements that are important in structural prevention—for example, major limitations on highly destructive weapons via international agreements and internal restraints—I focus here on democratic development because it tends to pull the other factors along. The many, inter-related socioeconomic facets of democratic development come together in ways that foster security, well-being, and justice even for large and diverse pop-ulations—not perfectly, not comprehensively, yet generally in constructive di-rections with a realistic basis for hopeful lives.

Democratic traditions evolve in ways that build ongoing mechanisms for dealing with the ubiquitous conflicts that arise in the course of human ex-perience. Democracy seeks ways to deal fairly with conflicts and to resolve them below the threshold of mass violence. This is a difficult process, there are failures, and the transition from a closed authoritarian society to a fully viable, open democratic society can be stormy, but this is the best chance for dealing justly and peacefully with the tensions of humanity.

The attitudes, beliefs, and procedures of democratic societies are useful in resolving intergroup conflict within and beyond state borders. There are effective means for promoting democracy and outside help can be crucial in these efforts. A recent assessment shows that, despite many obstacles, much can be accomplished.[14] The worldwide movement toward democracy is not simple or linear, but it is powerful and encouraging to those who value hu-man dignity, opportunity, creativity—and, yes—survival. Building demo-cratic societies with market economies in a technically competent and ethi-cally sound way is a clear path to structural prevention of deadly conflict. However arduous the task, and however great the flaws of established democracies, the game is worth the candle. This is the best antidote to the murderous rampages of tyrants that have so marred human history.

These great tasks of operational and structural prevention require sub-stantial international cooperation. This is because the problems they ad-dress are formidable and widely scattered around the world. Predisposing and precipitating factors for human conflict are ubiquitous. Homo sapiens is a highly contentious species with a dramatically destructive track record. Moreover, the tasks of prevention are complex, demanding, sometimes ex-pensive, often dangerous. Thus, the effective pursuit of these tasks requires pooling strengths, sharing burdens, and dividing labor.

At present, it is not obvious how this is to be done. Individual states, groups of states, the United Nations, regional organizations, nongovern-mental organizations, and eminent individuals typically approach preven-tive actions in a groping, uncoordinated way. This reflects the lack of any agreed international violence prevention system. Even though no single, worldwide, integrated system is yet feasible, more widely accepted and reg-ularized arrangements are necessary. Indeed, as a practical matter, such arrangements are beginning to emerge.

Notable successes (e.g., the OSCE high commissioner on national mi-norities) have resulted from adaptable efforts, working directly and closely with adversarial groups. OSCE is a significant paradigm because of its focus on very early conflict prevention, the willingness to become deeply involved, and the multiple mechanisms available. It has ways to start a process of conflict resolution through politics, legislation, or roundtable discussion. Other European institutions also offer promise in this respect. For example, the Council of Europe is involved in conflict prevention. Its focus is on establishing and to a certain extent enforcing norms of civilized and democratic national behavior. It underscores minority rights as an antidote to secessionism. It offers transitional countries a promising pathway to democracy. In order to implement democratic norms, it uses confidence-building projects, workshops, and technical assistance. Similarly, democracy, respect for human rights, the rule of law, and a market economy are the basic requirements for membership in the economically powerful European Union. It maintains that these norms are conducive to peaceful living, and the EU is beginning to consider violence prevention explicitly, as we shall see shortly. These cooperative European institutions have been a strong magnet for Eastern European countries emerging from authoritarian regimes—and in the process moving toward peaceful conflict resolution as well as economic benefits. These European examples, in the context of that continent's bloody history, suggest what might be done on other continents, each in its own way.

To achieve coordination of complex preventive efforts with input from multiple sources, it is necessary to consider geographic jurisdictions, functional responsibilities, norms, and procedures for preventive action. The essence is to achieve predictable, dependable arrangements for sustained joint action. This approach relies on flexible grouping of actors with relevant competencies, acting in terms of international laws to the extent possible or at least on the basis of widely shared norms relating to peace and justice.[15] Obstacles exist in each case, and we identify them here, but any difficulties are far outweighed by the potential benefits from several different (though overlapping) ways of organizing an international regime for prevention. We interrogate all of the systems discussed in this book, giving space to criticisms of each, providing a balance sheet for prevention that clearly shows the profits of pursuing an internationally cooperative regime of prevention.

A UN-Centered System

How could the UN be strengthened to foster international cooperation for prevention? Gareth Evans, former foreign minister of Australia and member of the Carnegie Commission, suggests making the UN Secretariat the main headquarters of an international early warning system.[16] We have discussed his approach in the chapter on preventive diplomacy. He proposes focusing on the Department of Political Affairs in the UN Secretariat, adding more staff to monitor the world's six major geographic regions, as well as adding teams of well-trained mediators for deployment to troubled areas when necessary. The UN regional offices could also arrange and monitor negotiations, aid disputants with other UN resources, direct contending parties to other channels if needed, and supervise adherence to agreements made. Such a unit could be fortified by permanent staff in the regions located at proposed Peace and Security Resource Centers, which could be located in the same cities as the headquarters of regional organizations. However, officials would report to the UN Secretary-General, not to the regional organization. This UN regional approach is further developed in Connie Peck's important book for the Carnegie Commission.[17] A particularly important feature of Peck's work is the emphasis on regional promotion of capable democratic governments concomitantly with operational prevention in time of intense stress.

While the UN has an important role to play in a preventive system, it has several significant disadvantages that need to be addressed in the manner that Secretary-General Annan is currently doing.

- Due to their limited resources and massive agenda, the Secretary-General and the Security Council are overloaded and are prone to focusing on crisis situations rather than preventive actions; the good offices, special envoys, and regional fact-finding missions have become overburdened.
- Although UN Charter Articles 39 through 42 enable the UN to respond to potential threats or breaches of peace within or among states, it often has trouble dealing with conflicts entailing nonofficial parties and internal disputes; and, so far, has had problems with very early prevention.
- Since significant security endeavors require the Security Council's approval, the UN is hindered by the possibility of a veto from one or more members of the Security Council.
- There are high stakes surrounding the UN's involvement in a conflict, so states are sometimes apprehensive about bringing their conflict to the United Nations. The Security Council may be inflexible or partisan or pass resolutions that cannot be implemented.
- The United Nations struggles to be organizationally efficient and still has the image of being wasteful.

The UN regional centers suggested by Evans and Peck do not yet exist and may require years of development—although this process could be accelerated. Nevertheless, a comprehensive preventive system grounded in the *United Nations* holds strong potential and considerable actual ability now. Despite any shortcomings, the UN has considerable resources that make it an indispensable part of any regime of prevention.

- It has the benefit of the resources of its worldwide organizational network.
- The Secretary-General has good offices and various diplomatic means that allow him to bring disputing parties together.
- The UN can bring issues to the attention of the international community and bring moral and other pressure to bear on disputing parties.
- It has the resources of experienced diplomats.
- It can assemble the political power and resources from major powers to constitute a package of preventive action.
- It can, in principle, make available to any troubled country or region the entire world's experience, knowledge, and skills—for example, pertinent to building durable mechanisms for conflict resolution.
- As the only universal organization, it has a distinctive, worldwide legitimacy.
- It has considerable capacity through several of its departments, agencies, and programs—especially in cooperation with international financial institutions—to foster democratic socioeconomic development.

Strengthening the United Nations' capacity to fulfill its potential for preventing deadly conflict deserves urgent consideration. Can the UN create paths to conflict resolution that are visible, attractive, and useful before conflicts become large and lethal? The obstacles are formidable, but the stakes are so high that serious and sustained effort is well justified. An important part of the effort is independent analytical work and forward-looking ideas arising outside the UN from observers who are well informed and sympathetic to the enterprise, yet objective with respect to constraints on the institution.

Recent studies by experts on international relations suggest ways to improve the UN's capacity to address the challenges of the post–Cold War international system. They have two basic propositions. First, that the end of the Cold War has created an unprecedented opportunity for the UN to function in a constructive atmosphere. Second, that pivotal change has occurred in the international community's conception of national sovereignty.[18] There is now a growing consensus that national sovereignty is not and cannot be a shield behind which governments are free to conduct their affairs with impunity—if they engage in horrific acts—and therefore members of the international community have, through the UN, a legitimate basis for intervening in "internal affairs" in order to prevent or resolve deadly conflict, avoid terroristic or other spread of killing, render humanitarian assistance, aid transitions to more democratic systems of governance, and offer technical assistance to build capacity for problem solving.

The actual and potential demands for such engagement are high. In the 1990s, there was a dramatic upsurge in the cost associated with the various UN peacekeeping missions and other expanded responsibilities. No single nation, not even the most powerful, wants to constitute the world's police force; and so the UN is increasingly being used to respond to international needs. If member states want vital functions of international security carried out by the UN, all will somehow have to pay. The international community will have to agree on fair, reasonable principles, criteria, and procedures for settling disputes among the UN's member states about the payment for vital functions.

The UN with its unique scope and legitimacy can be strengthened in ways that would permit it to play a valuable role in fostering political, social, and economic conditions in which a civil and just international society can evolve in due course.[19] The highest priority should be given to developing the UN's abilities for early action in order to prevent large-scale violence. In recent years, a basic extension of prior doctrine has occurred. The international community is now seen as having not only a justifiable rationale but also a constructive responsibility for engaging in serious international disputes.

To clarify the opportunities and approaches for action, a system to provide early alert and analysis by the Secretary-General would inform consideration of plausible options by the Security Council and might well head off some conflicts before serious damage is done. As noted previously, a number of circumstances provide the appropriate precipitating events for Security Council action following an alert by the Secretary-General. These include the possibility that a regional dispute might entail weapons of mass destruction, evidence of emerging genocide or terrorism, large flows of refugees threatening to destabilize neighboring countries, strong evidence of systematic and widespread human rights violations, forcible overthrow of democratically elected governments, serious and growing damage to the environment, and rapid arms buildup in tense situations. Such a system would help to clarify the role of the UN and that of the international community in other ways, to engage early in internal disputes of a grave nature. This cannot mean a constant intrusion into the internal affairs of every country or the domination of the weaker by the stronger. A key part of any regime of prevention is the establishment of a set of equitable criteria for engagement, procedures for action, the scope of accepted measures, and constructive follow-up. These must be transparent, fair-minded, deeply informed, and based on humane democratic values.

The Secretary-General needs an international panel of conflict resolution experts. They should be people of such extensive relevant experience, intellect, integrity, and distinction that they would be widely recognized throughout the world as suitable for missions on behalf of the Secretary-General. At the same time, such people need essential staff with expertise in different regions of the world. The Secretary-General should have such personnel available either directly in the Secretariat (such as a group of senior staff) or through a collaborative relationship with NGOs. In either case, the special envoys of the Secretary-General and the senior staff collaborators should combine expertise in two fundamental bodies of knowledge. They should be versed in the principles and techniques of conflict resolution and couple this with in-depth knowledge of a particular region, including the main historical and cultural factors bearing on a specific conflict.

Regional Centers for Sustainable Peace could be established under the auspices of regional organizations or the UN or, preferably, a combination of both acting in conjunction. This would be one important way of bringing together the UN, regional organizations, nongovernmental organizations, and regional analytical centers. This structure could integrate the most successful conflict prevention instruments, drawing widely on international experience and expertise, but ensure that they are tailored to local needs and circumstances. The horizontal transfer of knowledge and experience within regions would also be a distinctive feature of this approach, in which regional actors who have found solutions to their problems or evolved successful models of good governance could assist their neighbors within the context of a regional effort, aided, as necessary, by the international community. Regional centers could help establish a more solid international foundation on which, step-by-step, sustainable peace could be built.[20]

Regional centers would have two major foci. The first would be ongoing assistance in developing the structural processes for sustainable peace (good governance at all levels of society is fundamental here). The second would be maintaining peace through assistance in dispute resolution and the building of institutions that would allow groups to become more effective at resolving their own problems. While the main emphasis of regional centers would be at a very early phase of a conflict, they could also provide assistance in a time of impending crisis. Each center would provide an ongoing analysis of existing disputes and underlying problems to both the regional organization and the UN.

The United Nations Environment Program has become increasingly effective and deserves strong support from member states. We now know that environmental resource issues combine with other factors to threaten the lives of millions worldwide.[21] In a variety of ways, the misuse of natural resources lies at the heart of some conflicts that hold the potential for mass violence. Tensions can be deepened by the deliberate manipulation of resource shortages for hostile purposes (for example, using food or water as a weapon). When nations put forward competing claims of sovereignty over resource endowments (such as rivers or fossil fuel deposits), there is a distinct possibility of conflict. The role played by environmental degradation and resource depletion in areas characterized by political instability, rapid population growth, chronic economic deprivation, and societal stress has a history of promoting violence. With continuing environmental ills, this pressure is bound to continue.

A critical environmental challenge is constraining the emissions of carbon dioxide associated with fossil fuel consumption. The lion's share of such emissions comes from the developed countries. But increasing numbers of people in the developing world are demanding improved standards of living, and that will lead to higher levels of fossil fuel use. Experience from past international security negotiations may be useful in achieving the required arrangements to control CO_2 emissions. The UN can play a vital role in fostering the diplomatic and scientific cooperation to tackle such problems.

While serious problems remain within the United Nations, there simply must be a worldwide forum in which all kinds of information can be shared, ideas tried out, and views exchanged. The organization is so large, so multifaceted, so disparate in its composition and outlook of its members, so emotionally charged from its past history and from current difficulties in the world, that it will be no simple matter to fulfill its potential. Nevertheless, if it did not exist, something very much like it would have to be invented. It is a difficult but vital challenge to consider how effective components of the United Nations might be extended (and perhaps new ones created) in order to strengthen its role in preventing violence throughout the world.

Regional Organizations

As noted earlier, the UN is not the only important mechanism for prevention. A number of other types of organizations have a vital role in extending and enhancing any approach to prevention—notable among these are *regional organizations*. They could be an alternative to the new regional centers at decentralized levels of the United Nations—or they could be supplementary. The OSCE, OAU, and OAS have already created mechanisms for conflict prevention and management. Regional organizations have also taken ad hoc initiatives directed at particular conflicts. What are the obstacles they must find ways to overcome?

While there is potential for regional organizations to play an important preventive role in the future, they now lack the financial and political resources to be the sole leaders in preventive action. They have several limitations.

- Regional organizations in several parts of the world have so far been largely ineffective.
- Regional organizations mostly do not have the necessary financial, logistical, and human resources for effective preventive action.
- They have difficulty mobilizing any kind of military force because of the need for unanimous consent.
- Any action can be hindered by member states' desire to retain their individual sovereign privileges.
- Regional organizations may be biased in certain conflicts, as their own politics may reflect the disputes they are trying to settle.

- The need to satisfy the hegemonic regional power restrains their ability to mobilize support in disputes in which such powers have an interest.

Despite these obstacles, the Evans–Peck approach is a path with true promise. There are clear advantages to a preventive system rooted in such institutions that make it worthwhile to help them to establish or expand their capabilities to become participants in any culture of prevention.

- Since they are geographically close to an emerging conflict and have local knowledge, they may receive early warning before a full-blown crisis emerges.
- They may be able to respond more rapidly than the UN since they do not have as many partners to reach consensus with and because they do not have as many demands on them.
- They can create peer pressure and appeal to a state's pride in membership.
- The norms the regional organization promotes are probably more acceptable than those of a distant entity.
- A regional organization can serve a legitimizing function under which outside governments or NGOs can become effectively involved in settling a conflict; and it is likely to have substantial understanding of regional history and culture pertaining to a specific conflict.
- In the past few years, a variety of regional organizations have taken a serious interest in violence prevention.
- They can foster structural prevention through regional economic cooperation and promotion of democracy.

An NGO Preventive Network

Another possibility for a leading role (or least a major coordinating role) is the creation of a network of NGOs that would work with the United Nations and regional organizations. These burgeoning organizations have much promise, but they are mostly very young and immensely variable in relevance to violence prevention.

There are a number of obstacles in the path of an NGO system. Their lack of financial resources and their dependence on donors commonly means many of them are unable to provide services for as long as other entities. Most lack the ability to offer the needed logistical and communications capabilities that multilateral organizations or states can supply. NGOs have agendas that are often in conflict with governments, even democratic ones. At the extreme, some NGOs carry self-righteous moralism to the point of harshly deprecating others (including other NGOs) and even sometimes stray into the territory of revenge. They are also not required to answer to political constituencies, and NGOs typically do not coordinate closely with one another. Indeed, a number of scholars have recently challenged the overly optimistic assertions of the mid- and late 1990s that NGOs were a leading and possibly the best mechanism to carry out many international programs.

There is validity in these critiques, but they do not eliminate the considerable and indispensable capabilities the vast and varied nature of the NGO world brings to questions of conflict prevention. Many have grassroots connections and intimate knowledge of particular areas, often giving them the ability to sense the path that local disputes may take. Their independence provides the flexibility to bypass governments and cut across national boundaries through their links among professional, commercial, and educational groups as well as to involve disputants in low-key, nonthreatening dialogues that do not commit the parties to adopt any agreement. Frequently, NGOs are able to carry out these tasks because they have high-quality, dedicated professional personnel. Finally, we should not overlook the fact that many hold organizing principles that emphasize humane and democratic problem solving. NGOs may not be able to go it alone on numerous issues but they are an irreplaceable component of a larger international regime of prevention.

Individual States and Coalitions of the Willing

There is much potential here, too, for example, in formidable resources and flexible groupings for prompt attention. Yet, their track record in prevention is not inspiring. Indeed, a focus on prevention here is just beginning to emerge.

There are significant drawbacks to individual states acting unilaterally. They are not likely to help prevent conflicts in more than a few circumstances since they do not have a strong interest in all areas abroad; a state may not be welcome in a particular region due to past animosity; states need the support of their publics and political leaders—often assumed to be reluctant; and states may not act in the interest of the international community, but only in their own national interest, narrowly conceived.

Nevertheless, individual states still maintain several advantages over multilateral organizations when it comes to taking action. A state may be highly motivated to prevent disputes in a particular area because of a direct concern over the danger inherent in the conflict. In contrast to other groupings, states do not need international consensus, so their reaction time can be faster as many states have diplomatic, military, and technical resources at the ready. If they are unwilling to act alone, they still have the attractive option to establish a Friends group or other internationally cooperative "coalition of the willing."

These are Lund's basic elements for a proactive, cost-effective multilateral preventive regime:

- Proactive monitoring to prepare for an early response to previolent or low levels of conflict.
- Preventive action to settle interstate and internal disputes without force.
- A policy perspective focusing resources and attention on especially troubled areas.
- Assertion of the normative primacy of the peaceful transformation of societies and governments undergoing destabilizing change.
- Authorizing and enabling local and subregional actors as the first line of prevention.
- Coherent local conflict strategies.
- A graduated sequence of contingent responses.
- When necessary, higher-level and, if essential, more coercive responses by major powers and other global actors.
- International cooperation and coordination at all levels led by prime movers such as major powers.
- Public–private partnership between official bodies and NGOs.
- U.S. leadership in promoting a coordinated system within the fora of the United Nations and regional bodies.

The tasks of prevention are just too complex to be the exclusive responsibility of any one institution or nation. By practical necessity, the prevention of deadly conflict is a broadly international and cooperative enterprise. I firmly believe that established democracies have special responsibility and opportunities in the prevention mission. The important study by Allison and Owada makes this clear.[24] Within this group, the United States has a distinctive responsibility at the outset of the twenty-first century. This reflects the reality of its preeminent technological, political, economic, and military power in the world at large.

On this score, however, America's performance in recent years has been worrisome. Under the corrosive influence of strident neoisolationist and intense unilateralist voices at home, U.S. decisionmakers have been reluctant to use political capital to mobilize the support of the generally international-minded American majority behind principled preventive action. To some extent, America has neglected the responsibilities that flow from its status as primus inter pares and the support that it owes the international organizations to which it belongs and from which it continues to reap major benefits. There has been a growing reliance on aggressive unilateral statements and actions, dressed only with a thin veneer of allied consultation. Not only is this approach an inadequate substitute for genuine and sustained international cooperation in the difficult task of preventing deadly conflicts, but it also carries a high price in terms of America's international credibility. If the United States should find itself unable to bring along its friends and allies to address international challenges the world faces, there is a greater risk that today's problems will become tomorrow's threats to vital interests.

During the twentieth century, the United States accumulated substantial experience, knowledge, and skill in managing difficult domestic conflicts without falling into the trap of mass violence.[25] This was accomplished not only by governmental means, but also through strong institutions of civil society. Similarly, the United States has gained hard-won experience in working with others throughout the world to avert disaster in situations fraught with tension and potential violence—most notably in the Cold War but in other circumstances as well.

It is, therefore, reasonable to ask whether Americans—acting through government and nongovernmental organizations—can undertake a far-sighted responsible role within the international community to enhance current capacities to prevent the deadliest conflicts. Can the United States help to recognize serious dangers early enough, help adversaries to understand the risks of violence before they have crossed the Rubicon, help them strengthen their own capacities for conflict resolution, mobilize international resources to pool strengths, share burdens, and divide labor cooperatively in averting disaster and achieving just outcomes?

The United States is in a strong position to undertake preventive diplomacy, preventive defense, fostering of democracy, and socioeconomic development. Among its other endowments, the United States has a sophisticated information-gathering capacity and a cadre of diplomats well experienced in conflict management. As human rights and democracy have gained broader acceptance around the world, the United States has earned respect as a major promoter of these ideals and has the combined intellectual, technical, economic, political, and moral strength to help in their implementation.

Yet, preventing deadly conflict is a problem for the entire world, not just the United States by any means. The predisposing and precipitating factors for mass violence are widely distributed. Lethal weapons and the tools of incitement are available everywhere. International terrorism has a *worldwide* reach. International cooperation is a practical necessity for doing the work of prevention. There is admiration in the world for American freedom, science and technology, ingenuity, democratic standards, rich diversity, even entertainment media. All that gives the United States an excellent opportunity to elicit cooperation from others in preventing deadly conflict.

Yet, Americans cannot be everywhere and do everything. Certainly, Americans should not and do not wish to be (or be seen as) the world's hegemony or some kind of neoimperialist power. Ideally, American leadership in this context should mean drawing on the nation's best resources: intellectual, technical, and moral as well as material resources; being thoughtful, well-informed, active, creative, and respectful of others in helping to figure out where are the great dangers and how to cope with them and what is the moral and operational basis for preventing deadly conflict in each distinctive instance.

The United States must do its part. That surely includes support of relevant international institutions and strengthening them for this great mission. In the individual hot spot, different nations and different organizations will take leadership in different situations. There will be novel configurations for different cases. Sometimes the American role will be large, and sometimes small. But it should never be indifferent, insensitive, isolationist, or xenophobic. Interestingly, this view is consistent with the most recent careful surveys of American public opinion.[26] The American public understands that we live closely together with other peoples in a world of great diversity. Like families, nations need friends and social supports in the context of a mutual-aid ethic. The United States has only begun to fulfill its vast potential as an agent for preventing deadly conflict.

In my view, important leadership for violence prevention may also come from Europe, Japan, Canada, and other major democracies. In areas of serious conflict, multilateral task forces or contact groups can be created from local actors as well as agencies of the UN, major states, regional organizations, and NGOs—and a "prime mover" with the appropriate resources and status. Such a group can be headed by a highly esteemed individual with local or regional ties. A group organized on these lines has the ability to assess local resources that are available, decide on a cogent preventive strategy, and divide tasks based on the strengths of the members of the group. The multilateral task force can then develop a preventive package that suits the local area and make decisions on what assignments each third party should handle in order to start conflict resolution processes with attention to implementation.

Putting It All Together: Leadership for Prevention

Even if all the components described for an integrated multilateral regime are established and cultivated there is still a pressing need for the leadership to bring these sometimes disparate institutions, ideas, and groups together to work effectively for prevention. The Carnegie Commission on Preventing Deadly Conflict concluded that "although the prevention of deadly conflict requires many tools and strategies, bold leadership and an active constituency for prevention are essential for these tools and strategies to be effective."[27] Leadership is a sine qua non for success.

International leaders can do a lot to prevent deadly conflict by mediating disputes, mobilizing international coalitions and domestic constituencies in

support of peaceful solutions, and supplying the resources to make such solutions durable. They can vividly illuminate the dangers posed by intergroup violence, tap into latent public inclinations for prevention, and educate the public about nonviolent ways to settle disputes. They are especially
important in building the political will necessary to mount an effective response to conflict-prone situations—in effect, a constituency for prevention.
Though political leaders are vital in such efforts, leaders of other powerful
institutions and sectors, such as religion, business, the media, and the scientific community, can also make a profound difference. Effective leadership for violence prevention means drawing on the best intellectual, technical, and moral resources available and applying them with determination to
tackle the predisposing and precipitating factors in deadly conflict.[28] The
recurrent observation that negative leaders are crucial to the mobilization
of intergroup conflict—playing on ethnic, religious, and ideological differences—opens the way to influence on them by positive leaders through
third-party mediation, sometimes to marginalize them in their own societies, and other interventions to avoid war and seek just solutions.

Political will must be generated, in large part by the conscious deliberation of policymakers. We need deeper understanding of ways in which this
can be accomplished. Just as more attention has been given to the causes of
conflict rather than to its prevention, so too we know more about the role
of leaders in stimulating intergroup conflict than in diminishing the dangers. Research has already given useful clues to improving on present leadership operations.

Study of decision making under the stress of intergroup and international
conflict revealed cognitive pathologies such as "groupthink."[29] These are
more pronounced in some settings than others, depending on the institutional arrangements, advisory functions, personal dynamics, and policy
problems specific to particular leaders. Tendencies such as groupthink are
exacerbated by leaders who draw back into small groups of advisors under
stress, thereby obtaining relief from the pressures of risk, urgency, and ambiguity. In so doing, they tend to restrict the information available and narrow the range of policy options from which they can choose.[30] There are
ways to offset these tendencies so as to anticipate and interpret imminent
conflicts and to ensure a wide range of timely and appropriate responses.
For example, foreign ministries can be organized so as to permit regular
communication between a large number of official and informal sources of
early warning, especially those with greatest local knowledge of potential
violence situations. Similarly, a wide range of sound policy options linking
early warning to early response can be fostered by a leader in an emerging
crisis situation—and for the long term can be stimulated by introducing career incentives which reward professionals for initiative, creativity, and innovation. Leaders should devote substantial institutional resources to ad-

dressing long-term structural prevention as well as a repertoire of operational contingencies for dealing with dangerous situations—and doing so when there is opportunity for thoughtful reflection and considered analysis of policy options, requisite resources, and foreseeable trade-offs.

Leadership involves the vision to recognize real dangers and the courage to address them thoughtfully. It requires the ability to transcend wishful thinking. It can be greatly enhanced by building professional competence in the small advisory group and the institutional setting in which leaders make decisions—so that they can get the best available information, analyze it carefully, weigh their options, and reach conclusions for the general well-being. Moreover, authentic leaders must have the capacity to build constituencies for prevention through a base of public information and skill in forming political coalitions.

In practice, good policymakers engage in analytic problem solving, working to the best of their abilities within the limits of available organizational resources, trying to avoid serious mistakes in the essential tasks of information search, deliberation, and planning. Organizational, procedural, and staff arrangements supporting leadership decision making can be institutionalized in ways that foster these problem-solving processes.

There are several procedural tasks that must be well executed within a policy-making system if the leader is to receive information, analysis, and advice of high quality. These procedures do not guarantee high-quality decisions, but they increase their probability. The first task is to ensure that sufficient information about the current situation is obtained and analyzed adequately. Second, the policy-making process should facilitate consideration of all the major values and interests affected by the policy issue at hand. Third, the process should ensure a search for a relatively wide range of options and a reasonably thorough evaluation of the expected consequences of each. Fourth, the policy-making process should carefully consider the problems that might arise in implementing the options under consideration. Finally, the process should remain receptive to indications that current policies are not working: It is vitally important to learn from experience.[31]

There is a growing body of knowledge on these matters, derived from systematic research on leadership decision making as well as sharp observation by expert practitioners who have served in leadership capacities.[32] This knowledge can be put to use in organizations to tackle hard problems and take advantage of important opportunities—in short, providing a highly informative, supportive, problem-solving context for leadership decision making on matters of utmost consequence.

By virtue of their power and public prominence, eminent leaders in major sectors of society—not only in government—bear a serious responsibility for utilizing their public influence for constructive purposes. They can shape an agenda for cooperation, caring, and mutual accommodation of diversity.

They can build mechanisms for dealing with ongoing or emerging conflicts that rest on widely understood and agreed procedures.

One function of leadership is periodically to reassess formulations of national interest. In the new century there will be a need for a broader than conventional conception of national interests, one which strives for enlightened self-interest in a realistic appraisal of the contemporary world. When almost every violent conflict is dismissed as distant and inconsequential, we run the risk of allowing a series of conflict episodes to undermine hard-won international norms. In a world of growing economic and political interdependence, in which national well-being increasingly depends on the security and prosperity of other states and peoples, indifference of this sort could have corrosive effects for everyone. Rather than rely on narrow, obsolescent notions of national interest, leaders must develop formulations that reflect the new reality of economic globalization, intimate interdependence, widespread democratization, drastic technological changes, huge inequities, and the reach of international terrorism.

It is important that leaders make clear to their publics the terrible outcomes associated with degraded conditions in some developing countries, not only intergroup violence but also fostering of hatred and exportable terrorism, of infectious pandemics, of massive refugee flows, of dangerous environmental effects. All these risks must be taken into account in a world of unprecedented proximity and interdependence. Increasingly, they will have a bearing on realistic appraisals of national interest and the interest of the international community. Preventing deadly conflict must be understood publicly as a service to the most vital human interest—survival.

Leaders in democratic societies strive to build constituencies for important policy orientations. In practical terms, an enduring constituency for prevention could be fostered through measures that identify latent popular inclinations toward prevention; reinforce these impulses with substantive explanations of rationales, approaches, and successful examples; make the message clear by developing analogies from familiar contexts such as the home and community; and demonstrate the linkage between preventing deadly conflict and vital public interests, including protection against terrorism.

Among the general public, there are already dispositions, interests, and organizations that can be tapped for support. In a variety of democratic countries, a strong constituency for prevention in medicine and public health has emerged over the last several decades. Public awareness campaigns and the provision of readily accessible information about health risks and preventive behavior have led to remarkable improvements in public health. Concepts like "an ounce of prevention is worth a pound of cure" have taken hold in the public imagination of many countries and are reflected positively in improved rates of immunization, better diet and exercise practices, and reduced cigarette smoking. In short, sustained public efforts at disease prevention have proven highly effective. This model of dedicated leadership and public education can be usefully applied to the prevention of deadly conflict.

Community fire prevention provides another useful model for public understanding. Communities are interested in putting out fires when they are small, before they get out of hand. This is now a familiar, well-accepted notion of public safety. But we are also concerned with eliminating conditions that make fires likely in the first place. To put out fires early, communities need operational tools such as fire alarms, reliable telephones, adequate supplies of water and firefighting equipment, and well-trained professionals. When it comes to the structural conditions that minimize the likelihood of fires in the first place, additional tools are needed—for example, specialized knowledge about hazardous substances and the skills to dispose of them safely and public education about the perils of high-risk behavior. All this involves developing technically competent professional organizations functioning in the context of sympathetic public understanding. And it works. Over time, as fire prevention strategies have become the norm not only through the actions of fire departments but by businesses (who reap benefits by lowering liability costs), government (which has to deal with less disruption and eventually can cut its expenditures on firefighting), and individuals (who suffer less from the risk of fire), society in general has benefited. In the United States, where a culture of fire prevention has taken root, local fire companies spend less time than at any point in their history fighting fires, freeing them to perform other necessary services.

In short, there are ways in which leaders can stimulate interest and help the public to understand why prevention is necessary and feasible. Moreover, as emphasized throughout this book, the international community can do much more than it has previously done to help moderate, socially tolerant and pragmatic leaders build constituencies for prevention in hot spots.

President Roosevelt employed this kind of approach, utilizing familiar examples to clarify the necessity for international cooperative security during and after World War II. This strategy eventually helped the United States overcome deeply engrained isolationist sentiments that constituted an enormous obstacle to rational public policy in the face of aggressive, unscrupulous, and heavily armed dictators.[33]

Political leaders have been reluctant to try mobilizing broad-based support for concerted action to prevent deadly conflict. In modern democratic states, the constraints that competitive domestic politics impose on leaders as they contemplate whether and how to act in the face of deadly conflicts can be formidable. The conventional wisdom dictates caution because mass publics are assumed to be apathetic about global affairs and presumably reluctant to get involved in other people's quarrels. Research suggests that much of this view rests on questionable assumptions about the putative isolationist content of popular attitudes.[34] In fact, numerous surveys of American public opinion indicate that instead of rigid isolationism and/or widespread apathy, most Americans are reasonably well informed about global affairs and are supportive of U.S. participation in multilateral endeavors for peace and the relief of massive suffering. Public evaluation of any particular proposal for intervention abroad depends on several factors, such as the scope and intensity of the conflict, the severity of the regional and global threat it poses, the feasibility of the preventive action, its anticipated costs, and, above all, how cogently these issues are presented by leaders for public consideration. These findings have important implications for leadership.[35] Public opinion, if adequately mobilized, can offer crucial support for leaders who engage in preventive actions. Leaders can make use of the media for public education on these matters, especially when clear explanations are given repeatedly over time in relation to ongoing, newsworthy events.

The Long Sweep of Human Adaptation: A Basis for Hope

Within only a moment of evolutionary time, human ingenuity has produced a huge increase in destructive power available to our species—in the twenty-first century available to almost all countries everywhere and to many subnational groups. *In a few decades, there will be no part of the earth so remote that it cannot do immense damage to itself and to others far away.* This is a new kind of world we have made for ourselves—full of discovery, innovation, fascination, and opportunity; yet also extreme danger.

For many, many millennia, our prehuman and human ancestors lived in small groups in which they learned the rules of adaptation for survival and reproduction. They used simple tools to aid in adaptation. They were highly vulnerable to the vicissitudes of nature—food, water, weather, predators, infections, other humans. Their way of life changed with the onset of agriculture and changed even more drastically with the industrial revolution two centuries ago. Since then, science and technology have facilitated a profound and continuing transformation. Suddenly, the human species has drastically changed the world of its ancestors. Natural selection over millions of years shaped our ancestors in ways that were adaptive in earlier environments. We simply do not know how well we are suited to the world we have made. Some of our own ancient emotional response tendencies, inherited genetically and culturally, may now be maladaptive. These are tendencies in the mode of frustration and aggression; readiness to form harsh in-group versus out-group distinctions; and our susceptibility to authoritative leaders inciting to violence.

Warfare has a long and deadly tradition, which is often the outgrowth of serious errors, traps, and destructive cycles. And some of these problems are getting worse. Not only is the technology and destructive power of weaponry accelerating rapidly, but also other exacerbating factors have emerged. Massive social-technical-economic transformation affects the probability of fear, hostility, and war—for example, huge and uprooting migrations, the crowding of strangers, fear of the unknown, the vast, impersonal scale of a globalized economy, the loss of previous social supports, contagion of violence through mass media, easy availability of highly destructive weapons, and fanatical religious beliefs. Institutional restraints on aggression are weak. Institutional adaptation is altogether slow and difficult as compared with technological change—and nowhere more so than in international organizations. So, there is an urgent need for fundamental reassessment of approaches to war and peace. We must move beyond long entrenched bad habits and dangerous traditional assumptions.

The earth is no longer believed to be flat. But our intergroup attitudes often have a flat-earth nature. Likewise, the intimate, slowly changing world of our ancient ancestors is gone now. So, too, is the small and relatively simple world of our recent ancestors in agrarian societies. The world we have lately made is crowded, heterogeneous, impersonal, superarmed, rapidly changing beyond all previous experience. There is not much in the very long history of the human species to prepare us for this world we have suddenly made. Yet the fantastic adaptability of the human species rests heavily on our remarkable learning capacities. Now we must turn those capacities to the deepest problem of humanity.

The evolution that is distinctively human centers around our increasing capacity for learning, for communication chiefly by language, for cooperative problem solving, and for complex social organization as well as for advanced toolmaking and tool use. These attributes have gotten us here by enormously enhancing our capabilities, not only to adapt to a wide variety of habitats, but also by permitting us recently to modify our habitats profoundly in ways that suit our human purposes.

Now we are challenged as never before to find ways in which these unique capacities may be used to stop killing ourselves, especially to prevent the final epidemic of nuclear or bacteriological war, to provide a decent quality of life for people everywhere, and to preserve the life-sustaining attributes of the planet's environment. If we have lost our sense of purpose and human solidarity in the modern world, perhaps this perspective can help us regain it.

Indeed, there is much in the second half of the twentieth century that offers legitimate basis for hope.[36] Many of the tragic events have, despite their costs, spurred important changes within the world community. These have left landmarks in the form of the worldwide spread of human rights and democracy; the termination of aggressive tyrannies in Germany, Italy, Japan, and the Soviet Union; the end of the Cold War; the dissolution of the Soviet empire; the end of apartheid in South Africa; the growth of international cooperation. The unifying tendencies of global telecommunications, a heightened awareness of our shared natural habitat within the earth's environment, and great advances in science and technology have served to accentuate these dramatic changes. All of this and more suggest the vast constructive potential that exists within humanity. Perhaps in the twenty-first century these capacities will at last be brought comprehensively to bear on our ancient and fundamental problem of human relationships.

Notes

1. Boutros Boutros-Ghali, George Bush, Jimmy Carter, Mikhail Gorbachev, and Desmond Tutu, *Essays on Leadership* (New York: Carnegie Corporation of New York, 1998).
2. Eric Hobswam, *The Age of Extremes: A History of the World, 1914–1991* (New York: Pantheon, 1994); Michael Howard and William Roger Louis, *The Oxford History of the Twentieth Century* (New York: Oxford University Press, 1998); J. M. Roberts, *The Twentieth Century: The History of the World, 1901–2000* (New York: Viking, 1999).
3. Hamburg, "Human Rights."
4. John P. Steinbruner, *Principles of Global Security* (Washington, D.C.: Brookings, 2000).
5. Michael Mandelbaum, *The Dawn of Peace in Europe* (New York: Twentieth Century Fund Press, 1996).
6. William McNeill, *A History of the Human Community: Prehistory to the Present* (Upper Saddle River, N.J.: Prentice Hall, 1997); Arno Mayer, *The Furies: Violence and Terror in the French and Russian Revolutions* (Princeton, N.J.: Princeton University Press, 2000); Michael Howard, *War in European History* (New York: Oxford University Press, 1976).
7. William Ury, *Getting to Peace* (New York: Penguin, 1999).
8. Miles Hewstone, Wolfgang Stroebe, and Geoffrey Stephanson, *Introduction to Social Psychology*, 2d ed. (London: Blackwell, 1996); David Myers, *Social Psychology*, 2d ed. (New York: McGraw-Hill, 1987).
9. Staub, *Roots of Evil.*
10. Anthony Jackson and Willis Hawley, *Toward a Common Destiny: Improving Race and Ethnic Relations in America* (San Francisco: Jossey-Bass, 1995).
11. David A. Hamburg, *Preventing Contemporary Intergroup Violence and Education for Conflict Resolution* (Carnegie Corporation of New York Annual Report Essay, 1984, 25–40.
12. Ury, *Getting to Peace.*
13. *Conflict Prevention.*
14. Thomas Carothers, *Aiding Democracy Abroad: The Learning Curve* (Washington, D.C.: Carnegie Endowment for International Peace, 1999).

15. Michael Lund, *Preventing Violent Conflicts: A Strategy for Preventive Diplomacy* (Washington, D.C.: U.S. Institute of Peace Press, 1996).

16. Evans, *Cooperating for Peace.*

17. Peck, *Sustainable Peace.*

18. Milton J. Esman and Shibley Telhami, eds., *International Organizations and Ethnic Conflict* (Ithaca, N.Y.: Cornell University Press, 1995).

19. Kofi Annan, *We the Peoples: The Role of the United Nations in the Twenty-First Century* (New York: United Nations, 2000).

20. Peck, *Sustainable Peace.*

21. Kennedy, *Environmental Quality.*

22. Harlan Cleveland, *Birth of a New World: An Open Moment for International Leadership* (San Francisco: Jossey-Bass, 1993).

23. John Baylis and Steve Smith, eds., *The Globalization of World Politics* (New York: Oxford University Press, 1997).

24. Allison and Owada, *Responsibilities of Democracies.*

25. Carl Degler, *Out of Our Past: The Forces That Shaped Modern America,* 3d ed. (New York: Harper Collins, 1984).

26. Steven Kull, "What the Public Knows That Washington Doesn't," *Foreign Policy* (winter 1995/1996): 102–15.

27. *Preventing Deadly Conflict,* xlvi.

28. Alexander George, *Presidential Decisionmaking in Foreign Policy: The Effective Use of Information and Advice* (Boulder, Colo.: Westview, 1980).

29. I. Janis, *Crucial Decisions: Leadership in Policy Making and Crisis Management* (New York: Free Press, 1989).

30. Hamburg, George, and Ballentine, "Preventing Deadly Conflict: The Critical Role of Leadership."

31. Graham Allison and Philip Zelikow, *Essence of Decision: Explaining the Cuban Missile Crisis,* 2d ed. (New York: Longman, 1999).

32. Elliot Richardson, *Reflections of a Radical Moderate* (New York: Pantheon, 1996).

33. Kennedy, *Freedom from Fear,* ch. 13.

34. Kull, "What the Public Knows."

35. John W. Gardner, *On Leadership* (New York: The Free Press, 1993).

36. Akira Iriye, "The International Order," in Richard Bullet, ed., *The Columbia History of the Twentieth Century* (New York: Columbia University Press, 1998), 245–47.

9

Preventing Catastrophic Terrorism: International Cooperation, Weapons of Mass Destruction, and Democratic Development

September 11, 2001:
A Horrific Wake-up Call for Preventing Deadly Conflict

Some major themes of this book are reinforced by the hideous terrorist attacks on New York and Washington that occurred on September 11, 2001. It is far better to *prevent* mass violence, including terrorist violence, than to pick up the tragic pieces afterward and mourn for the thousands of good people irrevocably lost with families shattered.

In this book, I refer briefly to my own direct involvement in an international terrorist episode in Africa in 1975. Since then, I have several times been drawn into an advisory role in international terrorist episodes. In a similar vein, I have been concerned with assassination of presidents and presidential candidates since I served on a scientific advisory panel shortly after President Kennedy's assassination. During my presidency of the Institute of Medicine, National Academy of Sciences, the United State Secret Service contracted with the Institute of Medicine to study ways of preventing such assassinations. In the years of my participation in joint study groups with Soviet scientists on arms control and crisis prevention, I periodically raised the issue of mutual benefit in U.S.–Soviet (later Russia) cooperation to prevent terrorism. So, concern with terrorism has been a grim "hobby" of mine for four decades.

I have been warning policymakers and scholars that it *can* happen *here*. The United States has long been vulnerable to large-scale casualties from well-organized, *fanatical haters, ideologues,* or *deeply troubled young men.* Yet, as so often in human affairs, we have tended to deny this reality. Now we must face it. But the threat is one that already involves *many* countries and, in principle, could involve all. This makes possible the building of internationally cooperative efforts to overcome the serious terrorism problem.

251

As a practical matter, the problem simply cannot be overcome without a high degree of international cooperation.

One of the principal themes of this book is that preventing deadly conflict in all its major forms—including terrorist attacks—requires *extensive and sophisticated international cooperation*. This is not a matter of altruism or brotherly love, but a hardheaded practical requirement for effective action. This thesis surely applies to the September 11 catastrophe. If any antidote were needed for contemptuous unilateralism or other egocentric, ethnocentric attitudes and policies, the challenge of international terrorism provides it. It appears that we are at last beginning to get the message of this global reality.

One of the most heartening developments to come out of the September 11 tragedy is the prompt response of Secretary of State Colin Powell and of President George W. Bush to reach out to leaders of many countries and a wide range of international organizations to elicit their cooperation. The high degree of reciprocity has been encouraging. While it is too early to say whether a genuinely cooperative coalition built on shared concerns, mutual benefit, and mutual respect will emerge on an enduring basis, the first phase has been remarkable. Rarely if ever can I recall such a nearly worldwide response—not only of sympathy but of solidarity. Within the first week, many significant international institutions and world leaders made powerful statements. For example, there were strong resolutions from the UN Security Council and the UN General Assembly as well as a powerful, unequivocal statement by the Secretary-General; strong official statements from the European Union and from NATO. The latter included the first-ever invocation of Article V: An attack on one is an attack on all. This leads to serious international consultations that should involve genuine sharing of information, ideas, and policy options. Shortly thereafter, the UN Security Council passed a set of universal guidelines for counter terrorism that were powerful in their scope. If American diplomacy in the next few years is wise, sensitive, respectful, and resourceful, a unique coalition may develop in the widely shared interests of survival. It will surely not be easy, but it is possible.

What do we hope to gain by international cooperation? In the near term (measured in years), we can strive for a variety of initiatives to counteract, incapacitate, or overwhelm the terrorist violence. In the long term (measured in decades), there could be significant progress through initiatives of democratic, socioeconomic development to change the conditions that breed violence in tyrannical, degraded nations.

The near-term measures include international cooperation in: (1) intelligence collection and analysis; (2) coordination of policing in local areas, relating information about terrorists in different countries so as to bring networks out of deep cover; (3) political pressure on regimes that harbor or foster terrorists; (4) economic leverage on such regimes, including "smart sanctions"; (5) military action if necessary, including use of bases, permission for overflights, staging areas, and in some cases the deployment of joint forces. Different coalition members would make different contributions.

The long-term measures to stop the breeding of terrorists include all of the considerations reviewed in chapter 7 to promote competent, decent, prosperous nation-states. As I have pointed out repeatedly, it is in the national interest of advanced, affluent countries to help prevent degraded conditions in poor, undemocratic countries that breed hatred, violence, and exportable terrorism. This is much more than a matter of humanitarian altruism. It centers on developing decent human relations at every level conducive to peaceful living and indeed to human survival.

Thus, the ghastly terrorism of September 11 might possibly—just possibly—be a powerful stimulus for cooperative international action in the same way that World War II and the Holocaust taught us painful lessons that have been partially implemented in the intervening half century. If so, the current nightmare could provide compensatory benefits for the children of those lost in the September 11 madness.

Over decades, with strong international stimulation, guidance, and support, some (perhaps many or most) degraded regimes can become competent, decent, and relatively prosperous countries. After all, most people in most countries are not enthusiastic about being repressed, even persecuted and tortured by their own governments. Nor are many happy with abject poverty when they can see in movies, on television, and among their own elites the opportunities available to so many other people elsewhere. These conditions make for profound and pervasive frustration, day in and day out over years of growth and development.

It is in the nature of the human organism, as much research has shown, that frustration induces aggression.[1] Thus, some young people come to maturity full of anger, looking for scapegoats to blame. This anger can readily be directed by ruthless charismatic leaders to hatred of other peoples—whether designated by religion or ethnicity or level of affluence. "He causes our troubles so we must hate him." From here it is a short step to violence.

A determined international effort to foster democratic socioeconomic development in these countries, with culturally meaningful inducements of economic, political, and psychological benefit, can do much in the long run to turn around such miserable and dangerous conditions. Young people can then see a basis for hope, can acquire constructive, useful, marketable skills and take advantage of tangible opportunities for a better life.[2] They can develop at least a rudimentary sense of solidarity with the international community and feel that they have a respectful place in the world. Then, their need for scapegoats would diminish and their susceptibility to hate-inciting demagogues would be less than before.

This must be accompanied by broadly international efforts far exceeding prior experience to diminish ethnocentrism, prejudice, and the glorification of violence in all forms of education—from schools to religious institutions to universities to media to community organizations.³ In this respect, the world in general is somewhat primitive, nowhere more so than in autocratic or tyrannical regimes steeped in religious justification for hatred and violence toward out-groups—the fanatical behavior that makes possible the scourge of holy wars in one form or another. To change this is very difficult and slow. Yet the motivation to improve the quality of life in poor, repressive countries is strong, human ingenuity is great, and the capacity to learn from good examples is powerful. In chapter 7, I described the way such processes occurred in South Korea, over a half century of dedicated efforts, with heartening results. It can happen elsewhere. But not without international help—maybe "tough love" at first—but a genuine long-run commitment to help build better lives for today's equivalent of the Hitler youth and thereby offset the conditions favorable to terrorism. This is not a task for one country, but for many in joint efforts. Nor is it a task for the impatient or the fainthearted.

This viewpoint is well summarized by Gareth Evans, president of the International Crisis Group and a valuable member of the Carnegie Commission.

If the emerging facts identify deserving military targets—including one or more foreign governments—there can be no argument with a tough and decisive reaction, in as broad a coalition as is possible to build . . . it is absolutely critical that the targets be thoroughly justified. . . .

There is a larger message about the U.S. diplomatic role. As Washington moves with its allies to search out and destroy the perpetrators of these horrific attacks, it must begin again with a sustained effort to resolve the agonizing conflicts around the world from which the desperation and hatred that lead to those attacks grow. There has to be a focus on the conditions creating individuals able to believe that killing thousands of civilians is not only acceptable, but also heroic.

The job of fighting terrorism cannot be separated from the task of preventing, containing and ending conflict. All too often the places that generate terrorism—as well as drug trafficking, health pandemics, refugee outflows and environmental disasters—are shattered societies where grievance, greed, repression and poverty have led to violence, despair and extremism. . . .

Far better under these circumstances to mobilize U.S. ingenuity, will and power—in cooperation with the legion of countries that keenly want to work with Washington—to tackle constructively the issues festering in crisis breeding grounds.⁴

It is a consummation devoutly to be wished!

Practical Steps to Reduce the Risk of Catastrophic Terrorism

Professor William Perry of Stanford, a great public servant and one of the finest secretaries of defense the United States ever had, recently considered preventive approaches in this context. He highlights the gravity of the problem, counteracting the wishful thinking that has so permeated the field of deadly conflict, as I have tried to show throughout this book.

> Since the end of the Cold War, the barriers to success have been lowered. The know-how for making nuclear weapons is increasingly available through the Internet. Security controls on the huge supply of nuclear weapons (which number in the tens of thousands) and fissile material (amounting to hundreds of tons) are becoming increasingly uncertain. And the thriving black market in fissile material suggests that demand is high. In the next few years this combination of forces could result in a nuclear incident with results more catastrophic than the destruction wreaked by the Hiroshima and Nagasaki bombs, which together killed an estimated 200,000 people. . . .
>
> Hostile groups that cannot develop their own weapons, meanwhile, may be able to buy them through illicit channels. The Soviet Union produced a large supply of biological weapons during the Cold War, some of which may still be available. . . .
>
> Considering the level of catastrophe that could occur in a nuclear or biological attack, mitigating such threats should be an overriding security priority today, just as heading off a nuclear attack was an overriding priority during the Cold War. In that era the United States essentially depended on a single strategy: deterrence. Now it can add two other strategies to the mix—prevention (curbing emergent threats before they can spread) and defense. Rather than relying exclusively on any one strategy, the sensible approach is to deploy a balanced mix of all three.
>
> Prevention is the first line of defense against the proliferation of weapons of mass destruction, but it requires cooperation from the other nuclear powers. Any actions that the United States takes to stop the spread of weapons can easily be nullified if Russia, for example, decides to sell its nuclear technology, weapons, or fissile material. Russian leaders know that it is in their national interest to fight proliferation.[5]

Perry points out that some programs have been remarkably successful in reducing the risk of nuclear proliferation and terrorism. For example, the Nunn–Lugar initiative for cooperative threat reduction, in concert with other measures, has already been responsible for the dismantling of more than 5,000 nuclear warheads and the complete elimination of nuclear weapons in Ukraine, Kazakhstan, and Belarus. It has flourished for a decade despite obstacles in the United States and Soviet Union. Programs to immobilize or commercialize leftover Soviet plutonium and weapons-grade uranium, material that was once intended for Soviet bombs, are now meeting the needs of peaceful power reactors producing energy. He proposes strengthening these proven programs, especially by extending the fruitful Nunn–Lugar efforts to *tactical* nuclear weapons (which are particularly dangerous in the context of terrorism) and by funding efforts to immobilize plutonium.

In his practical view, he points out the low-tech and nonglamorous ways in which catastrophes can happen. For example, the most immediate danger is of a terrorist group delivering a nuclear bomb or biological weapon with a truck, cargo ship, airplane, or boat. The first line of defense against this kind of threat is to develop an intelligence network able to give the government advance warning of an attack so that it can be stopped before it is launched. In this regard, human intelligence is as important as technical means.

> At the same time, Washington should pursue an aggressive campaign against the bases of terrorist groups and their possible state sponsors. Terrorist groups often have activities and support scattered in several countries, so the United States needs *joint* intelligence collection and analysis efforts with other nations, particularly those where terrorist cells are located.[6] (italics mine)

Having worked cooperatively with Russian and Chinese leaders, Perry emphasizes the importance of eliciting their cooperation in these measures noting that "success in preventing nuclear proliferation will require joint programs with Russia and China, so will success in collecting intelligence on multinational terrorist groups."

I have referred repeatedly to Senator Sam Nunn, now co-chair with Ted Turner and CEO of the Nuclear Threat Initiative, a foundation focusing on diminishing the dangers of weapons of mass destruction. Ted Turner is an ingenious, humane, and generous philanthropist. Senator Nunn is one of the best-informed, wisest, and most creative statesmen I have ever known. He has offered a new security framework in which to stimulate our thinking about these profoundly critical issues. So, I quote a few passages here that can promote guidance in the prevention of catastrophic terrorism.

> We have an imperative now to integrate this accelerated fight against terrorism into a new security framework that addresses the full range of dangers we face. This strategy must contain both short-term urgent initiatives and longer-term strategic thinking. . . .
> The most significant, clear and present danger we face is the threat posed by nuclear, biological and chemical weapons.
> We must understand that threat reduction, diplomacy, cooperation, military power and intelligence are our first lines of defense against the spread of weapons of mass destruction and terrorism.

... Presidents Bush and Vladimir Putin could use the occasion to commit each nation to a course of action ensuring that our nuclear weapons and nuclear, chemical and biological weapons materials are safe, secure and accounted for with reciprocal monitoring.[7]

Finally, when Russia was developing biological weapons, it also was developing vaccines and other pharmaceuticals. When it was devising dissemination mechanisms, it also was working on detectors and protective devices. At this moment, the United States and Russia could combine their biodefense knowledge and scientific expertise and apply these considerable joint resources to defensive and peaceful biological purposes. The two presidents could promote a research endeavor that could motivate other nations to join.[8]

Professor Graham Allison of Harvard has been an authentic pioneer in the study of these problems and in formulating action plans to prevent nuclear disasters induced by terrorists and proliferation to highly irresponsible states. He has brought together a superb group of collaborators—Americans such as Professors Ashton Carter (who also works closely with William Perry), John Holdren, and Joseph Nye and Russians such as Andrei Kokoshin (a fine scholar and former high security official in the Russian government). It is worth quoting here some well-formulated passages from Professor Allison's recent work:

Preventing nuclear terrorist attacks on the American homeland will require a serious, comprehensive defense—not for months or years, but far into the future. The response must stretch from aggressive prevention and pre-emption to deterrence and active defenses. Strict border controls to keep out smuggled containers will be as important to America as ballistic-missile defenses.

To fight the immediate threat, the United States must move smartly on two fronts. First, no effort can be spared in the military, economic and diplomatic campaign to defeat and destroy al-Qaeda. Simultaneously, the unprecedented international effort of intelligence and law-enforcement agencies must seek to discover and disrupt al-Qaeda sleeper cells and interrupt attempted shipments of weapons.

Second, the United States must seize the opportunity of a more cooperative Russia to "go to the source" of the greatest danger today: the 99 percent or more of the world's nuclear, biological and chemical weapons of mass destruction that are stored in Russia and the United States. The surest way to prevent nuclear assaults on Russia, America and the world is to prevent terrorists from gaining control of these weapons or materials to make them.

The readiest sources of such weapons and materials are the vast arsenals accumulated over four decades of cold-war competition. . . .

Mr. Bush and Vladimir Putin should pledge to make all nuclear weapons and material as secure as technically possible as fast as possible. Their best course would be to follow the recommendations of the Baker-Cutler taskforce. Within Russia, the programme should be jointly financed by the United States, its allies in the war against terrorism, and Russia.[9]

A recent commission co-chaired by experienced, highly respected statesmen—former senator and White House chief of staff Howard Baker, and former White House counselor Lloyd Cutler—studied these matters very carefully. Allison incisively summarizes their recommendations.

1. Make nuclear weapons and nuclear materials safer.

    Drastically cut the number of sites where nuclear materials are stored. Close vulnerable nuclear-storage sites.

    Speed up the improvement of security, using the latest technologies, for buildings that continue to house nuclear weapons and materials.

    Identify, label, and seal all warheads and materials, and keep a check on them.

    Extract highly enriched uranium (HEU) from Soviet-built research reactors, especially in ex-communist Eastern Europe.

2. Get rid of all HEU not needed for current weapons.

    Speed up the purchase of Russian HEU.

    Get an agreement to make the remaining HEU militarily unusable.

3. Control excess Russian plutonium.

    Make an inventory of all Russia's plutonium, and get it in one place.

    Using those new technologies, improve safety at all places where plutonium is stored.

    Stop production of plutonium.

    Buy and/or destroy excess plutonium by blending it as mixed-oxide fuel and burning it in civilian reactors.

4. Cut Russia's nuclear complex.

    Shut unneeded weapons plants soon.

    Pay key Russian nuclear scientists money for "contract research," to prevent the flow of expertise to other countries—and terrorists—seeking nuclear weapons.

    Provide private capital for businesses that employ nuclear scientists from the "closed cities" of the Russian nuclear complex.

    Help Russia pay for other long-term safety measures.[10]

Rose Gottemoeller, a distinguished scholar of international security who served effectively in government, has recently analyzed threat reduction cooperation in counter-terrorism with reference to reducing the nuclear danger.[11]

Threat reduction cooperation with Russia and the other newly independent states (NIS) of the former Soviet Union is practically ten years old, and has matured immeasurably in that time. The maturity of the programs can be seen in the range of facilities, especially highly sensitive ones, where they operate. It can also be seen in the variety of procedures that have been developed to implement and even, in latter years, accelerate the programs. Finally, it can be seen in the solidity of the working relationships that have developed among the program managers from both the U.S. and the NIS.

Now the question arises, is the maturity of the cooperation such that it can be extended to solving other policy problems confronting the international community? . . .

Indeed would Russia and the other former Soviet states, as their circumstances improved, want to continue the threat reduction relationship?[12]

She concludes that the September 11 tragedies are likely to answer these questions in the affirmative. South Asia faces a crisis that could ease the acquisition of weapons of mass destruction by terrorists or highly irresponsible states. Moreover, the explicit devotion of major terrorists to acquiring nuclear and biological weapons by any means possible emphasizes the necessity of speeding threat reduction work in countries of the former Soviet Union.

She states incisively key principles and practical prospects flowing from these considerations.

Principles for a New Stage of Threat Reduction

1. Consider what threats will be particularly attractive or accessible to terrorists and decide whether and in what way they should receive a higher priority.
2. Develop situation- and country-specific partnerships with other countries that will enable the cooperation to develop more quickly and efficiently.
3. Incorporate new and especially cooperatively developed technologies that enable new areas of threat reduction cooperation or enhance the efficiency and sustainability of older projects.
4. Undertake cooperation in a way that will strengthen and reinforce arms control and nonproliferation regimes. . . .[13]

In light of these principles, Gottemoeller proposes projects.

1. Projects should be set to match counter-terrorism priorities. . . .
2. Projects should draw on international partnerships. . . .
3. Projects should incorporate new technologies for improved effectiveness in threat reduction. . . .
4. Projects should reinforce international arms control and nonproliferation regimes.[14]

She emphasizes that a consensus has emerged about the necessity of accelerating work to lessen the threat of weapons of mass destruction, especially nuclear weapons and materials. This consensus focuses on (1) accelerating disposition of weapons-usable nuclear materials; (2) accelerating protection, control, and accounting of those materials; (3) addressing brain drain of nuclear-capable scientists and engineers (and similar biological scientists) from the former Soviet Union weapons complex to terrorist groups and very dangerous states. We now can move beyond the original brain drain concept of keeping scientists at work in their weapons facilities and put an innovative emphasis on moving scientists out of those facilities while accelerating the shutdown of those facilities. In this process, these scientists and engineers can be helped to find opportunities in civilian employment.

Gottemoeller's conclusion is powerful.

> If we are to move in a new way to emphasizing the counter-terrorism problem, it is clear that the successes and failures of the past decade of threat reduction projects have created extensive precedents and a wide experience base that is ripe for expansion. If the United States and Russian Federation, to begin with, are ready to take on this task, then the potential for threat reduction work in the counter-terrorism struggle is serious and wide-ranging.[15]

The Distinctive and Grave Problem of Bioterrorism

It is exceedingly important to note that bioterrorism has, until recently, been neglected in public and policy considerations of contemporary threats. A half century of intensive analytical, technological, and political work has been devoted to the horrendous problems of nuclear weapons. The highly dangerous biological weapons, though considered seriously by such pioneers as the eminent scientists Joshua Lederberg and Matthew Meselson and a few political leaders (notably President Richard Nixon), have been the subject of less attention and concern. But this is now changing. I quote a few passages here from a highly informative overview paper prepared for the National Academy of Sciences 2002 publication, *Issues in Science and Technology,* by Dr. Margaret Hamburg. She was an early leader in practical preparation for biological attacks while serving as commissioner of health for New York City; she later helped to interest President Clinton in this problem—leading to a substantial upgrading of resources and efforts in this field. She is currently vice president for biological affairs of the Nuclear Threat Initiative.

In a recent article, she clarifies the need for cooperation and communication among doctors and the public health community, in combination with increased resources to manage effectively the challenge of bioterrorism in the United States. She focuses also on international cooperation among medical, scientific, and intelligence communities to control and destroy potentially hazardous biological materials before they unleash their deadly damage.

It is no longer a remote possibility that the use of biological agents may be purposely used to cause widespread disease and even death among the population. In order to reasonably control such an outbreak, an understanding and investment among many partners on the nature of epidemic disease is vital. Otherwise, the nation's preparedness programs will be insufficient, resulting in a missed opportunity for preventing such an attack.

Public health officials and health care workers must be the first to respond to a bioterrorism event. They must have adequate preparation to recognize an incipient disease outbreak and to deal with it adequately and early enough to minimize casualties.

> Today, experts agree that there is an *urgent need to increase the core capacities of the public health system to detect, track, and contain infectious disease.* State and local public health departments represent the backbone of our ability to respond effectively to a major outbreak of disease, including bioterrorist attack. Yet these public health agencies have never been adequately supported or equipped to fulfill this mission. (italics mine)[16]

She further emphasizes an urgent need to upgrade public health capacities. This implies a significant increase in investments. Resources must be provided to strengthen and broaden surveillance systems used to quickly detect and investigate unusual clusters of disease or symptoms. Epidemiological capabilities must be strengthened as well as trained personnel and laboratory capacity to be able to identify and analyze biological agents promptly. Communication among public health officials and officials at local, state, and federal levels must be improved by upgrading systems, which include computer links that facilitate collection, analysis, and sharing of information. These are critical domestic needs, but attention must also be focused on the *"renewed commitment to improving global public health"* (italics mine).

Physicians must be able to understand their responsibility to report unusual disease or symptoms to the public health department. Moreover they must be aware of whom to call and trust that their contributions are actually put to good use. Success hinges on the working partnerships among health care professional organizations, academic medical institutions, and public health officials, who could jointly develop training curricula and other informational guidelines.

She points out that countries at risk—and there are many—should strengthen their pharmaceutical stockpile so that vital drugs and equipment can be rapidly mobilized as needed. This should include contractual agreements with pharmaceutical manufacturers to ensure extra production capability for drugs and vaccines in a crisis as well as effective security at storage sites.

> Stopping a biological attack before it happens is obviously the most desirable way to avoid a crisis. *The first step in blocking the proliferation and use of biological weapons is to significantly bolster our intelligence.* The intelligence community could use additional scientific and medical expertise to help enhance the quality of data collection and analysis. This will require greater *partnership and trust between the intelligence community, law enforcement, and public health and biomedical science.*[17] (italics mine)

Hamburg emphasizes control of access to dangerous pathogens. The scientific community must ensure the safe storage and handling of these organisms. International cooperation will be essential to achieving these goals. Safety and control methods should be shared on a worldwide basis. Moreover, the scientific community, with help from governments, should enhance efforts to provide socially useful professional opportunities to scientists who had been employed in the former Soviet Union's bioweapons program so that economic need does not drive them into the arms of terrorists.

> We must also support efforts to help them secure or destroy potentially dangerous materials. The U.S. government has supported such efforts through the Cooperative Threat Reduction (CTR) program, but these programs desperately need to be strengthened and expanded. Opportunities to extend the reach of the program to include university and industry R&D collaborations will also be essential to long-term success.[18]

David Franz, a leading military bioscientist with extraordinary international experience in bioterrorism-related matters, has recently analyzed the value of scientist-to-scientist collaboration across U.S.–Russian boundaries.

He describes the improvement when these efforts were placed under the auspices of the Cooperative Threat Reduction Program. A major change was to drop demands that the Russian scientists formally admit to the past illegality of their offensive program. In recent years, U.S. participants held productive meetings, visited laboratories, and had in-depth discussions with former weaponeers. They oriented these scientists to business opportunities. Enthusiastic discussions of science, public health, and business have been pursued with the gradual emergence of mutual trust. It is now seven years into the biological program of U.S.–Russia cooperation. The American scientists are attempting to help these Russian scientists break into the world market for human and veterinary pharmaceuticals, food products, cosmetics, and other consumer goods.

> Enormous progress has occurred, especially in scientist-to-scientist relationship building. We now exchange ideas regularly; electronically and face to face. We are collaborating on fundamental and applied science . . . and many collaborators have become friends. We are building transparency in the former biological weapons labs.[19]

Franz lists the gains of these efforts.

1. Physical access to most of the former weapons facilities.
2. Transparency that has reduced the likelihood of biological weapons being made in these sites.
3. Personal relationships that have reduced the likelihood that the collaborating scientists are involved with any undiscovered remnants of the massive former bioweapons program.
4. Refocused basic and applied research programs of high quality in Russia, oriented toward constructive purposes.
5. An increased likelihood that former weapons scientists will contribute to the Russian economy and to better public health for Russian citizens.
6. A reduction in the likelihood of brain drain to potential terrorists or their supporters.
7. A generation of Russian scientists who are less likely to have the intent to make biological weapons.
8. Technical assistance in biodefense and public health programs in the United States.
9. A cadre of highly qualified Russian weapons scientists willing to help with the current bioterrorist threat to America.[20]

> They are now not only seriously interested, but also willing to assist during our time of difficulty. As we discuss our experience and concern, we observe a new frankness with regard to their vast experience as bioweaponeers. . . .
> Clinical medicine, public health, epidemiology, biotechnology and medical education may also hold opportunities for collaboration which could lead to better understanding between our peoples and help change intent among the professionals whose intent really matters. . . .
> Can any part of this Russian model be applied to other countries of BW proliferation concern? Likely not as effectively, however, we should not dismiss the possibility. There are undoubtedly areas in which minimal U.S. government support to academia or industry might leverage the unique energy that scientists of all nations share. When humans communicate, walls of fear, mistrust and hatred are torn down. Scientists not only hold the key

to controlling the proliferation of biological weapons, but we also speak a common language.[21]

From Franz's experience, and other leading scientists in this field, international collaborative efforts in research, education, and scientific exchange offer the best opportunities for achieving openness, breaking down secrecy, converting military to civilian work, and creating a mutual aid ethic for dealing with critical questions and crisis situations.

Opportunities for Global Leadership

In effect, the United States and Russia have an overwhelming preponderance of nuclear and biological weapons and the expertise that makes them possible. By the same token, these countries have a huge responsibility to safeguard their own weapons from theft, bribery, or serious accident—and to help other nations such as Pakistan do the same. Given the apparently excellent relationship of Presidents Bush and Putin, and the powerful superordinate goal of preventing catastrophic terrorism that can only be achieved by their cooperation, there is a new and crucial opportunity arising. Immediate steps to reduce the terrorists' chances of success in getting and using weapons of mass destruction are imperative in view of the terrorists' desperate urgency to strike again—in a jump step of violence—in response to their humiliating defeat in Afghanistan and the world's deep resentment of the September 11 events. But more is needed: long-term cooperative arrangements built into the functioning of both superpowers, and the availability of participation in such arrangements by countries throughout the world.

In light of these considerations, I had the opportunity in late 2001 of working closely with a group of long-standing collaborators—especially Graham Allison, Ashton Carter, Margaret Hamburg, Richard Lugar, Sam Nunn, and William Perry—to formulate a plan that would incorporate these observations. Our hope is to stimulate thinking and clarify policy options that strongly enhance prevention of the greatest nuclear and biological dangers—particularly in an effort to be helpful to the U.S. government and its partners in threat reduction.

We worked with the previous Bush administration a decade ago in the creation of the Nunn–Lugar program and strongly support expanding the scope of the existing programs of cooperative threat reduction. We do so in response to changed circumstances: The attacks of September 11; the clear desire and ability of Presidents Bush and Putin to move U.S.–Russian relations beyond the Cold War and its backwash in the 1990s; the clear and present danger that terrorists will gain the capability to carry out a catastrophic attack on the United States or other friendly countries, using either nuclear, biological, or chemical weapons; the urgent need for effective action on a global scale to deny terrorist access to weapons of mass destruction. This will require more resources, ingenious diplomacy, and presidential leadership in the United States and Russia (perhaps other leaders as well) to get this vital job done. The present leadership in both countries has the ability and public support to accomplish such tasks.

Our group of veteran collaborators proposes a coalition against catastrophic terrorism. In early 2002, President Bush and his colleagues are successfully leading a global coalition to defeat terrorists. They have elicited the cooperation of many governments to suppress terrorism within their own countries. He has made strong statements on the critical dangers, including one jointly with President Putin, to the effect that the United States and Russia, together, must keep the world's most dangerous technologies out of the hands of the world's most dangerous people.

President Putin has also made clear his desire to move beyond the Cold War relationship and find new forms of cooperation with the United States. This is manifested clearly with the war on terrorism in Afghanistan and in cooperation on bioterrorism. He leads a nation with abundant, relevant expertise in countering catastrophic terrorism. A coalition led by the two presidents could dramatically broaden the scope and enhance the effectiveness of the Nunn–Lugar program, going beyond cooperation in coping with Russian "loose nukes" to global security for nuclear materials and weapons on a worldwide basis as well as comparable bioweapons.

The central fact is that many nations have accessible, inadequately protected nuclear weapons and nuclear materials, with disastrous potential for nuclear terrorism. Thus, Presidents Bush and Putin could help other leaders understand the dangers and form a global coalition against nuclear terrorism.

China provides an important example. It could benefit for its own nuclear infrastructure and for its value as a contributor to the global effort, especially in Pakistan, with which it has long had a close relationship. Europe and Japan could contribute greatly with their own formidable capabilities and their own stocks of weapons, as well as nonweapons fissile materials. Many other nations could usefully join. Forty-three nations have research reactors that employ weapons-grade uranium as fuel, including nondeclared nuclear states.

What forms of U.S.–Russian cooperation could be particularly helpful? One would be development of world-class standards of nuclear security, with each country pledging to meet these standards, and interdiction of diverted weapons or materials through cooperative emergency response teams. On a global scale, it would be valuable to have agreed-upon high standards of inventory accounting, security of fissile materials and weapons, border and export controls, and adequate international transparency with respect to harboring the means of nuclear and biological terrorism.

With the help of this influential coalition, each country could achieve world-class standards in its own way. Here are a few examples: Pakistan's nuclear arsenal is in urgent need of protection; China's nuclear establishment needs to be brought into a cooperative safety and security framework; Kazakhstan still has unsecured fissile material on its territory despite President Nursultan Nazarbayev's excellent record of creating a nonnuclear state; many countries continue to operate research reactors using weapons-grade fuel; many countries have weapons-usable plutonium from nuclear power production projects. In the United States, leaders of the stature of Nunn, Lugar, Perry, and Allison could work constructively with the administration and the Congress in building this coalition.

Such a coalition could be valuable in counteracting bioterrorism and other infectious disease threats—even including prevention of a global pandemic. Russia has great expertise of much potential value to protection against bioterrorism, at home and abroad. This grows out of the very large, longstanding Russian bioweapons programs. As noted, there is now opportunity to engage Russian civilian and military bioscience experts in cooperative efforts. This is a critical time to share insights into the nature of threats, vulnerabilities, and how to address them across a range of critical domains, starting with prevention, early detection, and treatment. Early identification is key to preventing massive casualties.

Prevention efforts should include the following: safeguarding biological materials and strain collections; preventing brain drain of scientific expertise of former bioweaponeers; developing normative standards for scientific practice; implementing requirements for safe transfer and handling of dangerous pathogenic organisms; improving systems of intelligence collection, analysis, and sharing, including better use of human intelligence and emphasis on cooperative scientific expertise, including international research collaboration.

Early recognition/warning/protections efforts may include (1) strengthening core public health and medical capacity to detect, investigate, and respond to infectious disease threats—whether naturally occurring or terroristic; (2) developing new tools for rapid detection and diagnosis; (3) promoting development of preventive technologies such as air filtration and mail irradiation through international cooperation.

Prevention and treatment could both be strengthened by an internationally collaborative research agenda to address future needs: (1) develop new drugs, vaccines, and antidotes; (2) develop new vaccine delivery strategies; (3) research to understand how dangerous bioagents cause disease and how the immune system responds to such diseases.

Specific forms of global effort should (1) address public health and safety of populations worldwide; (2) improve global infectious disease surveillance; (3) safeguard dangerous organisms and establish a code of ethics focusing on these problems; (4) create explicit penalties for creation and/or use of bioweapons.

Thus, the great strengths of the United States and Russia in science and technology could, through cooperative efforts with each other and with the international scientific community, do much to reduce the risks of catastrophic terrorism.

A Long View of Prevention in the Hardest Cases

There is much concern in the world today about a virulent strain of Islamic extremism that fosters hatred and violence, not only toward the United States, but also toward much of the world—virtually all the democracies and all non-Muslims. This arouses fear and anger among non-Muslims. And in the case of mass violence, such as the September 11 attacks, it stimulates strong, forceful responses.

Yet much empirical evidence indicates that most Muslims are not committed to hatred as an organizing principle in their lives. Indeed, many non-Muslims take a compassionate view of the suffering of so many Muslims in the context of their own countries' severe poverty, oppression, and tyranny. In thinking about possible long-term solutions to such problems that are related to the enduring prevention of mega-terrorism, it is helpful to see this problem in historical and cultural perspective.

In his lecture on the occasion of receiving the 2001 Nobel Peace Prize on December 10, 2001, Kofi Annan put the world's current dilemma in context.

> The idea that there is one people in possession of the truth, one answer to the world's ills, or one solution to humanity's needs has done untold harm throughout history—especially in the last century. Today, however, even amidst continuing ethnic conflict around the world, there is a growing understanding that human diversity is both the reality that makes dialogue necessary, and the very basis for that dialogue.
>
> We understand, as never before, that each of us is fully worthy of the respect and dignity essential to our common humanity. We recognize that we are the products of many cultures, traditions and memories; that mutual respect allows us to study and learn from other cultures; and that we gain strength by combining the foreign with the familiar.
>
> In every great faith and tradition one can find the values of tolerance and mutual understanding. The Qur'an, for example, tells us that "We created you from a single pair of male and female and made you into nations and tribes, that you may know each other." Confucius urged his followers: "when the good way prevails in the state, speak boldly and act boldly. When the state has lost the way, act boldly and speak softly." In the Jewish

tradition, the injunction to "love thy neighbour as thyself" is considered to be the very essence of the Torah.

This thought is reflected in the Christian Gospel, which also teaches us to love our enemies and pray for those who wish to persecute us. Hindus are taught that "truth is one, the sages give it various names." And in the Buddhist tradition, individuals are urged to act with compassion in every facet of life.

People of different religions and cultures live side by side in almost every part of the world, and most of us have overlapping identities, which unite us with very different groups. We can love what we *are*, without hating what—and who—we are *not*. We can thrive in our own tradition, even as we learn from others, and come to respect their teachings.

This will not be possible, however, without freedom of religion, of expression, of assembly, and basic equality under the law. Indeed, the lesson of the past century has been that where the dignity of the individual has been trampled or threatened—where citizens have not enjoyed the basic right to choose their government, or the right to change it regularly—conflict has too often followed, with innocent civilians paying the price, in lives cut short and communities destroyed.

The obstacles to democracy have little to do with culture or religion, and much more to do with the desire of those in power to maintain their position at any cost. This is neither a new phenomenon nor one confined to any particular part of the world. People of all cultures value their freedom of choice and feel the need to have a say in decisions affecting their lives.[22]

Professor Bernard Lewis of Princeton University, one of the world's most respected scholars of Islam, clarifies the historical and cultural context of contemporary Islamic extremist terrorism in two recent articles.[23]

In the course of the twentieth century it became abundantly clear that things had gone badly wrong in the Middle East—and, indeed, in all the lands of Islam. Compared with Christendom, its rival for more than a millennium, the world of Islam had become poor, weak, and ignorant. The primacy and therefore the dominance of the West was clear for all to see, invading every aspect of the Muslim's public and even—more painfully—his private life.

Muslim modernizers—by reform or revolution—concentrated their efforts in three main areas: military, economic, and political. The results achieved were, to say the least, disappointing.

There was worse to come. It was bad enough for Muslims to feel poor and weak after centuries of being rich and strong, to lose the position of leadership that they had come to regard as their right, and to be reduced to the role of followers of the West. But the twentieth century, particularly the second half, brought further humiliation—the awareness that they were no longer even the first among followers but were falling back in a lengthening line of eager and more successful Westernizers, notably in East Asia.

By all standards that matter in the modern world—economic development and job creation, literacy, educational and scientific achievement, political freedom and respect for human rights—what was once a mighty civilization has indeed fallen low.

"Who did this to us?" is of course a common human response when things are going badly, and many in the Middle East, past and present, have asked this question. They have found several different answers. It is usually easier and always more satisfying to blame others for one's misfortunes.

The rise of nationalism—itself an import from Europe—produced new perceptions. Arabs could lay the blame for their troubles on the Turks, who had ruled them for many centuries. Turks could lay the blame for the stagnation of their civilization on the dead weight of the Arab past, in which the creative energies of the Turkish people were caught and immobilized. Persians could lay the blame for the loss of their ancient glories on Arabs, Turks, and Mongols impartially.

In the nineteenth and twentieth centuries British and French paramountcy in much of the Arab world produced a new and more plausible scapegoat—Western imperialism. . . .

But the Anglo-French interlude was comparatively brief, and ended half a century ago; Islam's change for the worse began long before and continued unabated afterward. Inevitably, the role of the British and the French as villains was taken over by the United States, along with other aspects of Western leadership. . . .

Another European contribution to this debate is anti-Semitism, and blaming "the Jews" for all that goes wrong.[24]

So, in the wake of the Nazi experience, it was not difficult to take up the stereotype of Jew as evil and a source of suffering for others. The 1948 Arab defeat at the hands of an emerging Israel—then seeming to be little more than pitiful remnants of the Holocaust—was humiliating. Blaming the Jews for all sorts of troubles far removed from Israel has thus become a kind of comfort for many Muslims in respect to their problems at home as well as abroad. Indeed, close observers of Muslim countries note that oppressive governments frequently shift the blame for their people's suffering elsewhere—to the modernizers, to the democracies, to the Jews, to the United States.

This, of course, is an old maneuver of tyrants and is surely not limited to the Muslim world. History teaches us that this is not a constructive way for people to deal with their own problems. Indeed, it tends to make matters worse by eliciting negative responses from those who are the objects of such hatred and violence.

Lewis believes that the lack of freedom in most Muslim countries under-
lies many of their troubles. The creative energy of the people is repressed;
innovative solutions to social and economic problems are blocked. Recognizing the long, hard road to democracy, he nevertheless believes it is the
road most likely to bring relief from suffering for Muslims and for others.

> If they can abandon grievance and victimhood, settle their differences, and
> join their talents, energies, and resources in a common creative endeavor,
> they can once again make the Middle East, in modern times as it was in
> antiquity and in the Middle Ages, a major center of civilization. For the
> time being, the choice is theirs.[25]

This analysis helps to offset the deep pessimism surrounding the Islamic,
especially Arab, countries in much of the world today. Perhaps there is a
way out of darkness and hatred after all—not quick, not easy, but hopeful
in the long run.

From my own experience, I am convinced that there is much diversity in
the world of Islam. Friends I have made over the years from Egypt, Pakistan, Jordan, Turkey, and Indonesia provide impressive personal evidence
of wise, peaceful, constructive, humane, problem-solving people of Muslim
religion. Carnegie-supported conferences have elicited systematic evidence
of the diversity within Islam.[26] Unfortunately, the moderate Islamic leaders
in various fields, like the moderate leaders of other faiths that I have referred to in this book, are often in a vulnerable position, and their voices
are less forceful than they would prefer under more secure circumstances.
This is another issue with which the international community can help—by
vigorously and persistently doing everything possible to support, protect,
and foster the moderate, pragmatic, tolerant voices of Islam.

Fareed Zakaria pursues Lewis's line of reasoning in a recent article.

> Even if viewed from a narrow strategic perspective it is in America's im-
> mediate security interests to try to make the regimes of the Middle East
> less prone to breed fanaticism and terror. And the only way to do this is
> to make these regimes more legitimate in the eyes of their people.[27]

He emphasizes the preconditions for democracy: the rule of law, individual rights, private property, independent courts, the separation of church
and state. He puts weight on the motivation for economic well-being—the
remarkable progress made in recent decades by such countries as Spain,
Portugal, Chile, Taiwan, South Korea, and Mexico—and the value of liber-
alizing the economy. In his view, this has spillover effects. Economic reform
brings an impetus toward a relatively democratic rule of law. Market
economies require reliable contracts, considerable openness to the outside

world, access to information, and the development of a business class. Such a class has elsewhere advocated and benefited from economic and political reform in a democratic direction.

He sees Jordan as a promising model, having become a member of the World Trade Organization, signed a free-trade pact with the United States, privatized some industries, and encouraged cross-border business activity with Israel. He extends this reasoning to Egypt as the prime locus for reform because he considers it to be "the intellectual soul of the Arab world." Economic and political progress there would show that Islam is compatible with modernity. He gives the Clinton administration credit for a high-level economic initiative toward Egypt along these lines, but the Egyptian government did not respond well. He believes that a vigorous renewal of this effort could be effective with persistent pressure for gradual reform in Egypt—and that this would have a stimulating effect on other countries.[28]

Ray Takeyh offers a further addition to this difficult but promising long-term approach.

> This simplistic choice between "Islam" and "modernity" ignores a third option that is emerging throughout the Middle East. Lost amidst the din of cultural saber-rattling are the voices calling for an Islamic reformation: A new generation of theological thinkers, led by figures such as Iranian President Muhammad Khatami and Tunisian activist Rached Ghannouchi, is reconsidering the orthodoxies of Islamic politics. In the process, such leaders are demonstrating that the region may be capable of generating a genuinely democratic order, one based on indigenous values. For the Middle East today, moderate Islam may be democracy's last hope. For the West, it might represent one of the best long-term solutions to "winning" the war against Middle East terrorism.[29]

The gravity of the problem and the interest of the international community are illustrated by a new report from Freedom House and commentary on it by the excellent international democracy-promoting NGO, International Institute for Democracy and Electoral Assistance, based in Stockholm. The former has an established track record in assessing democratic and antidemocratic trends. The latter, a more recent entry, has been particularly ingenious and respected under its secretary general, Bengt Save-Soderbergh of Sweden. It represents a collaboration of experts on democracy from many countries. These new observations are well summarized by Barbara Crossette.

Since the early 1970s, Freedom House reports, when the third major historical wave of democratization began, the Islamic world, and especially the Arab countries, have shown very little evidence of improvement in political openness, respect for human rights, and transparency. Indeed, in countries with an Islamic majority, there is just one free country, Mali; eighteen are rated partly free; twenty-eight are not free at all. Those Muslim countries after Mali that have shown democratic tendencies are Bangladesh, Indonesia, Jordan, Kuwait, Turkey, and Morocco.

Bengt Save-Soderbergh, commenting on this report, observes that there are hopeful developments under the surface in many Muslim nations. They need help from the established democracies. The democratically inclined reformers face very difficult conditions; a combination of corrupt governments, rigid fundamentalists, and a paucity of help from outside.[30]

Several valuable scholarly publications relevant to terrorism have recently been published. They deal with many facets of this complex problem and help to provide essential illumination of a previously neglected problem area:

- *To Prevail: An American Strategy for the Campaign Against Terrorism*[31]
- *The New Terrorism: Fanaticism and the Arms of Mass Destruction*[32]
- *Terrorism and America: A Commonsense Strategy for a Democratic Society*[33]
- *Origins of Terrorism: Psychologies, Ideologies, Theologies, States of Mind*[34]
- *Terror in the Mind of God: The Global Rise of Religious Violence*[35]
- *Planning the Unthinkable*[36]
- *Terrorism and U.S. Foreign Policy*[37]
- *The New Terror: Facing the Threat of Biological and Chemical Weapons*[38]
- *How Did This Happen? Terrorism and the New Year*[39]
- *Avoiding Nuclear Anarchy: Containing the Threat of Loose Russian Nuclear and Fissile Material*[40]
- "Bioterror: What Can Be Done?"[41]
- *The Age of Terror: America and the World after September 11*[42]
- *Biological Weapons: Limiting the Threat*[43]
- "Occidentalism"[44]
- *The New Great Power Coalition*[45]
- "The Sentry's Solitude"[46]
- *What Went Wrong? Western Impact and Middle Eastern Response*[47]

In general, they do not put strong emphasis on *prevention*, especially in overcoming the fundamental, long-term problems that breed terrorism. But I hope this chapter helps to stimulate serious, in-depth consideration of preventing catastrophic terrorism by pursuing these basic issues.

International Cooperation for Democratic Development

Overall, the emphasis I put on democratic socioeconomic development in this book has an important bearing even on the hardest cases. To pursue this exceedingly promising, though very difficult, path requires serious attention to research evidence, continuing interplay of scholars and policymakers, sophisticated international cooperation with sensitivity to the history and culture of each country and region, involving a judicious mix of carrots and sticks for socioeconomic reform. No easy task! But surely not beyond human capability if we as a species—and especially the established democracies in all parts of the world—can understand the urgency of the problem and the necessity for appropriate human, technical, and financial resources.

On this latter point, we must face the widespread distaste for "foreign aid" and growing "compassion fatigue"; this critical issue must be reexamined. Perhaps we should use an accurate and informative term such as *international cooperation for democratic development* rather than *foreign aid*? Do we really want a decent, healthy, peaceful, nonterroristic world? I am deeply convinced that most of us do. If so, we must be prepared to pay and work for it in keeping with the most hardheaded analysis of what really works and the most decent feelings for ourselves, our families, our countries, and the humanity in which we are deeply embedded, for better or worse. Surely we cannot be indifferent to the possibility of making it truly better for our children and their children.

This problem was tackled head on at the end of 2001 by one of the world's well-informed financial leaders, Gordon Brown, Britain's chancellor of the exchequer.

After World War II, American visionaries seized an unprecedented moment of opportunity. They created not only a new military and political settlement but a new economic and social order that tackled, in their words, hunger, poverty, desperation and chaos.

And their plan, the Marshall Plan, transferred 1 percent of national income every year, for four years, from America to poverty-stricken countries—not as an act of charity but in recognition that, like peace, prosperity was indivisible, and to be sustained it had to be shared.

America's postwar achievement should be our inspiration today both for rebuilding Afghanistan and for a new global alliance for prosperity between developed and developing worlds.

Just like our predecessors, we recognize that national safety and global reconstruction are inextricably linked. And like them we see that the gains are not simply the spread of prosperity but the spread of democracy. . . .

Fifty years on, we see more clearly that what happens to the poorest citizen in the poorest country can affect the richest citizen in the richest one. And we are challenged by the yawning gap between what technology enables us to do—abolish poverty—and the reality of 110 million children without schooling, 7 million avoidable child deaths each year, and a billion people in poverty.

That is why the whole international community has committed to ambitious development targets for 2015; halving world poverty, cutting child mortality by two-thirds and guaranteeing every child primary education.

My plan is this: In return for the developing countries' pursuit of corruption-free policies for stability, opening up trade and encouraging private investment, wealthier countries should be prepared to increase development funds by $50 billion a year—the resources needed to achieve these agreed-upon development goals. This funding would not be aid in the traditional sense but investment in the future.[48]

Brown emphasizes that this kind of approach requires responsibilities of both developing and developed countries. The nations of the world must agree on standards for fiscal and monetary policy that are sound macroeconomically, deter corruption, and enhance investor confidence. Developing countries must have reliable legal systems for contracts and business forums to foster trade and investment by cooperation of public and private sectors. To accomplish these fundamental long-term goals—following the Marshall Plan but adapted to different circumstances—Brown proposes that the international community establish a $50-billion-a-year investment fund that fosters high-quality efforts to improve health, education, and economic opportunity. All this would be oriented toward building capacity in very poor countries for sustainable development in the context of a just and inclusive world economy.[49]

Such a fund, if administered in a rigorous way, could help greatly to move today's dictatorships and failed states toward decent, competent governance on a path toward eventual prosperity. It would have to be substantially supported by all the established democracies and some of the emerging democracies as well. It would require superb leadership at the highest levels to sustain interest and understanding—akin to Marshall and Truman and Acheson a half century ago. It would require a high degree of donor coordination and world-class technical cooperation among developed and developing countries. In short, pooling strengths, sharing burdens, dividing labor over many years for a great purpose.

To a large extent, we in the world's most educated, technically competent, affluent, and democratic countries can decide what kind of world we want to have, even in the hardest cases. The twenty-first could be the century that turns the corner into a world far better than any we have known before. If that is what we want, we will have to think seriously about and work hard with people all over this precious globe. We will find that hardheaded practicality in preventing catastrophic terrorism merges with humane concern for people everywhere.

Notes

1. David A. Hamburg and Michelle B. Trudeau, *Biobehavioral Aspects of Aggression* (New York: Alan R. Liss, 1981).

2. *Great Transitions: Preparing Adolescents for a New Century,* concluding report of the Carnegie Council on Adolescent Development (New York: Carnegie Corporation of New York, 1995).

3. *Preventing Contemporary Intergroup Violence and Education for Conflict Resolution* (New York: Carnegie Commission Publication, December 1999).

4. Gareth Evans, *International Herald Tribune* (Paris), September 15, 2001.

5. William J. Perry, "Preparing for the Next Attack," *Foreign Affairs*, November/December 2001.

6. Perry, "Preparing."

7. Sam Nunn, "Our New Security Framework," *Washington Post*, October 7, 2001.

8. Nunn, "Our New Security Framework."

9. Graham Allison, "Fighting Terrorism," *The Economist*, November 3, 2001.

10. Allison, "Fighting Terrorism."

11. In Gottemoeller's paper the term *threat reduction cooperation* refers to all programs of the U.S. government devoted to reducing the threat of weapons of mass destruction and furthering nonproliferation goals, whether they are located in the Department of Defense, Department of Energy, Department of State, or elsewhere.

12. Rose Gottemoeller, *Threat Reduction Cooperation in the Counter-Terrorism Struggle*, draft paper prepared for Nuclear Threat Initiative, Washington, D.C., December 2001.

13. Gottemoeller, *Threat Reduction Cooperation*.

14. Gottemoeller, *Threat Reduction Cooperation*.

15. Gottemoeller, *Threat Reduction Cooperation*.

16. Margaret Hamburg, "Preparing for and Preventing Bioterrorism," *Issues in Science and Technology* XVIII, no. 2 (winter 2001–2002):27–30.

17. Hamburg, "Preparing for and Preventing Bioterrorism."

18. Hamburg, "Preparing for and Preventing Bioterrorism."

19. David R. Franz, "Targeting Intent: Scientist-to-Scientist Threat Reduction Programs," paper for Nuclear Threat Initiative, Washington, D.C., December 2001.

20. Franz, "Targeting Intent."

21. Franz, "Targeting Intent."

22. Kofi Annan, lecture given upon receiving the 2001 Nobel Peace Prize, December 10, 2001.

23. Bernard Lewis, "The Revolt of Islam," *The New Yorker*, November 19, 2001, 50–62.

24. Bernard Lewis, "What Went Wrong?" *Atlantic Monthly*, January 2002, 43–45.

25. Lewis, "What Went Wrong?"

26. Sam Afridi, "Muslims in America: Identity, Diversity and the Challenge of Understanding," paper presented at Carnegie Corporation meeting on Muslims in America, New York, June 2001.

27. Fareed Zakaria, "How to Save the Arab World," *Newsweek*, December 24, 2001, 25–28.

28. Zakaria, "How to Save the Arab World."

29. Ray Takeyh, "Can Islam Bring Democracy to the Middle East?" *Foreign Policy* (December 2001): 68.

30. Barbara Crossette, "As Democracies Spread, Islamic World Hesitates," *New York Times*, December 23, 2001.

31. Kurt M. Campbell and Michele A. Fluornoy, *To Prevail: An American Strategy for the Campaign Against Terrorism* (Washington, D.C.: Center for Strategic and International Studies Press, 2001).

32. Walter Laqueur, *The New Terrorism: Fanaticism and the Arms of Mass Destruction* (New York: Oxford University Press, 1999).

33. Philip B. Heymann, *Terrorism and America: A Commonsense Strategy for a Democratic Society* (Cambridge, Mass.: MIT Press, 1998).

34. Walter Reich, ed., *Origins of Terrorism: Psychologies, Ideologies, Theologies, States of Mind* (Cambridge, England: Woodrow Wilson International Center for Scholars and Cambridge University Press, 1990).

35. Mark Juergensmeyer, *Terror in the Mind of God: The Global Rise of Religious Violence* (Berkeley, Calif.: University of California Press, 2000).

36. Peter Lavoy, Scott Sagan, and James Wirtz, eds., *Planning the Unthinkable* (Ithaca, N.Y.: Cornell University Press, 2000).

37. Paul Pillar, *Terrorism and U.S. Foreign Policy* (Washington, D.C.: Brookings, 2001).

38. Sidney Drell, Abraham Sofaer, and George Wilson, eds., *The New Terror: Facing the Threat of Biological and Chemical Weapons* (Stanford, Calif.: Hoover Institution Press, 1999).

39. James Hoge Jr. and Gideon Rose, *How Did This Happen? Terrorism and the New Year* (New York: Public Affairs, 2001).

40. Graham T. Allison, Owen R. Cote Jr., Richard A. Falkenrath, and Steven E. Miller, *Avoiding Nuclear Anarchy: Containing the Threat of Loose Russian Nuclear and Fissile Material* (Cambridge, Mass.: MIT Press, 1996).

41. Matthew Meselson, "Bioterror: What Can Be Done?" *New York Review*, December 20, 2001.

42. Strobe Talbot and Nayan Chanda, eds., *The Age of Terror: America and the World After September 11* (New York: Basic Books, 2001).

43. Joshua Lederberg, ed., *Biological Weapons: Limiting the Threat.* (Cambridge, Mass.: MIT Press, 1999).

44. Ian Buruma and Avishai Margalit, "Occidentalism," *New York Review*, January 17, 2002.

45. Richard Rosencrance, ed., *The New Great Power Coalition: Toward a World Concert of Nations* (Lanham, Md.: Rowman & Littlefield, 2001).

46. Fouad Ajami, "The Sentry's Solitude," *Foreign Affairs*, November/December 2001, 2–16.

47. Bernard Lewis, *What Went Wrong? Western Impact and Middle Eastern Response.* (New York: Oxford University Press, 2002).

48. Gordon Brown, "A Yearly $50 Billion Safe Investment in Prosperity," *International Herald Tribune*, December 18, 2001.

49. Brown, "Yearly $50 Billion."

10

Prognosis for Prevention: Promising Developments in the First Two Years of the Twenty-First Century

An Awakening to Preventive Opportunities

At the first session of the Carnegie Commission on Preventing Deadly Conflict in 1994, and on subsequent occasions, I said we should mark progress toward prevention not in years, but perhaps in decades and more likely in generations.

If prevention were easy, it would have been set in motion seriously—perhaps even solidly accomplished—many years ago. But when we began our global view of prevention opportunities in the early 1990s, one rarely even heard the term *prevention*, let alone any serious analysis in leadership circles concerned with international relations and human conflict. For many reasons that we have touched on in these pages, prevention was virtually a nonexistent topic. Today, writing in the year 2002, prevention is pervasive in discussions of war and peace. What is clear is the rapid emergence of an intellectual, technical, and moral ferment in many parts of the world to consider seriously the possibilities of preventing civil and international wars, including terrorist wars, as the new century unfolds. The growing danger, powerfully reflected in the worldwide spread of deadly weapons (including those of mass destruction), the concomitant spread of communication capabilities that can incite hatred and violence, and the worldwide reach of fanatical haters no matter how remote, make it increasingly clear to many kinds of organizations and institutions (governmental and nongovernmental) that serious efforts must be made to transcend traditional intellectual habits, emotional stereotypes, and organizational legacies in striving to prevent catastrophes that could easily exceed the horrors of the twentieth century and might even lead to human extinction, once and for all.

In this chapter, we briefly consider a number of new efforts that were scarcely in sight a decade ago but show dynamic promise in 2002. Some of these efforts were clearly and strongly influenced by the Carnegie Commission, others less so, and the relation in some cases is simply unknown to me. But there is no question that the Commission's many reports and meetings have changed the zeitgeist. This is made explicit by such distinguished leaders of prevention as Kofi Annan, Secretary-General of the United Nations, and Jan Eliasson, ambassador of Sweden to the United States. The atmosphere is a very different one than it was less than a decade ago. Now, many thoughtful dedicated people in diverse settings are seeking ways to prevent deadly conflict.

Early in the history of the Carnegie Commission, Jane Holl, Cyrus Vance, and I agreed to follow up on our publications—seeking to encourage implementation. One way to do this is to form or strengthen relationships with key people in dynamic organizations, for example, foreign ministers in government or leaders of NGOs and IGOs, to encourage them to think preventively. We assumed that if they got into it seriously, they would find ways to improve on our ideas, generate their own approaches, and move toward implementation.

We particularly encouraged the formation of specific, dedicated units to deal with prevention full-time. They would, for example, alert governments to dangerous situations; mobilize ministries, departments, or agencies; link independent experts with policymakers; and generally provide a focal point for developing ways to prevent catastrophe. Similar focal points in universities, research institutes, and various NGOs would be similarly helpful. Much has happened along these lines, and this chapter is devoted to those examples with which I am most familiar from some personal involvement. No doubt there are other—and perhaps better—examples with which I am not so familiar. A reflection of the considerable expansion of support for prevention internationally is the number of prominent institutions that have made significant statements and taken action on the issue in the last several years.

The United Nations

Elements of the UN are now shaping a long-term culture of prevention. The Secretary-General's strong, visible, and thoughtful interest in this approach has activated many people at the UN who might have been interested anyway, but they are certainly motivated by the Secretary-General's leadership. We have earlier referred to several foci within the UN for prevention analysis and policy formation—for example, UNITAR. Through the disastrous wars of the 1990s, the United Nations Security Council (UNSC) was not a focal point of prevention activities. A rethinking of basic orientations of this very important body was undertaken in 1999 in a Security Council retreat in Princeton, New Jersey—the first activity of its kind in the history of the

UN. At the request of Kofi Annan, I opened the meeting with remarks on the need for the UN to take a leading role in preventing deadly conflict and some ways in which this could be done, especially in a farsighted interplay of the Secretary-General (SG) and the UNSC in preventive diplomacy. There ensued a highly constructive discussion on ways of strengthening these functions. Participants felt this was based on the principles on which the Security Council and the UN itself were founded in the aftermath of World War II. This realization has helped maintain a serious level of interest in prevention within the UNSC and shaped some promising initiatives. In the spring of 2001, the UNSC held its third retreat in two years. Prevention has been prominent in these discussions as the UNSC moves toward a more effective, professional way of functioning.

Since the Princeton meeting, the UNSC has become more proactive in setting the agenda for prevention. On July 20, 2000, the president of the Council, with the consent of the other members, issued a statement on "The Role of the Security Council in the Prevention of Armed Conflicts," which outlined the need for preventive action and how capabilities to assure its success can be expanded.[1] The statement on the role of the UNSC in prevention shows that the body is in general agreement with the basic themes that surround the idea of prevention. The final document is mostly focused on ways to expand UN capabilities and how to forge new alliances with other organizations that will support an interdependent and interlocking "culture of prevention." Importantly, the UNSC also called on the Secretary-General to prepare a comprehensive report on the UN's role in conflict prevention. This important report emerged in the spring of 2001, and we consider it in the epilogue.

Understanding that it holds the primary responsibility for maintaining international peace and security under Chapter VI of the UN Charter, the statement by the UNSC affirms its central role in preventing armed conflicts. It also calls on member-states to live up to their obligations under the charter and support preventive efforts by the UNSC. However, it also restates its commitment to the principles of sovereign equality and territorial integrity of all states. This reflects the sensitivity of member states to matters of "intervention."

The critical foundation for preventing violent conflict in the view of the Security Council is cultivating a "culture of prevention." The UNSC states that early warning, preventive diplomacy, preventive deployment, preventive disarmament, and postconflict peace building are "interdependent and complementary components of a comprehensive conflict prevention strategy." Indeed, the UNSC sees the origin of armed conflict lying in a battery of economic, social, cultural, and humanitarian problems, and, therefore, any international response must recognize this complexity and be coordinated in a way that deals with it.

Part of establishing this culture of prevention is an acknowledgment that human beings harbor the causes of violence, and they are addressed in the "Declaration and Programme of Action on a Culture of Peace" (now a UN-ESCO program). The council encourages ongoing efforts to enhance early warning capacity within the UN while emphasizing the need to link early warning with early response. The body also reiterates a call for the UN and regional organizations to forge closer relationships. This would involve sharing information that can be useful for developing strategies and programs to be employed in actual operations. Part of this cooperation would be a mechanism for expanding the capacities of some regional organizations for prevention, in particular the Organization of African Unity.

Linked to prevention is postconflict peace building to prevent the reemergence of violence. UN mandates that take into account operational military requirements and other relevant local conditions can help interventions succeed and also facilitate long-term peace building. UNSC efforts for peace building demand closer cooperation among the UN specialized agencies as well as other actors. Connected to this are programs for disarmament, demobilization, and reintegration that can help prevent the recurrence of violence.

Beyond peace building, the UNSC statement gestures toward a number of other issues important to conflict prevention. It calls for action to curb the exploitation and illegal trade in natural resources, particularly diamonds, that often fuel conflicts. The Council also underlines the importance of preventive deployment as a means for prevention and expressed its willingness to consider these operations with the consent of the host country. Recognizing the important role of women in prevention and conflict resolution, the UNSC calls for their increased participation in these efforts. The statement welcomes initiatives to control the illicit trade in small arms and light weapons, particularly those endeavors that come from regional bodies. Proliferation of small arms is seen as a global concern, and there is a vital need for national regulations to govern small arms transfers that include supply- and demand-side measures that control illegal diversion and reexport of weapons. States also need to enforce all existing arms interdiction measures. Related to this is the importance of disarmament and nonproliferation in regard to weapons of mass destruction.

The UNSC statement highlights the need for adequate and dependable resources for preventive action. This is crucial to ensure smooth transitions from emergency humanitarian assistance to development and peace-building endeavors in the postconflict stage of a crisis. The UNSC therefore encourages further contributions by member states to the Trust Fund for Preventive Action. Another resource vital to peacekeeping and postconflict situations is international civilian police, and the UNSC asks that member-states explore ways to supply personnel to meet the growing demand.

The UNSC concludes its statement by declaring that a "reformed, strengthened, and effective United Nations remains central to the maintenance of peace and security of which prevention is a key component and underlines the importance of enhancing the capacity of the Organization in preventive action, peacekeeping, and peace-building."

Overall, the UNSC statement shows that the most powerful body in the UN system has embraced prevention as one its priorities and is more inclined than ever before to work cooperatively with the Secretary-General in seeking effective ways to implement prevention policies.

The Secretary-General's 2001 report is responsive to the UNSC's main thrusts. It builds on the existing ferment of ideas and innovations for preventing deadly conflict. It discusses the role of all the main organs of conflict prevention and how they can be enhanced to better perform this task. There is primary focus on the role of the UN and its agencies with missions that impact prevention. But it also sites the UN within larger international efforts for prevention, including a discussion of civil society institutions working toward peace. The report goes some distance in helping the UN clarify its own institutional arrangements for prevention and in fleshing out how it can collaborate with other organizations seeking similar goals.

In my judgment, this is the most important statement on prevention made by the UN since the promulgation of its charter and the Universal Declaration of Human Rights. It has many suggestions of practical value. Its approach is entirely consistent with that of the Carnegie Commission. This report is likely to be a landmark in the history of prevention and the UN. Therefore, we look at it more closely in the epilogue.

Regional and Other International Organizations

European Union

The UN is not alone among international bodies in exploring and expanding its potential to act preventively. The European Union has taken the question extremely seriously. The economically powerful EU is itself a strikingly successful example of how close cooperation and understanding between nations, which waged massive wars against one another within living memory, can lead to reconciliation that is the basis for peace and prosperity. As the most prominent representative body in one of the wealthiest and most influential areas of the globe, the EU realizes it is well positioned to play a major role in preventing conflict. It can use not only its civilian and military crisis management capabilities but also the diplomatic instruments of its members. It can also wield trade policy instruments, cooperation agreements, development assistance, economic cooperation, social and environmental policies as mechanisms and incentives to assure peace. What the EU is currently seeking to achieve is a thoroughgoing coordination of these different capabilities with an explicit focus on prevention. This is an innovative approach to international affairs.

A report presented to the European Council at Nice in 2000 gives concrete recommendations to improve the EU's capabilities for conflict prevention.[2] Since it has groundbreaking significance for this important institution, we summarize here its important findings and recommendations. Prevention requires the EU to foster better relationships with the UN, NGOs, regional organizations, and other states to further prevention. For the EU itself, there are considerable long-term (development) and short-term steps (focused largely on diplomacy) on the road to creating a sustained and coordinated conflict prevention apparatus.

The report emphasizes economic incentives bearing on early conflict resolution. Although the report does not highlight the important ability of the EU, because of its power and influence, to put issues on the world agenda, this is in fact one of its strongest assets. Paradoxically, the EU's embarrassment of riches poses a problem for concerted action. Not only will a wide array of nations, institutions, and departments have to be coordinated but also a variety of very different situations in very different parts of the world may require attention. Greater coherence and complementary action are therefore necessary at all levels from the member states to the organization as a whole. New policies should be grounded in a proactive approach to opportunities for prevention.

Since the causes of conflict are broad and complex, the response must be equally extensive and comprehensive. This requires collaboration with other international, regional, and nongovernmental organizations. Leading the way are the UN and its specialized agencies. The EU can play an important role in expanding the UN's reach in conflict prevention by offering political and financial support.

The EU should also support the OAS, Southern African Development Community (SADC), ECOWAS, ASEAN, and other regional actors in efforts to prevent conflict. Nearby stand international organizations such as the G8, IMF, and World Bank, which have an important role in mitigating the structural factors that can lead to conflict.

Cooperation with NGOs is also a valuable part of the EU's program. NGOs are well placed to provide information that identifies root causes of problems as well as to work directly with parties on the ground or with victims. They should be part of any larger system. The EU's wide-ranging "political dialogue" also offers a regularized opportunity to address contentious situations in a timely manner. This can benefit both those who are at risk for conflict and those actors who can assist in defusing a situation.

The report recognizes that pervasive *lack* of opportunity, illegitimate and ineffective government, and weak civil society are conducive to the descent into violence. Therefore, the EU should undertake long-term peace-building measures that address these deficiencies. It must support the creation of political and mediation efforts, democratic institutions, the rule of law and administration of justice, an impartial police force, and reintegration of ex-combatants into societies (for countries emerging from violence). Following this path, the EU must join with nonstate actors that also work to strengthen democracy, social tolerance, and peaceful resolution of disputes. All operations designed to dampen conflict should begin at an early stage.

A more sustained and flexible approach is needed. More informal means of contact need to be cultivated. Mandates should be constructed with an eye to using the privileged relationships that some member states of the EU have with other nations. There must be a proactive orientation of the EU's policy making.

This integrated and comprehensive policy must deal with the aftereffects of interrelated problems such as discrimination against minorities, forced displacement, abuse of human rights, weak institutions, the exclusion of international organizations, and the curtailment of media freedom.

A wide range of authorities, procedures, and activities may be deployed to undertake preventive action. For example, trade policy for sanctions falls to the EU itself while other civilian and military capabilities are the responsibility of its member states. Achieving coherence of these overlapping efforts is a challenge but necessary to success.

This wide-ranging and farsighted report emphasizes that sustained political will is the prerequisite for effective conflict prevention. There is a need to acknowledge failures and to learn from them but also to build on successes, such as the example of EU action in East Timor. Watchwords are *coherence* and *integration* in the use of what is a very broad range of resources that can be employed in the quest for conflict prevention. If successful, the benefits in terms of human life, political stability, budgetary savings, and trade will far outweigh the investments.

Overall, this report shows that the EU is taking very seriously not only the idea of prevention but also the necessary steps to construct an effective policy. As the emphasis on "building" partnerships and capacity indicates, there is still a long way to go, but the report stimulates comprehensive and workable plans in one of the most significant international institutions to support conflict prevention. Indeed, in the first two years of the new century the member governments of the European Union have been consistently more vigorous in exploring prevention possibilities than their counterparts in the United States.

Renata Dwan, a distinguished scholar at the Stockholm International Institute for Peace Research (SIPRI) in 2001, also explored the issues around

creating a cohesive European Union prevention policy.³ This is indicative of
the EU's intellectual ferment on prevention. She notes the union's recent attention to short-term prevention and crisis management but emphasizes
that the greatest strengths of the EU lie in structural prevention. Comparative advantage for the organization rests on its authority, influence, wealth,
and ability to encourage member states to adopt certain preventive strategies. Long-term structural prevention is where the EU can bring its best assets to bear, and it is in this area that the EU should concentrate its efforts.
Its crisis prevention activities should be placed within a broader prevention
framework that fosters the molding of competent, decent states and
strengthens mechanisms for handling grievances fairly.

The EU is unmatched in the breath of policy instruments within its grasp
for prevention activities. Long-term efforts at prevention, especially development assistance, are essential. Here, the EU holds distinct advantages because of the relative wealth of its member states; the potential to encourage
these member states to increase their development budgets; the ability to
provide coherence, linkage, and greater efficiency among national development policies and its own financial and assistance policies, particularly in
the area of capacity building; the powerful international trading position of
the EU, and its member states' influence in other trading organizations; and
the moral authority in terms of human rights values and policies as well as
peace and security issues.

There is a need to further clarify how development assistance can address
root causes of conflict. What is needed is a body that can coordinate the development programs of the different EU members, train staff, and carry out
structural prevention programs in a more systematic way.

Dwan points out that another way the EU can support prevention is
through partnerships with other international, regional, and private organizations. Many EU members are touchy about signing on to general policies—particularly interventionist ones. Also, prevention as policy, particularly in the hands of the EU, runs the risk of being seen as purely a Western
policy imposed on others. Building links with other groups can overcome
these hurdles. The multiplicity of mechanisms and institutions that can contribute to prevention internationally requires the construction of collaborative relationships. Dwan emphasizes building bridges to regional organizations (such as the OAU and ECOWAS), businesses, and NGOs.
Coordination with these groups along with the provision of EU financial
support and technical assistance could be the largest contribution to a coherent prevention policy.

These new prevention structures need to include an early-warning capacity; a forum for coordination necessary between the different phases of activity; a flexible "situation center" that in moments of crisis could provide
operational guidance and deploy other tools of prevention; as well as the

means for monitoring and reviewing prevention policies in order to figure out what tactics and programs have been successful and which have not.

Taking these steps would go a long way in allowing Europe to effectively employ those assets that give it the greatest comparative advantage in preventing deadly conflict. A strong political vision for prevention needs to be articulated in which crisis management is not abandoned but it is set within a phased context of crisis response—a balanced mix of crisis prevention, management, and peace building that is supported by effective coordinating structures integrating the EU's strong assets for fundamental, long-term contributions to just peace. Sweden used its recent presidency of the EU to promote such measures.

This work at SIPRI as well as work at the University of Bradford in England and other independent outstanding European institutions provides a powerful stimulus for ongoing improvements in the EU's work on preventing deadly conflict. Today, this is a higher priority for the EU than ever before.

Activity in the European Union is not limited to writing reports. In various areas there has been constructive activity to prevent conflict. One illustrative area is light weapons. These weapons, ranging from pistols, machine guns, and assault rifles to mortars and portable missiles, have been the major killers in recent conflicts. By and large, the international community has been slow to control the trade in these arms. The EU has taken concrete steps to limit the flow of arms with a 1998 Code of Conduct on arms exports that not only limits sales but also the stocks of small arms. It has also provided direct assistance to troubled regions. For example, the EU has supported programs for the collection and destruction of weaponry in Cambodia in recent years.

There is still much to do on this issue. There is support for greater controls on the suppliers of weapons, improved border controls, and encouragement for greater regional initiative. To this end, the EU and its member states (notably Sweden) helped convene the July 2001 UN Conference on Small Arms and Light Weapons in All Its Aspects to bring further attention to this dangerous issue. This conference drew on the activities of other international bodies and states on the issue of light weapons, including those of the G8 and Japan, which are discussed in the following section. This activity shows that issues of concern to deadly conflict are not the exclusive province of any one organization or group, and, indeed, they are best and most effectively confronted by multisided and cooperative efforts.[4] A crucial need is stronger commitment from the United States.

The Group of 8 Industrialized Nations

The EU effort described previously emphasizes cooperative activities with other regional, nongovernmental, and international bodies. Key among

these is the UN but also important is collaboration with regional organizations such as the OAS, ECOWAS, and ASEAN. In addition, the G8, IMF,
and World Bank are also seen as potentially valuable partners.

Among these international bodies, the G8 has recently put conflict prevention high on its agenda. At its meeting in Berlin in 1999, the member states
sought to make the prevention of armed conflict a priority by nurturing a
"Culture of Prevention." As host, the government of Germany convened prevention experts in advance, including Jane Holl of the Carnegie Commission,
to give priority to prevention and promote forward-looking measures.

The following year those basic ideas were built upon in a declaration by
the host, Japanese Foreign Minister Miyazaki, at the G8's 2000 meeting on
Okinawa.[5] The "Miyazaki Initiatives" stress five global topics that include
small arms and light weapons, the link between conflict and development,
the illicit trade in diamonds, children and armed conflict, and international
civilian police. Each of these issues was selected because the G8's member
states have a comparative advantage in confronting them.

Both the German G8 meeting of 1999 and the Japanese G8 meeting in
2000 declared a determination to make the prevention of armed conflict a
priority by nurturing a Culture of Prevention. Such a culture is based in the
principles of democracy, the rule of law, human rights, human security, and
an open economy. This comprehensive approach of the G8 sees the UN as
playing a central role. However, it also sees conflict prevention as a joint effort undertaken by an international community of regional institutions,
states, business, and NGOs. The proposals put forward are part of an in-
terconnected approach to prevention. Thus, both the G8 and the European
Union are in agreement with the Carnegie concept of mobilizing an array
of pivotal institutions to make prevention effective.

Japan has been a strong advocate of the control of light weapons (which
include highly destructive weapons such as mortars, rocket launchers, and
smaller missiles along with small arms) in recent years, so it is no surprise
that Miyazaki's initiative in this area is the most detailed. It sees light
weapons and their proliferation as inherently destabilizing, often devastating, and it urges action to control exports, crackdown on illegal trafficking,
increase law enforcement resources, as well as emphasize demobilization of
combatants and postconflict reconstruction. The G8 declaration makes
nine major recommendations to specifically implement this approach. The
G8's awakening from its long slumber on prevention is a dramatic development; and in its ending of decades-long psychological denial of the dangers of "small" and "light" weapons, there is an opportunity for effective
action. No one should expect this to be quick and easy, but at least some
great powers are facing the problem.

Seeing that international cooperation for democratic socioeconomic development is important in promoting durable peace, the G8 plans to use its

position as the major provider of development assistance to push programs in this area. It plans to maintain the fundamental goals of development assistance but will also push for consideration of conflict prevention in development assistance, with the focus toward ensuring quick action to prevent violence and a smooth transition from emergency humanitarian assistance to development assistance in the postconflict stage. These efforts will recognize that the participation of local government and civil society is vital. The major recommendations set forward to implement this basic approach go well beyond prior G8 policies.

The G8 also plans to take steps to curb the illicit trade in diamonds, often used to fund arms purchases that feed conflicts in Africa. Since the G8 is by far the largest segment of the world market for diamonds, it urges coordinated efforts by states, producers, and distributors to block the illicit trade; support for UN initiatives and sanctions on this issue; and support for other pragmatic solutions. This G8 emphasis on diamonds helped to stimulate major UN activity in 2000 and 2001, especially in the Security Council.

The G8 also aims to establish standards to end the plight of children involved in armed conflict by targeting those who involve children in conflict, support of international standards, outreach, and reintegration and rehabilitation by advocating a variety of new policies. Here again, G8 attention to children and war has helped the UN to take serious action, led by the distinguished Olara Otunnu, a crucial member of the Carnegie Commission. He was appointed to the position of special representative of the Secretary-General for children and armed conflict. Even though implementation will take many years, this painful problem is now seriously on the world's agenda.

Understanding that a UN-deployed civilian police force (CIVPOL) is a critical component of any peacekeeping operation, the G8 proposes to support and develop this capacity by getting member states to help the UN meet the demand for civilian police and enhancing UN capabilities to support CIVPOL activities in the field through improved training and coordination.

In these G8 meetings and documents, prevention is *the* centerpiece and is being approached through initiatives that can work in an interlocking manner. This is an important departure from past G8 thinking and practice. These various declarations show that G8 activities on prevention have a momentum that is likely to be maintained in the future even if some of the G8 members lag behind in their commitments. Important leadership has emerged, understanding of the prevention approach is growing, and the moral responsibility of the G8 is becoming clear.

The Organization for Security and Cooperation in Europe

Earlier in this book, we gave much attention and credit to the work of the Organization for Security and Cooperation in Europe (OSCE), especially the work of its high commissioner on national minorities. A more comprehensive view of the OSCE's potential is given by the recent work of Terrence Hopmann.[6] He was a Fulbright Fellow at the OSCE during 1997 to 1998. There, he saw Max van der Stoel and the OSCE dispense accurate warnings of impending conflict in Kosovo some eighteen months before NATO took action in 1999.

Despite the fact that the OSCE's calls went unheeded in the Kosovo case, Hopmann has come to see the body as *a model for preventive diplomacy.* With a membership larger than the EU and with a reach that stretches from "Vancouver to Vladivostok," the organization has considerable potential. It has the flexibility to adapt to a new international atmosphere and an agility to intercede in a variety of situations.

Hopmann sees encouraging democratization, preventive diplomacy, conflict resolution, and postconflict security building as primary missions for the OSCE. These efforts, in one form or another, have been undertaken in the Baltics, the Ukraine, Moldova, Georgia, Azerbaijan, the Russian Federation, Central Asia, and the Balkans with varying degrees of success. There have been clear failures to prevent violence in Chechnya and Kosovo, but dividends have been paid in minimizing or preempting violence in Macedonia, the Crimea, and the Baltics.

The lessons from Hopmann are that missions need clear goals and must develop complementary strategies to achieve those goals. This means that missions must communicate and coordinate closely on planning and implementing interventions with interested NGOs. Missions are also most effective when they pay close attention to issues such as human rights, rights of persons belonging to minorities, democratization, freedom of the media, and the rule of law. Just as crucial to remember is the fact that missions are only as strong as their members. Successes are directly related to personnel. Thorough training in negotiation, mediation, conflict resolution, cultural sensitivity, with an eye to gender balance on the team, is valuable.

Taken as a whole, the OSCE's momentum continues in the new century as an innovative and useful regional organization that now includes fifty-three countries. It can be further strengthened in its own region and also highlight similar opportunities for other areas of the globe. In my view, peer learning in collaboration with the Organization of African Unity could have mutual benefit.

Governments

Individual governments have been active in building momentum for prevention. Sweden, in particular, has shown the influence that a single, relatively small state can have internationally on this issue. Holding the presidency of the EU during 2001, Sweden used the position to further highlight the potential this strong organization has for prevention. The Swedish Foreign Ministry has taken steps not only to clarify the possibilities of prevention but also to take the necessary step of institutionalizing prevention as part of its operations. We have described Sweden's institutional arrangements in an earlier chapter, providing a basis for dynamic action.

Crucially, the Swedes view prevention as transnational activity. They have not only taken steps to orient their own national policies to support prevention but they have also supported institutions outside Sweden that work for prevention. An example of this is the Swedish government's support for a program at the International Peace Academy on prevention. This seeding of overseas institutions plays an important role in expanding capabilities. Prevention of deadly conflict is a global question, and collaborative efforts like these are one of the best means to assure that viewpoints from across the globe are brought into the discussion. Other states, such as Canada, Japan, and Norway, have taken similar paths, and these nations can serve as examples for the rest of the international community. We consider this further in the section discussing the recent actions of prominent NGOs.

On June 26–27, 2000, dignitaries from governments of 133 countries gathered in Warsaw, Poland, to affirm their basic support for democratic principles "set forth in the Charter of the United Nations and the Universal Declaration of Human Rights."[7] Perhaps the key point of the document lay in its emphasis that peace, development, human rights, and democracy are all interdependent. Therefore, the 133 states (calling themselves a "Community of Democracies") committed themselves to support democracy around the world and promised to undertake activities that continue to foster it. The meeting was sponsored by Poland, the United States, the Czech Republic, Chile, India, Mali, and South Korea. It presages a larger meeting on the topic to be held in Seoul in 2002.

The roster of nations that affirmed their support for the principles is impressive; the nations not only noted the "universality of democratic principles" but also agreed to respect and uphold these "core democratic principles and practices." These included the right of people to choose their government, equal protection under the law, free expression, the right to education, freedom of the press, and due process of law. The declaration urged that all human rights as set down by the Universal Declaration and other human rights instruments be promoted and protected. All participants agreed to a substantial set of nineteen basic points.

The support of these nineteen points is important because of the interdependence of development, human rights, and peace with democracy. By signing, all the members of this community of democracies promise to promote and strengthen democracy. The overall goal is to establish a set of common democratic values and standards. This is an active process that may include forums and dialogues on the subjects sponsored by the community's member states. There is also a promise to cooperate to meet any threat posed by the overthrow of democratically elected governments as well as other transnational threats (drug trafficking, terrorism, organized crime, the illegal arms trade, trafficking in human beings) within the bounds of international law. There is also a call for leaders to respect and promote pluralism and for the community itself to support the development of civil society institutions that buttress democracy around the world. This action will also focus on emerging democratic states. Democracy is seen as mutually reinforcing to economic growth; and, therefore, efforts here will have an impact in economic and social arenas and can help to alleviate poverty.

One limiting factor to this set of interlocking activities designed to support democracy is a statement that follows the nineteen points. The Warsaw Declaration clearly states that the signatories "will cooperate to consolidate and strengthen democratic institutions, *with due respect to sovereignty and the principle of non-interference in internal affairs*" (italics added). This clearly sets the norm of sovereignty on an equal footing with democracy. Also, the signatories only promise to correct states where democracy has been overthrown rather than to curb abuses by nondemocratic states. Thus, the nineteen points are viewed primarily as a mechanism to preserve and strengthen preexisting democracies; more is required to meet the vital needs of states that have only recently emerged as democracies and remain fragile.

While the United States fostered the idea initially, the most powerful advocate was Polish Foreign Minister Bronislaw Geremek, himself a former dissident. The U.S. secretary of state, Madeline Albright, who led the U.S. delegation, did not push for the American model to be the global standard for democracy. Rather, the other six sponsors of the conference did much to mold the draft declaration that was sent to each invitee. In fact, the draft document was carefully prepared on an international basis and widely accepted. Overall, the world press portrayed the conference as a serious international effort to which many nations made substantial contributions.[8] Convening committee members hoped that their declaration would eventually carry as much international significance as the 1975 Helsinki declaration of human rights did during the Cold War—a worthy goal and an attractive model considered earlier in this book.

Even though the declaration itself commits the community of democracies to limited action, the fact that 133 states can sign such a document is impressive. The basic fact that so many states want to be signatories to such a declaration, even if it is simply to please the court of international public opinion, is a significant development in itself.

Also, the fact that the UN Charter and Universal Declaration of Human Rights along with UN membership served as major benchmarks for writing the declaration and deciding on participants shows the critical presence of the UN in discussions of this type. The UN's basic documents in the case of the Warsaw Declaration provide the solid ground from which to further develop norms, practices, and consensus on democracy. Altogether, this is an ongoing effort, fostering cooperative efforts by democratic states both within and beyond the UN.

An interesting follow-up to the Warsaw meeting, undertaken by the Council on Foreign Relations (an NGO), is a series of annual conferences on the relation between democracy and development.[9] These annual conferences are a joint effort of its new GeoEconomic Center and its equally new Center on Democracy and Free Markets. The core belief is grounded in the concept that a better understanding of the interrelationship between democracy and development will advance more effective policies of these important objectives. Institutions in which economic development is promoted must be provided along with the rationale for democracy in furthering their objectives. Likewise, those interested in democracy must realize that development (including the reduction of poverty) is needed for democracy to be sustained in poor countries. This initiative also shows the constructive interplay of governments and NGOs.

The Warsaw Declaration makes a strong statement about the clear relationship between democracy and meeting economic aspirations. Indeed, democracy cannot survive in many countries where prevalent economic standards are at the poverty level. The plan is to give insights from the council to the participating members in the community of democracies by holding the second annual conference on the eve of the Second Ministerial Conference of the Community of Democracies, which will take place in Seoul, Korea, in October 2002. It promises to be a large international follow-up to the Warsaw meeting of 2000, thus helping to consolidate the global community of democracies. A major thrust of the effort is prevention of deadly conflict.

On July 13, 2000, a group of high-level representatives of foreign ministers from nine leading democracies together with independent experts met in Stockholm. Their aim was to sharpen the concept of preventing deadly conflict while considering how best to organize and cooperate for prevention. Earlier, the Swedish Foreign Ministry organized a stimulating meeting at the UN in conjunction with the Carnegie Commission.

The question posed at the outset of the seminar was a simple one—why not prevention? In terms of lives, costs, reputation, and interests, the arguments for greater international efforts are clear. Conflict prevention is undoubtedly demanding, requiring extensive understanding of the causes of conflict and the tools that can be used to prevent violence, insightful analysis of particular crises, the will to act preventively, and the capability of effective action.

There is a growing view that prevention serves national and international interests. The benefits to be accrued have to be measured against the risk of being accused of interference. Yet, such accusations must not lead to paralysis. It is here that certain states and governments can play a valuable role as norm entrepreneurs, introducing prevention into the international debate and taking a lead in initiating practical policies of prevention. The significance of leadership for the development of an international culture of prevention was one of the central themes to emerge in discussions.

Such leadership should lead to the institutionalization of prevention within national and international structures and decision-making processes. In this context, while the UN will continue to play a central role in conflict prevention, the world organization is not always the most suitable actor to take practical preventive action. This poses a challenge to the traditional organization and working methods of the international system. Here, elicitation of cooperation among this group of highly regarded democracies (most of whom are medium-sized states) becomes operationally valuable.

The building of political will requires changing perceptions of the possibility of action to prevent violent conflict. At the national and international level, this process of change can only come about through the leadership of a relatively small group of committed individuals and/or governments. Participants agreed that such a "coalition of the willing" must initiate and lead a learning process of prevention that would identify potential violent conflicts and identify acceptable third parties as well as potential subjects for preventive engagement.

The goal of this learning process should be the "routinization" of preventive thinking within decision-making processes. The broadening understanding of human security—already evident in the policy agendas and discussions of international organizations, such as the UN and OSCE, as well as some national governments—is a positive step in this direction. Policymakers often do not have access to a wide range of preventive policy options from which to choose an action. The prevention constituency, both domestic and international, must take the responsibility of providing decisionmakers with credible options for action and reliable bases of support.

Positive incentives, "carrots," were considered more efficient than the "stick" that may be needed at a later stage. Here, institutions such as the EU, World Bank, and the IMF could play a more important role. A recurring theme was the need for better coordination within and between various actors. One idea was to make better use of development roundtables, in order to draw on the clout of major donors and international financial institutions, acting in a coordinated way to help build *competent, decent states*.

The challenge now is to develop partnerships between the different types of players in prevention and to achieve higher levels of coordination between traditional state efforts and initiatives sponsored by nonstate actors. There is a need to distinguish the roles of track-two players (mainly NGOs) to map existing available resources and, crucially, to identify the areas of comparative advantage for the various NGOs, private individuals, media, business, and academic communities. The parties to a conflict should be incorporated into prevention efforts at an early stage.

This meeting, primarily a loose consortium of foreign ministries, reflects the emergence of a leadership coalition of early prevention actors. The discussions in Stockholm show that a group of intellectually vital democracies with high moral standing is working to stimulate many elements of the international community to focus on effective prevention. It is particularly interesting that this group is arriving at a consensus on basic concepts of prevention as well as institutional roles, including a significant part for nongovernmental organizations. It is a very different situation from just a decade ago.

Business, Human Rights, and Mass Violence

The UN Secretary-General has promoted a compact of the UN with the business community to reduce the risk of mass violence. At his request, Juliette Bennett recently drew together a considerable body of information on the emerging situation.[10]

Bennett looks at the shifts in the past few years that have moved many large multinational corporations (mostly those dealing with the extraction of raw materials) to embrace human rights, violence prevention, and postconflict peace building in the countries where they operate. Using a few recent illustrative cases, the report gives an overview of initiatives addressing these businesses' role in prevention. A general change may be underway, caused not only by criticism of the behavior of multinationals in various countries but also by the recognition that it is good business to promote and preserve peace through preventive action as the Carnegie Commission envisioned. Many of the initiatives lately are focused on business–NGO collaborative efforts in which businesses show their commitment to human rights and violence prevention through their adherence to a set of principles or guidelines worked out in consultation with an advocacy NGO. Connected to these efforts are several government- and UN-sponsored voluntary agreements with NGOs and businesses. Notable among these is the "Global Compact," fostered by Kofi Annan, in which businesses show their commitment to one of the building blocks of prevention, human rights, by publicly committing to maintaining them in their operations worldwide.

These actions spring from the belief that has emerged in recent years that business and human rights are intertwined. In part this is due to NGO and media coverage of the excesses and abuses of multinationals but also to the growing realization that it is simply good business for a company to be seen as authentically respectful of human rights. Preventing and controlling human rights abuses not only provides for decency within the countries where the multinationals operate but also protects the good name of the company itself.

Bennett's focus is on extraction companies (here, oil, mining, and diamonds) that are often the most vulnerable to national turbulence and criticism of their policies. Royal/Dutch Shell is held up as an example of the changing attitudes of business toward human rights. In 1994, Shell was subjected to a hailstorm of criticism for its de facto support of the Nigerian government's execution of Ken Saro-Wiwa and eight other Ogoni tribe members who had protested Shell's environmental policies. In the wake of this public relations disaster, Shell teamed up with Amnesty International to work out a corporate human rights program.

Freeport-McMoRan's (a gold- and copper-mining concern) Indonesian operation has been subject to considerable criticism for its close relation to the then-repressive Indonesian government. Often, abuses perpetrated by security forces were connected to Freeport. In response, Freeport joined the "Global Mining Initiative" that explores the impact of mining operations on the environment and communities. It also developed its own environmental policy as well as a social and human rights policy with the Robert F. Kennedy Center on Human Rights and Amnesty International.

Occidental Petroleum also stirred up opposition with its plans to drill for oil in the Samore Block in northern Colombia. This huge project threatened the U'wa tribe, which protested; it also came under violent attack by leftist rebels of the Colombian National Liberation Army, which caused huge financial losses. Occidental's situation shows the costs that a company can endure when its policies do not recognize rights of local people.

In the Sudan, a Canadian company, Talisman Energy, has been severely criticized by NGOs, religious groups, and its own government for helping to fuel the civil war with its oil operations, which supply the regime in Khartoum with funds while turning a blind eye to abuses that include slavery. Talisman responded with a corporate responsibility report by PricewaterhouseCoopers and its own human rights–monitoring program.

Diamonds, even more than oil and other commodities, have come to have a tragic role in underwriting civil wars in Angola, Congo, and Sierra Leone. A number of NGOs were instrumental in raising international awareness of this issue. The UN, and a number of government-financed studies (notably one by Finland) that followed, investigated the illicit trade. Reacting to this ferment, DeBeers, the largest diamond producer, formally ended its purchases of Angolan stones.

These activities highlight a number of emerging strategies to deal with these issues that involve government and NGO collaboration with business on rights issues. These activities by member states have been conducted in cooperation with the UN and have, to some extent, been stimulated by the

UN commitment to the issue. Topping the list of these new strategies is the "Voluntary Principles on Security and Human Rights" put forward by the governments of the United Kingdom and the United States and signed by several mining and oil companies (BP, Chevron, Conoco, Freeport, Rio Tinto, Shell, Texaco). Such NGOs as Amnesty International, Business for Social Responsibility, Council on Economic Priorities, Human Rights Watch, International Alert, the Lawyers Committee for Human Rights, and the Prince of Wales Business Leaders Forum are also parties to the agreement. These principles provide for a dialogue on how businesses can voluntarily maintain the safety and security of their operations while respecting human rights and fundamental freedoms. A particular emphasis is on preventing security forces connected to the companies from committing human rights abuses. The principles hold promise for hammering out practical solutions to human rights problems. They can provide ready-made guidance on these issues for companies faced with troubling situations.

Along with these more general agreements there are a number of examples of direct NGO and business partnerships. Illustrating the benefits of such cooperation is a report created by the Council on Economic Priorities, the Prince of Wales Business Leaders Forum, and International Alert. Their "Business of Peace" puts forward six broad principles that, if followed by business, can make a positive contribution to conflict prevention and resolution. In their activities, the multinationals should be guided by policies grounded in a sense of strategic commitment, risk and impact analysis, dialogue and consultation, partnership and collective action, effective evaluation, and accountability.

Bennett's report also provides a number of examples that show how companies have contributed to prevention and postconflict peace building. Notable among these efforts were Microsoft's aid to the UN High Commission for Refugees (UNHCR) in Kosovo; Oracle's donation of 100 computers to help with coexistence projects in Northern Ireland; NetAid.org's work with thousands of NGOs and its efforts to raise $12 million for humanitarian aid; and Ericsson's partnership with the UN and Red Cross for disaster relief.

Such cooperation shows that opportunities exist. In line with these programs, the NGO Fund for Peace has established a "Business and Human Rights Roundtable" that brings activists, business leaders, and government leaders together to discuss shared interests in human rights and peace building. These discussions have attracted such multinational powerhouses as Mobil, Motorola, and Texaco and have sat them down at the table with such important NGOs as Amnesty International, the Lawyers Committee for Human Rights, and Transparency International. The roundtable recently put forward six "Joint Statements of Principles of Representatives of the Business and Human Rights Communities" that are to be used to develop practical solutions for business and human rights. These principles urge business to organize their policies around:

- Promoting the Universal Declaration of Human Rights.
- Recognizing the mutual goals between human rights and the business community, for example, that human rights and maximizing shareholder returns are complementary.
- Committing to the promotion of rule of law and the promotion of open societies.
- Recognizing the role of multilateral institutions in advancing human rights and promoting "the Joint Statement of Common Interests" that includes international promotion of good governance, efforts to strengthen institutions and infrastructure, eradication of poverty, and the development of human resources.

All these are critical to the creation of a business-friendly environment;

- Recognition by the corporate community of human rights standards, including the need to avoid complicity in governmental human rights abuses in the countries in which they operate.
- The need to uphold human rights in the corporation's own operations.

A number of NGOs, from the Carter Center to the Search for Common Ground to Harvard's Program on Strengthening Democratic Institutions, are available to provide collaboration with business in violence prevention.

Business partnerships with NGOs are matched by their increasing engagement with multilateral organizations for postconflict peace building. The World Bank's Post-Conflict Unit has built alliances with food companies in its work in Guatemala. The Institute for Multi-Track Diplomacy has also tapped business leaders in difficult attempts to improve relations between Taiwan and China as well as Pakistan and India.

Bennett's illuminating overview of these many recent activities interrelating business with the UN, governments, and NGOs leaves no doubt that business has an interest in preventing conflict and that real progress has come from the recognition of this fact. She makes a good case that there has been a sea change in this area over the past few years; multinationals are cooperating with many well-respected and international NGOs that have a focus on human rights and social justice. The report also makes plain that this is happening internationally with, for example, European companies cooperating with American NGOs. It is also not simply a case of private groups (business and NGOs) working together, but working with IGOs and governments as well. This has the potential to increase the chance of success. Emphatic public commitments by business to foster a culture of prevention that can be sustained reflect a remarkable emerging change in the attitude of the business community. If this can be maintained—and spread widely—it could make a highly significant difference in the outlook for peace even though many significant companies have not yet joined these efforts.

There will have to be monitoring by the UN, NGOs, the media, and by business to describe any clear, identifiable results this change has brought about. Will these endeavors produce practical shifts in the day-to-day activities of these multinationals? Will they increasingly use their formidable expertise and clout in effective ways to reduce severe poverty, foster conflict resolution, and exemplify decent standards of human behavior? Their continuing cooperation with top UN leadership, major governments, and strong NGOs can surely enhance the likelihood of positive outcomes. The experience is quite limited, the subject controversial, and the results uncertain. But the potential for prevention, including democratic socioeconomic development, is great.

Nongovernmental Organizations

The government of Sweden and the International Peace Academy (IPA) teamed up for a groundbreaking joint project, which they entitled "Reaction to Prevention: Opportunities for the UN System in the Millennium." It delineated a range of prevention strategies from the diplomatic and political to the military to the social and economic aspects of development. At the same time, it considered the impact of the important facets of timing, resources, legitimacy, information, and coordination of these strategies.

This international meeting in April 2000 was preceded by two major reviews of the research literature. The final report concluded that the UN is uniquely placed to shift international action from a culture of reaction to one of prevention, facing up to the difficulties along the way: (1) mobilizing member states to provide adequate resources for prevention, and (2) improving information flow and coordination within the organization.

The notable opportunities for preventive action by the UN include its broadly defined mandate, an international presence, unique staff, and institutional strengths, plus virtually worldwide moral authority and legitimacy for preventive action. Among efforts that highlight the UN's comparative advantage, the UNDP and the World Bank are developing new practices to bridge the development–security divide and focus more specifically on local needs. These organizations are ideally placed to help create an integrated, long-term strategy for preventive action by managing resource scarcity and abundance, processes of political change such as democratization, and socioeconomic issues such as horizontal inequality. Furthermore, the World Bank could also be an important provider of prevention resources by increasing collaboration with other organizations in the UN system.

The Security Council has a primary but not exclusive role in conflict prevention. The council has dramatically increased the volume of its activity since the end of the Cold War—thus providing an opportunity to advance a prevention agenda within the council but also making determination of exactly which preventive initiatives to undertake somewhat difficult. Furthermore, the Security Council has tools at its disposal (e.g., fact-finding missions, observer missions, preventive disarmament, the establishment of demilitarized zones, postconflict peace building, and targeted sanctions) that could be used more frequently and more effectively.

The Secretary-General is widely perceived to have a high degree of moral authority. This is utilized, at forums such as the Millennium Assembly, to promote a prevention agenda acceptable to member states and other relevant actors. The Secretary-General can also play a key role in influencing the General Assembly and the Security Council regarding the need for long-term, structural prevention initiatives. Finally, through the use of Article 99 of the UN Charter, more systematic fact finding can be undertaken and more frequent, case-specific advice given to the Security Council. Altogether this joint effort of an important government, Sweden, and an important NGO, the International Peace Academy, gave a strong push to prevention efforts in and around the UN.

An IPA conference in February 2001 reflected further analysis of the UN's capacities for prevention—again with support from the government of Sweden. Impetus for serious engagement in preventive action at the United Nations came directly after Boutros Boutros-Ghali's 1992 report, *An Agenda for Peace*. This was strongly reinforced by Kofi Annan in his keynote address at the launching of the Carnegie Commission's report at the UN in early 1998. Unprecedented Security Council presidential statements, in November 1999 and July 2000, closed by asking for a major report from UN Secretary-General Kofi Annan to be submitted on the topic in the spring of 2001.

The International Peace Academy convened a meeting to contribute to the formulation of this report.[11] Participants included members of the Security Council and permanent missions of other member states, representatives from UN departments and agencies, foreign ministry representatives, and experts in the field of prevention. The meeting covered a broad range of topics, including the United Nation's role in prevention, differentiating prevention from intervention, development, tools for prevention, the importance of analysis, and, finally, UN actors and their roles and strengthening the capacities of the UN for the future. Their analysis and recommendations contributed to the Secretary-General's landmark report that I highlight in the epilogue. The various cooperative efforts of the Swedish government and the IPA illuminate the growing tendency of government–NGO cooperation in this field.

During 2000 to 2001, there has been a sharp intensification of work on prevention by other leading NGOs. Independent work by NGOs has fed the growing interest in prevention. A number of leading U.S. nongovernmental institutions have recently begun dedicated programs that focus explicitly and systematically on prevention. The Woodrow Wilson Center for International Scholars launched in 2000 has its own Conflict Prevention Project. The center has distinguished leadership in Lee Hamilton, who was a champion of prevention during his leadership years in Congress. Taking up from the Carnegie Commission on Preventing Deadly Conflict, the Wilson Center's program seeks to evolve effective strategies for prevention. Its emphasis is on rigorous analysis and research that can be transferred into the realm of policy making and planning. In Washington, the Center provides an excellent interface between the scholarly and policy communities on a worldwide basis.

With an emphasis on prevention as policy, the center shows how rigorous policy analysis of conflict prevention may be infused into decision making and planning at the highest levels of governments. The project has created a forum for dialogue between policymakers, scholars, and practitioners. Special attention is given to implementing conflict prevention strategies and encouraging coordination in the conflict prevention community. Speaking engagements, forums, conferences, monographs, and edited volumes serve as the products of this stimulating endeavor.

The Woodrow Wilson Center is an appropriate place for extending the work of the Carnegie Commission. It is home to an international cadre of carefully vetted scholars and practitioners who bring not only the highest-caliber professional credentials, but also an essential international outlook and historical policy perspective. Additional assets are the center's nonpartisan nature and close association with U.S. policymakers in the legislative and executive branches and an international reputation for fine scholarship on timely subjects.

Like the Wilson Center, other institutions are endeavoring to deepen the public's knowledge of prevention issues. In 2001, the Foreign Policy Association of the United States held a series of high-profile lectures in New York on preventing deadly conflict, which were dedicated to Cyrus Vance. The speakers included Kofi Annan, Brian Urquhardt, Eason Jordan (of CNN), and me. This was the first time in the history of the organization that it focused such sustained attention on one subject, and the responses were very positive.

As mentioned previously, another well-respected institution has recently intensified its work on prevention. The Council on Foreign Relations (CFR), a complex mixture of leaders from several sectors, had a five-year initial phase in its Center for Preventive Action, led by Barnett Rubin and supported by the Carnegie Corporation. This activity studied several hot spots in considerable detail and made recommendations for prevention based on what was learned. It oriented leading foreign policy people to the concepts and techniques of prevention and held stimulating annual meetings that helped build a community of prevention specialists from different backgrounds. A valuable new book in preparation by Rubin undertakes a fundamental analysis of prevention issues and lessons from the Center's analysis of specific conflicts.

Following this initial phase, the council undertook a second step with the Center for Preventive Action, supported by the Hewlett Foundation and led by the CFR's president, Leslie Gelb, who has worked closely with Frederick Tipson and General William Nash. This process is currently underway with the goal of drawing together the lessons of the 1990s for general use. It is also setting up a series of task forces that will study dangerous situations in the field, formulate action recommendations for prevention, and pursue these recommendations with the United States, other governments, the UN, and the business community.

Outside the United States there are excellent NGOs that are hard at work on the problem of deadly conflict. One with a global reach is the International Crisis Group (ICG), which has emerged dramatically in the past few years. A multinational organization, its goal is to broaden international capabilities to anticipate and then prevent violent conflict. Headquartered in Brussels, with advocacy offices in Washington, D.C., New York, and Paris, the organization operates field projects in eighteen crisis-affected countries and regions across Africa, Asia, North America, and southwest Europe. Its staff monitor and report on dangerous situations in various trouble spots. Its independence helps to bring certain issues that otherwise would receive scant notice to the attention of governments and international bodies. ICG also provides fresh perspectives to leaders and advocates that can be vital in providing new approaches to problems that may otherwise appear intractable.

Founded by Morton Abramowitz, a highly respected diplomat, it has built financial and political support over the past few years. Currently heading the ICG is the Honorable Gareth Evans, Australian foreign minister from the late 1980s to mid-1990s, who became president and chief executive in January 2000. He was a strong member of the Carnegie Commission on Preventing Deadly Conflict and has written extensively and deeply on preventing deadly conflict, especially the United Nation's role. In ICG's most recent annual report, 2001, Evans writes about its mission of prevention and ways to fulfill it.[12]

The International Crisis Group carries out its mission in three ways. Experts are put on the ground in crisis situations to examine what is happening and why. From their work, policy options are developed in consultation with their highly experienced board members. The ICG then supports appropriate policy responses by going directly to policymakers, the media, and other potential sources of constructive influence. At a minimum, ICG can be instrumental in achieving better understanding of dangerous situations and contribute ideas and proposals that are seriously considered and sometimes put into action. Evidence that its work matters is reflected in the growing support of many governments and foundations. During 2001, its analytical output has been prolific and its impact growing.

An illustration of the ICG's efforts is given by the events in Montenegro in early 2001. An extraordinary parliamentary election took place in Montenegro in April 2001, which focused on the future status of the republic— would it continue as a federal union with Serbia or as an independent state? ICG provided a strategy for preventing deadly conflict in a briefing paper produced a month prior to the election. It carefully examined fundamental issues and strategies of the main players in the election and considered the various likely postelection outcomes. Based on this analysis, it made recommendations to the world community and to the political actors in Montenegro and Serbia about possible choices during and after the election period. The report offered a range of likely options for the future relationship of Montenegro with Serbia, types of issues that may need to be resolved in defining a new relationship, and consequences for Montenegro and for the region in the event that it opted for independence. In the spring of 2001, this was followed by a valuable major report on the Balkans after Milosevic with special attention to structural prevention.[13]

Universities and Prevention

There is a general upsurge of interest in the area of education in preventing deadly conflict. Activity is widespread enough that here we can only give a few impressionistic examples. Several prominent universities in the United States, Canada, South Africa, Japan, and Europe currently offer such courses and programs.

In the spring of 2001, a meeting of international experts was held at the United Nations to discuss the possibility for the University for Peace (UP-EACE) to have a stronger role in peace studies as part of a recommitment of the university under the guidance of Maurice Strong to expand its programs worldwide. The United Nations University in Tokyo is another example of an institution that puts significant focus on peace education and conflict resolution. It is part of the UN system. The university makes use of research and capacity building to clarify and help resolve world problems of concern to the UN and member states.

An example of current offerings in higher education on prevention is a course recently taught at Columbia University entitled "Preventive Diplomacy and Conflict Resolution in the United Nations: Integrating Theory and Practice." It is a combined effort of several programs within the School of International Affairs as well as Teachers College at Columbia. In addition, it was planned and executed with the help of the office of the Secretary-General, the Carnegie Council on Ethics and International Affairs, and Parliamentarians for Global Action (PGA).[14]

The objective of the course was to draw together "theory of conflict, negotiation, mediation and conflict management with the practice of the United Nations" and underscores the capacity of international and governmental officials along with academics to understand ways in which preventive diplomacy and peacemaking can prevent or halt deadly conflict. By the end of the course, students were expected to possess the necessary skill of analysis and practical perspective to enable them to enhance peacemaking in the types of situations likely to arise in the international community within the next ten years. This course reflects the recent emphasis of the UN on coordination for prevention.

Over the course of three months, students were required to review at least one of five books; among them were the Carnegie Commission's *Final Report* and *The Handbook of Conflict Resolution*. Student papers were supposed to reflect the findings of theoretical literature as well as the analysis of actual cases.

Other innovative course offerings in the area of prevention can be found at the University of Victoria, at Harvard, and Stanford. Dr. Gordon Smith, director of the Centre for Global Studies at the University of Victoria, taught a course at the University of British Columbia built on the course outline and reading list developed by the Carnegie Commission on Preventing Deadly Conflict (CCPDC). As an expert in international policy from his experiences as deputy foreign minister of Canada, Smith used CCPDC's outline as a basis for the students to gain practical experience in proposing concise and concrete measures that would either prevent conflict, help resolve it, or aid in peace building. Two students went on to join the Canadian Foreign Service, an institution that only accepts fifty individuals per year.

At Harvard, the Center for Science and International affairs, headed by Professor Graham Allison, has brought together an outstanding group of scholars and practitioners with deep interest in violence prevention. Stanford's Institute for International Studies, headed by Professor David Holloway, includes a major program on Preventive Defense headed by former secretary of defense, William Perry. Many other good examples could also be given, including a strong program at the University of Bradford in England. Professor John Stremlau, a senior staff member of the Carnegie Commission, and Dr. Chris Hansberg, formerly a Hamburg Fellow at Stanford, head a new program at the University of Witwatersrand in South Africa.

A meeting was held at the United Nations in March 2001 at which world-wide experts from various fields met to discuss the potential role of the University for Peace (UPEACE).[15] Based in San José, Costa Rica, it was founded by an act of the General Assembly of the United Nations in 1980. Since 1999, a plan for the expansion of UPEACE's programs and an enhancement of its curriculum has been developed to make the university more a focus for global efforts in education for peace. Secretary-General Kofi Annan opened the session. Scholars from academia, prominent UN officials, and experts from nongovernmental, governmental, and multilateral organizations convened to discuss ways in which UPEACE might be able to fill a void found in the field of peace education. In addition, participants considered the current state of peace education internationally. All concurred that the current concerns posed by human conflict in the twenty-first century must be more adequately addressed. There was a strong consensus for international interuniversity collaboration to strengthen and widen education on ways to prevent mass violence.

New Communication Technologies and Democracy Building

A prominent example of an organization making use of the new communication technologies is the National Endowment for Democracy, ably led by Carl Gershman. It is actively pursuing the extraordinary potential of new communications technologies to help build democracy.[16] It stems from the connection between democracy and the flow of information. The Internet is not the only medium for this rush of information; books, newspapers, phones, faxes, television, posters, and flyers all have their roles. However, today's world, with its increasing complexity and interactivity, is now more than ever suited to the interactive nature of the Internet. The Internet both enhances this complexity and provides a way to cope with it. Its impact is inescapable. Already, the Internet is playing a large role in the promotion of democracy in ingenious and unexpected ways—often in remote areas of the earth that have been little associated with democracy.

A number of factors determine how the Internet helps to build democracy, including the condition and needs of the country and the relevance of the technology to their objectives. An indigenous community creatively responding to its own problems archives some of the best projects around the world. In an autocracy, the Internet can be used to help open a closed information system controlled by the regime. In a new democracy it can be used as a tool to make governance more accessible. Humans are inherently creative—so, if technology is available, people will figure out a way of making use of it, even if the circumstances are difficult.

Dictatorial or semiauthoritarian systems are the toughest cases, where democracy groups fight for more political space against unfriendly governments.

A classic example is found in the role of Radio B-92, other independent media, and NGOs in the former Yugoslavia during the Dayton peace agreement and the ouster in autumn 2000 of Slobodan Milosevic. The Milosevic regime closed down the radio station in December 1996 only to confront the effects of B-92 using the Internet to reach an even wider audience, which forced the regime to lift the ban in just over two days. This same model was used by a network of fifty local radio and television stations, thereby circumventing continued regime restrictions. Signal transmission via Internet and telephone to London BBC were then rebroadcast back to Yugoslavia via BBC satellite. News broadcasting was not the only way that B-92 used the Internet. It also transmitted via the Internet magazines, books, articles, movies, documentaries, and television programs to international stations for broadcast to foreign countries.

Other groups used the Internet to organize rallies and demonstrations during the disruptive period leading up to the election in September 2000. Two organizations cooperated closely to preserve important election data during the tense period following the vote.

Internet activity has extended to Belarus, Ukraine, China, and parts of Africa. Belarus democrats take advantage of the fact that there are over 100,000 Internet users domestically—more than the circulation of the largest newspaper—and these users are primarily young people. In order to reach and mobilize this young audience, the local financial newspaper set up an election Web site that gave profiles of candidates and election-related news. Before the close of the campaign, later in 2001, it held a "virtual election," enabling users to nominate candidates, debate issues, and cast ballots. Another Web site operated by an NGO led the opposition reports on violations of human rights. It also reported activities of the united opposition as well as political and economic changes.

The Ukraine's first Internet newspaper, *Ukrainska Pravda* (UP), reaches 60,000 readers and offers unbiased coverage of politics in both the Ukraine and Russia. It is widely believed that the murder of UP's editor, Heorhyi Gongadze, was due to the newspaper's exposition of the incompetence and corruption of the government. Subsequently, tape recordings allegedly caught the president, Leonid Kuchma, ordering Gongadze to be silenced. This caused an explosion of mass demonstrations and demands for Kuchma's resignation. This story illustrates the power of the Internet to disseminate information widely—overcoming regime censorship to some extent. It also illustrates the risks inherent in the struggle for democracy everywhere.

In China, a huge contradiction exists where the regime is concurrently trying to expand the use of the Internet to promote economic development, while also attempting to limit its subversive political potential through controlling its use. There has been a vast increase in Internet use over the past four years—from 120,000 users to 22,000,000. It is expected to grow to over 100,000,000 by the year 2004. The legitimacy of the Chinese regime relies mostly on controlling what people believe and the information they receive, so it has logically developed different mechanisms to control the Internet use, ranging from blocking access to independent Web sites, spreading false information or rumors, or publicizing arrests to intimidate Web users. These restrictive efforts have only been marginally successful because the regime's enforcement would also hinder economic growth. As more Chinese citizens gain access to the Web, the Internet will provide alternative (shadow) media and a possible tool for organizing independent social and political groups.

The Internet has also helped activists come out of isolation in Africa, where new technologies are not as widely used. Even so, in Sudan, sixty women's organizations made use of e-mail to form a group and enlist international partners to help force the government to repeal a law forbidding women from being engaged in public employment.

Because of its ability to link people across great distances for minimal cost, the Internet has grown to be a tool for bringing about decentralization and civic engagement across regions. Examples can be found in U.S.–South Africa partnership in an online data management and communication system that ensures participation of provincial and local government in the policy making at the national level. In Russia, a group has formed linking human rights centers across many time zones. Each center has computer equipment and training and access to databases and reports on political and legislative developments. Turkey and Slovenia have youth-oriented Web-based networking. In Turkey, young people join discussion groups and are exposed to NGO activities. Slovenia has a successful program encouraging young people to get out and vote.

In Latin America, a particularly interesting initiative called Journalists Against Corruption uses the Internet as a networking and communications tool while also making government and business dealings more visible. It also provides critical help to American journalists who investigate and report on corruption. For example, the Center for International Private Enterprise, the supporting organization of the initiative, helped to release journalists in Bolivia and Mexico. Women are being empowered in the Middle East through training in new technologies. Two groups in the Middle East, Sisterhood is Global International (SIGI) and Women's Learning Partnership (WLP), defend women's human rights, battle so-called honor crimes and rape, help women become self-reliant, and develop leadership skills.

NED was inspired to create the World Movement for Democracy in 1999 because of the overwhelming capacity of the new communications technologies to give ordinary citizens the ability to access information and to network with each other at a grassroots level. In conjunction with other democracy assistance groups, it launched the World Movement to form a loose association of groups and practitioners from around the world to work in areas of democracy building. Some work on governance issues while others concentrate on human rights. Journalists, educators, entrepreneurs, and academics who specialize in democracy along with political party leaders and activists in civil society work mostly within their own countries and essentially interact over the Web.

One network focused specifically on the theme of using the Internet and other media to promote democracy. It started by establishing a listserv to aid communication and exchange of information. In addition, it promoted training and resources for NGOs and helped them to design their Web sites. It also dealt with government restriction by helping international groups use pressure to lift censorship and develop better Internet policies and communications infrastructure.

Democracy-building organizations (governmental, nongovernmental, and mixed) are being well received in much of the world. They are building informative and supportive networks and facilitating the work of democratic reformers far and wide. Certainly, the prominence of the Internet does not guarantee the democratic process, but it can be a powerful influence for human freedom and democracy.

The burst of new possibilities and widening acceptance for NED is by no means unique. The same may be said of most of the NGOs we have described earlier in the chapter on civil society, such as the Carter Center and the Project on Ethnic Relations. Similarly, NED's "cousins" supported by European governments are thriving. The net effect of all this is an unprecedented moral commitment, intellectual ferment, and organizational creativity in the service of democracy, justice, and closer human relationships around the globe. This provides better prospects for preventing mass violence than ever before. But the coalescence of the ingenious and dedicated forces for just peace can still only be distantly perceived on the horizon, and the long, hard struggle will go on. Still, there is basis for hope in the new century that has rarely, if ever, been achieved in the past.

Philanthropy

Several important developments bearing on the prevention of deadly conflict have occurred in the world of philanthropy. One is the United Nations Foundation (UNF), created by Ted Turner (founder of CNN). This foundation is headed by Timothy Wirth, formerly a distinguished member of the United States Senate and then head of a major new program of the U.S. State Department on global problems. In 2000, the UNF created a new program on peace, security, and human rights headed by Jane Holl Lute, former executive director of the Carnegie Commission.

The Secretary-General's strong commitment to conflict prevention, the considerable weight of UN field experience, and growing political support both within the UN and among member states have combined to generate a consensus that the UN must take a leading and sustaining role in preventing violent conflict. Within its Peace, Security and Human Rights program, UNF works to strengthen the UN for this purpose.

The UNF emphasizes that effective prevention requires both long-term and short-term efforts. Structural prevention highlights the importance of long-term engagement and rests on the idea of the capable society or capable state—one characterized by representative governance, widespread market economic activity, robust civil society, and one grounded on the rule of law. Capable states provide conditions of security, well-being, and justice, inhibiting the tendency to resort to violence to settle differences. Operational prevention relies on urgent, often more assertive, measures to preempt fatal decisions and avert crises. Operational prevention rests on the effectiveness of early action on receipt of timely warning. The UNF is helping the UN to become more effective in both kinds of prevention.

In 2000, Ted Turner created another new foundation, this one focusing on the critical dangers of weapons of mass destruction. The new organization is headed by former U.S. Senator Sam Nunn, who served for many years as chairman of the Senate Armed Services Committee and is one of the most highly respected people in the entire field of international security. Although the name of the new foundation is Nuclear Threat Initiative, it will also focus on biological weapons of mass destruction. Throughout the emerging program of this organization is an emphasis on prevention, and, indeed, Senator Nunn was a highly contributory member of the Carnegie Commission's advisory board.[17] During his years in the Senate, he was central in bringing the crisis prevention viewpoint to the Cold War and making it operational. Together with Senator Richard Lugar, he instituted the largest and most effective cooperative threat reduction program between the United States and Russia. The Nunn-Lugar program has accomplished much in preventing the proliferation of nuclear states and weapons, for example, helping Belarus, Ukraine, and Kazakhstan to become nonnuclear states.

The transformation of the Hewlett Foundation has been another major development in the world of philanthropy. For years it has been distinguished in conflict resolution, but recent changes in its program are dramatic. With a new president, Paul Brest, former dean of Stanford University's Law School and an individual long interested in the problem of conflict, and the appointment of Melanie Greenberg, a distinguished lawyer, as chief program officer for conflict resolution and violence prevention, Hewlett has taken a highly significant role in the field. Greenberg is the senior author of one of the Carnegie Commission's most important books, *Words Over War*. With the passing of the foundation's eminent

founder, William Hewlett, it now becomes one of the largest of all foundations and one of the best. Like the UN Foundation and the Nuclear Threat
Initiative, the Hewlett Foundation will be a major supporter of inquiry and
innovation at the interface between research, policy, and practice, with special attention to prevention of deadly conflict.

Concluding Comment

Altogether, it is clear that there has been a burst of prevention activity in the
early years of the twenty-first century that stands in dramatic contrast to
the early years of the 1990s—not to mention the early years of the twentieth century. There is a conjunction of new moral commitment, new ideas,
new organizations, and new departures for existing institutions. Tools and
strategies are being developed beyond prior experience and tried out in
highly innovative ways across many nations and sectors. No one can be
sure how far and how fast this movement will go; the near-term prognosis
is encouraging and the long-term prognosis has great potential for a healthy
humanity.

Notes

1. Statement by the president of the Security Council, *Role of the Security
Council in the Prevention of Armed Conflicts*, UN Document: S/PRST/2000/25,
July 20, 2000.

2. *Improving the Coherence and Effectiveness of European Union Action in
the Field of Conflict Prevention* (Report presented to the Nice European Council by the Secretary-General/High Representative and the Commission, Nice,
France, 2001).

3. Renata Dwan, "Conflict Prevention and CFSP Coherence" (Stockholm
International Peace Research Institute, 2001).

4. Chris Patten and Anna Lindh, "Let's Control the Small Arms Trade," *International Herald Tribune*, June 30, 2001.

5. G8 Miyazaki Initiatives for Conflict Prevention and Conclusions of the
G8 Foreign Ministers' Meeting, July 13, 2000.

6. P. Terrence Hopmann, "The Organization for Security and Cooperation
in Europe: Its Contribution to Conflict Prevention and Resolution," in Paul C.
Stern and Daniel Druckman, eds., *International Conflict Resolution After the
Cold War* (Washington, D.C.: National Academy Press, 2000), 569–616;
"Scholar Searches for Long-Lasting Security in Postcommunist Regions," *Briefings* (Watson Institute for International Studies at Brown University,
winter/spring 2000).

7. U.S. Department of State, "Toward a Community of Democracies," Final Warsaw Declaration (Warsaw, Poland, June 27, 2000).

8. Beata Pasek, "Nations Discuss Democracy, Rights," *Washington Post*, June 26, 2000; Jane Perlez, "Vast Rally for Democracy Opens in a Polish Castle," *New York Times*, June 26, 2000; British Broadcasting Corporation, "France Refuses to Sign Democracy Charter," June 27, 2000 <www.news.bbc.co.uk>; British Broadcasting Corporation, "Officials Gather for Democracy Conference," June 25, 2000 <www.news.bbc.co.uk>; Jim Hoagland, "Democracies Will Gather to Make a Big Statement," *International Herald Tribune*, June 22, 2000.

9. Paraphrase of letter from Morton H. Halperin and Michael M. Weinstein, (May 2, 2001) of the Council on Foreign Relations.

10. Juliette Bennett, *Business in Conflict Zones: The Role of the Multinational in Promoting Regional Stability* (report prepared for the United Nations Office of the Global Compact, January 2001).

11. Lekha Sriram, "From Promise to Practice: Strengthening UN Capacities for the Prevention of Violent Conflict" (International Peace Academy, Security Council Workshop Report, February 2001), 1–11.

12. Gareth Evans, "President's Essay" (Annual Report of the International Crisis Group, 2001), 3.

13. International Crisis Group, *After Milosevic: A Practical Agenda for Lasting Balkans Peace* (Brussels: International Crisis Group Press, 2001).

14. School of International and Public Affairs, Columbia University, International Affairs, course U8556, "Preventive Diplomacy and Conflict Resolution in the United Nations: Integrating Theory and Practice" <www.columbia.edu/cu/sipa/COURSES/2000-2001/u8556.html>.

15. David Ekbladh, *Education for Peace in the Twenty-First Century: A Report on the Advisory Meeting on the Academic Program of the University for Peace*, United Nations, New York, March 23–24, 2001 (University for Peace, 2001).

16. Carl Gershman, "The Internet and Democracy Building—The NED Experience" Paper presented at the meeting on democracy, Wilton Park, U.K., April 27–28, 2001 (National Endowment for Democracy, Washington, D.C., 2001).

17. *US–Russian Cooperation to Prevent Deadly Conflict: Reports of a Commission Task Force*, Sam Nunn, chairman (Carnegie Commission on Preventing Deadly Conflict, Perspectives on Prevention, December 1999).

Epilogue

A Landmark Report on Fulfillment of the UN's Potential for Prevention

During the Cold War and since, it has been my great privilege to work with many distinguished scientists, scholars, and world leaders—in my own country and beyond. Among these, none has been more significant than Kofi Annan, the current Secretary-General of the UN. While I have emphasized strongly—perhaps as much as anyone in the prevention field—the necessity of engaging many institutions and organizations in this great mission, it is clear that the UN must become one of the strong players to make a preventive system work.

In my first conversation with Boutros Boutros-Ghali a short while after he became Secretary-General, we discussed the prevention approach. He was exceedingly thoughtful and stimulating. When Cyrus Vance and I organized the Commission, Boutros Ghali was helpful in many ways. We, in turn, tried to be helpful to him, particularly in his leadership in preparing three key documents: *An Agenda for Peace*; *An Agenda for Development*; and *An Agenda for Democratization*. All these pointed in the direction of prevention, bringing the UN back to the basic orientation formulated by Franklin Roosevelt and others at its inception.

Earlier in these pages, I have put strong emphasis on the growing community of established democracies. I tried to make clear their strong assets and their special responsibility for prevention of war—acting partly within the UN system and partly outside it, but always in a way that values international cooperation for peace and justice. I have also pointed out the inherent constraints on efficacy of UN action. Yet, it is the truly universal organization, the one with the largest body of experience in helping countries sort out their differences. Our case studies show that, for all its faults, it has time and again been helpful in resolving disputes and reducing violence. But its full potential for averting mass violence can only be achieved if the member states—and especially the established democracies—want it to do so and if it has superb leadership.

When Kofi Annan became Secretary-General, he immediately took a keen interest in the Carnegie Commission's work and was exceedingly helpful and wise. The first international presentation of the Commission's main report was made at the UN shortly after its publication. Kofi Annan opened the meeting with a memorable address, which the Commission later published along with several of his other key statements.

Shortly thereafter, he proposed the first-ever retreat of the Security Council with prevention of deadly conflict as the central topic. When the retreat occurred, he asked me to give an opening statement, an overview of the Commission's work bearing directly on strengthening the UN for prevention. The response of the Security Council was positive. During 2000 to 2001, there has been a remarkable, constructive interplay between the Secretary-General, the Security Council, and the General Assembly on the subject of prevention, reflecting a steadily increasing level of interest and concern. This culminated on June 18, 2001, with a report of the Secretary-General that may in time come to be seen as a landmark in the history of the UN, comparable to the great documents of the period from 1945 to 1948. Its functional significance for prevention has extraordinary potential.

In a forward-looking way, it deals with the UN mandate for prevention of armed conflicts; the role of the principal organs of the UN; the activities of UN departments, agencies, and programs; interactions between the UN and other international actors; enhancing the UN's capacity for prevention in all of these spheres. It combines conceptual sophistication with organizational ingenuity. It recognizes the importance of other players and makes practical suggestions for cooperative efforts. Since the potential importance of this document for the preventive mission is so great, I now quote several key passages.

"Perhaps the most pitiful lesson of the past decade has been that the prevention of violent conflict is far better and more cost-effective than cure. The challenge is to apply that lesson so that prevention exists not just at the rhetorical level but also practically. This is easier said than done; existing problems usually take precedence over potential ones and, while the benefits of prevention lie in the future and are difficult to quantify, the costs must be paid in the present. On the other hand, the costs of not preventing violence are enormous. The human costs of war include not only the visible and immediate deaths, injury, destruction, displacement—but also the distant and indirect repercussion for families, communities, local and national institutions and economies, and neighboring countries. They are counted not only in damage inflicted but also in opportunities lost.

"The 1997 Carnegie Commission on Preventing Deadly Conflict found, for example, that the gross domestic product (GDP) in Lebanon in the early

1990s remained 50 percent lower than it was before fighting broke out in 1974; that civil war and widespread use of landmines was widely blamed for the abandonment of an estimated 80 percent of Angola's agricultural land; and that already inadequate food production in Burundi dropped 17 percent during recent periods of conflict. We also need to factor in the costs of external actors who intervene to stem the violence. A Carnegie Commission study estimated that the international community spent about $200 billion on the seven major interventions of the 1990s, in Bosnia and Herzegovina, Somalia, Rwanda, Haiti, the Persian Gulf, Cambodia and El Salvador, exclusive of Kosovo and East Timor. The study calculated the cost differentials between these conflict management activities and potential preventive action, and concluded that a preventive approach would have saved the international community almost $130 billion. . . .

"The Carnegie Commission on Preventing Deadly Conflict described strategies or prevention as falling into two categories: *operational prevention*, which refers to measures applicable in the face of immediate crisis, and *structural prevention*, which consists of measures to ensure that crises do not arise in the first place or, if they do, that they do not recur. The present report will consider the broad spectrum of assistance offered to States by the United Nations system in the realm of both short-term operational prevention and long-term structural prevention. . . .

"Since assuming office, I have pledged to move the United Nations from a culture of reaction to a culture of prevention. In its presidential statement of 20 July 2000, the Security Council invited me to submit a report on the prevention of armed conflict, containing an analysis and recommendations on initiatives within the United Nations, taking into account previous experience and the views and considerations expressed by Member States. My first objective in the present report is to review the progress that has been achieved in developing the conflict prevention capacity of the United Nations as called for by both the General Assembly and the Security Council. My second aim is to present specific recommendations on how the efforts of the United Nations system in this field could be further enhanced, with the cooperation and active involvement of Member States, who ultimately have the primary responsibility for conflict prevention.

"In drafting the present report, I have endeavoured to take into account the many different views and considerations of Member States expressed in recent debates of the General Assembly and the Security Council on conflict prevention. It is axiomatic that the active support and cooperation of Member States will be needed for conflict prevention efforts to succeed. The specific contributions that can be made by the General Assembly, the Security Council, the Economic and Social Council, the International Court of Justice and the Secretary-General are explored in the present report, as is the cooperation between the United Nations and outside actors, such as regional organizations, NGOs, civil society and the business community. . . .

"My emphasis here is to show how the United Nations family of departments, programmes, offices and agencies (which have all contributed to the present report) interact in the furtherance of the prevention of armed conflict. Of particular importance are United Nations efforts of enhancing the capacity of Member States for conflict prevention. The challenge before us is how to mobilize the collective potential of the United Nations system with greater coherence and focus for conflict prevention, without necessarily requiring new resources:

"The basic premises of the present report are the following:

- Conflict prevention is one of the primary obligations of Member States set forth in the Charter of the United Nations, and United Nations efforts in conflict prevention must be in conformity with the purposes and principles of the Charter. Conflict prevention is also an activity best undertaken under Chapter VI of the Charter.
- The primary responsibility for conflict prevention rests with national Governments, with civil society playing an important role. The main role of the United Nations and the international community is to support national efforts for conflict prevention and assist in building national capacity in this field.
- Preventive action should be initiated at the earliest possible stage of a conflict cycle in order be most effective. One of the principal aims of preventive action should be to address the deep-rooted socio-economic, cultural, environmental, institutional and other structural causes that often underlie the immediate political symptoms of conflicts.
- An effective preventive strategy requires a comprehensive approach that encompasses both short-term and long-term political, diplomatic, humanitarian, human rights, developmental, institutional and other measures taken by the international community, in cooperation with national and regional actors.
- Conflict prevention and sustainable and equitable development are mutually reinforcing activities. An investment in national and international efforts for conflict prevention must be seen as a simultaneous investment in sustainable development since the latter can best take place in an environment of sustainable peace.
- A successful preventive strategy depends on the cooperation of many United Nations actors, including the Secretary-General, the Security Council, the General Assembly, the Economic and Social Council, the International Court of Justice and United Nations agencies, offices, funds and programmes, as well as the Bretton Woods institutions. The United Nations is not the only actor in prevention and may often not

be the actor best suited to take the lead. Therefore, Member States, international, regional and subregional organizations, private sector, nongovernmental organizations, and other civil society actors also have very important roles to play in this field. . . .

"The main lesson to be drawn from past United Nations experiences in this regard is that the earlier the root causes of a potential conflict are identified and effectively addressed, the more likely it is that the parties to a conflict will be ready to engage in a constructive dialogue, address the actual grievances that lie at the root of the potential conflict and refrain from the use of force to achieve their aims. . . .

"In the present report, I have stressed that conflict prevention lies at the heart of the mandate of the United Nations in the maintenance of international peace and security, and that a general consensus is emerging among Member States that comprehensive and coherent conflict prevention strategies offer the greatest potential for promoting lasting peace and creating an enabling environment for sustainable development. The imperative for effective conflict prevention goes beyond creating a culture, establishing mechanisms or summoning political will. The United Nations also has a moral responsibility to ensure that genocides such as that perpetrated in Rwanda are prevented from ever happening again.

"The time has come to translate the rhetoric of conflict prevention into concrete action. It is my earnest hope that the United Nations system and Member States will be able to work together in developing a practical road map to implement the specific recommendations contained in the present report. It is axiomatic that effective preventive action will require sustained political will and a long-term commitment of resources by Member States and the United Nations system as a whole if a genuine culture of prevention is to take root in the international community. The present report marks a beginning in that direction. . . .

"The present report provides ample testimony to the fact that the time has come to intensify our efforts to move from a culture of reaction to a culture of prevention. Based on the lessons learned and analysis presented in the present report, I propose the following 10 principles, which in my view should guide the future approach of the United Nations to conflict prevention:

- Conflict prevention is one of the primary obligations of Member States set forth in the Charter of the United Nations, and United Nations efforts in conflict prevention must be in conformity with the purposes and principles of the Charter.
- Conflict prevention must have national ownership. The primary responsibility for conflict prevention rests with national Governments, with civil society playing an important role. The United Nations and

the international community should support national efforts for conflict prevention and should assist in building national capacity in this field. Conflict prevention activities of the United Nations can therefore help to support the sovereignty of Member States.

- Conflict prevention is an activity best undertaken under Chapter VI of the Charter. In this regard, the means described in the Charter, for the peaceful settlement of disputes are an important instrument for conflict prevention, including such means as negotiation, inquiry, mediation, conciliation, arbitration, judicial settlement or other peaceful means, as set forth in Article 33 of the Charter. It must also be recognized that certain measures under Chapter VII of the Charter such as sanctions, can have an important deterrent effect.
- Preventive action should be initiated at the earliest possible stage of a conflict cycle in order to be most effective.
- The primary focus of preventive action should be in addressing the deep-rooted socio-economic, cultural, environmental, institutional, political and other structural causes that often underlie the immediate symptoms of conflicts.
- An effective preventive strategy requires a comprehensive approach that encompasses both short-term and long-term political, diplomatic, humanitarian, human rights, developmental, institutional and other measures taken by the international community, in cooperation with national and regional actors. It also requires a strong focus on gender equality and the situation of children.
- Conflict prevention and sustainable and equitable development are mutually reinforcing activities. An investment in national and international efforts for conflict prevention must be seen as a simultaneous investment in sustainable development since the latter can best take place in an environment of sustainable peace.
- The preceding suggests that there is a clear need for introducing a conflict prevention element into the United Nations system's multifaceted development programmes and activities so that they contribute to the prevention of conflict by design and not by default. This in turn, requires greater coherence and coordination in the United Nations system, with a specific focus on conflict prevention.
- A successful preventive strategy depends upon the cooperation of many United Nations actors, including the Secretary-General, the Security Council, the General Assembly, the Economic and Social Council, the International Court of Justice and United Nations agencies, offices, funds and programmes as well as the Bretton Wood institutions. However, the United Nations is not the only actor in prevention and may often not be the actor best suited to take the lead. Therefore, Member States, international, regional and subregional organizations,

the private sector, nongovernmental organizations, and other civil society actors also have very important roles to play in this field.
• Effective preventive action by the United Nations requires sustained political will on the part of Member States. First and foremost, this includes a readiness by the membership as a whole to provide the United Nations with the necessary political support and resources for undertaking effective preventive action in specific situations.

"It is high time that we translate the promise of prevention into concrete action. Let us make this endeavour a testament to future generations that our generation had the political vision and will to transform our perception of a just international order from a vision of the absence of war to a vision of sustainable peace and development for all."

I emphasize this landmark report because it should, in due course, provide a powerful stimulus for governments, regional organizations, nongovernmental organizations, and the institutions of civil society. As the UN's potential for prevention becomes clearer, and its principles laid out, this formulation should provide worldwide inspiration for many organizations, institutions, and individuals to go beyond present efforts and take up this challenge creatively. Not least, this should stimulate us to seek much wider and deeper public understanding, to build constituencies for preventing deadly conflicts and creating the conditions for durable, just peace.

The Earth Is Not Flat

Today, humanity is engaged in the proliferation of lethal weaponry, including nuclear, biological, and chemical weapons of mass destruction, as well as worldwide, wall-to-wall spread of deadly small arms. We see in all parts of the world abundant prejudice, hatred, and threats of mass violence, now enhanced by use of modern telecommunications. International terrorism is vividly in our minds. The historical record is full of every sort of slaughter based on invidious distinctions pertaining to religion, ethnicity, nationality, and other group characteristics. We inherit these attitudes from our ancient past and search for ways of overcoming them. They come from the flat-earth era and are no longer compatible with human survival.

In this kind of world, the scientific and educational communities have a great responsibility to disseminate reliable information on these serious problems and ways to cope with them. Education must provide understanding, insight, and constructive ways of dealing with the profound dangers of deadly conflict. In a world so full of hatred and violence, past and present, human conflict and its resolution is a subject that deserves major educational efforts—not only in schools and universities, but also in community organizations, religious institutions, print and nonprint media, and international organizations.

Historically, education everywhere has to some degree been ethnocentric—and all too often flagrantly prejudicial. If we humans are ever to live together amicably, it will be a drastic change from past practices that can only be achieved by using the unique learning capacities that have made the human species so distinctively and remarkably effective in adaptation even under very adverse conditions.

Fundamentally, the problem is learning how to live together—at all levels: family, community, intergroup relations within a country, and international relations. This calls for very widespread understanding of human relations, sources of stress, and ways of coping at every level.

The central fact is the nature of the human condition: We are a single, worldwide, highly interdependent species, now driven more closely together than ever before by the forces of technoeconomic globalization. We need to understand why some of our old habits are much more dangerous than ever before and why mutual accommodation is essential for survival.

People need decent life chances in every country for a quality of life compatible with human dignity; arrangements within each country to protect human rights, respect pluralism, avoid oppression, give children and youth a good start.

To the extent that many countries cannot yet do this, the international community should reach out in friendship to help (1) put out fires when they are just starting, and (2) build capacity to cope with their own problems in nonviolent ways.

The international community needs attitudes, insights, institutions, and resources to implement a farsighted proactive approach of assistance, cooperation, and education for countries in bad shape. Many will welcome such an approach—even if ambivalently.

The hardest problem is a small number of countries that are intransigent toward outsiders, mired in hatred, controlled by rulers who are no more than tyrants. For them, the international community must seek repeatedly to draw them into the community of responsible nations, while containing and deterring as may be necessary with forceful means.

The most fundamental aspiration is that all of us concerned with intergroup and international relations—including war and peace issues—come to think preventively. We need to be aware of what is possible now and also to push the limits of present knowledge and skill; to develop new research and innovations, concepts and techniques. Organizations and institutions must come to use this information and experience to strengthen our capacities for preventing deadly conflict, to learn to live together amicably in search of shared benefits across our common humanity.

The most pervasive need is for the international community to be prepared and proactive in helping nations or groups in trouble rather than waiting for disaster to strike. For the longer term, this essentially means help in acquiring attitudes, concepts, skills, and institutions for resolving internal and external conflict. It means help in building political and economic institutions of democracy. There can be—and of necessity will be—many different international configurations through which such help is provided. And it can be done in a way that is sensitive to cultural traditions and regional circumstances.

To offer such help will especially involve relating to moderate, constructive, pragmatic leaders who are oriented to humane and democratic values. They exist all over the world but their situation is often precarious. The international community can reach out to them and provide recognition in the context of an international support network—and in the long run help such leaders to build institutions capable of meeting basic human needs and coping with the conflicts that arise in the course of human interactions.

Thus, intervention in problematic situations need not be military in nature. Indeed, if reasonable measures are taken in other spheres—political, economic, social, psychological—military intervention will rarely be necessary. Still, military capability is essential—above all, in coping with aggressive dictators and fanatical haters.

Overall, the prevention of disastrous outcomes involves providing conditions under which it is possible to meet the essential requirements for decent human relations and socioeconomic development through the cooperative efforts of pivotal institutions that have the salience and the capacity to do the job. The application of such concepts in the public health sphere is familiar and effective. A wider view of the prevention process is useful in preventing deadly conflict.

There is now a powerful convergence of moral commitment to prevention among many different kinds of organizations and institutions. It is a commitment that cuts across governmental, intergovernmental, and nongovernmental bodies around the world. An equally powerful convergence of facts, concepts, and techniques is occurring in the realm of implementing prevention.

Yet, none of these efforts can assume the success of the enterprise in the long run. Ancient and ubiquitous human tendencies toward hatred and violence may triumph yet again. Will we need another series of catastrophes—more terrible than Rwanda and Bosnia or even, if the fearful potential of modern technology is again turned toward the annihilation of others, worse than the Holocaust? Let us hope that humanity will not need another tragic lesson on the scale of World War II to bring it to an appreciation that humankind must act collectively to prevent mass violence. It was the painful schooling of the 1930s and 1940s that gave the world some of the imperfect yet important means to act for prevention. We have taken some significant steps in the last decade to learn from the exposed shortcomings of the institutions and agendas of this earlier period as well as the Cold War and as the warning from recent history. At the very least, the developments of recent years provide, perhaps for the first time, the basic intellectual, technical, organizational, and moral capacities to make the prevention of deadly conflict a genuine and realistic possibility in human relationships.

Appendix 1

Carnegie Commission on Preventing Deadly Conflict Publications

Commission publications fall into several categories, identified in the individual listings. Only reports of the Commission are endorsed by all commissioners. Other Commission publications—reports to the Commission, Commission books, perspectives on prevention, and discussion papers—express the views of their authors and are not attributable to the Commission as a whole or to individual commissioners or Commission staff.

Commission Final Report

Preventing Deadly Conflict: Executive Summary of the Final Report. December 1997. Also available in French and Spanish.
Preventing Deadly Conflict: Final Report (Full Report and Executive Summary). Report of the Commission. December 1997.

Reports and Papers

The following reports and papers can be obtained from the Commission's Web site at www.ccpdc.org.

Allison, Graham, and Hisashi Owada. *The Responsibilities of Democracies in Preventing Deadly Conflict: Reflections and Recommendations.* Discussion Paper. July 1999.
Annan, Kofi. *The Challenge to Prevent Deadly Conflict: Selected Speeches by the Secretary-General of the United Nations.* Perspectives on Prevention. December 1999.

Boutros-Ghali, Boutros, George Bush, Jimmy Carter, Mikhail Gorbachev, and Desmond Tutu. *Essays on Leadership*. Perspectives on Prevention. December 1998.

Comprehensive Disclosure of Fissionable Materials: A Suggested Initiative. Discussion Paper. June 1995.

Diamond, Larry. *Promoting Democracy in the 1990s: Actors and Instruments, Issues and Imperatives*. Report to the Commission. December 1995.

Feil, Scott R. *Preventing Genocide: How the Early Use of Force Might Have Succeeded in Rwanda*. Report to the Commission. April 1998.

George, Alexander, and Jane F. Holl. *The Warning-Response Problem and Missed Opportunities in Preventive Diplomacy*. Report to the Commission. May 1997.

Gjelten, Tom. *Professionalism in War Reporting: A Correspondent's View*. Report to the Commission. July 1998.

Goodpaster, Andrew I. *When Diplomacy Is Not Enough: Managing Multinational Military Interventions*. Report to the Commission. July 1996.

Gowing, Nik. *Media Coverage: Help or Hindrance in Conflict Prevention*. Report to the Commission. September 1997.

Hamburg, David A. *Preventing Contemporary Intergroup Violence* and *Education for Conflict Resolution*. Perspectives on Prevention. December 1999.

Joulwan, George A., and Christopher C. Shoemaker. *Civilian-Military Cooperation in the Prevention of Deadly Conflict: Implementing Agreements in Bosnia and Beyond*. Report to the Commission. December 1998.

Kennedy, Donald. *Environmental Quality and Regional Conflict*. Report to the Commission. December 1998.

Lapidus, Gail W., with Svetlana Tsalik, eds. *Preventing Deadly Conflict: Strategies and Institutions*. Proceedings of a conference in Moscow. Report to the Commission. April 1998.

Laurance, Edward J. *Light Weapons and Intrastate Conflict: Early Warning Factors and Preventive Action*. Report to the Commission. August 1998.

Lute, Douglas F. *Improving National Capacity to Respond to Complex Emergencies: The US Experience*. Report to the Commission. April 1998.

Preventive Diplomacy, Preventive Defense, and Conflict Resolution: A Report of Two Conferences at Stanford University and the Ditchley Foundation. Perspectives on Prevention. October 1999.

Stremlau, John. *People in Peril: Human Rights, Humanitarian Action, and Preventing Deadly Conflict*. Report to the Commission. May 1998.

———. *Sharpening International Sanctions: Toward a Stronger Role for the United Nations*. Report to the Commission. November 1996.

Stremlau, John, and Francisco Sagasti, *Preventing Deadly Conflict: Does the World Bank Have a Role?* Report to the Commission. July 1998.

Stremlau, John, with Helen Zille. *A House No Longer Divided: Progress and Prospects for Democratic Peace in South Africa*. Report to the Commission. July 1997.

US–Russian Cooperation to Prevent Deadly Conflict: Reports of a Commission Task Force. Sam Nunn, chairman. Perspectives on Prevention. December 1999.

Valenzuela, Arturo. *The Collective Defense of Democracy: Lessons from the Paraguayan Crisis of 1996.* Report to the Commission. December 1999.

Vance, Cyrus R., and David A. Hamburg, *Pathfinders for Peace: A Report to the UN Secretary-General on the Role of Special Representatives and Personal Envoys.* Report of the Commission. September 1997.

Wilkinson, M. James. *Moving beyond Conflict Prevention to Reconciliation: Tackling Greek–Turkish Hostility.* Report to the Commission. June 1999.

Commission Books

To order books in the Carnegie Commission Series published by Rowman & Littlefield, call 1-800-462-6420 (toll-free in United States only) or 301-459-3366.

Appleby, R. Scott. *The Ambivalence of the Sacred: Religion, Violence, and Reconciliation.* Carnegie Commission Series, Rowman & Littlefield, 2000.

Barkey, Henri J., and Graham E. Fuller. *Turkey's Kurdish Question.* Carnegie Commission Series, Rowman & Littlefield, 1998.

Boutwell, Jeffrey. and Michael T. Klare, eds. *Light Weapons and Civil Conflict: Controlling the Tools of Violence.* Carnegie Commission Series, Rowman & Littlefield, 1999.

Brown, Michael E., and Richard N. Rosecrance, eds. *The Costs of Conflict: Prevention and Cure in the Global Arena.* Carnegie Commission Series, Rowman & Littlefield, 1999.

Cortright, David, ed. *The Price of Peace: Incentives and International Conflict Prevention.* Carnegie Commission Series, Rowman & Littlefield, 1997.

Feldman, Shai, and Abdullah Toukan. *Bridging the Gap: A Future Security Architecture for the Middle East.* Carnegie Commission Series, Rowman & Littlefield, 1997.

Greenberg, Melanie, John H. Barton, and Margaret E. McGuinness. *Words over War: Mediation and Arbitration to Prevent Deadly Conflict.* Carnegie Commission Series, Rowman & Littlefield, 2000.

Jentleson, Bruce W. *Opportunities Missed, Opportunities Seized: Preventive Diplomacy in the Post–Cold War World.* Carnegie Commission Series, Rowman & Littlefield, 1999.

Peck, Connie. *Sustainable Peace: The Role of the UN and Regional Organizations in Preventing Conflict.* Carnegie Commission Series, Rowman & Littlefield, 1998.

Zartman, I. William, ed. *Preventive Negotiation: Avoiding Conflict Escalation.* Carnegie Commission Series, Rowman & Littlefield, 2001.

Carnegie Commission Web Publications

These are available at www.ccpdc.org.

Aklaev, Airat. *Causes and Prevention of Ethnic Conflict: An Overview of Post-Soviet Russian-Language Literature.* 1999.
Arthur, Paul. *Peer Learning Northern Ireland As A Case Study.* 1999.
Arutiunov, S. A. *Ethnicity on the Caucasus: Ethnic Relations and Quasi-Ethnic Conflicts.* 1999.
Krasno, Jean E. *The Group of Friends of the Secretary-General: A Useful Diplomatic Tool.* 1998.
Mares, David R. *Latin American Perspectives on the Causes, Prevention and Resolution of Deadly Intra- and Interstate Conflicts. 1982–1996,* 1999.

Selected Publications of Carnegie Corporation's Grant-Making Program on Preventing Deadly Conflict

Allison, Graham T., Owen R. Cote Jr., Richard R. Falkenrath, and Steven E. Miller. *Avoiding Nuclear Anarchy: Containing the Threat of Loose Russian Nuclear Weapons and Fissile Material.* Cambridge, Mass.: MIT Press, 1996.
Arbotov, Alexei, Abram Chayes, Antonia Handler Chayes, and Lara Olson, eds. *Managing Conflict in the Former Soviet Union: Russian and American Perspectives.* Cambridge, Mass.: MIT Press, 1997.
Brown, Michael E., ed. *The International Dimensions of Internal Conflict.* Cambridge, Mass.: MIT Press, 1996.
Brown, Michael E., Sean M. Lynn-Jones, and Steven E. Miller, eds. *Debating the Democratic Peace.* Cambridge, Mass.: MIT Press, 1996.
Brown, Michael E., Owen R. Cote Jr., Sean M. Lynn-Jones, and Steven E. Miller, eds. *Nationalism and Ethnic Conflict.* Cambridge, Mass.: MIT Press, 1997.
Chayes, Abraham, and Antonia Handler Chayes, eds. *Preventing Conflict in the Post-Communist World: Mobilizing International and Regional Organizations.* Washington, D.C.: Brookings, 1996.
Committee on International Security and Arms Control, Managing and Disposition of Excess Weapons Plutonium: Reactor-Related Options. Washington, D.C.: National Academy of Sciences, 1995.
Diamond, Larry, and Marc F. Plattner, eds. *Civil-Military Relations and Democracy.* Baltimore: Johns Hopkins University Press, 1996.
Drohobycky, Maria, ed. *Crimea: Dynamics, Challenges, and Prospects.* Lanham, Md.: Rowman & Littlefield, 1995.
———. *Managing Ethnic Tension in the Post-Soviet Space: The Examples of Kazakhstan and Ukraine.* Washington, D.C.: American Association for the Advancement of Science, 1995.

Elman, Miriam, ed. *Paths to Peace: Is Democracy the Answer?* Cambridge, Mass.: MIT Press, 1997.

Haass, Richard N., and Gideon Rose. *A New U.S. Policy toward India and Pakistan.* New York: Council on Foreign Relations, 1997.

Handler, Antonia, Abraham Chayes, and George Raach. *Beyond Reform: Restructuring for More Effective Conflict Intervention.* Cambridge, Mass.: Conflict Management Group, 1996.

Marks, John, and Eran Fraenkel. "Working to Prevent Conflict in the New Nation of Macedonia." *Harvard Negotiation Journal* 13, no. 3 (July 1997).

Maynes, Charles William, and Richard S. Williamson, eds. *U.S. Foreign Policy and the United Nations System.* New York: Norton, 1996.

Sagdeev, Roald Z., and Susan Eisenhower. *Central Asia: Conflict, Resolution, and Change.* Chevy Chase, Md.: CPSS Press, 1995.

Varas, Augusto, James A. Schear, and Lisa Owens, eds. *Confidence-Building Measures in Latin America, Central America and the Southern Cone.* Washington, D.C.: Stimson Center; Chile: LASCO-Chile, 1995.

To order the following books that were published, copublished, or cosponsored by the Commission, contact the publishers indicated in the individual book listings.

de Cerreño, Allison L. C., and Alexander Keynan. *Scientific Cooperation, State Conflict: The Roles of Scientists in Mitigating International Discord.* Cosponsored by the Carnegie Commission on Preventing Deadly Conflict, published by New York Academy of Sciences, New York, 1998. Available in libraries as Volume 866 of the *Annals of the New York Academy of Sciences.* To obtain this book, call the academy at 1-800-843-6927, ext. 342; or access the academy's Web site (www.nyas.org).

Oakley, Robert B., Michael J. Dziedzic, and Eliot M. Goldberg. *Policing the New World Disorder: Peace Operations and Public Security.* Cosponsored by the Carnegie Commission on Preventing Deadly Conflict, published by the National Defense University, Washington, D.C., 1998. To obtain this book, call the Government Printing Office at 202-512-1800; or write to the Superintendent of Documents, U.S. Government Printing Office, Washington, DC 20402; or access the Government Printing Office's Web site (www.ndu.edu).

Sisk, Timothy D. *Power Sharing and International Mediation in Ethnic Conflicts.* Copublished with United States Institute of Peace, Washington, D.C., 1996. To obtain this book, call USIP at 1-800-868-8064 (toll-free in the United States); or 202-429-3816; or access USIP's Web site (www.usip.org).

Appendix 2

Additional Valuable Sources of Information and Concepts Pertinent to Preventing Deadly Conflict

Ackerman, Peter, and Christopher Kruegler. *Strategic Nonviolent Conflict.* Westport, Conn.: Praeger, 1994.

Anderson, Lisa. *Transitions to Democracy.* New York: Columbia University Press, 1999.

Asch, Solomon E. *Social Psychology.* New York: Prentice Hall, 1952.

Ashton, Carter B., William J. Perry, and John D. Steinbruner. *A New Concept of Cooperative Security.* Washington, D.C.: Brookings Institution, 1992.

Bandura, A. *Aggression: A Social Learning Analysis.* Englewood Cliffs, N.J.: Prentice Hall, 1973.

Barash, David P. *Introduction to Peace Studies.* Belmont, Calif.: Wadsworth, 1991.

Barkey, Karen, and Mark Von Hagen, eds. *After Empire: Multiethnic Societies and Nation-Building.* Boulder, Colo.: Westview, 1997.

Bauer, Yehuda. *Rethinking the Holocaust,* New Haven, Conn.: Yale University Press, 2000.

Betts, Richard K., ed. *Conflict After the Cold War: Arguments on Causes of War and Peace.* New York: Macmillan, 1994.

Bloomfield, Lincoln P. "The Premature Burial of Global Law and Order: Looking beyond the Three Cases from Hell." *Washington Quarterly* (summer 1994): 145–61.

Bok, Sissela. *Mayhem: Violence as Public Entertainment.* Reading, Mass.: Perseus, 1998.

Brewer, Marilynn B., and Norman Miller. *Intergroup Relations.* Pacific Grove, Calif.: Brooks/Cole, 1996.

Brown, Michael E., ed. *The International Dimensions of Internal Conflict.* Cambridge, Mass.: MIT Press, 1996.

Brown, Michael E., Sean M. Lynn-Jones, and Steven E. Miller, eds. *Debating the Democratic Peace.* Cambridge, Mass.: MIT Press, 1996.

Brown, Seyom. *International Relations in a Changing Global System.* Boulder, Colo.: Westview, 1992.

Burg, Steven L. *War or Peace? Nationalism, Democracy, and American Foreign Policy in Post-Communist Europe.* New York: New York University Press, 1996.

Burton, John. *Conflict: Resolution and Prevention.* New York: St. Martin's, 1990.

———. *Violence Explained.* Manchester, England: Manchester University Press, 1997.

Cahill, Kevin M., ed. *Stopping Wars Before They Start: Preventive Diplomacy.* New York: Basic, 1994.

Carothers, Thomas. *Aiding Democracy Abroad: The Learning Curve.* Washington, D.C.: Carnegie Endowment for International Peace, 1999.

Carter, Jimmy. *Talking Peace: A Vision for the Next Generation.* New York: Dutton Children's Book, 1993.

Chalk, Frank, and Kurt Jonassohn. *The History and Sociology of Genocide: Analysis and Case Studies.* New Haven, Conn.: Yale University Press, 1990.

Clements, Kevin, and Robin Ward. *Building International Community.* St. Leonards, NSW Australia: Allen & Unwin, 1994.

Committee on International Security and Arms Control, National Academy of Sciences. *The Future of US Nuclear Weapons Policy.* Washington, D.C.: National Academy Press, 1997.

Conflict Prevention: Strategies to Sustain Peace in the Post–Cold War World. Washington, D.C.: Aspen Institute, 1997.

Cooperative Threat Reduction. Washington, D.C.: United States Department of Defense, April 1995.

Crocker, Chester A. *Herding Cats, Multiparty Mediation in a Complex World.* Washington, D.C.: United States Institute of Peace Press, 1999.

Dahl, Robert A. *Modern Political Analysis.* 5th ed. Upper Saddle River, N.J.: Prentice Hall, 1991.

Damrosch, Lori Fisher. *Enforcing Restraint: Collective Intervention in Internal Conflicts.* New York: Council on Foreign Relations Press, 1994.

Dean, Jonathan. *Ending Europe's Wars: The Continuing Search for Peace and Security.* New York: Twentieth Century Fund Press, 1994.

Deutsch, Karl W. *The Analysis of International Relations.* 3d ed. Upper Saddle River, N.J.: Prentice Hall, 1988.

Deutsch, M. *The Resolution of Conflict.* New Haven, Conn.: Yale University Press, 1973.

Diamond, Jared. *Gun, Germs, and Steel: The Fates of Human Societies.* New York: Norton, 1999.

Diamond, Louise, and John McDonald. *Multi-Track Diplomacy: A Systems Approach to Peace.* Hartford, Conn.: Kumarian, 1996.

Elliott, Delbert S., Beatrix A. Hamburg, and Kirk R. Williams. *Violence in American Schools.* New York: Cambridge University Press, 1998.

Franck, Thomas M., and Georg Nolte. "The Good Offices Function of the UN Secretary-General." In A. Roberts and B. Kingsbury, eds. *The UN and International Security after the Cold War: The UN's Roles in International Relations.* Oxford, U.K.: Clarendon Press, 1993.

Gardner, John W. *On Leadership*. New York: The Free Press, 1993.

Glover, Jonathan. *Humanity: A Moral History of the Twentieth Century*. New Haven, Conn.: Yale University Press, 2000.

Goodby, James, Petrus Buwalda, and Dmitri Trenin. "A Strategy for Stable Peace: Toward a Euroatlantic Security Community." Washington, D.C.: United States Institute of Peace Press, 2002.

Grobel, J., and R. Hinde. *Aggression and War: Their Biological and Social Bases*. Cambridge, England: Cambridge University Press, 1989.

Gurr, Ted Robert. *Minorities at Risk: A Geopolitical View of Ethnopolitical Conflicts*. Washington, D.C.: United States Institute of Peace Press, 1993.

Gurr, Ted R., Monty G. Marshall, Deepa Khosia. *Peace and Conflict 2001—A Global Survey of Armed Conflicts, Self-Determination Movements, and Democracy*. Report of the Center for International Development and Conflict Management (CIDCM). College Park: University of Maryland, 2001.

Hamburg, David A. "An Evolutionary Perspective on Human Aggression." In P. Bateson, ed. *The Development and Integration of Behavior: Essays in Honor of Robert Hinde*. Cambridge, England: Cambridge University Press, 1991.

Hamilton, Lee, Gareth Evans, Lord Carver, and Stanley Hoffman. "A UN Volunteer Military Force—Four Views." *New York Review of Books*, June 24, 1993.

Hammond, Allen. *Which World? Scenarios for the Twenty-First Century*. Washington, D.C.: Island Press/Shearwater Books, 1998.

Harris, Peter, and Ben Reilly, eds. *Democracy and Deep-Rooted Conflict: Options for Negotiators*. Stockholm: IDEA, 1998.

Henkin, Louis, Righard Crawford Pugh, Oscar Schachter, and Hans Smit. *International Law: Cases and Materials*. 3d ed. St. Paul, Minn.: West, 1993.

Herman, Charles, Harold Jacobson, and Anne S. Moffat, eds. *Violent Conflict in the Twenty-First Century*. Chicago: American Academy of Arts and Sciences, 1999.

Holsti, Kalevi J. *Peace and War: Armed Conflicts and International Order 1648–1989*. Cambridge, England: Cambridge University Press, 1991.

Horowitz, Donald. "Democracy in Divided Societies." *Journal of Democracy* 4, no. 4 (1993).

———. *Ethnic Groups in Conflict*. Berkeley: University of California Press, 1985.

———. "Making Moderation Pay." In Joseph V. Montville, ed. *Conflict and Peacemaking in Multiethnic Societies*. Lexington, Mass.: Lexington, 1990.

Howard, Michael. *The Invention of Peace*. New Haven, Conn.: Yale University Press, 2000.

International Task Force on the Enforcement of UN Security Council Resolutions. *Words to Deeds: Strengthening the UN's Enforcement Capabilities*. New York: United Nations Association of the United States of America, 1997.

Kaldor, Mary. *New and Old Wars*. Stanford, Calif.: Stanford University Press, 1999.

Krasner, Stephen D. *Sovereignty: Organized Hypocrisy*. Princeton, N.J.: Princeton University Press, 1999.

Kressel, Neil J. *Mass Hate: The Global Rise of Genocide and Terror*. New York: Plenum Press, 1996.

Lancaster, Carol. *Aid to Africa: So Much to Do, So Little Done*. Chicago: University of Chicago Press, 1999.

Larson, Welch Deborah. *Anatomy of Mistrust: US–Soviet Relations during the Cold War*. Ithaca, N.Y.: Cornell University Press, 1997.

Lifton, Robert Jay, and Eric Markusen. *The Genocidal Mentality: Nazi Holocaust and the Nuclear Threat*. New York: Basic Books, 1990.

Linz, Juan J., and Alfred Stepan. *Problems of Democratic Transition and Consolidation: Southern Europe, South America, and Post-Communist Europe*. Baltimore: Johns Hopkins University Press, 1996.

Mandelbaum, Michael, ed. *The New European Diasporas: National Minorities and Conflict in Eastern Europe*. New York: Council on Foreign Relations Press, 2000.

Mathews, Jessica T. "Power Shift." *Foreign Affairs* 76:1 (January/February 1997): 50–66.

Matlock, Jack F., Jr. *Autopsy on an Empire: The American Ambassador's Account of the Collapse of the Soviet Union*. New York: Random House, 1995.

McDonald, John W., Jr., and Diane B. Bendahmane, eds. *Conflict Resolution: Track Two Diplomacy*. Washington, D.C.: U.S. Government Printing Office, 1987.

McNamara, Robert, and J. G. Blight. *Wilson's Ghost: Reducing the Risk of Conflict, Killing, and Catastrophe in the 21st Century*. New York: Public Affairs, 2001.

Melson, Robert F. *Revolution and Genocide: On the Origins of the Armenian Genocide and the Holocaust*. Chicago: University of Chicago Press, 1992.

National Research Council. *Our Common Journey: Transition toward Sustainability*. Washington, D.C.: National Academy Press, 1999.

Newman, Frank, and David Weissbrodt. *International Human Rights: Law, Policy and Process*. 2d ed. Cincinnati, Ohio: Anderson, 1996.

Nichols, Rodney W. *Linking Science and Technology with Global Economic Development*. Chennai, India: International Council for Science, 1999.

Nye, Joseph S., Jr. *Understanding International Conflicts*. 2d ed. New York: Longman 1997.

Oakley, Robert B., McGeorge Bundy, Sadruddin Aga Khan, Olusegun Obasanjo, and Marion Donhoff. "A UN Volunteer Force: The Prospects." *New York Review of Books,* July 15, 1993.

Organization for Security and Cooperation in Europe. *Vade Mecum: An Introduction to the OSCE*. Berne: Organization for Security and Cooperation in Europe, May 1996.

Organization of African Unity. *African Charter on Human and Peoples' Rights*. Organization of African Unity Doc. CAB/LEG/67/3Rev.5.

Our Global Neighborhood. Governance Commission on Global. Oxford, England: Oxford University Press. 1995.

Owen, David. *Balkan Odyssey.* London: Victor Gollancz, 1995.

Patchen, Martin, *Resolving Disputes between Nations: Coercion or Conciliation?* Durham, N.C.: Duke University Press, 1988.

Perez de Cuellar, Javier, ed. *Our Creative Diversity.* Report of the World Commission on Culture and Development. Paris: UNESCO Publishing, 1995.

Pruitt, Dean G., and Jeffrey Z. Rubin. *Social Conflict: Escalation, Stalemate, and Settlement.* New York: Random House, 1986.

Ramphele, Mamphela, and Francis Wilson. *Uprooting Poverty: The South Africana Challenge.* Report for the Second Carnegie Inquiry into Poverty and Development in Southern Africa. New York: Norton, 1989.

Rothchild, Donald. *Managing Ethnic Conflict in Africa.* Washington, D.C.: Brookings, 1997.

Rubin, Barnett R. *Blood on the Doorstep: The Politics of Preventive Action.* (To be published in 2002.)

Russett, Bruce. *Grasping the Democratic Peace: Principles for a Post–Cold War World.* Princeton: Princeton University Press, 1993.

Sagan, Scott. "The Perils of Proliferation." *International Security* 18 (spring 1994).

Shawcross, William. *Deliver Us from Evil: Peacekeepers, Warlords and a World of Endless Conflict.* New York: Simon & Schuster, 2000.

Sisk, Timothy. *Democratization in South Africa: The Elusive Social Contract.* Princeton, N.J.: Princeton University Press, 1995.

Sivard, Ruth Leger. *World Military and Social Expenditures 1996.* Washington, D.C.: World Priorities, 1996.

Smuts, Barbara, Dorothy Cheney, Robert Seyfarth, Richard Wrangham, and Thomas Struhsaker, eds. *Primate Societies.* Chicago: University of Chicago Press, 1986.

State of World Conflict Report, 1994–1995. Atlanta, Ga.: Carter Center, 1995.

Stern, Paul C., and Daniel Druckman, eds. *International Conflict Resolution After the Cold War.* Commission on Behavioral and Social Sciences and Education, National Research Council. Washington, D.C.: National Academy Press, 2000.

Swedish Ministry for Foreign Affairs. *Preventing Violent Conflict: A Study.* Stockholm: Ministry of Foreign Affairs, 1997.

Tipson, Frederick S. *Preventing Deadly Conflicts: Taking Stock and Taking Hold (Lessons for Americans from the Last Decade).* Council on Foreign Relations, in press.

United Nations. *Universal Declaration of Human Rights,* DPI/876. New York: United Nations Department of Public Information, 1995.

United Nations Development Program. *Human Development Report.* New York: Oxford University Press, 1995, 1996 and 1997.

United Nations High Commission for Refugees. *The State of the World's Refugees 1995: In Search of Solutions.* New York: Oxford University Press, 1995.

————. *The State of the World's Refugees*. New York: Oxford University Press, 1997.

Urquhart, Brian. *A Life in Peace & War*. New York: Norton, 1991.

————. "The Role of the Secretary-General." In Charles William Maynes and Richard S. Williamson, eds. *US Foreign Policy and the United Nations System*. New York: Norton, 1996.

Van de Walle, Nicolas. *Economic Globalization and Political Stability in Developing Countries*. New York: Rockefeller Brothers Fund, 1998.

Wallensteen, Peter, ed. *Preventing Violent Conflicts: Past Record and Future Challenges*. Uppsala, Sweden: Uppsala University, 1998.

Wilson, Ernest J., III. *Globalization, Information Technology, and Conflict in the Second and Third World: A Critical Review of Literature*. New York: Rockefeller Brothers Fund, 1998.

Wistrich, Roberts S. *Antisemitism: The Longest Hatred*. New York: Pantheon, 1989.

World Commission on Environment and Development. *Our Common Future*. Oxford, England: Oxford University Press, 1987.

Wright, Robert. *Nonzero: The Logic of Human Destiny*. New York: Vintage Books, 2000.

Bibliography

Ackerman, Peter, and Jack Duvall. *A Force More Powerful: A Century of Nonviolent Action*. New York: St. Martin's, 2000.

Afridi, Sam. "Muslims in America: Identity, Diversity and the Challenge of Understanding." Paper presented at Carnegie Corporation Meeting on Muslims in America, New York, June 2001.

Ajami, Fouad. "The Sentry's Solitude." *Foreign Affairs*, November/December 2001, 2–16.

Allison, Graham. "Fighting Terrorism." *The Economist*, November 3, 2001.

Allison, Graham, and Hisashi Owada. *The Responsibilities of Democracies in Preventing Deadly Conflict: Reflections and Recommendations*. Carnegie Commission on Preventing Deadly Conflict Discussion Paper, July 1999.

Allison, Graham, Owen R. Cote Jr., Richard A. Falkenrath, and Steven E. Miller. *Avoiding Nuclear Anarchy: Containing the Threat of Loose Russian Nuclear and Fissile Material*. Cambridge, Mass.: MIT Press, 1996.

Allison, Graham, and Philip Zelikow. *Essence of Decision: Explaining the Cuban Missile Crisis*. 2d ed. New York: Longman, 1999.

Allison, Graham, W. L. Ury, and B. J. Allyn, eds. *Windows of Opportunity: From Cold War to Peaceful Competition in US–Soviet Relations*. Cambridge, Mass.: Ballinger, 1989.

Allport, G. W. *The Nature of Prejudice*. New York: Doubleday, 1958.

Alvarez, Alex. *Governments, Citizens, and Genocide*. Bloomington: Indiana University Press, 2001.

Aly, Gotz. *"Final Solution": Nazi Population Policy and the Murder of the European Jews*. New York: Oxford University Press, 1999.

Anderson, Lisa. *Transitions to Democracy*. New York: Columbia University Press, 1999.

Annan, Kofi. *Towards a Culture of Prevention: Statements by the Secretary-General of the United Nations*. Carnegie Commission Publication, 1999.

————. *We the Peoples: The Role of the United Nations in the Twenty-First Century.* New York: United Nations, 2000.

Annan, Kofi, and Rita Hauser. *International Peace Academy 2001 Annual Report.* New York: International Peace Academy, 2001.

Appleby, R. Scott. *The Ambivalence of the Sacred: Religion, Violence, and Reconciliation.* Carnegie Commission Series, Rowman & Littlefield, 2000.

Aster, Sidney. "'Guilty Men': The Case of Neville Chamberlain," Pp. 62–78 in Patrick Finney, ed. *The Origins of the Second World War.* New York: Arnold, 1997.

Axworthy, Lloyd. "Human Security and Global Governance: Putting People First." *Global Governance* 7 (January–March 2001): 19–23.

Barnett, R. Rubin, ed. *Cases and Strategies for Preventive Action Plan.* New York: Century Foundation Press, 1998.

Barraclough, Geoffrey. *An Introduction to Contemporary History.* New York: Penguin, 1973.

Baylis, John, and Steve Smith, eds. *The Globalization of World Politics.* New York: Oxford University Press, 1997.

Beddard, Ralph. *Human Rights and Europe.* 3d ed. Cambridge, England: Grotius, 1993.

Bennett, Andrew. *Condemned to Repetition? The Rise, Fall, and Reprise of Soviet-Russian Military Interventionism, 1973–1996.* Cambridge, Mass.: MIT Press, 1999.

Bennett, Juliette. *Business in Conflict Zones: The Role of the Multinational in Promoting Regional Stability.* Report prepared for the United Nations Office of the Global Compact, January 2001.

Birdsall, Nancy, and Augusto de la Torre with Rachel Menezes. *Washington Contentious: Economic Policies for Social Equity in Latin America.* Carnegie Endowment for International Peace and Inter-American Dialogue, 2001.

Boutros-Ghali, Boutros. "An Agenda for Democratization." Report of the Secretary-General. Support by the United Nations System of the Efforts of Governments to Promote and Consolidate New or Restored Democracies, December 17, 1996.

Boutros-Ghali, Boutros, George Bush, Jimmy Carter, Mikhail Gorbachev, and Desmond Tutu. *Essays on Leadership.* Perspectives on Prevention. New York: Carnegie Corporation of New York, 1998.

Brewer, Marilynn B., and Norman Miller. *Intergroup Relations.* Pacific Grove, Calif.: Brooks/Cole Publishing, 1996.

British Broadcasting Corporation. "France Refuses to Sign Democracy Charter." June 27, 2000 <www.news.bbc.co.uk>

————. "Officials Gather for Democracy Conference." June 25, 2000 <www.news.bbc.co.uk>

Brodie, Bernard, and Fawn Brodie. *From Crossbow to H-Bomb: The Evolution of Weapons and Tactics of Warfare.* Bloomington: Indiana University Press, 1973.

Brody, J. Kenneth. *The Avoidable War: Lord Cecil and the Policy of Principle, 1933–1935.* Vol. 1. New Brunswick, N.J.: Transaction, 1999.

Brown, Archie. *The Gorbachev Factor.* New York: Oxford University Press, 1996.

Brown, Gordon. "A Yearly $50 Billion Safe Investment in Prosperity," *International Herald Tribune*, December 18, 2001.

Brown, Michael E., and Richard N. Rosecrance, eds. *The Costs of Conflict: Prevention and Cure in the Global Arena.* Carnegie Commission Series, Rowman & Littlefield, 1999.

Brown, Michael E., Owen Cote Jr., Sean Lynn-Jones, and Steven E. Miller, eds. *Nationalism and Ethnic Conflict.* Cambridge, Mass.: MIT Press, 1997.

Bundy, McGeorge, William J. Crowe, and Sidney Drell. *Reducing Nuclear Danger: The Road Away from the Brink.* New York: Council on Foreign Relations Press, 1993.

Burg, Steven. *War or Peace?: Nationalism, Democracy and American Foreign Policy in Post-Communist Europe.* New York: New York University Press, 1996.

Buruma, Ian, and Avishai Margalit. "Occidentalism." *New York Review*, January 17, 2002.

Campbell, Kurt M., and Michele A. Fluornoy. *To Prevail: An American Strategy for the Campaign Against Terrorism.* Washington, D.C.: Center for Strategic and International Studies Press, 2001.

Carley, Michael Jabara. *1939: The Alliance That Never Was and the Coming of World War II.* New York: Ivan Dee, 1999.

Carnegie Commission on Preventing Deadly Conflict. *Preventing Deadly Conflict, Final Report.* Carnegie Commission Publication, December 1997.

Carothers, Thomas. *Aiding Democracy Abroad: The Learning Curve.* Washington, D.C.: Carnegie Endowment for International Peace, 1999.

Carter, Ashton, and William Perry. *Preventive Defense: A New Security Strategy for America.* Washington, D.C.: Brookings, 1999.

Cevallos, Albert. *Whither the Bulldozer? Nonviolent Revolution and the Transition to Democracy in Serbia.* United States Institute of Peace Special Report, August 6, 2001.

Chayes, Abram, and Antonia Handler Chayes, eds. *Preventing Conflict in the Post-Communist World: Mobilizing International and Regional Organizations.* Washington, D.C.: Brookings, 1996.

Christopher, Warren. *The Negotiator.* The Jackson H. Ralston Lecture, Stanford Law School, 1998.

Clark, Margaret S., ed. *Prosocial Behavior.* New York: Sage, 1991.

Cleveland, Harlan. *Birth of a New World: An Open Moment for International Leadership.* San Francisco: Jossey-Bass, 1993.

Conflict Prevention: Strategies to Sustain Peace in the Post–Cold War World. Washington, D.C.: Aspen Institute, 1997.

Cortright, David, ed. *The Price of Peace: Incentives and International Conflict Prevention.* Carnegie Commission Series, Rowman & Littlefield, 1997.

Craig, Gordon. *Europe Since 1815.* New York: Holt, Rinehart & Winston, 1961.

———. *Germany, 1866–1945.* New York: Oxford University Press, 1978.

Craig, Gordon, and Alexander George. *Force and Statecraft: Diplomatic Problems of Our Time.* 3d. ed. New York: Oxford University Press, 1995.

Crossette, Barbara. "As Democracies Spread, Islamic World Hesitates." *New York Times,* December 23, 2001.

Crozier, Andrew. *The Causes of the Second World War.* Malden, England: Blackwell, 1997.

Dahl, Robert A. *On Democracy.* New Haven, Conn.: Yale University Press, 1998.

Dawidowicz, Lucy S. *The War Against the Jews.* New York: Bantam, 1976.

De Cerrano, Allison L. C., and Alexander Keynan. *Scientific Cooperation, State Conflict: The Roles of Scientists in Mitigating International Discord.* New York: New York Academy of Sciences, 1998.

Degler, Carl. *Out of Our Past: The Forces That Shaped Modern America.* 3d ed. New York: Harper Collins, 1984.

Delman, Howard, and Astri Suhrke. "Early Warning and Conflict Management, Study 2: The International Response to Conflict and Genocide: Lessons from the Rwanda Experience." Steering Committee of the Joint Evaluation of Emergency Assistance to Rwanda, March 1996.

Deng, Francis M. "Further Promotion and Encouragement of Human Rights and Fundamental Freedoms, Including the Question of the Programme and Methods of Work of the Commission." Study to the Economic and Social Council, Commission on Human Rights, 1993.

———. *Protecting the Dispossessed: A Challenge for the International Community.* Washington, D.C.: Brookings, 1993.

Denman, Roy. *Missed Chances: Britain and Europe in the Twentieth Century.* London: Indigo, 1997.

Deutsch, Morton. "Educating for a Peaceful World." *American Psychologist,* May 1993.

Diamond, Larry. *Developing Democracy Toward Consolidation.* Baltimore: Johns Hopkins University Press, 1999.

———. *Promoting Democracy in the 1990s: Actors and Instruments, Issues and Imperatives.* Report to the Carnegie Commission on Preventing Deadly Conflict, July 1996.

Drell, Sidney D. *Facing the Threat of Nuclear Weapons, With an Open Letter on the Danger of Thermonuclear War from Andrei Sakharov.* Seattle: University of Washington Press, 1983.

Drell, Sidney D., Abraham Sofaer, and George Wilson, eds. *The New Terror: Facing the Threat of Biological and Chemical Weapons.* Stanford, Calif.: Hoover Institution Press, 1999.

Dunlop, J. T. *Dispute Resolution.* Dover, Mass.: Auburn House, 1984.

Dwan, Renata. "Conflict Prevention and CFSP Coherence." Stockholm International Peace Research Institute, 2001. Available from SIPRI.

Ekbladh, David. *Education for Peace in the Twenty-First Century: A Report on the Advisory Meeting on the Academic Program of the University for Peace.* United Nations, New York, March 23–24, 2001, University for Peace, 2001.

Encyclopedia Britannica Online. "Table 7: World War II Casualties" and "World War II: Costs of the War." <www.eb.com> Accessed March 29, 2000.

Esman, Milton J., and Shibley Telhami, eds. *International Organizations and Ethnic Conflict.* Ithaca, N.Y.: Cornell University Press, 1995.

Evangelista, Matthew. *Unarmed Forces: The Transnational Movement to End the Cold War.* Ithaca, N.Y.: Cornell University Press, 1999.

Evans, Gareth. *Cooperating for Peace: The Global Agenda for the 1990s and Beyond.* St. Leonards, Australia: Allen and Unwin, 1993.

———. *International Herald Tribune* (Paris), September 15, 2001.

———. "President's Essay." Annual report of the International Crisis Group, 2001.

Falk, Richard. *On Human Governance: Toward a New Global Politics.* University Park: Pennsylvania State University Press, 1995.

Farnham, Barbara. *Roosevelt and the Munich Crisis: A Study of Political Decision Making.* Princeton, N.J.: Princeton University Press, 1997.

Feil, Scott R. *Preventing Genocide: How the Early Use of Force Might Have Succeeded in Rwanda.* Report to the Carnegie Commission on Preventing Deadly Conflict, April 1998.

Fischer, Klaus P. *Nazi Germany: A New History.* New York: Continuum, 1995.

Fisher, Roger, and William Ury. *Getting to Yes: Negotiating Agreement Without Giving In.* New York: Penguin, 1983.

Fitzpatrick, Sheila. "Socialism and Communism." In Richard Bullet, ed. *The Columbia History of the Twentieth Century.* New York: Columbia, 1998.

Forsythe, David P. *The Internationalization of Human Rights.* Lexington, Mass.: Lexington Books, 1991.

Franz, David R. "Targeting Intent: Scientist-to-Scientist Threat Reduction Programs." Paper for Nuclear Threat Initiative, Washington, D.C., December 2001.

Fromkin, David. *The Way of the World: From the Dawn of Civilization to the Eve of the Twenty-First Century.* New York: Knopf, 1999.

G8 Miyazaki Initiatives for Conflict Prevention and Conclusions of G8 Foreign Ministers' Meeting, July 13, 2000.

Gardner, John W. *On Leadership.* New York: The Free Press, 1993.

George, Alexander. *Avoiding War: Problems of Crisis Management.* Boulder, Colo.: Westview, 1991.

———. *Bridging the Gap: Theory and Practice in Foreign Policy.* Washington, D.C.: United States Institute of Peace, 1993.

———. *Forceful Persuasion: Coercive Diplomacy as an Alternative to War.* Washington, D.C.: United States Institute of Peace Press, 1991.

———. *Presidential Decisionmaking in Foreign Policy: The Effective Use of Information and Advice.* Boulder, Colo.: Westview, 1980.

George, Alexander, and Jane F. Holl. *The Warning-Response Problem and Missed Opportunities in Preventive Diplomacy.* Report to the Carnegie Commission on Preventing Deadly Conflict, May 1997.

George, Alexander, Philip J. Farley, and Alexander Dallin. *US–Soviet Security Cooperation: Achievements, Failures, Lessons.* New York: Oxford University Press, 1988.

Gershman, Carl. "The Internet and Democracy Building—The NED Experience." Paper presented at the meeting on democracy, Wilton Park, U.K., April 27–28, 2001.

Glass, James M. *"Life Unworthy of Life": Racial Phobia and Mass Murder in Hitler's Germany.* New York: Basic, 1997.

Glendon, Mary Ann. *A World Made New: Eleanor Roosevelt and the Universal Declaration of Human Rights.* New York: Random House, 2001.

Goldstein, J. S. *International Relations.* 3d. ed. New York: Longman, 1999.

Goncharov, S. N., John Lewis, Litai Xue. *Uncertain Partners: Stalin, Mao, and the Korean War.* Stanford, Calif.: Stanford University Press, 1993.

Goodall, Jane. *The Chimpanzees of Gombe: Patterns of Behavior.* Cambridge, Mass.: Belknap Press, 1986.

Goodpaster, Andrew J. *When Diplomacy Is Not Enough: Managing Multinational Military Interventions.* Report to the Carnegie Commission on Preventing Deadly Conflict, July 1996.

Gorbachev, Mikhail. *Gorbachev: On My Country and the World.* New York: Columbia University Press, 2000.

Gottemoeller, Rose. *Threat Reduction Cooperation in the Counter-Terrorism Struggle.* Draft paper prepared for Nuclear Threat Initiative, Washington, D.C., December 2001.

Great Transitions: Preparing Adolescents for a New Century. Concluding report of the Carnegie Council on Adolescent Development. New York: Carnegie Corporation of New York, 1995.

Greenberg, Melanie C., John H. Barton, and Margaret E. McGuinness. *Words Over War: Mediation and Arbitration to Prevent Deadly Conflict.* Carnegie Commission Series, Rowman & Littlefield, 2000.

Gunn, Giles. *Beyond Solidarity.* Chicago: University of Chicago Press, 2001.

Gurr, Ted R. *Minorities at Risk: A Global View of Ethnopolitical Conflicts.* Washington, D.C.: United States Institute of Peace Press, 1993.

Hamburg, David A. "Human Rights and Warfare: An Ounce of Prevention Is Worth a Pound of Cure." In Samantha Powers and Graham Allison, eds. *Realizing Human Rights from Inspiration to Impact.* New York: St. Martin's, 2000.

———. "New Risks of Prejudice, Ethnocentrism, and Violence." *Science* 231, February 7, 1986, 533.

———. "Prejudice, Ethnocentrism and Violence in an Age of High Technology." Carnegie Corporation of New York Annual Report Essay, 1984.

———. *Preventing Contemporary Intergroup Violence and Education for Conflict Resolution.* Carnegie Commission Publication, December 1999.

———. "Understanding and Preventing Nuclear War: The Expanding Role of the Scientific Community." In *The Medical Implications of Nuclear War.* Washington, D.C.: National Academy Press, 1986.

———, ed. *Great Transitions: Preparing Adolescents for a New Century.* Concluding report of the Carnegie Council on Adolescent Development, Carnegie Corporation of New York, 1995.

Hamburg, David A., and Elizabeth McCown. *The Great Apes.* Menlo Park, Calif.: Benjamin Cummings, 1979.

Hamburg David A., and Michelle B. Trudeau. *Biobehavioral Aspects of Aggression.* New York: Alan R. Liss, 1981.

Hamburg, David A., Alexander George, and Karen Ballentine. "Preventing Deadly Conflict: The Critical Role of Leadership." *Archives of General Psychiatry* 56 (November 1999): 971–76.

Hamburg, David A., Sidney Drell, Alexander George, John Holdren, Jane Holl, John Steinbruner, John Stremlau, and Cyrus Vance. *Preventing Deadly Conflict: What Can the Scientific Community Do?* Report of the President's Committee of Advisors on Science and Technology to the President of the United States, Office of Science and Technology Policy, White House, Washington, D.C., 1996.

Hamburg, Margaret. "Preparing for and Preventing Bioterrorism." *Issues in Science and Technology* XVIII, no. 2 (winter 2001–2002): 27–30.

———. "Youth Violence Is a Public Health Concern." In Delbert S. Elliot, Beatrix A. Hamburg, and Kirk R. Williams, eds. *Violence in American Schools.* New York: Cambridge University Press, 1998.

Hassan, Mohamed H.A. "Can Science Save Africa?" *Science* 292 (June 2001): 1609.

Hayward, Steven F. *Churchill on Leadership: Executive Success in the Face of Adversity.* Rocklin, Calif.: Forum Prima, 1997.

Heilbroner, Robert. *Visions of the Future, The Distant Past, Today, and Tomorrow.* New York: Oxford University Press, 1995.

Henig, Ruth. *The Origins of the Second World War, 1933–1939.* New York: Routledge, 1991.

Hewstone, Miles, Wolfgang Stroebe, and Geoffrey Stephanson. *Introduction to Social Psychology.* 2d. ed. London: Blackwell, 1996.

Heymann, Philip B. *Terrorism in America: A Commonsense Strategy for a Democratic Society.* Cambridge, Mass.: MIT Press, 1998.

Hinde, Robert A., and Donald A. Parry. *Education for Peace.* Nottingham, England: Spokesman, Bertrand Russell House, 1989.

Hitler, Adolf. *Mein Kampf.* Ralph Manheim, trans. New York: Houghton Mifflin, 1943.

Hoagland, Jim. "Democracy Will Gather to Make a Big Statement." *International Herald Tribune*, June 22, 2000.

Hobswam, Eric. *The Age of Extremes: A History of the World, 1914–1991.* New York: Pantheon, 1994.

Hoge, James Jr., and Gideon Rose. *How Did This Happen? Terrorism and the New Year.* New York: Public Affairs, 2001.

Hopmann, P. Terrence. "The Organization for Security and Cooperation in Europe: Its Contribution to Conflict Prevention and Resolution." In Paul C. Stern and Daniel Druckman, eds. *International Conflict and Resolution After the Cold War.* Washington, D.C.: National Academy Press, 2000.

Howard, Michael. *War in European History.* New York: Oxford University Press, 1976.

Howard, Michael, and William Roger Louis. *The Oxford History of the Twentieth Century.* New York: Oxford University Press, 1998.

Hurlburt, Heather F. "Preventive Diplomacy: Success in the Baltics." In Bruce Jentleson, ed. *Opportunities Missed, Opportunities Seized: Preventive Diplomacy in Post–Cold War World.* Carnegie Commission Series, Rowman & Littlefield, 1999.

Improving the Coherence and Effectiveness of European Union Action in the Field of Conflict Prevention. Report presented to the Nice European Council by the Secretary General/High Representative and the Commission, Nice, France, 2001.

International Crisis Group, *After Milosevic: A Practical Agenda for Lasting Balkans Peace.* Brussels: International Crisis Group Press, 2001.

Iriye, Akira. *Cultural Internationalism and World Order.* Baltimore: Johns Hopkins University Press, 1997.

———. "The International Order." Pp. 229–47 in Richard Bullet, ed. *The Columbia History of the Twentieth Century.* New York: Columbia University Press, 1998.

Jackson, Anthony, and Willis Hawley. *Toward a Common Destiny: Improving Race and Ethnic Relations in America.* San Francisco: Jossey-Bass, 1995.

Janis, I. *Crucial Decisions: Leadership in Policy Making and Crisis Management.* New York: Free Press, 1989.

Jentleson, Bruce. *Coercive Prevention: Normative, Political and Policy Dilemmas.* Peaceworks No. 35, United States Institute of Peace, 2000.

———. "Economic Sanctions and Post–Cold War Conflicts: Challenges for Theory and Policy." In Paul C. Stern and Daniel Druckman, eds., *International Conflict Resolution After the Cold War.* Washington, D.C.: National Academy Press, 2000.

———, ed. *Opportunities Missed, Opportunities Seized: Preventive Diplomacy in the Post–Cold War World.* Carnegie Commission Series, Rowman & Littlefield, 1999.

Joulwan, George A., and Christopher C. Shoemaker. *Civilian-Military Cooperation in the Prevention of Deadly Conflict: Implementing Agreements in Bosnia and Beyond.* Report to the Carnegie Commission on Preventing Deadly Conflict, December 1998.

Juergensmeyer, Mark. *Terror in the Mind of God: The Global Rise of Religious Violence.* Berkeley, Calif.: University of California Press, 2000.

Kagan, Donald. *On the Origins of War and the Preservation of Peace.* New York: Doubleday, 1995.

Keegan, John. *A History of Warfare.* New York: Knopf, 1994.

———. *War and Our World.* New York: Vintage, 1998.

Kennedy, David. *Freedom from Fear: The American People in Depression and War, 1929–1945.* New York: Oxford University Press, 1999.

Kennedy, Donald. *Environmental Quality and Regional Conflict.* Report to the Carnegie Commission on Preventing Deadly Conflict, December 1998.

Kennedy, Paul. *The Rise and Fall of the Great Powers: Economic Change and Military Conflict from 1500 to 2000.* New York: Random House, 1987.

Kershaw, Ian. *Hitler, 1889–1936: Hubris.* New York: Norton, 1998.

King, Mary. *Mahatma Gandhi and Martin Luther King, Jr.: The Power of Nonviolent Action.* Paris: UNESCO, 1999.

Korey, William. *The Promises We Keep: Human Rights, the Helsinki Process and American Foreign Policy.* New York: Institute for East–West Studies, 1993.

Krueger, Anne O. *The Developmental Role of the Foreign Sector and Aid.* Cambridge, Mass.: Harvard University Press, 1982.

Krugman, Paul. "The Scrooge Syndrome." *New York Times,* December 25, 2001.

Kull, Steven. "What the Public Knows That Washington Doesn't." *Foreign Policy* (winter 1995/1996).

Lapidus, Gail. "The War in Chechnya: Opportunities Missed, Lessons to Be Learned." In Bruce Jentleson, ed. *Opportunities Missed, Opportunities Seized: Preventive Diplomacy in the Post–Cold War World.* Carnegie Commission Series, Rowman & Littlefield, 1999.

Laquer, Walter. *Fascism: Past, Present, Future.* New York: Oxford University Press, 1996.

———. *The New Terrorism: Fanaticism and the Arms of Mass Destruction.* New York: Oxford University Press, 1999.

Lavoy, Peter, Scott Sagan, and James Wirtz, eds. *Planning the Unthinkable.* Ithaca, N.Y.: Cornell University Press, 2000.

Lederberg, Joshua, ed. *Biological Weapons: Limiting the Threat.* Cambridge, Mass.: MIT Press, 1999.

Lenski, Gerhard, Patrick Nolan, and Jean Lenski. *Human Societies: An Introduction to Macrosocieties.* 7th ed. New York: McGraw-Hill, 1995.

Lesser, Gerald. "The Role of Television in Moving Beyond Hate." Paper presented at Conference on Beyond Hate, initiated by Elie Wiesel, Boston University, March 19, 1989.

Levine, R., and D. Campbell. *Ethnocentrism: Theories of Conflict, Ethnic Attitudes and Group Behavior.* New York: McGraw-Hill, 1972.

Lewis, Bernard. "The Revolt of Islam." *The New Yorker,* November 19, 2001, 50–62.

———. *Semites and Anti-Semites: An Inquiry into Conflict and Prejudice.* New York: Norton, 1999.

———. "What Went Wrong?" *Atlantic Monthly,* January 2002, 43–45.

———. *What Went Wrong? Western Impact and Middle Eastern Response.* New York: Oxford University Press, 2002.

Linz, Juan, and Alfred Stepan. *Problems of Democratic Transition and Consolidation.* Baltimore: Johns Hopkins University Press, 1996.

Lund, Michael. *Preventing Violent Conflicts: A Strategy for Preventive Diplomacy.* Washington, D.C.: U.S. Institute of Peace Press, 1996.

Mandelbaum, Michael. *The Dawn of Peace in Europe.* New York: Twentieth Century Fund Press, 1996.

Mason Edward S., Mahn J. Kim, Dwight Perkins, Kwang Suk Kim, and David C. Cole. *The Economic and Social Modernization of Korea.* Cambridge, Mass.: Harvard University Press, 1980.

Matthews, Jessica T.. "Power Shift." *Foreign Affairs* 76:1 (January/February 1997).

Mayer, Arno. *The Furies: Violence and Terror in the French and Russian Revolutions.* Princeton, N.J.: Princeton University Press, 2000.

McNeill, William. *A History of the Human Community: Prehistory to the Present.* Upper Saddle River, N.J.: Prentice Hall, 1997.

———. *The Pursuit of Power: Technology, Armed Force and Society Since* A.D. *1000.* Chicago: University of Chicago Press, 1982.

———. *A World History.* 4th ed. New York: Oxford University Press, 1999.

Mendelson, Sarah E., and John K. Glenn. *Democracy Assistance and NGO Strategies in Post-Communist Societies.* Working paper of the Carnegie Endowment for International Peace, 2000.

Meselson, Matthew. "Bioterror: What Can Be Done?" *New York Review*, December 20, 2001.

Myers, David. *Social Psychology.* 2d. ed. New York: McGraw-Hill, 1987.

Naimark, Norman. *Fires of Hatred.* Cambridge, Mass.: Harvard University Press, 2001.

Nichols, Rodney W. *Linking Science and Technology with Global Economic Development: A US Perspective.* COSTED Occasional Paper No.5, Committee on Science and Technology in Developing Countries, September 1999.

Nunn, Sam. "Our New Security Framework." *Washington Post*, October 7, 2001.

Ostrower, Gary B. *The United Nations and the United States.* New York: Twayne, 1998.

Overy, Richard. "Misjudging Hitler: A. J. P. Taylor and the Third Reich." In Gordon Martel, ed. *The Origins of the Second World War Reconsidered: A. J. P. Taylor and the Historians.* 2d ed. New York: Routledge, 1999.

———. *The Origins of the Second World War.* 2d ed. New York: Longman, 1998.

Parker, R. A. C. *Churchill and Appeasement.* London: Macmillan, 2000.

Partnerships for Global Development: The Clearing Horizon. Report of the Carnegie Commission on Science Technology and Government, 1992.

Pasek, Beata. "Nations Discuss Democracy, Rights." *Washington Post*, June 26, 2000.

Patten, Chris, and Anna Lindh. "Let's Control the Small Arms Trade." *International Herald Tribune*, June 30, 2001.

Peck, Connie. *Sustainable Peace: The Role of the UN and Regional Organizations in Preventing Conflict.* Carnegie Commission Series, Rowman & Littlefield, 1998.

Perlez, Jane. "Vast Rally for Democracy Opens in a Polish Castle." *New York Times*, June 26, 2000.

Perry, William J. "Preparing for the Next Attack." *Foreign Affairs*, November/December 2001.

Peukert, Detlev J. K. *The Weimar Republic: The Crisis of Classical Modernity.* Richard Deveson, trans. New York: Hill and Wang, 1989.

Pillar, Paul. *Terrorism and U.S. Foreign Policy.* Washington, D.C.: Brookings, 2001.

Prevention of Armed Conflict. Report of the Secretary-General, A/55/985-S2001/574, United Nations, June 7, 2001.

Preventive Diplomacy, Preventive Defense, and Conflict Resolution: A Report of Two Conferences at Stanford University and the Ditchley Foundation. Report to the Carnegie Commission on Preventing Deadly Conflict, October 1999.

Preventing Contemporary Intergroup Violence and Education for Conflict Resolution. New York: Carnegie Commission Publication, December 1999.

Raiffa, H. *The Art and Science of Negotiation.* Cambridge, Mass.: Belknap, 1982.

Redlich, Fritz. *Hitler: Diagnosis of a Destructive Prophet.* New York: Oxford University Press, 1999.

Reich, Walter, ed. *Origins of Terrorism: Psychologies, Ideologies, Theologies, States of Mind.* Cambridge, England: Woodrow Wilson International Center for Scholars and Cambridge University Press, 1990.

Reilly, Ben, and Andrew Reynolds. "Electoral Systems and Conflict in Divided Socities." In Paul C. Stern and Daniel Druckman, eds. *International Conflict Resolution After the Cold War.* Washington, D.C.: National Academy Press, 2000.

Report of the Independent Inquiry into the Actions of the United Nations during the 1994 Genocide in Rwanda. UN Doc. S/1999/1257, December 15, 1999.

Richardson, Elliot. *Reflections of a Radical Moderate.* New York: Pantheon, 1996.

Roberts, J. M. *The Penguin History of the World.* New York: Penguin, 1995.

———. *The Twentieth Century: The History of the World, 1901–2000* New York: Viking, 1999.

Robinson, Mary. "The Next Human Rights Agenda: Preventing Conflict." *New Perspectives Quarterly* 16 (fall 1999): 23–28.

The Role of Foreign Assistance in Conflict Prevention. Woodrow Wilson Center for International Scholars Conference Report. Washington D.C., January 8, 2001.

Role of the Security Council in the Prevention of Armed Conflicts. UN Doc. S/PRST/2000/25, July 20, 2000.

Roosevelt, Franklin Delano. "Quarantine the Aggressors." October 5, 1937. <www.homer.providence.edu/wcb/schools/PC1/his/mmanches/12/files/fdrqua rspch.htm> Accessed April 2000.

Rosencrance, Richard, ed. *The New Great Power Coalition: Toward a World Concert of Nations.* Lanham, Md.: Rowman & Littlefield, 2001.

Rotberg, Robert I. *Vigilance and Vengeance: NGOs Preventing Ethnic Conflict in Divided Societies.* Washington, D.C.: Brookings, 1996.

Rubin, Barnett R., ed. *Cases and Strategies for Preventive Action.* New York: Century Foundation Press, 1998.

Ruggie, John. "The Past as Prologue? Interests, Identity and American Foreign Policy." *International Security* 21(4): 89–125.

Sachs, Jeffrey. "A New Global Consensus on Helping the Poorest of the Poor." Address to the Annual Bank Conference on Development Economics, World Bank, Washington, D.C., 2000.

Sagasti, Francisco, and Gonzalo Alcalde. *Development Cooperation in a Fractured Global Order.* Ottawa, Canada: International Development Research Center, 1999.

Sagasti, Francisco, Pepi Patron, Max Hernandez, and Nicholas Lynch. *Democracy and Good Government: Towards Democratic Governance in Peru.* Lima, Peru: Agenda Peru, 1995.

Saunders, Harold H. "Interactive Conflict Resolution: A View for Policy Makers on Making and Building Peace." In Paul C. Stern and Daniel Druckman, eds. *International Conflict After the Cold War.* Washington, D.C.: National Academy Press, 2000.

Schellenberg, J. A. *The Science of Conflict.* New York: Oxford University Press, 1982.

"Scholar Searches for Long-Lasting Security in Postcommunist Regions." *Briefings* (Watson Institute for International Studies at Brown University winter/spring 2000).

School of International and Public Affairs, Columbia University, International Affairs course U8556. "Preventive Diplomacy and Conflict Resolution in the United Nations: Integrating Theory and Practice." <www.columbia.edu/cu/sipa/COURSES/2000-2001/U8556.html>

Schuker, Stephan A. "France and the Remilitarization of the Rhineland, 1936." Pp. 222–45 in Patrick Finney, ed. *The Origins of the Second World War.* New York: Arnold, 1997.

Schulz, William F., and Mary Robinson. *In Our Own Best Interest: How Defending Human Rights Benefits All Americans.* Boston, Mass.: Beacon, 2001.

Sen, Amartya. *Development as Freedom.* New York: Knopf, 1999.

Sherif, M., and C. Sherif. *Groups in Harmony and Tension: An Integration of Studies on Intergroup Relations.* New York: Octagon, 1966.

Shirer, William L. *The Rise and Fall of the Third Reich.* New York: Simon & Schuster, 1960.

Sidanius, Jim, and Felicia Pratto. *Social Dominance.* New York: Cambridge University Press, 1999.

Sisk, Timothy D. *Power Sharing and International Mediation in Ethnic Conflicts.* Washington, D.C.: United States Institute of Peace, 1996.

Slavin, Robert E., and Robert Cooper. "Improving Intergroup Relations: Lessons Learned from Cooperative Learning Programs." *Journal of Social Issues 55*, no. 4 (winter 1999): 647–66.

Smoch, David. *Training to Prevent: Conflict Management*. Washington, D.C.: United States Institute of Peace, 1999.

Snyder, Jack. *From Voting to Violence: Democratization and Nationalist Conflict*. New York: Norton, 2000.

Sriram, Lekha. "From Promise to Practice: Strengthening UN Capacities for the Prevention of Violent Conflict." International Peace Academy, Security Council Workshop Report, West Point, New York, 2001, 1–11.

Staub, Ervin. *The Roots of Evil: The Origins of Genocide and Other Group Violence*. New York: Cambridge University Press, 1989.

Stedman, Stephan John. "Spoiler Problems in Peace Processes." In Paul C. Stern and Daniel Druckman, eds. *International Conflict Resolution After the Cold War*. Washington, D.C.: National Academy Press, 2001.

Steinbruner, John P. *Principles of Global Security*. Washington, D.C.: Brookings, 2000.

Stern, Fritz. *Dreams and Delusions: National Socialism in the Drama of the German Past*. New York: Vintage, 1987.

Stern, Paul C., and Daniel Druckman, eds. *International Conflict Resolution After the Cold War*. Washington, D.C.: National Academy Press, 2000.

Stiglitz, Joseph E., and L. Squire. "International Development: Is It Possible?" *Foreign Policy* (spring 1998): 138–51.

Stremlau, John. *People in Peril: Human Rights, Humanitarian Action, and Preventing Deadly Conflict*. Report to the Carnegie Commission on Preventing Deadly Conflict, May 1998.

———. *Sharpening International Sanctions: Toward a Stronger Role for the United Nations*. Report to the Carnegie Commission on Preventing Deadly Conflict, November 1996.

Stremlau, John, and Francisco Sagasti. *Preventing Deadly Conflict: Does the World Bank Have a Role?* Report to the Carnegie Commission on Preventing Deadly Conflict, July 1998.

Swedish Foreign Ministry. *Preventing Violent Conflict—A Swedish Action Plan*. Stockholm: Regeringskansliet UD, Printing Works of the Government Offices, 1999.

Takeyh, Ray. "Can Islam Bring Democracy to the Middle East?" *Foreign Policy* (December 2001): 68.

Talbot, Strobe, and Nayan Chanda, eds. *The Age of Terror: America and the World After September 11*. New York: Basic Books, 2001.

Tharoor, Shashi. "Are Human Rights Universal?" *World Policy Journal* 26 (winter 1999/2000): 1–6.

Thomas, Hugh. *A History of the World*. New York: Harper and Row, 1982.

"Toward a Community of Democracies." Final Warsaw Declaration, Warsaw, Poland, June 27, 2000.

Ury, William. *Getting to Peace.* New York: Penguin, 1999.

U.S. Department of State. "Toward a Community of Democracies." Final Warsaw Declaration. Warsaw, Poland: June 27, 2000.

US–Russian Cooperation to Prevent Deadly Conflict: Reports of a Commission Task Force. Sam Nunn, chairman. Carnegie Commission on Preventing Deadly Conflict, Perspectives on Prevention, December 1999.

Valenzuela, Arturo. *The Collective Defense of Democracy: Lessons from the Paraguayan Crisis of 1996.* Report to the Carnegie Commission on Preventing Deadly Conflict, December 1999.

Vance, Cyrus R., and David A. Hamburg. *Pathfinders for Peace: A Report to the UN Secretary-General on the Role of Special Representatives and Personal Envoys.* Report of the Carnegie Commission on Preventing Deadly Conflict, September 1997.

van der Stoel, Max. "Democracy and Human Rights. On the Work of the High Commissioner on National Minorities of the OSCE"; "Early Warning and Early Action: Preventing Inter-Ethnic Conflict"; and "The Involvement of the High Commissioner Is No Stigma, But an Act of Solidarity." In Wolfgang Zellner and Falk Lange, eds. *Peace and Stability through Human and Minority Rights.* Baden-Baden, Germany: Nomos, 1999.

Van Evera, Stephan. *Causes of War: Power and the Roots of Conflict.* Ithaca, N.Y.: Cornell University Press, 1999.

Vick, Karl. "Death Toll in Congo War May Approach 3 Million." *Washington Post,* April 30, 2001.

Walzer, Michael. *On Toleration.* New Haven, Conn.: Yale University Press, 1997.

Washburn, S. L., and David A. Hamburg. "Aggressive Behavior in Old World Monkeys and Apes." In P. Jay, ed. *Primates: Studies in Adaptation and Variability.* New York: Holt, Rinehart & Winston, 1968.

Weiss-Wik, Stephen. "Enhancing Negotiator's Successfulness: Self-Help Books and Related Empirical Research." *Journal of Conflict Resolution* 27 (December 1983): 706–35.

Williams, R. M. *Mutual Accommodation: Ethnic Conflict and Cooperation.* Minneapolis: University of Minnesota Press, 1977.

Wolfenson, James D. *A Proposal for a Comprehensive Development Framework.* World Bank, Washington, D.C. January 21, 1999.

Woo, Jung-En. *Race to the Swift: State and Finance in Korean Industrialization.* New York: Columbia University Press, 1991.

World Bank. *World Development Report 1996.* New York: Oxford University Press, 1996.

———. *World Development Report 1999/2000.* New York: Oxford University Press, 2000.

Wrangham, Richard, and Dale Peterson. *Demonic Males.* New York: Houghton Mifflin, 1996.

Zakaria, Fareed. "How to Save the Arab World." *Newsweek,* December 24, 2001, 25–28.

Zartman, I. William, ed., *Preventive Negotiation: Avoiding Conflict Escalation.* Carnegie Commission Series, Rowman & Littlefield, 2000.

———. "Ripeness: The Hurting Stalemate and Beyond." In Paul C. Stern and Daniel Druckman, eds. *International Conflict Resolution After the Cold War*. Washington, D.C.: National Academy Press, 2000.

Zimmerman, Warren. *Origins of a Catastrophe*. New York: Times Books, 1996.

Index

ADB. *See* Asian Development Bank
An Agenda for Democratization
  (Boutros-Ghali), 164, 311, 312
An Agenda for Development (Boutros-
  Ghali), 311
An Agenda for Peace (Boutros-Ghali),
  311
aggressive behavior: contributing
  factors, 44, 98, 253; effects of
  inaction on, 56–57; research on,
  106–7
Alberts, Bruce, xx, xxv, 215
Allison, Graham, v, 239; democracies
  in preventing deadly conflict study,
  72–75; on nuclear terrorist attacks,
  257–58; Strengthening Democratic
  Institutions Project, 90–92
Annan, Kofi (UN Secretary-General):
  on equitable economic development,
  195–96; highlights of speeches and
  reports, 77–79; on International
  Peace Academy (IPA), 94; leadership
  abilities, 81; lecture when receiving
  Nobel Peace Prize, 267–68
appeasement, 34, 37, 38, 45
Appleby, R. Scott, 96
Aral Sea Basin conflict, 138–39, 140
arms reduction: efforts of Carnegie
  Corporation, 7–9; efforts of
  scientific community, 107–8;
  leadership in, 264–67; light

weapons, 280, 285, 286; steps
  toward, 255–60. *See also* Cold War
Asian Development Bank (ADB), 201,
  205
authoritarianism: in Korea, 202–3;
  relapse to, 156; and transition to
  market economy, 155–56, 202–3

Baker, Howard, 258
Baldwin, Stanley, 35
Ballentine, Karen, 100
Barchas, Jack, xvii
Barthou, Jean-Louis, 29
Barton, John, 136–41
BBC. *See* British Broadcasting
  Corporation
Bennett, Juliette, 293
Bergstrom, Sune, xx, 188
bioterrorism, 260–64
Birdsall, Nancy, 213
Boutros-Ghali, Boutros, 164, 220, 311
British Broadcasting Corporation
  (BBC), 98, 99
British Commonwealth's Harare
  Declaration of 1991, 163
Brodie, Keith, xvii, xxiii
Brown, Gordon, 273–74
Brown, Michael, 13
Brundtland, Gro Harlem, xviii, xx, 145
Bundy, McGeorge, xviii, xxi, xxiv
Bush, George W., 265

349

About the Author

David A. Hamburg, M.D is president emeritus at Carnegie Corporation of New York, after having been president from 1982 to 1997. He received his A.B. (1944) and his M.D. (1947) degrees from Indiana University. He was professor and chairman of the Department of Psychiatry and Behavioral Sciences from 1961 to 1972 and Reed-Hodgson professor of Human Biology at Stanford University from 1972 to 1976; president of the Institute of Medicine, National Academy of Sciences, 1975 to 1980; director of the Division of Health Policy Research and Education and John D. MacArthur professor of Health Policy at Harvard University, 1980 to 1983. He served as president and then chairman of the board of the American Association for the Advancement of Science (1984–1986).

His research contributions have dealt with biological responses and adaptive behavior in stressful circumstances and with several aspects of human aggression and conflict resolution. He has been concerned with the conjunction of biomedical and behavioral sciences—first in the context of building an interdisciplinary scientific approach to psychiatric problems, then in research on the links of behavior and health as a major component in the contemporary burden of illness. In recent years, he has concentrated on child and adolescent development, as well as large-scale intergroup conflict.

Dr. Hamburg is the author of *Today's Children: Creating a Future for a Generation in Crisis* (1992). He was chairman of the Carnegie Council on Adolescent Development, which completed its decade-long activities with a report entitled *Great Transitions: Preparing Adolescents for a New Century*. The Council published reports and books on many aspects of adolescent development. It sponsored national and international meetings on ways to improve health, education, and life chances of youth, including problems of youth violence.

Dr. Hamburg has long been concerned with the problems of human aggression and violence, especially with violence prevention and conflict resolution, and he is the author or co-author of numerous publications on these subjects. He has studied human conflict at different levels: family, community, ethnic group, and international. Under his leadership, the Carnegie Corporation has played an active role in reducing the danger from nuclear weapons and moving toward the resolution of the Cold War and democracy in South Africa.

In 1994, he established the Carnegie Commission on Preventing Conflict, which he co-chaired with Cyrus Vance. It comprised international leaders and scholars long experienced in violence prevention and conflict resolution. The Commission asked fundamental questions: What are the problems posed by deadly conflict and why is outside help often necessary to deal with these problems? What can be done to resolve disputes at an early stage? What political, economic, military, and social tools are at the disposal of the international community? Which strategies work best? What institutions and organizations can effectively use those tools and strategies for prevention? What fundamental conditions are conducive to peaceful living? How can the international community help to create these conditions?

The Commission and the Carnegie Corporation published seventy-five reports and books on subjects related to the prevention approach. In addition, the Commission sponsored international meetings drawing together independent experts and policymakers from around the world to consider these issues carefully. It published a synthesis of these activities under the title *Preventing Deadly Conflict*. Taken together, the publications constitute a unique resource on prevention.

In addition to *No More Killing Fields: Preventing Deadly Conflict*, Dr. Hamburg and his wife, Dr. Beatrix Hamburg, are writing a book for Oxford University Press entitled *Learning to Live Together: Diminishing Prejudice and Hatred in Child and Adolescent Development*.

Dr. Hamburg has served on various boards, including Stanford University, Rockefeller University, Mount Sinai–New York University Medical Center, American Museum of Natural History, the Carter Center, the Leakey Foundation, the Jacobs Foundation of Zurich, the Federal Reserve Bank of New York, the International Peace Academy, the Project on Ethnic Relations, and the New York Academy of Medicine.

He has served on many policy advisory boards, as well. In the international security field, he served on the Chief of Naval Operations Executive Panel, the Secretary of Energy Advisory Board, the National Academy of Sciences Committee on International Security and Arms Control, the Center for Naval Analysis, the United States–Soviet Joint Study Group on Crisis Prevention, and the Defense Policy Board, United States Department of Defense.

In science policy, he has served as chairman of several national and international groups, including the Science Policy Committee of the Institute of Medicine and both the intramural and extramural scientific advisory boards of the National Institute of Mental Health, as well as the Science Education Advisory Committee of the National Science Foundation. He served on the Advisory Committee on Medical Research of the World Health Organization and the International Development Research Center. He was the founder of the Carnegie Commission on Science, Technology and Government. From 1994 to 2001, he served on the President's Committee of Advisors on Science and Technology, the White House.

He is a member of the National Academy of Sciences, the Institute of Medicine, the American Philosophical Society, and the American Academy of Arts and Sciences. He is the past president of the Academy for Research in Behavioral Medicine, the International Society for Research on Aggression, and the Association for Research on Nervous and Mental Disorders.

Dr. Hamburg received the American Psychiatric Association's Distinguished Service Award, the International Peace Academy's 25th Anniversary Special Award, the Achievement in Children and Public Policy Award from the Society for Research in Child Development, the National Academy of Science's Public Welfare Medal (its highest award), and the Presidential Medal of Freedom, the highest civilian award of the United States.